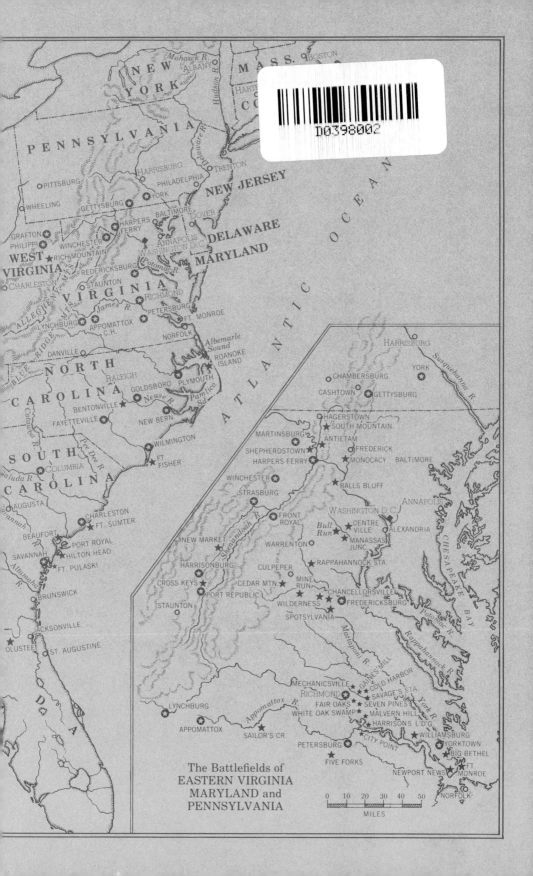

The Battlefields of
EASTERN VIRGINIA
MARYLAND and
PENNSYLVANIA

0 10 20 30 40 50
MILES

The Deep Waters
of the Proud

VOLUME 1
OF
THE IMPERILED UNION:
1861–1865

The Deep Waters
of the Proud

VOLUME 1
OF
THE IMPERILED UNION:
1861–1865

WILLIAM C. DAVIS

DOUBLEDAY & COMPANY, INC.
Garden City, New York
1982

Library of Congress Cataloging in Publication Data

Davis, William C., 1946–
The Deep Waters of the Proud.

(The Imperiled Union; v. 1)
Includes bibliographical references and index.
1. United States—History—Civil War, 1861–1865—
Causes.   I. Title.   II. Series: Davis, William C.,
1946–   . Imperiled Union; v. 1.
E459.D27   973.7
AACR2
ISBN: 0-385-14894-1
Library of Congress Catalog Card Number 81–43303

CONTENTS

LIST OF PHOTOGRAPHS

AUTHOR'S PREFACE

The people of every great nation look back to some great divide in their past, a watershed that parted the old from the new, and so, too, do Americans. Through more than two centuries of national existence, centuries filled with drama and excitement, still there is one transcendent event by which all others pale in the measure. Our American Civil War. It is our Waterloo and Magna Carta, the Glorious Revolution, 1066, the Exodus, and more, all in one. We look back to it for inspiration, for example, for studies of Americans at their best, and worst. Public figures and popular leaders harken to it, seeking in its experience support for the causes of today. Indeed, there can be no greater testimony to the continuing impact upon the conscious and subconscious American mind of this four-year war than the fact that it is used, and more often misused, in the political and social arguments of the day more than any other era in our past. So accustomed are we to finding analogy to our times in the events of the 1860s, or the perfectly apt phrase for any cause in the words of Lincoln and his peers, that when they are not to be found we invent them. Winston Churchill wrote of the Arthurian legend, if it were not so, it should have been. If it did not happen in the Civil War, still it should have happened. More than anything else, the Civil War is our measure of ourselves. We cannot escape it. To do so would be to abandon elements of our basic American character, and our own perception of that character. The two are not always the same, incidentally, and even that, too, we owe in large part to the conflict of North and South. We are as much prisoners of that war as any poor Yank or Reb who languished at Andersonville or Fort Delaware.

For this reason alone, if for no other, the Civil War is a story that demands telling and retelling as each succeeding generation tries for itself to deal with the events and the meaning of that terrible war. Different Americans see their Civil War in varying ways, which is hardly a surprise, yet differing generations have viewed it through contrary eyes as well. Sometimes they saw it only for justification, or retribution, or glory, or shame. Like all epochal events, it was a war whose story can be molded to suit almost any purpose, to attack or defend any cause. Yet beyond all that, surely there are some basic truths about what happened and why, and how it revealed or changed the America of its time and Americans for all time.

In this first volume, and in the two that will follow (*Stand in the Day of Battle* and *Rebuke the Raging Winds*), some of these truths emerge. Many are new, many are not. Most will stand time's challenge, some may not for, as with our forebears of the 1860s, the search for the truth is often as close as we can come to achieving it. Yet surely there is one verity to be found in this trilogy that should not be challenged. It treats a "total" war as just that. What emerges is a picture of America at war with itself that goes beyond the long-treasured clichés of Blue and Gray deciding the fate of their nations in heroic battle. That they surely did. But it was a war between civilians as well, and they perhaps more than the soldiers determined the outcome of the war. It was a war of the politicians and failed statesmen who brought on the conflict in the first place, in many cases men whose attitudes had been predestined for them by two centuries of American experience. It was a war of money against money, of industry growing to meet its demands—or failing to—of diplomat against diplomat, of thousands of blacks struggling to freedom and thousands more afraid of it, of hundreds of thousands of women beginning to climb out of their old roles however briefly, and of America itself undergoing a subtle yet pervasive revolution of society and economy.

Each one is a story filled with as much drama and excitement as the bloody encounters in Virginia and Tennessee, yet in the past they have been too often buried or ignored. In this first volume these stories begin, and with them as well the undeniable adventure of the growing great armies as they sought each other out to make war, brother upon brother. No book or series of books can do justice to all the individuals involved. But as Americans North and South began their journey to wade out of "the deep waters of the proud" in the first eighteen months of the war, several who are representative of their caste emerge, and the story of the war both on and off the battlefield is told largely through their actions. The deeds of Wade Hampton of South Carolina serve as well for those of hundreds of the *beaux sabreurs*. The efforts of Owen Lovejoy account nicely for those of a mass of the men who made and maintained the party of Lincoln. The agony of John C. Breckinridge of Kentucky speaks well for that suffered by thousands torn between duty to country and loyalty to state. Not every Confederate woman could approach the erudition of Mary Chesnut nor did every Southern firebrand speak with the venom of Edmund Ruffin, but they spoke well enough for almost all.

And in the two volumes to follow, they and others reveal what happened to bring the Union to disunion, what made the conflict repressible or irrepressible, and the impact it had upon them and the American personality. From the epic clash of mighty armies at Antietam to the forgotten efforts of a single diplomat in London, from the encounter of formidable ironclad warships at Hampton Roads to the seemingly lackluster meetings of a Yankee financier with investors, they all made the total story of the "total" war. This was no war in a vacuum. The soldiers in blue and gray, many as they were, were yet the smallest part of the numbers truly engaged. Without placing the compellingly dramatic role of the armies into the perspective of two entire nations in conflict, the story of the Civil War is reduced to a hollow sphere, the armies snaking about the surface with nothing beneath them for support.

And that would be an irony not to be borne. For if there is a single great lesson to be drawn from this first volume especially, it is that the one most pervasive force impelling the men and women who populated the surface of that sphere in the 1860s, was gravity. Always it drew them toward the center. Radicals there were at all extremes, yet the overgoverning influence of all lay toward the middle. As always in the history of this continent, the ideas that set great and terrible events in motion came from extremists. It is no different with North and South. But once turned into practical movements, those ideas came increasingly into the hands of moderates who, in their search for solution and resolution, sought the guiding principle of the Republic from its earliest days. Consensus. It is customary in three-volume works on the Civil War for the first book to end around the time of the Battle of Antietam and the Emancipation Proclamation. This one does, too, and even that represents something of a consensus, yet the reasons for its ending after the first eighteen months of the war have little to do with those that have impelled previous historians. Antietam is often regarded as a military and diplomatic turning point of the war. That it most certainly was not.

To the contrary, those final months of 1862 marked a *returning* point, for only by then had control of the affairs of America, North and South, come back securely in the hands of a distinctly American impulse. To be sure there was still a madness abroad in the land, else how could section battle against section in the face of all the ancestral ties that bound them. But the reins that guided their course, that aimed toward some resolution of this horrible war, had passed once again from the hands of the extremists and returned to those who led by consensus. The irresistible pull of the center took control once more in late 1862, after a year and one half of chaos, yet with it came as well the subtle revolution that so often accompanies the American center. Surely North and South still had a long way to go as 1863 approached, yet by that time the struggles of their first eighteen months apart had resolved their future direction. They had struggled through the deep waters of the proud and found their beacon identities once more. Yet still a wide gulf lay between them and the peace of a much distant shore.

INTRODUCTION

Prophecy is, after all, a matter of mathematics. Given a sufficient population disposed toward speculation, any state may surely expect that some among its citizens, by the pure law of averages, will foretell with considerable accuracy its national destiny.

Yet still the prescience of the Reverend William Jenks is hard to explain. In 1808 under the sobriquet Williamson Jahnsenykes, he wrote six letters to his fictitious son Julius, ostensibly published in Quebec in 1901. They were reflective in nature, looking backward over troubled decades through which the clergyman passed. Their forward vision is frightening.

The son Julius commented upon the letters in a preface. "Whatever sources of information may have been opened in general histories," he began, "it is plain that private memoirs, separate from the circumstance of authenticity, must enter more into the detail of those causes, which, though they develope [sic] themselves only to the curious eye of an intelligent and attentive observer, produce ultimately the greatest events." His father's letters "faithfully paint the miseries of former times," he said. Perhaps their message might serve warning upon the present generation. "For the Republick is a prey to the dissentions of her ambitious chiefs."[1]

The story went back many years as unfolded in Jahnsenykes's letters, and it began in human impulses. "Whatever motives and principles may justly be ascribed to individuals, it is a fact, that nations act on a plan totally selfish." The essence of patriotism lies in preferring the benefit of one's own country to that of all others. "In the collision of separate national interests, that of our own nation lies nearest to the heart." Yet even in this he found that leaders rarely conducted na-

tional concerns consistently for very long, "and nothing but the un-
varying motive of self-interest can be assumed, as the clue to every
state labyrinth." The origins of that self-interest went back to the beginnings of the Union and before, to the nature of the varied peoples
who settled the untamed land.

"There was a very great difference in character between the several
citizens, and even the several States of the former Union," he said.
Former Union! By 1901 the old United States of Washington and
Jefferson was no more? Indeed it was not. In its place two nations and
nearly a third divided the once happy territory of the Union. The title
of Jahnsenykes's pamphlet told all too well how that division sundered the land. *Memoir of the Northern Kingdom,* he called it. The
Union had split into North and South.

It was that selfishness he spoke of that had done it. It was not peculiar to nations but rather sprang from the men who governed. "I
have very much questioned, whether most of the Republicks, which
have been constituted in the world, did not take their origin from the
ambition, jealousy, envy and pride of leading men." Indeed, prior to
the establishment of the Northern and Southern kingdoms in America,
he found it had been common for men in both sections "to deny merit
to any, but themselves." Even men of good and long family, men of
the American aristocracy, were denied recognition of worth by men
whose fortunes were newly made.

Worse was the American press. The political and commercial newspapers, "those vehicles of truth and falsehood so indeterminately and
promiscuously" combined, were reliable for nothing on the real state
of the nation. "In them abuse generated abuse, and the contention
never closed, till language was exhausted of its epithets of slander. The
American newspapers were the vilest, that ever disgraced a nation." No
sooner did one sheet compliment a public man than its opponent
"blackened his character with aspersion on aspersion." Looking back,
Jahnsenykes could recall only two works of real importance and worth
written in the times leading up to the sectional split. One was President
John Adams's "Defence of the American Constitutions," and the other
Chief Justice John Marshall's biography of Washington. All else was
dross.

Viewing all this, "such a chaotick state of character, such a mixture
of Dutch phlegm, the sanguine complexion of the Englishman, French
choler and vanity, Irish rapidity, German sensibility and patient industry, Negro indifference, and Indian indolence, there was a 'pabu-
lum', as say the naturalists, for any plant whatever." And a virulent,
discordant weed to thrive on that food "was not long wanting."

In the Southern states particularly there had long been a looking toward Europe, toward that more aristocratic than democratic mode of
thought, toward rule by birth rather than worth. "As might naturally
be expected," said the Reverend Jahnsenykes, "native Americans, and

especially those of the middle and northern States, conceived a disgust at these measures." That disgust would grow, "and since politically as well, as philosophically, action and reaction are equal, this conduct created resentment, and paved the way for a separation of interests."

The leader of that separation was Virginia. "She had ever been indifferent to the Federal Union, except when she herself was the acknowledged head of it." Fearful of uprising among her large slave population, she resented all the more her declining influence in the government that might at any time threaten her hold over Negro property. Virginia "set up, by her writers, the hue and cry," said Jahnsenykes. "It was now too late to recede, and the cry of war resounded from the south." Those states not in sympathy with Virginia, those of the North, "they too, who were disaffected to Virginia and her interests, demanded war." The journalists of North and South both feverishly editorialized for defense, for battle. Virginia lay charged with willfully seeking to dissolve the national compact. She did not deny it. As a state "she claimed her right," a state's right. That spirit of self-interest, which the clergyman said set nation against nation, now brought war between the states. Virginia and her sisters to the south "cast the gauntlet of civil war at the feet of the yet confederated States."[2]

How America could come to sectional strife, to secession and internal warfare, baffled Jahnsenykes. "In the political contests and discussions of that day the disputants seemed to have forgotten, that the government was decidedly and legally a creation of the majority, and that of course it was the duty of a minority to submit with cheerful loyalty." The Constitution even provided an opportunity to change administrations periodically "that mutual dependence might beget and nurture mutual charity." But the growth of parties divided the loyalties of men and split them along sectional lines. Before long, instead of bending to the will of the majority, the minority party spoke of oppression and secession. "The question of separation ought never to have been debated. Behold now the consequences! To utter the idea should, from the first, have been deemed implicit treason; and the man, who broached the plan of it, should have been held up, as an enemy to his country, whether he were a Virginian or New Englander."

Yet the very nature of the men populating North and South dictated conflict. Virginians and other Southerners "were generally bred in habits of superiority, and accustomed to deference from early years, owing to the great prevalence of slavery in those times." The Northerner, on the opposite hand, was not usually the creation of his estate but, rather, its creator. "Hence the planters were, in fact, a kind of lords; and so too were the merchants, another body of 'honourable men'; and between the two there obtained not only a domestick rivalry, but a civil competition."

No sooner did Virginia and her sisters give indications that "a political sovereignty, of whatever name, was about to be formed in the South, than every exertion was made among influential men of the North, to increase their influence, and form a separate dominion." Meanwhile, the middle states, Pennsylvania, Delaware, Maryland, firmly adhered to the old course of Republicanism, the old notion of Union. They were wooed and courted by North and South to no avail.

And then came the war. "I will not enter into a detail of . . . that eventful period," wrote Jahnsenykes. "I look on all the scenes I have related with horror." The contest between North and South, he said, was "long and violent." It was briefly forestalled by a presidential election, "but for a short time only." In the North "a vigorous preparation for war immediately commenced. Rebellion had begun." Yet the clergyman hesitated to recount to his son "the murders, sieges, devastations and cruelties of a mode of warfare ever the most bloody. Why paint to you the rage, barbarity and brutal violence of a contest so deplorable and fatal?" Suffice it to say that "the war raged." And as it ravaged North and South, many, dissatisfied or compelled to leave, sought their future in the West. "And it is far more than probable, that there will be the last stand of American Republicanism," predicted Jahnsenykes.

"Quiet may be restored to this unhappy country in all its parts," he concluded, "a quiet, which for fifty years and more has been prostituted and abandoned." Indeed, he even believed that North and South, now split in twain, might "yet find their interest in uniting their force." He could but hope.[3]

His son Julius, in his preface, added further comment to his father's letters. They had been written in 1872, fifty years after the sectional conflict that began in the 1820s. Now Julius Jahnsenykes, writing in 1901, made reference briefly to the great war between North and South. It began, he said, in 1856, and the years of open warfare brought great changes to the land and its people. That sectional conflict, too, gave rise to a new group which he feared, the "Illinois Republicans." "These factious demagogues, for such must they be named, are for protracting a war" that should have ended long ago. Yet, curiously enough, out of the rise of these Republicans will come eventually a reunion of North and South.[4]

Of course, it was all a fairy tale. The Reverend Williamson Jahnsenykes was, in fact, William Jenks of Boston, and there he published his pamphlet, not in Quebec. This glimpse into the future came from the press, not in 1901, but in 1808. In fact, Jenks was writing a political tract against President Thomas Jefferson, "His Virginian Majesty," and his predilection for things French. Indeed, one of "Jahnsenykes's" letters even comments upon Jefferson. "I will not call him great," it read. History had indicted him with responsibility for the course taken by Virginia, and "I do not take it upon myself to exculpate him, for a review of his measures tends too evidently to a conviction." It would have been better for Jefferson's memory had he died in office as secretary of state, rather than go on to the presidency and disaster. Not that Jenks was all that much for the Federalists. They, too, he characterized without flattery, though they did, at least, have the benefit of a prejudice toward Great Britain. And as for those Illinois Republicans, Jenks referred to the broad group of those who fled the East to seek fortune, and power, in the trans-Appalachian West. "For many years, it is well known, their territory has been the common receptacle of intriguing, discontented and abandoned men," obviously a reference to onetime Vice-President Aaron Burr, whose recent presumed attempt to establish a Western nation collapsed in his capture and trial.

Yet there was startling prophecy here, prescience of a kind that even a careful study of the current state of the Union in 1808 could hardly match. The nation would be split in two, North and South, over sectional differences and, more than anything else, the unwillingness of the minority to submit to the majority. Slavery would be a significant issue. The press in both sections would exacerbate their differences. Virginia would be the premier state in the Southern confederation-to-be, and the great issue would be her rights, a state's rights. A species of nationalism, that selfish self-interest that animated nations, would arise within the individual states of the South, a Southern nationalism. From that and the unyielding position of the men of New England, would come the catalyst for civil war. A presidential election would bring out all the hostility, crystalize the feelings of the sections, and momentarily divert militant passions into political emotions. But in its path there followed a "long and violent" conflict, a civil war, "a mode of warfare ever the most bloody." The South would seek foreign alliances, chiefly with France.

And emerging from the ruin would come a new party, the Illinois Republicans, who would eventually cause the North and South to be joined again into one. Here was prophecy of a high order. Even as Jenks's pamphlet issued from the press, in November 1808, a woman named Nancy Hanks Lincoln was six months pregnant out in the Kentucky wilderness, in the West Jenks so feared. Her son to come would be a leader of those Illinois Republicans and would, more than any other man, reunite South to North.

Jenks even came close in predicting that the upheaval would come in 1856. He missed the mark by just one presidential election, four years. Yet many will argue in days to come that the first blows of civil war were, in fact, thrown in 1856, and that open warfare took five more years to erupt simply because of delayed reaction.

Surely, in his own time, in the Union of 1808, William Jenks's musings attracted little notice. "It has been too hastily written to preserve more than a momentary existence," wrote a reviewer, and he was right. "The idea of anticipating the events of futurity, is not new," the reviewer went on, yet "were we to occupy ourselves in speculations of this kind, we should not be disposed to predict the future fate of the country exactly as the author has done." Not even, he concluded, "if we admitted the notion of the destruction of the present Union."[5]

That notion this reviewer of 1808 did not admit. It simply could not happen.

"Yea, the waters had drowned us, and the stream had gone over our soul: the deep waters of the proud had gone over our soul."

From *The Psalter*, 124, in
THE BOOK OF COMMON PRAYER

CHAPTER 1

_____

"MAKE YOURSELVES ALL OF ONE MIND"

The first Americans were just that—Americans—long before they ever set foot on the unspoiled soil of the New World. America was an idea before it had a name. It was an idea of hope, of something better, of riches, land, trade, and plenty. For more millennia than history recorded, men and women of the Old World, of Europe, lived and died in the land of their ancestors. Their lot was given them at birth, their place, their social standing, even their names rigorously dictated by all that had gone before. The lives of forgotten millions could have been foretold from the moments of their conception, unchanging, immutable, wedded to the land, the law, the tradition of the Old World. For all but the privileged, it was a way of life in which one century was much like another. The clothing changed of course, as did the music and other arts. The occasional technological innovation altered life for the aristocracy from time to time. Yet for the rest of European humanity life in A.D. 1492 was little changed from life in 3000 B.C. It was work, life at barely the level of subsistence, and a way of living that discouraged, if it did not destroy, the idea of hope, of improvement, of something better.

The real miracle of the Renaissance is not the sudden blossoming of art and invention. So far as the *literati* and artists were concerned, the Dark Ages were not really so dark. The true wonder is not what happened among the privileged and educated. Rather it lies with the poor, the illiterate, those who were to form the nucleus of an emerging middle class. Bred for centuries not to look ahead, to live day to day, to expect no change for the better and certainly not to think that they themselves might have an influence on the improvement of their destinies, these people in the wake of Columbus suddenly began to think in ways not a part of their ancestral inheritance. Admittedly only a fraction of the common people of the Old World, this cadre still sensed somehow instinctively that there could be a better future for them, and that it lay with the setting sun in the West.

Others felt that same impulse, that same hope, thousands of years earlier, and found it in the same place. Yet for them it lay in the East, in the dawning sun. Long before Columbus, before Rome and Greece, before pharaohs ruled in Egypt, when a land bridge still connected North America to the easternmost reaches of Asia in the icy Bering Sea, men with dark skins moved across that passage and began the centuries of migration that led them to the warm and fertile and abundant plains and mountains and valleys of the heartland. They came for something better, for their own self-interest. Their coming made them Americans. Only the European made them Indians.

This is what would set America apart from the rest of the world, this expectation of something better. And thus it was that those who came to discover, to explore, and finally to settle, the new land, were men of like minds. They came because *they* looked for something better. For many it was merely quick profits, the exploitation of the virgin wilderness for riches that would bring a high price and improved status in the Old World. Yet even they, in their way, sought their future in America, though they did not essay to live there.

How much more American, then, were the men and women who made the truly epochal decision to abandon their millennial homes, to sever forever their ties of custom and culture, and move to make permanent cause in the new land. However casually some made that decision—and for many, their circumstances dictated the choice for them—it represented a closing of the door on everything they had known from their own experience and from ancestral memory. Never since the time when mammals abandoned the sea had human creatures taken so complete a departure from their known environment. Only the bold, the foolhardy, and the desperate, would take that departure in the first days of discovery and settlement. And it was their determination to go, their recognition that there might be something better for them in the West, and their intention to find it, that made them Americans from the moment of decision. Even before the first feet shuffled aboard the crowded decks of the naos and caravels to risk the uncertain passage west, the essential elements of the American mind were born among those now nervously stowing their few possessions for the voyage. They had hope. More than that, they had expectation, a belief that they could effect their destinies, that they could make their lives and their fortunes better by their own influence. Whether they came for greed, for adventure, to escape persecution, whether they were expelled from their homes as undesirables, or simply sought a better place to live, their expectations united them. Many would falter and return. More would die. Others saw their brief initiative dissolve against the hardships of the new country, and reverted to the unthinking, unhoping creatures they had been before America changed them, however briefly.

But for those who survived, who stayed, who conquered and prospered, the idea of America became ever more entrenched, more deeply rooted in their consciousness and that of their progeny. Here was the land of self-interest. They came and stayed not to gather themselves together for the common weal, but that each individually might reap what he himself had sown. They brought in their determination and enthusiasm, in their independence of mind, the seeds of unity, of future greatness, of mighty nationhood, of commerce and discovery and invention, social and technological, that would dazzle the world. Yet lurking dormant amid that seed, and itself the natural outgrowth of this new American mind, lay the germ of Fort Sumter.

Barely a decade after the first permanent English settlement was planted at Jamestown in the new country called Virginia, most of the influences that would bring discord to the immigrants' posterity were already present. Even now, despite hopes of finding precious minerals, agriculture and commerce were the only concrete means of support for the Virginians. And for their cash crop, their profit-making harvest, they looked to a plant that rapidly debilitated the soil. Tobacco, like the cotton that would follow it in later years, voraciously devoured acre upon acre. It could bring great wealth, but it demanded great land in return. Thus were born the baronial estates, the plantations, that burgeoned later in the 1600s. For those with the industry or the influence to acquire it, much land awaited the taking. Great estates begat considerable power in local affairs, and that power, naturally, was exerted for the benefit first of the estate, or else for a group of estates whose interests were common. That meant government.

Government came early to Jamestown. In 1619 the precursor of the House of Burgesses first met in council. Their concerns were for themselves and their fellow planters, for defense, for establishment of title to their properties, for laws of conduct and morality, and for their rights as Englishmen. And for their rights as Virginians. Already, so soon after landing on these shores, these Americans looked to government to further and to protect their interests, their rights. Here were first entwined the fibers of an incipient nationalism that runs thread-

like through the entire career of Virginia from colony to statehood to
rebellion. The same thread will for a time bind all of the New World
colonies in revolt against the Old, and into Union. But being a cotton
thread, it will bind even more to one another, the colonies and future
states of the South.

In 1619, as well, yet one more influence came to Jamestown, one
that will be bound up with Southern agriculture, government, and nationalism, in a way that will make it symbolic of all. In that year
Dutch traders landed in the James River and brought ashore a handful of Africans. Slaves.

Ironically, the slave trade had been inaugurated to Europeans
chiefly by one of the very same explorers and entrepreneurs who did
much to facilitate the opening of the New World, Sir John Hawkins.
Indeed, in recognition of bringing this new labor force to England
and Europe, he was allowed to add a Negro in chains to his family
arms. It is he as well, and not Walter Raleigh, who really introduced
the produce of the New World, tobacco, to the Old. The resulting
demand created America's first significant trade, yet to grow and tend
that difficult weed required time and care and many hands. Cheap
hands, else the profits would dissipate. What better to grow Hawkins's
tobacco than Hawkins's slaves? The extent of the legacy of John
Hawkins to the economy, culture, and society of the American South
would never be fully appreciated, particularly since he never set foot
on its soil nor actually sold slaves there. How sweet, then, the irony
that his own descendants who settled in America would one day take
arms to battle against the economy of slavery.

And so the settlers came to America. They declared their intentions
in memorials to their backers in London, "These being the true, and
essential ends of this *Plantation*." They paid the obligatory service to
the church, promising to baptize the heathens into the Christian
religion. But they were more interested in "the appearance and assurance of *Private commodity* to the *particular undertakers*, by recover-
ing and possessing to themselves a fruitfull land."[1] They came for
their own good, and the instructions of the London Company to the
Virginia settlers of 1607 amply enhanced that determination. "Lastly
and Chiefly," they said, "the way to prosper and to Obtain Good Success is to make yourselves all of one mind for the Good of your Country and your own." From the very instant of creation, then, America
was destined to be the land of self-interest, of local peoples being "all
of one mind" for their local good.[2]

Upon their landing in the New World, the colonists found a country that naturally encouraged a divergence of interest, a dispersion of
people into environments that made impossible any universality of
"one mind" among them. The northern regions of the Atlantic Sea-
board, though settled later, were immediately more inhospitable.
Great wooded wildernesses proved for a generation a seemingly im-

penetrable barrier, concentrating the population in villages and burgeoning cities along the coast. Boston and New Amsterdam (New York) will be prospering colonial metropolises long before Richmond or Charleston are even founded. For in the South the wilderness was more yielding. Further, the land seemed more fertile, less rocky, better adapted to agriculture and profit-making crops, than the soil of the Northern colonies, soon to be called New England.

The rivers ran from west to east, encouraging expansion and exploration for each colony independently of the others. Once settlement was made in the interior, the same river courses stimulated trade in a like manner. Because the Potomac ran west from the Virginia shore, it was chiefly Virginians who pushed westward their settlement along it. And thus Virginians traded with Virginians when once the waterway was used for commerce.

Nothing in the geography of the New World encouraged trade, expansion, or conquest, as a cooperative effort among the peoples of the several colonies. The land was simply too big, there was too much to conquer. Even the mountains encouraged an insular, provincial, "local" turn of mind. Running from North to South, the Appalachians provided a barrier from New York to the wilds of what will become Georgia. The peoples of each colony, at roughly the same point in their separate evolution and expansion, will come face to face with this wall of stone, and each will conquer it for themselves. Thus, they will regard what they find on the other side as their own, as theirs by the time-honored right of conquest and by an already developing sense of what in later years will be termed their "manifest destiny." The new land to the west was not there for the common benefit of all Americans as a whole. Rather, it was conceived immediately as an arena for the individual interests of the colonies separately. Virginia and Massachusetts, three hundred miles apart on the Atlantic coast, each laid claim to much of the same territory in the interior.

Just as the conquest of the land moved straight west, colony by colony, so did the conquest of a less stationary, more formidable foe, the first Americans. Indeed, it can be argued that the Europeans did not in fact settle "a virgin land," but that in fact they merely invaded and made their own a territory already settled by a resident population. Further, far from being uncivilized, the American Indians enjoyed a fairly rich culture, a highly stratified social order, and even a reasonably sophisticated political system. They traded among themselves, North and South, East to West, and in several parts of the land formed loose confederations for their common defense. They lived in houses little more rude than those the first settlers would build, gathered in cities, and tied themselves to the land, their land. They were far more "Western" in their civilization than the Europeans would ever realize.

They were also in the way. For two centuries, almost from the first

landings at Jamestown and Plymouth, the bloody work of pushing the
Indian westward, beyond the as yet unknown Mississippi, would continue unabated. Those who did not move were either dispossessed or
assimilated into poor white society. The result was a state of mind of
almost constant conquest. Not only did the colonists wrest their land
from the wilderness, as they perceived it, but also from a terrible, savage, unmerciful, and ungodly foe. And even as they pushed the na-
tives back, the whites began the unconscious creation of their conquest myth, begat their heroes, their legends.[3]

This myth of the frontier will become a primary element in the
building of a sense of cultural identity. While it operated throughout
the new country, it is most dominant in the South. Many Southerners
will find affinity with the savage, even as they kill him, affecting in
some manner his dress and custom. The early literature of the South
will speak favorably of the Indian and liken Southern men unto him
in warlike and manly pursuits. Yet at the same time this, for most
whites, first contact with a dark skinned people will also provide the
initial experiences from which will grow the belief that these peoples
were by their very color inferior to the white European. The rapidly
and widely spread myths of Indian savagery only added to this belief.
That plus the natural xenophobia of a frontier society, opened the
way for the growth of deep rooted racial prejudices. Put that handful
of captive Negro slaves brought by the Dutch in the middle of this,
and the result was inevitable. The Indians might come to be regarded
as inferior, but they were at least free, and could move West. The
blacks were not and could not. They and their masters were en-
trapped one with the other, an unhappy marriage, yet one not easily
dissolved.[4]

And so this conquest of the Indian became not just a punitive or
avaricious act. In time it will assume a religious quality, and its myth
will feed upon itself and ever grow. Because of the considerably
different nature of the struggle against Southern Indians with that of
those in the North, the mythology and its effects take different courses
in the two sections. Forced by their environment to gather more in
common, the New Englanders will be less expansive, enter less into
conflict with their red neighbors. Their preoccupation with religion, as
well, inclines them more to tolerance, and less to idealization, with
the Indian. Thus, the Indian will not have the unifying effect in the
North that he takes in the South. Among other things, the New
Englanders did not need it to bind them. Their colonies, and later
states, were so small in territory that all of them combined barely
equaled the territory of Virginia alone. Their very proximity in a
common landscape led to common interests.

But not so in the South. There the land and the Indian played a
major role in encouraging men toward common purpose. Virginians
fought the wilderness and the red men to cross the Appalachians and

grasp the land that Virginians will settle and call Kentucky. Virginians and North Carolinians crossed the same mountains, faced the same foes, to take and possess Tennessee. South Carolina and Georgia are not long settled before they carry their guns and their culture into Alabama and Mississippi. Men from every state cross the great river to settle Texas, Arkansas, and Missouri. In short, the conquest of the American South and its Indian population became, by necessity, rather a community effort, and with virtually no assistance from the Northern colonies and states. Conquest breeds pride, pride in self and community. Within that pride lie the seeds of nationalism. It is a spirit that will come to prevail in the South as in no other portion of the new country. It will become a part of the Southern mind, and slowly but steadily it will expand beyond the borders of the individual colonies and states to embrace all of the peoples of the South. It was *their* conquest, *their* pride, and no longer just Virginia's or North Carolina's. They and their guns won together a whole new land, one naturally and distinctly set apart from the rest by the waters that surrounded it. The Potomac and the Ohio rivers on the north, the Mississippi to the west, the salt waters of the Gulf of Mexico and the Atlantic on the south and east, seemed by their very courses to separate this land, the South, from the rest of America. And their conquest set Southerners apart. Fierce in their independence as men of their individual states, still they assumed more and more a collective consciousness, a sense that Southerners as a whole were different from the rest. Their centuries-long conflict with the Indian added a militance to that difference. Southerners were warriors, like the red men. They were conquerors. What New England sought ineffectually to accomplish with the Bible, they did all too successfully with the gun. It is no accident that the South came to outnumber the North in folk heroes. They are the natural children of frontier victory and national pride. Yet they, like the rifle-waving nationalism that spawned them, required conflict to survive. So long as there remained a frontier to conquer, there remained a seeming justification for the militant Southern jingo. Nurtured in a tradition of conflict, he seemed orphaned without it. Thus, by the early decades of the nineteenth century, when the last Southern Indian menace had been erased east of the Mississippi, and the British had already been twice "defeated" by Southern generals, it might have seemed that the Southern mind faced a crisis. Who or what to fight next? Other factors, as old as Southern nationalism and militance, already provided the adversary.

This new threat, this new opponent, followed a long procession in sable. Its issue was slavery. "About the latter end of August, a Dutch man of Warr . . . brought not any thing but 20. and odd Negroes, wch the Governor and Cape Marchant bought." So wrote John Rolfe early in 1620 from Jamestown. So began the long history of the black in America.

In fact, little is known of these early blacks in the colonies. What is certain, however, is that the first American "slaves" were in fact white. In 1610, and perhaps earlier, white indentured servants stepped ashore in Virginia, bonded in servitude for several years to their masters in return for their passage to the New World. Not infrequently the indentured were referred to as slaves, and thus "slavery" was already in practice years before the Dutch ship brought the first of uncountable thousands of cargoes of misery.

How the first Negroes were treated is largely mystery. Though they were "bought" from the Dutch, it appears that several of these first blacks became freemen not long thereafter. For the next half century the flow of slaves into the colonies was only a trickle. By 1649 a contemporary estimate placed their numbers in Virginia at only three hundred. And it is only at this time—actually around 1640—that signs appear of what will eventually become the story of slavery in the South for the next two centuries.

There is some argument that racial prejudice against blacks, far from being a reason for slavery, was instead the result of it. Yet it is apparent from the earliest extant records that the Virginia colonists and their fellows in other colonies, did indeed regard Negroes as something inferior. In 1630, in Jamestown, Hugh Davis was ordered whipped publicly "for abusing himself to the dishonor of God and shame of Christians, by defiling his body in lying with a negro." Similar punishments revealed not only that whites were to be chastised for cohabiting with blacks, but also that the presumably innocent servant received a harsher sentence. When Robert Sweet impregnated a Negro woman in 1640, he was ordered to go to church and do penance. The woman was whipped.[5]

After 1640 it is evident that slavery was in full sway. The term of service, unlike indentures, was for life. Even Indians captured by one tribe from another and sold to the English, were legally held to service only for twelve years. Further, the ruling bodies early on declared that the progeny of black slaves should take up their parents' burden, that they too, and their issue for all time, were to be slaves. And as one more evidence that distinction of race was no small factor, children born of Negro mothers were to be slaves even if fathered by whites. Miscegenation came to be abhorred; but it was not a special crime for a man to lie with his white bond servant, nor was it ever regarded so among Western peoples in earlier times when captured enemies were held in bondage. Clearly the primary issue was the condition of race, not of servitude. Probably even before coming to the New World, these Europeans regarded Negroes as inferiors, as little removed from the wild.[6]

What is important about this is its timing, and place. By the first decades of the seventeenth century the sailing ship had finally mastered all parts of the Atlantic almost from pole to pole. Though far from routine, still a voyage was now at least a secure enough venture that transoceanic trade promised enormous profits. The merchants took what was most easily found and most profitable. From the American coastline they took timber for ships' masts. From Central and South America they took the gold already mined by the Indians. From the shores of Africa they took slaves. By the mid-1600s circumstances were ripe for a burgeoning slave trade, needing only a hungry market. And at that very instant the most lucrative market of all opened in America, and particularly in the South. Thanks to the nature of the land and the selection of tobacco as the first cash crop, large amounts of cheap labor became necessary. No labor, so it seemed, was cheaper than slavery. Indeed, with the large numbers of indentures who came almost on the very first ships, bonded servitude was already accepted practice before the first blacks came. The switch to a labor system based on lifetime Negro servitude, then, required no adjustment at all. And here, the already prevailing disposition of the white to look down on the black as inferior, even subhuman, only provided further encouragement. The conjunction of all these influences at this time and this place virtually ensured that black slavery would take a hold in the American South as nowhere else in the New World or the Old.

Once that hold was taken, it tended, inevitably, to draw together those areas to which slavery was important, as opposed to those places where it was not. By the early eighteenth century, even as really significant numbers of slaves began to appear in the colonies, their presence already encouraged sectional feelings. And sectionalism is merely a synonym for a limited version of the age-old sentiment toward local self-interest, nationalism.

As each decade of the 1700s progressed, it was ever more clear that slavery was destined to be an essentially Southern institution. Northern geography discouraged its spread in significant numbers above Pennsylvania, and Northern sentiments did likewise. Even then Virginia and Maryland were less inextricably involved with slavery than the sister colonies to the south. Yet once the Revolution came and went, bringing in its wake a new nation and a new government, then a setting apart of the slave states precisely because they were *slave* states became inevitable.

For the first time, the American colonies-now-states were part of a unified whole, governed by its own people solely according to its own interests. Sectionalism within the colonies would never have been a major problem so long as they were ruled by England, for their greater combined interests tended to unite all of the colonies as a "section" against Great Britain. With their common antagonist disposed of, however, the colonies instantly found much of their commonality vanished. Even before they were a nation, during the debates in Philadelphia in 1776 leading to the Declaration of Independence, the specter of a sense of Southern nationalism arose over the issue of slavery, and the institution was ignored in the final document. Once the states were a United States, further agitation was inevitable, and it was America's newfound nationhood that made it so. It is no truism to state that to have sectionalism, there must first be a whole; to have disunion, there must first be union.

Within only a few years of the formation of that new Union, the old influences of geography, economy, and prejudice went even farther to entrench slavery as *the* Southern institution and, being distinctly Southern, it tended to set the South further apart from the North. While tobacco was still an important crop, cotton and indigo and rice grew in popularity and profitability. The cotton gin helped, but it only sped a trend that was already in motion. And that created an ever increasing need for slaves. It was served in the main by a continuing Atlantic slave trade, in the face of a Federal law in 1808 prohibiting such commerce. And it was served as well by an internal overland trade. Virginia, and to a lesser extent North Carolina, came in the early nineteenth century to abandon the labor intensive crops like tobacco and cotton and converted to more conventional agriculture. That required fewer field hands and created a troubling surplus of slaves. Soon Virginians began selling their extra hands into the lower South where cotton raising had spread rapidly and where the slave market burgeoned. Thus, while an expanding cotton economy made slavery ever more vital to the Deep South states, the trade in Negroes to those states from the Middle Atlantic slave owners tended to bind them in common interest. Slavery became the great single common denominator, the thread that bound the South together, its "peculiar institution." Thus, to attack slavery was to attack the South itself. To defend slavery was not an act of economic interest as much as an expression of "national" pride.[7]

The attacks began early. Despite the fact that Great Britain encouraged the slave trade and the expansion of slavery during most of the colonial period, there had also been consistent attempts to curtail the institution, and not all of them in the North. South Carolina, for instance, banned slave importation for several years after the Revolution, and there was always a significant, if minority, sentiment against bonded servitude in the South. But in the North it was far more outspoken, more numerous, and more successful. Whereas the antislavery movement never had the effect in the North of enhancing a Northern nationalism, as its opposite did in the South, still it came in time to assume the character of a religious movement. Throughout history the only impulse that has been able to stand toe to toe in battling with nationalism, has been religion.

Slavery became an issue in determining who should fight for freedom—for the whites, that is—and in how the states should be taxed and representation was to be apportioned in the Congress. Once the new nation began its inexorable march of acquisition and annexation, slavery once again stood as a major issue. Just as the colonists felt from the beginning that the lands directly west of their settlements should belong to them, even to the Pacific, so now the states felt that the territories that would be settled to make new states to their west should also reflect their particular, and peculiar, institutions. When the Northwest Territory came before Congress for organization in 1787, New Englanders, certain that the new land would be settled chiefly from the Northern states, demanded that slavery be banned there. The measure barely failed by one vote. Significantly, every Northern Congressman voted in favor of the ban; every Southern Congressman but two voted against. And thus was set the pattern. Even more significant is that this first major Congressional vote on the issue of slavery was not an attack on it as it existed in the South. Rather, it only sought to contain its spread to newly acquired territory. It is precisely this subject that will be the major point of contention between North and South for the next half century. Slavery was already secure in, and symbolic of, the South. To threaten its expansion into the new Federal territories, then, posed not just a threat to a system of labor. It was a direct affront to the South itself, an insult to the entire section, one more factor setting it apart from the Union as a whole, one more rallying point of common interest, one more stimulant to Southern nationalism.

Thus almost from the first the very existence of the Union posed a great threat to Southern interests. Before the Revolution the antislave interests in the North had no influence with Great Britain to threaten Southern slavery. But now the nation was ruled entirely from within itself, and by a representative assembly. Here, now, was a forum for the antislave people to use in direct assault. Worse, power in the House of Representatives lay in numbers of votes, and representation was based on population. If somehow slaveholders were prevented from taking their property into the new lands, then obviously they would not go. That meant settlement chiefly by nonslaveholders, who would send in turn antislave representatives to Congress, making an ever greater majority opposed to the South. Like a snowball rolling down a hill, the prolonged effect of such a course would increasingly discriminate against the South, eventually isolating it and its institutions until, with its finally overwhelming numbers, the antislave element could turn the power of the Union government against the South in an assault on slavery within its very borders. That this threat was foreseen and taken seriously almost from the inception of the Union is incontestable. The South even fought in the Constitutional Convention in 1787 to use its slaves as a deterrent, insisting that in apportioning representatives on the basis of population its slaves be partially included in the count. Thus the slaves unwittingly found

themselves used to help maintain a sufficient power in Congress to ensure that they would remain slaves.[8]

The slave men fought the antislavery forces by defending slavery as
a positive good. They were in fact defending the South, and there is
no better stimulant to an incipient nationalism than to put it on the
defensive. In the first three decades of the Union, of course, the South
was mostly preeminent in national politics, with four of five Presidents Virginians. But that ever present West, the tendency of Southern agriculture to exhaust its land and need more, and the rapid
growth in population and influence of a chiefly mercantile North,
quickly made the situation unstable. Every influence forced the South
further in on itself. On top of this, even the nonslaveholders in the
South came quickly to identify with their plantation neighbors. Those
who owned slaves did not, then, necessarily labor themselves. Thus,
work being the task of Negroes, it was degrading. This set the
slaveholders apart from the rest of their Southern brethren as superior
individuals. First, it brought resentment from the poor and unproper-
tied. Gradually, however, the slaveholder came to represent a certain
patrician status that was uniquely Southern, and if the poor white
could not afford to participate materially, still he could elevate himself by emulating the slaveholders' ideals. In time the abstract of slavery became as great a source of pride and honor and "national" identity for the poor white as for the plantation lord. Many of the most
vehement defenders of the peculiar institution hailed from the ranks
of those who never owned a single chattel.

Another effect of slavery was one early recognized and feared by
Thomas Jefferson, himself a prime example of a different kind of
Southerner—one who owned slaves yet opposed slavery. He believed
that living in a world where whites held absolute power, even to
death, over blacks, would encourage an imperiousness in the children
of the plantations that was incompatible with a democratic society.
These would be the children who would grow to rule their states in
coming years and sit in Congress. Yet, unaccustomed to being restrained or governed, they would, he feared, resent and recoil from
accepting limitations and government imposed by anyone but themselves.

All of these elements helped Southerners to overcome a significant
obstacle, their own lack of unity within themselves. There were several Souths as the region developed. By the first half of the nineteenth
century there was a planter South, a mercantile South, a Whig South
not too concerned with state rights, politics, and Southern nationalism, a poor white South whose only cheer in the social order was
that poor though they were they were still better than the Negro.
Many of these divergent groups felt a considerable antipathy toward
some or all of the others. All that each of them had in common was
that they were Southern, and they were white. Yet these two traits

were enough eventually to overcome all of the differences. For the increasing attacks on slavery from outside the South, coupled with a growing lag of the region's economy compared with the North, tended ever more to drive its people together despite their differences. And the ever present black, symbol of so much more than his actual labor represented, offered the greatest persuasion of all. One of the thousands of newly wealthy plantation lords whose fortunes were made in moving with their slaves to the trans-Appalachian west, was Jefferson Davis of Mississippi. With unusual candor, this most contentious of Southerners freely admitted that the greatest cement holding all white Southerners together in a single fraternity was the presence in their midst "of a lower race."

Thus driven together, the men of the South increasingly saw common cause among the several states. All of those many and irresistible influences that had worked on them and their grandsires since the first days at Jamestown came increasingly together as America in the 1800s marched toward mid-century. The sense of being different from the rest of the nation; the motivation of self-interest; the grounding of their economy in a few limited cash crops; the rapacious need for the cheap labor that those crops demanded; the use of government from the first as a means to protect their localized interests; the geography that made the westward movement to the Mississippi a topic for local and regional, not national, pride; the growth of a deep-rooted prejudice against nonwhite peoples, particularly the African; the repeatedly successful stands at arms, first the conquest of the Indians, and then the defeat of the British in two wars, the major defeats being administered in the South by Southerners; and finally the paranoia engendered by steady and increasing attacks from outside on the South's most cherished social and economic institution, slavery. The combination of all of these powerful elements inevitably produced in the South what other and sometimes similar influences effected in the colonies as a whole in the days leading to 1776. Nationalism. A feeling of sufficient distinction, of sufficient separation, of enough interests and institutions that were uncompatible with the rest of the nation, that the South was truly a separate nation in itself. Indeed, it was. Nationhood, like family, is more than a matter of blood. It is the perceived identity, the seat of interest and welfare, of loyalty, of affection and fraternity. In all of these things, the South prior to the Civil War turned in on itself rather than outward to the nation as a whole. Such a highly developed and militant sense of self was not alone, however, enough to lead to crisis. After all, even after the first firing in 1775, most colonists still felt that they were only asserting rights as Englishmen, not Americans. What is necessary to push nationalism to overt action is threat, threat to pride and property and institutions. Northern attitudes and Southern hysteria will provide all the danger necessary.[9]

Little has been said of the North, and not too much needs to be said. In the two and one half centuries of growth and development of America that followed the first landings at Plymouth and Jamestown, the North was consistently more a catalyst than a cause in the mushrooming growth of Southern nationalism. The elements that would lead the South to turn in on itself were there from the first; its Northern neighbors simply fed the fires of its own already smoldering fears.

The Northern colonies and states were frequently no less self-interested than those in the cotton kingdom. Indeed, it is in New England that the first feeble rumblings of secession or resistance to the Union are heard. In convention at Hartford, Connecticut, in 1814–15, Massachusetts, Rhode Island, Connecticut, New Hampshire, and Vermont, actually discussed withdrawing from the Union in opposition to the war with Great Britain. Much of their deliberation focused on the threats to New England from the South! More sanguine heads prevailed, but the incident still amply displayed that the states below Pennsylvania had no corner on hot temperaments, or on certain feelings of incipient nationalism.

And neither did the New England states exhibit a markedly more asectional attitude in their commerce and society than the South. Maine proved just as much concerned for the interests of Maine, as was Georgia for Georgia. Yet, with their many similarities, the North, unlike the South, lacked a single unifying element to bind its states consciously together into a part which felt greater than the whole. Its economy was far more diverse. Its industry gave it greater freedom from the land. Its carrying trade on ocean and navigable rivers and canals gave it an outward rather than inward thrust. Its educational advantages and prevailing Calvinism oriented its people more toward individual achievement and hard work, less toward family and station. And most significant, its soil did not require slaves. Even before the Revolution the movement against slavery in the North was widespread. By the middle of the next century slavery was virtually abolished everywhere north of Maryland. After all, it was not hard to give up what was not needed. This is not to discount the widespread moral antipathy toward slavery felt by many, but by and large Northerners believed just as much in the Negro's inferiority as their neighbors to the south. Slavery was not vital, and that made it much easier for the moral element to prevail. Yankee protestations against the peculiar institution may also have been rooted in a sense of guilt for, before abolition of the slave trade, most of those cargoes of living black gold were delivered to the wharves of Charleston and Savannah in the hulls of New England ships.

Yet by the 1830s a genuinely sincere and increasingly militant antislavery sentiment arose in the North, and its aggressive outcries, combined with the fears engendered by the South's increasing minority status in the government, put slaveholders ever more on the defensive. "I will be as harsh as truth and as uncompromising as justice," declared abolitionist William Lloyd Garrison. "I will not retreat a single inch, and I will be heard." There could hardly be a more threatening pronouncement than that. No matter that the virulently militant abolitionists like Garrison would always be a distinct minority in the North, and even more so in Congress. No matter that most of those opposed to slavery objected not so much to its existence in the South as to its extension into new territories in the West. The threat was uttered in mighty invective, and the South was primed to overreact. The threat to slavery, and to its right to extend into the West, was in fact a threat to the South. Editors like Garrison and his proslavery Southern counterparts would battle for three decades, ever increasingly inflaming passions. The Reverend Jahnsenykes's prediction of the irresponsibility of the press in bringing on the disaster was truly prophetic.

For the South, then, by 1850 crisis seemed inevitable. She perceived an imminent assault on the institution that represented not just her base of labor and economy, but as well her life-style, her social order, her very distinctiveness as the South. Slavery was the very identity of the South. And when one threatens a nation's institutions, its identity, its pride, its natural and inevitable course is defense, and ultimately arms.

CHAPTER 2

"SOUTH CAROLINA IS READY, SIR!"

Surely the worst place to be in the 1850s was the middle. John C. Breckinridge was in the middle. He was a Kentuckian, from a border state caught between the fretting sections, and like most border state men, the victim of conflicting loyalties. It was a malady besetting many like him, yet it was chiefly these men from the middle who would preserve national calm and stay the mailed fists as long as possible. He was a young state legislator in the assembly at Frankfort in 1850 when his first statement of his attitude came forth. It was on January 16, his birthday, his twenty-ninth. He was proud, a new father.

Breckinridge spoke in support of the abstract right of slavery, of the rights of Southerners under the Missouri Compromise of 1820 to take their slave property into any new territory formed south of an imaginary line drawn across the center of the continent to the Pacific. Yet he said as well that Congress did in fact have the right to legislate in the matter "in a manner just and equal to all the states." This the more strident Southern rights men from South Carolina and other states would never countenance. Yet Breckinridge was a moderate in all things. He recognized the many threats to national harmony then in the wind, yet for him as for most border men the welfare of the whole was of greater concern than that of the parts. "Kentucky does not look to disunion as a remedy for any of the evils which threaten our peace," he said. It was his credo.[1]

Could someone have taken a Southern rights man, a Southern Unionist, a Western expansionist, a Northern abolitionist, a Yankee entrepreneur, in short, one of every kind, and combined them to form a composite man, it would make a Breckinridge. In the 1850s he was the median man, the average American. The goods, the evils, hopes, and fears, are all blended in this one character, and all tempered by his unshakable moderation. It was the product of his heritage.

The Breckinridges were always moderates, neither revolutionary nor reactionary. They came from Scotland, passed time in Ireland like many Covenanters, then crossed the ocean to America in the late 1720s. They made themselves Virginians, and slaveowners. They partook of local politics. They became, and would remain, landed, but hardly wealthy. Their first pride was the first John Breckinridge, born in 1761. He began the family emphasis on education when he entered the College of William and Mary in 1780, there imbibing the enlightened views of men like George Wythe and the Reverend (later Bishop) James Madison. He took to the law, and late in 1780 to politics. Though he was just nineteen, he was elected to the House of Burgesses by Botetourt County. Early achievement, too, would become a family trait, and from this beginning he went on to the new lands in Kentucky where he soon became a leader in public affairs. He liked the stripe of Jefferson and his new Republican party, and in 1798 acted as Jefferson's agent in introducing the Kentucky Resolutions, the first boldly enunciated stand for the rights of states individually to judge the acts of the Federal government and, if found unjust, to nullify those acts and prevent their imposition. It was a reaction to the Federalist policies of President John Adams. It was also to be a cornerstone in the doctrine of secession.

But Breckinridge was first a Union man. President Jefferson made him his attorney general, but premature death ended a promising career. Breckinridge's progeny carried on his ideas in the Bluegrass, identifying with Henry Clay's Whig party when the old Republicans died away. In 1821 the attorney general's grandson and namesake, John C. Breckinridge was born in Lexington, and the family's brightest star began its ascent.

There is symbolism, perhaps, in the fact that Breckinridge was born in the commonwealth of Clay within months of the Great Pacificator's achievement in bringing about the Missouri Compromise, the first major national attempt to legislate an end to the growing sectional controversy over slavery and its extension. Thus Breckinridge the youngster was nurtured in an atmosphere of compromise, of negotiation, of Union first but Southern rights just over its shoulder. Clay himself was a personal friend to the Breckinridges, and in time an even closer friend to their young scion.

Education in the law grounded him well in the Constitution, and making his first practice in the then frontier of Iowa for two years gave young Breckinridge a healthy regard for raw democracy. His family circle of friends included abolitionists like James G. Birney, whose son was Breckinridge's closest childhood friend, Clay, John J. Crittenden, and prominent slaveholders as well. Eclectic influences surrounded him.

Wisely he returned to Kentucky in 1843 to seek his real fortune, but not before his flirtation with the West left its mark, and not before he narrowly averted a neat bit of irony. On his way to Iowa he had stopped in Jacksonville, Illinois, and was so taken with the community that he wanted at first to settle there. He soon found, however, that the Jacksonville bar was already crowded and offered little promise. Two other lawyers practicing in and around Jacksonville in that year were Stephen A. Douglas and Abraham Lincoln. In less than twenty years these two and Breckinridge will be midwives at the birth of civil war.

In 1849 Breckinridge entered politics, winning his seat in the state legislature, and the next year uttered his stand for Kentucky and the Union. This same year Henry Clay stepped onto the national stage again, along with Douglas and others, to once more avert sectional crisis with the Compromise of 1850. There had been a war with Mexico, successfully concluded two years before. Once again there were large territories open for settlement into which Southerners wanted to go with their slaves. By now, however, a substantial antislave Free-Soil party arose in the North. In 1846 and 1847 Congress had debated the Wilmot Proviso, which would have excluded slavery from all territory acquired from Mexico, even below the Missouri Compromise line. The South, incensed and on the defensive, cried out for John C. Calhoun's doctrine that all territory be open to all Americans *and* their property, since the territory was acquired with the blood and money of all Americans. Southern states called a convention for Nashville in June and secession threatened. Into this maelstrom went Henry Clay. Just two weeks after Breckinridge's "Kentucky does not look to disunion" speech, Clay proposed a series of compromises for the national difficulties. It took nine months for five separate pieces of legislation to pass. They were called the Compromise of 1850. Utah and New Mexico were organized as territories under Douglas's pet scheme of "popular sovereignty," whereby any territory about to apply for statehood would decide the slavery question by popular vote of its then inhabitants. A Fugitive Slave Act was also passed, providing means for slaveholders to recover their runaway slaves even if they sought shelter in free states. California was also admitted to the Union as a free state, and the slave trade abolished in the District of Columbia.

The compromise, in fact, hardly brought North and South together. Antislavery people were outraged at a statue that forced them to send escaped slaves back into bondage, and many resolved publicly to defy the law. Most Southerners, Breckinridge included, felt dismay that the nation's capital, the property and symbol of *all* the people, should deny the property rights of Southerners within its borders. In Georgia, Mississippi, and South Carolina, secession sentiment escalated in the wake of the legislation, and state conventions were called in which Union men narrowly prevailed. It was nearly two years before a relative calm returned to the adversary sections. And it would be only temporary.

Breckinridge happily believed the questions in contention were settled for good. Ever an optimist, he saw good people governing wisely and in good faith. First a Unionist, he did not entirely understand the deep-seated secessionist impulse of his Southern brethren. Like most Kentuckians, he was never a Southern nationalist and did not feel those yearnings for a separate identity from that of the Union. Yet he thought of himself proudly as a Southerner. At the same time he felt a genuine moral aversion to slavery, seldom owned blacks himself, and when he did he often as not manumitted them, as did many in his family. Yet he was not so committed to emancipation that he could fully understand the fervor of the antislave forces in the North and would not countenance tampering with an institution that was explicitly recognized and provided for in the Constitution. He stood squarely in the middle, which meant that when a time came to demand from him a clear choice for one side or the other, he would lose either way.

Thanks in small part to Clay's implicit endorsement of Breckinridge, the young Kentuckian won a seat in Congress in 1851, even though he ran as a Democrat in Clay's old predominantly Whig district. The days of Whiggery were done. It, not the Democracy, had been the patron party of slave men in the South for the past decades. The Democratic party, the party of Jackson, was in fact in its early days much more indifferent to the issue of slavery than to more attractive issues like commerce. But the Whig party in the North also included an increasing number of antislavery men, and the issues of the 1840s, annexation of Texas (as a slaveholding state), extension of slavery into the territories, began a split in the party along sectional lines that never healed. The crisis of 1850 further crystalized allegiances to section rather than party so that, by 1852, the Whigs no longer existed as a truly national fraternity. The Northern Whigs fragmented, those favoring slavery joining the Democrats, those opposing it aligning with the free-soilers. Southern Whigs went in either of two directions. Many of the numerous antislavery people gravitated

toward a burgeoning nativist movement, while the proslavery interests went en masse into the Democracy.

From the first time that Breckinridge stepped onto the House floor,
he was marked as a man of destiny. His family name would have no
less, and his own natural attributes made it inevitable. He stood tall,
over six feet, naturally graceful and erect in carriage. Some said his
head alone seemed "two-story and a half," and within it a handsome
face was illuminated by near-hypnotic, deep-set blue eyes. His appearance and manners, coupled with a born gift for oratory, made
him formidably persuasive on the stump or in the legislative hall. A
fellow Congressman listened to Breckinridge's first speech and mar-
veled. "Nature seemed to have favored him far beyond most men,"
wrote Thomas Bragg of North Carolina. "Of a mien and presence
vouchsafed to few, an eloquence rarely ever equalled, an address and
bearing truly inimitable, an harmonious blending of the *suaviter in
modo* with the *fortiter in re*. These, with the lofty integrity and proud
disdain of all the mean tricks 'of low ambition', marked him as the
very best type of Southern character, and the fittest representative of
the people who loved and trusted him so well." Certainly he was,
then, a force with which to reckon in the days ahead.[2]

When Breckinridge took the floor to make his first address "he was
almost unknown," said Representative Edward Marshall, yet "at the
expiration of the one hour he was recognized among the most formidable debaters in the house." Honors and advancement came rapidly.
In the summer of 1852, when Henry Clay finally ended his long career
by dying, the House of Representatives turned to the young Kentuckian to deliver the elegy. He quickly won the confidence of those
in high Democratic counsels, including Stephen Douglas, and worked
ably in Kentucky for the election of a Democratic President, Franklin
Pierce, in November. Already there were rumors that the Whigs in his
district were so desperate to defeat him that they were prepared to
take unusual measures. At the same time Pierce's people constantly
monitored Breckinridge's political horizon, one of the new President's
men writing the Kentuckian that "You stand no. 1 with the President,
and you can have what you want for the asking." Shortly before the
adjournment of this session a newspaperman asked another Congressman about the tall, graceful young Kentuckian. "That man is
John C. Breckinridge, of Kentucky," came the reply, "who will one
day, if he lives, be President of the United States." Something in
Breckinridge invited prophecy.[3]

But those powers of prescience might better have been used to cast
the future of the Union. Breckinridge would win his reelection in
1853, in a contest that attracted national attention, but it paled in
comparison with the first major issue faced by him and his fellow
Congressmen when they returned to Washington. By early 1854 the
Democratic party had so absorbed the slave interests in the South

that Southerners saw in it their only hope of preserving the peculiar institution and, thereby, their section. President Pierce, a Northern Democrat, felt sympathetic to Southern interests, as did leading Northern Democrats like Douglas. Yet even as 1854 dawned, fragmentation was beginning to attack the party. "I am in favor of the union of the Democratic party," Breckinridge said in a toast in January. "I believe it can exist, and believe that it ought to exist." For his fearful Southern brethren, the prospect of the party's disintegration would leave them seemingly with no remaining hope of survival within the Union.

It began on January 4, when Stephen A. Douglas reported to the Senate a bill to organize the Territory of Nebraska, a bill that eventually became known as the Kansas-Nebraska Act. Douglas's motives are complex. He wanted a railroad to the Pacific. He wanted an issue that might unify the Democratic party. Would-be settlers wanted to move into the fertile new land. And Douglas wanted to be President. The opening of Nebraska and its *proper* territorial organization would go far toward accomplishing all these goals, or so he thought. There were problems, most immediate of which was Nebraska's lying north of the Missouri Compromise line of 1820. So long as that statute remained in effect, slaveholders—most of them Democrats—were barred from taking their property into the new land. Without their property they would not go, Nebraska would be settled by free-staters, and almost certainly enter the Union eventually as a free state, thereby creating only more sectional discord and party dissolution.

The "Little Giant's" solution was his pet program of popular sovereignty, allowing the people who settled the territory to determine for themselves the issue of slavery at the time they applied for statehood. Implicit in this was an abrogation of the Missouri Compromise, which Douglas in fact regarded as unconstitutional anyhow. Under pressure from Southern politicians, Douglas had set off a volcano.

All Americans, Breckinridge among them, wanted Nebraska open to settlement, and in the battle that occupied the next several months, virtually the only issue of contention was this popular sovereignty issue. It divided the Union between slave and antislavery interests, and it divided the Democratic party in the same fashion. Breckinridge, like most Southerners and many moderates, never fully approved of the Missouri Compromise line. Rather than settling sectional passions, he felt, it only inflamed them. It was a constant barrier to Southern men posted "do not trespass." If the question of slavery could be settled by each territory for itself, then whether the institution was voted in or out it would nevertheless be in a manner more democratic. Slavery, thus, would cease to be a dangerous national problem and become, instead, a local one, territory by territory.

In consequence of the position he held on the Missouri Compromise, Breckinridge was dubious about the new Nebraska bill. "I never

would have voted for the Territorial organization of Kansas and Nebraska while that odious stigma remained on the statute book," he
said a few years later. Now he went to work to do something about it.
"While the bill struck at the spirit of the Missouri prohibition," he
said, "it did not meet the question fully. I thought it had to be met."

Others were working even then at an explicit repeal of the 1820
compromise line, and they consulted Breckinridge. He would act as a
go-between for them with Douglas, who opposed writing a repeal into
his bill, believing it to be implicit anyhow, and a move that would
arouse "the hell of a storm." The Kentuckian next brought together
Douglas and Philip Phillips of Alabama to prepare the wording of the
repeal section, and then he went to work on President Franklin
Pierce.

Pierce, too, opposed the Missouri line, but feared the outcry that
would attend an attempt at repeal. Indeed, when Senator Archibald
Dixon of Kentucky prematurely introduced repeal in the Senate, it
created immediate furor. Almost at once the Democrats split sec-
tionally over the issue. Caught in the middle, Pierce sought help from
Breckinridge. The Kentuckian went to him, outlined the repeal that
Phillips was drafting, and urged the President to accept it as an administration measure, or else propose an amendment of his own. To
bring the party back together and to save his presidency, Pierce could
not stand by while this crisis worked its way out. He must take the direction of it or appear to.

Pierce proposed putting the validity of the Missouri line to the
Supreme Court, convinced that the judges would find it unconstitutional. This would free him and his party from the wrath of the
antislave forces. Breckinridge and Douglas agreed, but the Southern
rights men backing the Nebraska bill would not. They demanded explicit repeal. Without it the Southern Democrats would defeat the
bill. With repeal, Pierce and the Northern Democrats would defeat it.
Breckinridge realized that the Nebraska measure, with a repeal, had
to be made an administration bill if it were to pass.

Pierce did not like to transact business on the Sabbath, yet with
time pressing, Breckinridge gathered Douglas, Phillips, David Rice
Atchison, R. M. T. Hunter and James Mason of Virginia, and two or
three others on a Sunday. Before the hour of church they called first
on Pierce's close friend and confidant, Secretary of War Jefferson
Davis of Mississippi. In company with him they went to the White
House. There, in an atmosphere described as "cold formality," Pierce
finally gave in to his visitors and accepted a repeal as part of the Nebraska bill. With administration backing, the measure now had every
good chance of passage.

Breckinridge was proud of the part he had played. "You may think
I have committed a great error," he wrote to an uncle, "yet I say to
you that I had more to do than any other man here, in putting it in its

present shape." This was not a sectional measure, he believed. It was national. It would not exacerbate the slavery issue, but rather remove it from the halls of Congress and put it where it belonged, in the hands of the settlers who would be opening and developing the new territories. Like many another Democrat North and South who supported the Nebraska bill, he believed that "if the Union cannot abide upon it, it cannot last under any form of settlement."[4]

The bill did pass, largely through Breckinridge's continued efforts as one of its floor managers in the House. Indeed, he came near to offering his life for it when a heated debate with another Representative resulted in the Kentuckian's being challenged to a duel. Abhorrent to the practice of dueling, Breckinridge settled the matter short of violence, yet his reputation was greatly enhanced by the affair. On May 30, 1854, Pierce signed the legislation. A Congressman from Georgia, Alexander H. Stephens, who found Breckinridge to be "a man of a high order of talents, of most fascinating manners," would later declare that "Very few contributed more than he did in the House, to the Kansas-Nebraska legislation of 1854."[5]

With the furor done, the rest of the session was anticlimax for Breckinridge but not for the Union. The Democracy had been seemingly united on the bill, but in fact the voting still followed largely sectional lines. For the South it seemed almost as if it was passing its own legislation, assisted by a few Northern friends. Yet the bill disaffected thousands of antislavery and free-soil men, and rallied together the fragments of the old Whig party in the North. On February 28, 1854, at Ripon, Wisconsin, a local meeting was held in opposition to the Nebraska measure. In honor of Jefferson and his antislavery stand in the old Republican party, these men now adopted to themselves the designation Republican. The same was done by countless other local gatherings throughout the North and Northwest. The remnants of the Free-Soil party of 1848, antislavery Whigs, and like-minded Democrats, coalesced almost simultaneously. Before the end of the year there was a real political party in existence out of seeming thin air. Its chief platform was opposition to the further extension of slavery. One of its early members was a man who once practiced law around Jacksonville, Illinois, Abraham Lincoln.

However pedestrian the remainder of his second term in Congress might have seemed for Breckinridge, it looked bright compared to his reelection prospects. The nativist movement that began a few years before sprang full on the national scene with the so-called Know-Nothing party, an anti-Catholic, anti-Semitic, anti-immigrant party, that was militantly xenophobic. The Kansas-Nebraska Act with its implicit encouragement for more Irish and Germans to come settle the West, brought the Know-Nothings out of the woodwork and gave them a particularly strong hold in the South. Southerners largely feared that

the free-soil sentiments of immigrants would outnumber the slave interests and bring the territories into the Union without slavery.

The new party gained a particularly strong hold in Kentucky,
whose large percentage of foreign-born inhabitants stimulated na-
tivists to action. By late 1854 they already held several important
offices in the state and, combined with the last vestiges of Whiggery,
gerrymandered Breckinridge's district out from under him. Reelection
would be nearly impossible. Pierce did not forget his friend, however,
and first proffered him the post as minister to Spain, and later the
governorship of Minnesota Territory. Neither position came about
however, and in 1855 Breckinridge retired to his law practice in Lexington. He was only thirty-four, yet had already enjoyed a remarkable, if brief, career. His retirement was even more brief and more restive.

The Kansas-Nebraska legislation could not possibly have taken
more the opposite effect than what Breckinridge hoped. It sent the
new territory into absolute turmoil. A bitter contest over the new
lands began between proslavery and antislavery men eager to control
the territory for their own ends. Arms and illegal voting were used by
both sides, but the Southern rights forces struck first and won a majority in the new territorial legislature in Kansas. At once they passed
a territorial slave code. Yet by late 1855 the free state men who continued to flock to the fertile plains of the territory outnumbered their
antagonists. They formed their own Free State party and moved toward initiating statehood. Thus "Bleeding Kansas" was born. Border
warfare threatened, and in 1856 proslavery forces would sack
Lawrence, Kansas, provoking retaliation by a fiery-eyed angel of
vengeance, John Brown of Ossawatomie.

So far as Breckinridge was concerned, there was great fault on both
sides, but the real culprit was the Republican party. It was in his eyes
strictly a sectional party, uncontent to abide by the Kansas-Nebraska
settlement. Instead, he and many other Southerners saw in the new
party a threat not only to slavery in the territories, but also in the
South itself. The outspoken rhetoric of its leaders led to exaggerated
fears among all proslavery men. The fate not only of their peculiar institution, but of the Union, seemed at stake. The presidential election
of 1856 would be the measure of all things.

Breckinridge himself began working in Kentucky toward two ends,
renomination of Pierce and placement of Kentucky's own Linn Boyd
in the second spot on the ticket. Others like James Buchanan of Pennsylvania and Douglas, of course, also coveted the Democratic nomination. And even Breckinridge was widely spoken of. "If the matter
could be properly managed," a friend wrote him, "*you* could call forth
and unite the strength of the party in 1856." Breckinridge's reply to
that was "Humbug." Even more pressure was applied to him to seek
the vice-presidential nomination. Buchanan put out hints that he

would be pleased to run on a ticket with the Kentuckian. Yet when Breckinridge entered Nixon's Hall in Cincinnati on June 2, 1856, for the opening session of the Democratic National Convention, he was still committed to Pierce and Boyd. Three days later, after refusing deals and compromises, and over his own attempt to decline, he was the vice-presidential nominee. Constitutionally, he was barely eligible for the job, having become thirty-five years old only four months earlier.

Buchanan and Breckinridge were elected in November, making the latter the youngest Vice-President in American history. Indeed, many there were during that campaign who would have preferred that the candidates and their offices be reversed, for the contrasts between them were remarkable. The "Kangaroo ticket" some called it, for in many ways Breckinridge seemed to be carrying Buchanan. While the elder Pennsylvanian remained aloof from the election, the Kentuckian broke with convention and actively campaigned in several states. There were other more marked differences between the two candidates. Breckinridge was little more than half the age of the sixty-five-year-old Buchanan. The former was vibrant, alive. Buchanan acted and thought like a man beyond his years. Steady, predictable, unfailingly mediocre in personality and character, he was the most ill-suited man ever to achieve the presidency. No one ever accused him of being exciting. He held grudges and probably nursed one against his running mate for not supporting him initially for the nomination. Certain it is that after their inauguration, the new President appears purposely to have alienated his running mate. When Breckinridge sought his first audience with Buchanan, the President declined. He told him, instead, to go see his niece Harriet Lane![6]

It was a bad time for Buchanan to be creating division in his own administration. He and Breckinridge won by a good majority, but still the new Republican party carried a significant number of states in the election, and every one of them in the North. The Democrats took the South solidly and a few marginal Northern states. The popular vote said even more. The Democrats defeated their Republican opponent John C. Frémont by a margin of 500,000 votes. A third party, the American, representing the Know-Nothing movement, polled 800,000 votes, 500,000 of them in distinctly Northern states. The Americans' ranks were disintegrating, and most of their Northern adherents could be expected to unite with the Republicans. Clearly, the once mighty Democratic party, split by sectional divisions, could no longer look with confidence toward control of the seats of power in Washington. And in the South, where the safety of Southern life and institutions was believed to be inextricably entwined with that party, the future looked bleak indeed should the Republicans take power.

Nothing during Buchanan's administration went very far to relieve those fears in the South. Provocation and agitation followed one another act by act for four years. Vice-President Breckinridge, thanks to close family and personal connections on both sides of Mason and Dixon's line, was in an excellent vantage point to observe the mounting passions and tremors. He also traveled the country frequently, observing, counseling, and himself becoming ever more concerned for the future.

In late 1857 the Vice-President took a trip by train from Baton Rouge to Washington. It was his first journey into the Deep South, his first encounter with those nationalistic hotbloods who soon would come to be called "fire-eaters." If his eyes needed any more opening, he got it here. While passing through South Carolina he stepped into the smoking car of the train and sat next to a man in militia uniform wearing "a cocked hat, with three ostrich plumes in it dyed a golden hue." Breckinridge was impressed with the comic opera aspect of his fellow passenger. "His epaulettes were as goldenly superb as his sash and sword," he said. "His martial mien of defiance would have humiliated Job's proudest war-horse sniffing the battle from afar." Somewhat meekly in the face of this sartorial splendor, Breckinridge dared speak.

"May I ask what is going on in this state?"

"Going on, sir? We won't stand it no mo', sir! The governor has sent for his staff to meet him and consult about it in Columbia, sir! I am one of his staff, sir! We won't stand it any longer, sir! No, sir! It is intolerable, sir! No, sir!"

Breckinridge would recall that in surprise "not unmixed with dread," he replied, "Stand what? What is going on?"

"Stand the encroachments on our Southern institutions, sir! The abolitionists must be crushed, sir! We will do it, sir! South Carolina is ready, sir!"

The Vice-President thought for a moment, and then told his companion quietly, with the mordant wit that generally characterized his conversation, that "there was a custom in the Indian Office at Washington, to *tote* at the public cost, a band of big Indian chiefs over the North and its marvelous cities; so that they would not go to war, when they saw what a big country they would have to whip!" The story was probably lost on the hotspur, but the incident did not fail to highlight for Breckinridge the danger facing the Union, and the catastrophic consequences to North and South if the martial spirit of this South Carolinian should ever come to more than bold talk. "We may not agree in all respects in our theories of the constitution," the Vice-President wrote to a Northern Republican that same year, "but I fear that the differences would not amount to much if the opposing views should ever come to the arbitration of the sword."[7]

Events seemed determined to make that judgment by the blade inevitable. Barely did Breckinridge reach Washington and take his seat as President of the Senate when Kansas began anew to smolder and flame. Free-soilers in the territory refused to participate in its government with the slavery men. Thus when a constitutional convention met, it was composed entirely of Southern rights people. When time came to elect a new territorial legislature, the antislavery forces did participate, but their opponents carried the election through gross frauds. The results were thrown out, giving the free-staters a majority in the new legislature. Frightened that their hold on Kansas was dissolving, the slave interests who still controlled the constitutional convention passed a document without requiring that it be voted upon by the people of the territory. The only choice that would be open to Kansans would be this constitution with slavery or without it. This was a flagrant violation of the popular sovereignty doctrine of Douglas and his friends, yet Buchanan made this Lecompton Constitution an administration measure and tried to push it through as a test of party loyalty. Instead it split the party even more and on sectional lines. Douglas struck out at the President and the Kansas constitution while the Southern men in Washington, who had largely forced Buchanan into this position, rallied to his defense. In the end, after referendums and voting boycotts by both sides in Kansas, the Lecompton Constitution came to Congress. The Senate approved it, but Douglas and the Republicans managed to engineer its defeat in the House. A compromise bill was passed referring the constitution to a general vote of the people of Kansas—precisely what the proslavery interests had not wanted—and it was defeated at the Kansas polls in August 1858.

For a full year Lecompton kept passions aroused, further dividing the Democrats, and pitting North and South against one another. Yet once more the national government seemed to pose a threat to distinctly Southern interests and rights. More and more the notion took hold that the only protection for Southern identity was a Southern nation.

Through all this, the Vice-President remained quiet about his feelings, though he favored the Lecompton Constitution since, rightly or wrongly, it was the product of a duly elected convention. He was even glad when the constitution was voted down, for at least the defeat removed a source of discord from the political forum. Even his political enemies, men like Republican Senator William Seward of New York, appreciated and applauded his impartiality. Seward himself moved a resolution in the Senate thanking Breckinridge for the manner in which he presided over the body. "He is a fine-looking man," a young Georgian wrote home after seeing the Vice-President in Washington, "universally esteemed and respected, deemed and taken to be a son of fortune, destined to rise."[8]

Indeed, Breckinridge himself, amid the trouble over Kansas, proved continually the center of a great deal of attention. More than that boy from Georgia thought him "destined to rise." For a Vice-President, a rise could mean only one thing. The Kentuckian was spoken of for the presidency as far back as 1856, when many hoped that he, not Buchanan, would lead the Democratic ticket. After Buchanan's inauguration, when he announced that he would be a one-term President, Breckinridge's backers were even more optimistic of his chances for 1860. Breckinridge was young, appealing, moderate, well liked in both North and South, and had a proven ability at the polls. People voted for him. Even Douglas, once Breckinridge's good friend but now an enemy of the Buchanan administration, still looked kindly upon the Kentuckian. As a sign of his conciliatory intentions, Breckinridge broke with the President by tacitly supporting Douglas in his 1858 bid for reelection to the Senate from Illinois. His opponent was a man who the Reverend Williamson Jahnsenykes never heard of, but one who was a good friend of Breckinridge, and whose wife was his cousin. He was Jahnsenykes's much feared catalyst of civil war, an Illinois Republican, Abraham Lincoln.

Douglas won, and with renewed assurances of his affection for Breckinridge. Yet the two seemed destined for a challenge in 1860, as Douglas surely had presidential aspirations, and the Kentuckian—who felt uncertain—was being pushed by many of his friends as well. Douglas could not carry the South. His alignment with the Republicans on Lecompton had cost him that. Breckinridge, on the other hand, could, and yet he enjoyed wide popularity among Northern Democrats as well. Here was the only prominent man, then, who might unite once more the party, the only party, that could defeat the Republicans and preserve to the South her interests within the Union.

During most of 1859, Breckinridge quietly sounded the support for him among men of all stripes in the party. New York and Pennsylvania looked good for him. "I have not at any time, and do not intend to take one step towards promoting myself in that direction," Breckinridge said of the White House in May, though admitting that "I have not the folly to affect perfect indifference on such a subject." If he should be nominated in 1860, however, it must be because the party as a whole wanted him and not, as with Douglas, because he wanted the presidency. More than anything else, the Kentuckian desired unanimity at the national convention, which would meet in Charleston to select a ticket. "I would not have one fourth of a convention to dissent," he said.[9]

By early 1860 Breckinridge all but abandoned any ideas of seeking the nomination. "I find my name a good deal discussed in connection with the Presidency," he wrote to his uncle Robert, "yet I have neither said or done anything to encourage it—and am firmly resolved not to do so. I do not think that I will be nominated, for . . . I know of no organization for me anywhere, and many of the friends of other gentlemen are actively whistling me down the wind." To a friend he was even more candid. "I do not anticipate being in the way of any body," he wrote, "for my old resolution is unchanged, to take no step to promote myself in that direction. If I were taken up it would be such an accident as does not occur in ages." Besides, the Kentuckian was feeling increasingly unsettled about the future of the country. It "almost tempts me to turn my back on the Capital in indignant despair." Worse, he ruefully admitted that a time was nearly in sight "at which some of the states will go off, or employ the State Governments to paralyze the regular action of the Federal Gov't—and a sad day it will be when it comes." He blamed extremists on both sides, but still laid the lion's share of responsibility at the feet of the Republicans. If there was no change of feeling among the "moral or fanatical element" in the North, he warned, "then according to all human experiences the present system is destined to fail." He could not countenance secession. Disunion was to him repugnant. "The duty, it seems to me of a public man now, is to proclaim honestly the dangers that threaten the country and yet to cling to the constitution and the Union to the last. . . . I look calmly and mournfully at the unhappy tendency of things—and if I had the capacity—and opportunity would make at least a manly effort to restore the feeling for a Constitutional Union." He would make that effort.[10]

As events in 1860 unfolded, the only way in which Breckinridge could attempt to restore unity and a sentiment for the Union was to do precisely what he had resolved against—seek the presidency. Douglas, threatened by the Kentuckian's popularity, now spoke out against him strongly, completing the break between the two. Several other men showed interest in the nomination, but none of them with the credentials or support to unify the Northern and Southern wings of the party. Only the Vice-President could do that. "Breckinridge is unquestionably thought [of], for he can, in my opinion, get the Southern vote. . . . Penn. is for him, and so will be New Jersey, and other scattering votes in the North," wrote a confidant of former President Franklin Pierce; "as against Douglas, I regard his chances as much the most certain. So thinks Douglas too." The Vice-President rather symbolically kept North and South from coming to blows in February when he chanced upon a Pennsylvania Republican and a Virginia Democrat with pistols drawn and ready for combat. He calmed the two Congressmen and prevented violence. But could he do the same with their sections?[11]

As the Charleston convention approached, Breckinridge still felt that his running would only help divide the party. As a result, he instructed all those who wanted to vote for him to support instead James Guthrie, a fellow Kentuckian. When the convention met, however, it was mayhem. The Douglas men came with a slight majority, but not enough to nominate him, particularly after delegates from six Southern states walked out. After fifty-seven ballots with no nominee, the convention adjourned to reconvene in Baltimore on June 18.

Breckinridge was worried. "The proceedings at Charleston threaten great calamities," he said, "unless there is wisdom and forbearance enough to redeem errors, at Baltimore." There was need for wisdom on his part, too. The fiasco at Charleston showed that Guthrie was not a good candidate, and that Douglas was losing ground. Indications were coming from New York, Pennsylvania, Connecticut, New Jersey, and all over the South, that the convention in Baltimore could not unite on either of those two, but that it could agree on Breckinridge. Buchanan would not help. "The President is not for me except as last necessity," wrote the Kentuckian, "that is to say not untill his help will not be worth a d——n." Now he allowed his friends a little more lee-way. They could put his name before the convention, but only after Guthrie had failed to garner any of the major Northern states. "I have some hope, but no great confidence in the general result at Balti-more," he told a friend. "If we can unite, *we will elect the nom-inees.*"[12]

They would not unite. Once more, even though Douglas did not have a majority of the convention behind him, his friends managed to take control of the rules and procedures. When they refused to allow two of the Southern delegations who withdrew at Charleston to re-turn, eight full state delegations walked out in protest along with indi-viduals from other state contingents. That same morning, now that it was too late, Guthrie had withdrawn. If it had been known then that Breckinridge would now allow his name to go before the convention, there might not have been a walkout. But it was too late. Left in a clear majority in Baltimore, Douglas's backers quickly gave him a meaningless nomination with considerably fewer than the two thirds of the total delegates that the rules required. The Democratic party was split.

The men who walked out of the convention quickly reconvened elsewhere in Baltimore. Northerners like Benjamin F. Butler of Mas-sachusetts had earlier received from Breckinridge his pledge that he was first and foremost for the Union, and that even in the event of the Republicans winning with their nominee Abraham Lincoln, there was no justification for the talk of secession. Thus assured, they joined with the Southern delegates in speedily nominating the Kentuckian for the presidency. A vote for Breckinridge, they felt, was a vote against secession. Yet there were those who served different ends in his nomination. The ardent Southern nationalists, the fire-eaters, saw in the Baltimore nominations the fatal division that would ensure Lin-coln's election in November. That, in turn, would mean secession and a new Southern nation. Old Edmund Ruffin of Virginia, a prominent agricultural scientist and vehement secessionist, rejoiced. "This, I trust, is the breaking down of the national democratic party," he wrote in his diary. Now he saw "good prospects of increased southern secession."[13]

Breckinridge was dismayed to receive a divided nomination, one that ensured Lincoln's victory. He decided at once not to accept, and told his friends that he would decline the nomination. But then Senator Jefferson Davis and Robert Toombs of Georgia met with the Kentuckian and made a proposal. He should accept, they said. By doing so, Douglas would know that he could not carry the South, and that he would be defeated. Thus, the only hope for the party would be if both withdrew in favor of a compromise candidate. Breckinridge agreed to accept on this understanding. Yet when Davis called on Douglas, the Little Giant refused to participate in the compromise. He would not withdraw. Despite his admirable stand for the Union a year later, Douglas undeniably allowed his own ambition to split his party, and the Union, in 1860.[14]

Breckinridge was trapped. With Douglas determined to run, and having himself already accepted his nomination, he had no choice but to run as well. In accepting the nomination he had said that men were sometimes "placed in a position where they are reluctant to act and expose themselves to censure, if not to execration they do not merit." Now he lamented to a friend that "My course has been surrounded by difficulties for which I am wholly blameless. We must each pursue what seems to be the path of duty." He was resigned. "I fear there is nothing left but a square fight," he said, "I deeply regret the state of things, but shall do my duty quietly & firmly." Soon it was rumored that he felt he had been lied to and cheated in being persuaded to accept the nomination, probably because Toombs and Davis would come to stand at the forefront of the secessionists. Such was the painful lot of the man in the middle. Like the state he came from, he was committed to moderation, tied alike to North and South and the Union by old bonds of affection, he would not place any one over the others. The prospect of the coming campaign, and its now inevitable denoument, depressed him. To a friend he lamented a few days after the nomination that "I trust I have the courage to lead a forlorn hope."[15]

It was forlorn. Through the summer and into the fall, as November approached, he steadfastly defended the Union and the Constitution, and frequently himself. Even his enemies, like the Republican New York *Times* saw manliness in his course. "Indeed," said the paper, "his conduct challenges a certain degree of admiration from the spirit of self-sacrifice which it indicates." Only once during the campaign did he make a major speech, and it was chiefly a personal defense, and a reiteration of his commitment for the Union. It rankled the Southern nationalists who had seen in his nomination a hope for a candidate who would represent their views. Ruffin was disgusted, calling it "a union-saving speech." "Breckinridge does not come up to my standard of what a southern candidate should be," he decided, "or a true & bold maintainer of the rights of the South." Yet Ruffin did vote for him on November 6, then left immediately for South Carolina. Confident of the election of Lincoln and the crisis that it would pre- cipitate, he wanted to be where "even my feeble aid may be worth something to forward the secession of that state, & consequently of the whole South."[16]

Of course Breckinridge lost, and so did Douglas. Lincoln received a plurality of the vote with 1,866,452, but not a majority. Douglas re- ceived 1,376,957, and Breckinridge 849,781. Yet Lincoln's vote was en- tirely in the North, as was most of Douglas's. Only Breckinridge re- ceived an even vote from North and South. He carried the latter section except for Virginia, Tennessee, and Kentucky, which went for yet a fourth candidate, John Bell. In the electoral college, his vote was second to Lincoln's. More significant, in the South the ardent slave in- terests had voted for Bell. Breckinridge's vote came primarily from the nonslaveholders, predominantly Union men. Clearly, he repre- sented in this election just what he said, moderation, Union. But now it did not matter, really. A Republican would be President. For the old Union, barely over a month remained. For men like Breckinridge, the moderates, their time was passed. The hysteria, the decades of mutual insult and threats in the press that the Reverend Jahnsenykes so decried, the rise of his much feared Republicans and the election of one from Illinois, their commitment to containment of slavery where it already existed, and the vocal minority in the North who called for abolition everywhere, all had combined to drive the South into a corner. Repeated threats from without brought greater unity within the section. To a people already disposed to strong feelings of regional nationalism, nothing could drive them even closer together than the paranoia engendered by Northern assaults on their cherished institution of slavery. No longer was a Southern nation logical simply from a social and geographical standpoint. Now it seemed imperative simply for self-preservation. Just a few weeks prior to the election Alexander H. Stephens, a Congressman from Georgia and friend both of Breckinridge and Lincoln, predicted that the election of the latter would mean that "no earthly power could prevent civil war."[17]

He proved a better prophet, even, than the good Reverend Jahn- senykes.

CHAPTER 3

"WE HAVE PULLED
A TEMPLE DOWN"

"Loyalty to the Union will be treason to the South!" So said Lawrence Keitt of South Carolina. He had once listened to Vice-President Breckinridge tell the story of the Indian chiefs and what they would have to whip if they battled the North, but it had no effect on him any more than it would have on any of the hundreds of other fire-eaters who flocked to their state conventions in the South after Lincoln's election. Certainly it would not have influenced old Ruffin as he sat listening to the delegates to South Carolina's state convention debating an ordinance of secession that December.[1]

He was getting on in years, nearly sixty-seven, a native Virginian and a planter aristocrat. As a young man he volunteered to fight against Great Britain in the War of 1812, and thereafter went on to a career as a nationally prominent agriculturist. That old cash crop tobacco had exhausted Virginia's soil east of the Blue Ridge, and Ruffin experimented with ways of making it once more productive. He was highly successful, and for the next forty years stood in the front rank of progressive farming. He published the highly respected *Farmers' Register* for nine years until his vicious editorializing against banks led to its downfall. He distrusted the democratic process, blamed it for the rise of abolition movements among low-born and immigrant classes. By the 1830s he was an outspoken proponent of slavery and defended it on every ground imaginable—racial inferiority, historical precedent, economic need, and even scientific proofs. By the early 1840s his extreme views had already persuaded him toward secession. His extreme views naturally bedded him with the Southern nationalists, they who spoke for an elitist government, white supremacy, slavery forever, and a separate Southern entity. By 1850 he embraced outright disunion, and for the next decade looked expectantly for more and more confrontations with the North that might unite the Southern states in a resolve to withdraw. He began to write editorials avowing secession and resolved that it should come even if it meant armed conflict.

He was hardly alone. A South Carolinian, Robert B. Rhett, and an Alabamian, William L. Yancey, were with Ruffin the chief movers in the Southern secession movement, a movement that went back with single-minded purpose for more than a decade. Yancey had once actually stood in defense of the Union, but the controversy over slavery in the land acquired from Mexico made him a secessionist. Rhett's state rights extremism dated back to the 1820s. By 1850, both men, along with Ruffin, stood loudly for disunion. All were disappointed when other Southern states failed to stand with South Carolina in the secession crisis in 1850. The three worked together at the Southern Commercial Convention in Montgomery, Alabama, in 1858, a front for chiefly secessionist views and debate on reopening the slave trade. That same year Yancey and Rhett organized the League of United Southerners, and Ruffin became its staunchest defender. It sought to unify Southerners upon a single course of action, and that tending toward secession. Rhett's newspaper, the Charleston *Mercury*, became the chief organ of disunion in the South, and Ruffin soon became a frequent contributor. These three, and others like them, did not bring about secession by themselves. They simply molded the Southern mind, already disposed to a nationalistic impulse, so that it required only external impulses like the Lecompton question, John Brown's 1859 raid on Harpers Ferry, Virginia (now West Virginia), the constant abolition agitation, and finally the election of Lincoln, to set that impulse to spontaneous action. Ruffin was delighted by Brown's attempt to foment a slave uprising in Virginia, for it galvanized Southern fears and belligerence. He proudly attended the hanging of Brown, then sent the weapons captured from Brown and his followers to the Southern governors as souvenirs, and reminders of what the Northern abolition mob wished to visit on the South. He was an able, if irrational, sculptor of public opinion. December 20, 1860, brought him the reward he coveted so long.[2]

At noon that day he attended the meeting of the secession convention in what would henceforward be known as Secession Hall. The appropriate committee reported their ordinance of secession for the convention to consider. "We, the people of the State of South Carolina, in Convention assembled, do declare and ordain . . . that the union now subsisting between South Carolina and other States under the name of the United States of America is hereby dissolved." It was a momentous occasion. Andrew P. Calhoun declared that "We have pulled a temple down that has been built three-quarters of a century. We must clear the rubbish away to reconstruct another. We are now houseless and homeless, and must secure ourselves against storms."

That evening the convention met again to sign and ratify the ordinance. The ceremony took more than two hours, with cheering and applause frequent. The signing done, the president of the convention held aloft the document and declared South Carolina to be "a free & independent community." Ruffin listened to cheer upon cheer as gentlemen tossed their hats to the ceiling and the ladies waved their handkerchiefs. Outside the hall, militia companies paraded and fired salutes. Every street flickered in the light of bonfires. Rockets pierced the dark sky and little boys threw firecrackers indiscriminately. As a memento of the occasion toward which he had bent his efforts for so long, Ruffin obtained one of the pens used to sign the secession ordinance. Was it indeed mightier than the sword? He would soon know.[3]

With the announcement of the Charleston action, other states in the South quickly followed. Mississippi on January 9, 1861, Florida the next day and Alabama the day after that, Georgia on January 19, Louisiana on the twenty-sixth, and Texas on February 1. "All Alabama is in a blaze," wrote Robert Rodes. "The State is now out of the Union, and we are all expecting a brush with the Federal troops." Men like Toombs finally showed their true colors. On December 23 he went home to Georgia to tell his constituents that "I came here to secure your constitutional rights, and to demonstrate to you that you can get no guarantee for those rights from your Northern confederates. . . . I tell you, upon the faith of a true man, that all further looking to the North for security for your constitutional rights in the Union ought to be instantly abandoned." Secession, he said, "will be your best guarantee for liberty, security, tranquillity, and glory." Similar speeches inflamed the rest of the South, coming from throats that proclaimed themselves just as "true" as the duplicitous Toombs. And already that word "glory," with all its ominous overtones, began more and more to appeal to the always present Southern bent toward the militant. Militia companies were marching in every major city and county. Martial fever ran high. And as everything else in the history of secession, the fire blazed the hottest in Charleston.[4]

The match to start the conflagration was a massive pile of bricks and mortar in Charleston Harbor, Fort Sumter. Ironically, it rested on a man-made island of rubble and granite brought from New England in 1829. Atop this foundation the war department spent the next thirty-one years lazily constructing a truly formidable fortress with walls fifty feet high and as much as twelve feet thick. In 1846 Jefferson Davis, then a Congressman, had suggested that United States Army troops manning coastal fortifications like Sumter be replaced with local militia. His motion failed; but if it had not, then there never would have been any trouble here.

Instead, the fort, and mainland defenses at Fort Moultrie, now held United States Regulars. The adoption of the secession ordinance made them foreigners, armed and potentially hostile, and occupiers of sovereign South Carolina soil. Their presence insulted the Palmetto State, and the South, and they must be removed. Governor Francis Pickens immediately appointed a commission to go to Washington and negotiate the removal of the soldiers at Moultrie and Sumter. On December 28, 1860, they petitioned Buchanan for the turning over to South Carolina of all "forts, magazines, light-houses, and other real estate, with their appurtenances" then held by the United States government. The next day, Buchanan, with uncharacteristic decision, declined. It happened, in part, because events in Charleston made the decision for him.[5]

The garrison which so affronted Southern dignity consisted of eighty-five men and officers, hardly a mighty host. Further, their commander was a man who himself held decided Southern sympathies, Major Robert Anderson of Kentucky. His father, Major Richard Anderson, stood in defense of Fort Moultrie exactly eighty years before when attacked by the British in 1780. Now his son, who took command at Moultrie in November 1860, would seemingly do likewise. A career soldier from West Point, fifty-five years old, a slave owner and married to a Georgia woman, his promotion to major had been facilitated some years before by Jefferson Davis himself. He would hardly, then, seem a threat to Southern interests, which may be why Buchanan's pro-secession secretary of war, John B. Floyd of Virginia, appointed him. But Floyd reckoned without Anderson's sense of duty, his allegiance first and foremost to the Union.

Immediately upon assuming command at Charleston, Anderson saw the dangers that awaited him. He found in South Carolina "a settled determination" to possess Moultrie. The friendly personal relations and intercourse between soldiers and citizens did nothing to belie his fears. And should the militia gathering by the hundreds in Charleston decide to act, Anderson's paltry garrison could do little to stop them. Further, if they should attack, he would have to defend himself. Armed conflict. War.

Anderson sought guidance from Secretary Floyd without getting it. The secretary was already culpable of treason in other regards, among them his order—without the President's knowledge—to send 124 cannon to Southern forts in Mississippi and Texas where they would undoubtedly fall into the hands of secessionists. The order went out on December 20, the day South Carolina seceded. Earlier Buchanan had asked—through Breckinridge—that Floyd resign because of financial frauds of which he was guilty. Floyd said he would but took his time, and the ever timorous Buchanan, with all the courage and forcefulness of a bowl of pudding, let him. Now Floyd seemed to be deliberately mismanaging the situation at Charleston. How could the Union possibly survive when the men at its very highest posts were either incompetents or, worse, dishonest. At the time in its history when the United States had its greatest need for statesmen and forceful leaders, it produced only hotheads and third-rate bureaucrats. They, as much as Southern nationalism, made conflict almost inevitable.

Anderson would do what he could to avoid that conflict, with or without help from Floyd. On December 23 he received a confidential dispatch from the secretary that actually, read between the lines, encouraged him to surrender Moultrie and Sumter rather than "expose your own life or that of your men in a hopeless conflict in defense of these forts." This was not what Anderson wanted to hear. Unaware that two weeks before Buchanan had promised Pickens's emissaries that he would make no change in the situation at Charleston, Anderson now decided to move on his own initiative. He would abandon Moultrie and withdraw to Sumter.[6]

He made his move on the night of December 26 and did not alert anyone in his command of it, for fear that word might leak to the Charlestonians who every day visited their works to talk and trade with the soldiers. "So completely did our Commander keep his own counsel, that none in the garrison officer or soldier ever dreamed that he contemplated a move," wrote Private John Thompson of Company E, 1st United States Artillery. Anderson formed the men shortly after sundown, they still thinking that they would defend Fort Moultrie. His first admission of his true plan had been to his surgeon, Samuel W. Crawford, that afternoon. Seeing a steamer lying off the harbor, he said he hoped it would not attempt to come into port that evening. "It would greatly embarrass me. I intend to move to Fort Sumter tonight." Then, around 5 P.M., he spoke to Captain Abner Doubleday who came up intending to invite the major to tea. "I have determined to evacuate this post immediately," said Anderson, "for the purpose of occupying Fort Sumter." He gave the officers twenty minutes to form the garrison and be ready to leave.[7]

The men and officers and their wives and baggage loaded three barges and two boats and in the moonlight cast off for Sumter. Anderson left Lieutenant Jefferson C. Davis—no relation to the Mississippi Senator—with a small detachment to cover the movement. Surgeon Crawford also remained at Moultrie as did Captain John G. Foster. Anderson had given them orders to spike all of the guns and burn their wooden carriages, and by morning most of the work was done.

Shortly after he reached Sumter Anderson wrote a report of his action to the war department. "The step which I have taken," he concluded, "was, in my opinion, necessary to prevent the effusion of blood." If South Carolinians could not attack him at Moultrie, then he would not have to defend himself, and there would be no bloodshed.[8]

His action brought a storm both North and South. When Charleston awoke on December 27 and discovered what had happened under its nose, and despite patrol boats cruising the harbor to prevent just such a movement, the citizenry became livid. Pickens, who was making his capital in the city now, immediately sent J. Johnston Pettigrew to Sumter to demand that Anderson return to Moultrie. The air of formal cordiality belied the serious, nay deadly, business at hand. Pettigrew complained of Buchanan's December 10 promise to keep the status quo, a promise of which Anderson was never informed. Anderson, in turn, cited his duty to protect his command from attack. "In this controversy between the North and South," he told Pettigrew, "my sympathies are entirely with the South." His officers knew that, but he and they knew where their first duty lay. When Pettigrew conveyed the governor's courteous but peremptory demand to return to Moultrie, Anderson declined. "I cannot and will not go back."[9]

Once informed of the major's decision, Pickens immediately ordered all Federal buildings in Charleston seized, and by so doing committed an act of genuine aggression. Anderson had done nothing to threaten South Carolina property. Indeed, he gave up some of it in Fort Moultrie. But now Pickens had unlawfully taken government property. It was the act required to give some little spine to the jellyfish in the White House. The very day that Anderson moved to Sumter, Buchanan agreed to meet with Pickens's commissioners, and to submit to Congress their request that Federal property in South Carolina be turned over to the state. The next day they learned of Anderson's movement and, joined by the slippery Floyd, demanded that the garrison return to Moultrie. Confronted with this, Buchanan hastened to deny any responsibility for Anderson's actions, and agreed to discuss the matter with his cabinet. Floyd had already protested to Anderson. "It is not believed, because there is no order for any such movement," he declared and demanded an explanation. Anderson gave him a simple one. "If attacked, the garrison would never have surrendered without a fight," said the major. Floyd continued his protest in the cabinet meeting, but no decision was reached, and a few days later he finally honored his promise to resign. As for Buchanan, he all but humbled himself before Pickens's commissioners. They pressed him too hard, he complained, they did not give him time to say his prayers! "I always say my prayers when required to act upon any great State affair." It postponed having to take a stand, and now, with only two months of his term as President left, Buchanan wanted nothing so much as to serve it out without taking a stand. He was a moral coward.

The seizure of Federal property in Charleston forced the President to live up to his oath. Even though he was inclined to accede to Pickens's demand, now he could not. Instead, he declared, Sumter would be defended. He gave in to a proposal from Lieutenant General Winfield Scott, general commanding the United States Army, to send a warship with 250 men and supplies to reinforce Sumter. He replaced Floyd as secretary of war with Joseph Holt of Kentucky. "It means war," wrote Senator Louis T. Wigfall of Texas to General Milledge L. Bonham of the South Carolina militia. "Cut off supplies from Anderson and take Sumter as soon as possible." Buchanan was bemused by all this activity. He asked Toombs why all this fuss over a single fort. "Sir," said the Georgian, "the cause of Charleston is the cause of the South."

"Good God, Mr. Toombs, do you mean that I am in the midst of a revolution?"

Toombs replied with appropriate sarcasm. "Yes, Sir—more than that, you have been there for a year and have not yet found it out."[10]

Certainly Anderson knew he was in the middle of something. The fort was not yet completed, many of its guns still unmounted and lying on the parade ground. Only fifteen cannon were actually in their embrasures. Powder and shell lay scattered in piles all over the parade along with the building materials yet needed to complete the works. Worse, the fort had been designed to withstand an attack from the ocean side of the harbor, which it guarded, not from Charleston. There was much work to do. "We are daily adding to the strength of our position," he reported to Washington on January 6, 1861. He believed that, given a little time, he could "hold this fort against any force which can be brought against me." He did not, consequently, ask for reinforcement but did fear that the South Carolinians might cut off his communications with Washington. Oddly enough, they did not, hoping always that one of the letters that they passed back and forth might be Anderson's order to give up Sumter.[11]

Meanwhile, they looked to their own defenses. Charleston ringed Sumter with a series of forts and works. Moultrie faced it from the northeast, at the upper edge of the channel while batteries at Cummings Point to the south, on the lower edge, also trained on the fort. Fort Johnson, directly west of Anderson, and Castle Pinckney to the northwest also commanded his position. Other batteries were spotted around the harbor, along with some new innovations being constructed, among them an iron-sheathed "floating battery" moored off Sullivan's Island, near Moultrie, and another "Iron-Clad Battery" sometimes called the Stevens battery, near Cummings Point. Eventually there would be forty-eight guns of varying dimensions trained on Sumter, among them the ones spiked at Moultrie and soon returned to service. The secessionists needed to be ready, not only to deal with Sumter, but also with any attempts to reinforce it by sea.

This last is precisely what Scott hoped to do, but how? He first intended to send 250 men aboard the warship USS *Brooklyn*, but thought better when he realized that the ship's deep draft might cause it to run aground. After consulting with the President, he changed his plan and determined instead to use the chartered paddle-wheel steamer *Star of the West*. It carried no guns, but was shallower and, it was hoped, would look more peaceful to the Charlestonians than a warship like the *Brooklyn*. It took time to load and provision the vessel, and it was not until January 5 that the *Star of the West* departed. Worse, no one informed Anderson that she was coming and, when the war department did, it was by letter sent through the usual post, even though all mail to Sumter was certainly being intercepted and opened before its delivery. Consequently, Anderson did not know of his imminent relief or of his orders to assist the ship with covering fire should she be fired upon. But if he did not know, Charleston did, and when the *Star of the West* appeared in the main channel on January 9, the city was ready. The ship got within two miles of the city when the battery on Morris Island opened fire, doing no injury. At the first sound of guns, Anderson ordered the garrison to quarters, the guns loaded and ready. Anderson stood with Crawford and other officers on the parapet and looked longingly toward the vessel through his glass. "Major Anderson was excited and uncertain what to do," said Crawford. Then the *Star of the West* apparently made a signal for support and Anderson ordered Lieutenant Davis down to a lower tier of guns to open fire on Fort Moultrie, which was now starting to shoot at the ship. Another lieutenant immediately protested that to do so would start civil war. Before Anderson could act further, the relief vessel gave in to the Confederate shore fire, turned about, and steamed back out to sea. The attempt to supply Sumter had failed.[12]

The men in the fort were distressed that they had not returned the enemy fire. Doubleday stamped his feet in frustration. He for one was ready for war. There had been quite enough pandering to the South. As for the Charlestonians, they rejoiced at this petty victory. It seemed a sure sign that the Yankees, as long believed, did not have the stomach for a fight. They could not have been more mistaken. The North felt outrage at the hostile act, and many chaffed that Buchanan did not take the obvious opportunity to declare that South Carolina had commenced hostilities and move at once to suppress the rebellion. In fact, such a move at this early stage might have halted the march of secession before events got out of hand. But even if successful, strong action now would only have treated the symptom, not the sickness. The nationalistic impulse behind what was happening in Charleston would still remain, to flare out once more another day.

Buchanan did the right thing, and did nothing. Indeed, the condition of the army was such that he could do little else. The Union frankly did not have the muscle to quell rebellion in South Carolina, not now. The silence hurt many loyal Union men. "The nation pockets this insult to the national flag," lamented a New Yorker, "a calm, dishonorable, vile submission."[13]

In the rest of the South, the attempt to succor Sumter was taken for a hostile act at best, at worst treachery. The result was swift. In Washington, Jefferson Davis and others planned to gather in Montgomery, Alabama, the next month to lay plans for a convention to establish a new government. Alabama seceded two days after the firing, and in Mobile there was "the wildest day of excitement in the annals of Mobile." Military companies paraded, and that night bonfires illuminated the city. Elsewhere more militant acts were taking place. In Georgia secessionists took Fort Pulaski on the seacoast near Savannah. In Mississippi they seized Ship Island. As each state in turn passed its secession ordinance, it followed South Carolina's lead by taking possession of Federal arsenals, customs houses, post offices, and forts. Only in Florida did Federal troops make a stand. Lieutenant Adam Slemmer, commanding at Fort Barrancas on the Florida mainland near Pensacola, knew that he could not hold his position, but instead he withdrew his garrison to Fort Pickens on nearby Santa Rosa Island. Here even with only forty-six men he would be secure. When the governors of Alabama and Florida demanded that he give up the place, he said bluntly that " a governor is nobody here." The fortress would remain in Federal hands for the duration of the war, a constant insult to the secessionists in Pensacola who could look each day across the bay to see the Stars and Stripes floating overhead.

Major Robert Anderson, relief or no relief, also intended to hold Fort Sumter. Instantly he lodged his protest with Pickens over the firing on the *Star of the West*. He could not believe that it had been done with the governor's sanction, he said, otherwise it would be an act of war. If so, then the major would retaliate by interdicting the passage of ships into and out of Charleston Harbor. He communicated with Pickens "In order to save, as far as is in my power, the shedding of blood." The governor responded that the hostile act was sending the ship in the first place, and that South Carolina was merely defending herself. "To repel such an attempt is too plainly its duty to allow it to be discussed." There the matter rested. Washington fully approved of Anderson's actions, and repeatedly assured him of its support. For his part, the major put his trust "in God that He will be pleased to save us from the horrors of civil war."[14]

He would be saved for a time. A truce ensued in Charleston. Anderson's messengers came and went. His quartermaster was allowed to buy provisions in Charleston's markets, and one courtly gentleman sent out to the fort several cases of wine. Here matters stayed for several weeks, while South Carolinians seethed beneath the calm. Pickens found Anderson's presence an affront, and it was costing him his popularity. From all sides he took pressure to attack and capture the fort. After all, it held less than ninety men. But Pickens did not have sufficient strength in Charleston to mount an assault, and his batteries were not yet all completed or manned. They would be his only hope of forcing the enemy to submit, for the fifty-foot walls of Sumter simply could not be stormed. Rhett of the *Mercury* raged into the governor's office one day, indignant that supplies were being sold to Anderson, and demanding that the fort be taken. Pickens replied, "Certainly, Mr. Rhett. I have no objection! I will furnish you with some men and you can storm the work yourself."

"But, sir, I am not a military man!" Rhett's ardor apparently did not extend to personal risk.

"Nor I, either," said Pickens, "and therefore I take the advice of those who are."

Pickens also took the counsel of Jefferson Davis who, though an ultra among the Southern nationalists, now played the role of moderate in trying to prevent South Carolina from provoking war before there was a new Southern government in power ready to meet the challenge with a unified command. Sumter, he told Pickens on January 20, "presses on nothing but a point of pride." Be still, he said, wait a month. "We shall then be in a condition to speak with a voice that all must hear and heed."[15]

Meanwhile, the Southerners continued their work on the batteries and earthworks ringing Fort Sumter, while the Federals chaffed at seeing themselves ever more thoroughly besieged. Doubleday, now a virtual hothead, urged Anderson to fire on workmen putting up the enemy defenses, but he would not. To the last extremity he would avoid provoking conflict, ever hopeful of compromise, of a peaceful accommodation. As a Kentuckian, it was almost an ancestral creed.

Then came February 4, 1861. In Montgomery, far away from the turmoil in Charleston, representatives from seven seceded states met in convention. Toombs was there, Francis Barlow, Howell Cobb, Stephens, Rhett, Keitt, and several others. There they organized the government of a new nation, the Confederate States of America, framed a Constitution, and chose a provisional President. Many coveted the new title, among them Toombs, but it went instead to a man who would have preferred to be a general, Jefferson Davis. On February 18 Davis took his oath of office on the steps of the Alabama state Capitol. Now the time was closer when he could take the steps he promised Pickens a month before. Soon the new Confederacy would speak with that "voice that all must hear and heed."

In Sumter, meanwhile, the work of preparing for an attack went on. "We are in daily expectation of a commencement, which must come from them, as our orders are to act strictly on the defensive." So wrote

Private Thompson to his father in Ireland. Anderson was being very candid with his men, telling them almost everything that he learned in dispatches from Washington. Considering the situation, simple fairness seemed to demand it. "That they intend to bombard us is evident," Thompson went on, "and that they will attempt to breach this work at its weakest point is equally sure, but we are sure their attempt will prove a failure." They might starve out Anderson, he concluded, and shell them continually, but the other men were confident that any attack would fail. "To tell the truth in spite of all their bluster I am almost sure they never will fire a shot at us." Thompson left something to be desired as a soothsayer.[16]

As for Anderson himself, he like Breckinridge, was finding the middle a damned uncomfortable place to be. "I have lost all sympathy with the people who govern this State. They are resolved to commence their secession with blood." He spent a lot of time answering the flood of correspondence that came in through courtesy of Charleston officials. His supplies were dwindling. Firewood was gone and they were slowly dismantling and burning temporary workers' sheds for heat and cooking. Anderson became silent and morose, weighted to the ground by the knowledge that the momentous issue of civil war rested entirely in his hands. Do what they might in Washington, and now Montgomery, the decision would be made here in Charleston.[17]

In Washington, both sides played for time. Davis sent a commission to the city to petition for the recognition of the new Confederacy's right to possess Sumter and Pickens. The commissioners arrived separately, the first reaching the Federal capital on Buchanan's last full day in office, March 3, 1861. He toyed with calling on the President in hope of forcing some last minute concession from him. He quickly relented. "His fears for his personal safety," Crawford wrote of Buchanan, "together with the cares of state and his advanced age, render him wholly disqualified for his present position. He is as incapable now of purpose as a child."[18]

The next day there was a new President, Abraham Lincoln. To the Confederate commissioners, as to most of the nation, he was an unknown quantity. Of course he was a Republican, an Illinois Republican. Of course he opposed the extension of slavery, but he also promised not to interfere with the institution where it already existed. Furthermore, like so many of the men who stood in pivotal positions this spring, he was a Kentuckian, a man of Southern antecedents. Perhaps he could be bargained with. Perhaps not. In his speech of inauguration he promised that he would not assail the South, that civil war, if there were to be one, rested in their hands alone.

The very next day President Lincoln learned that Anderson had supplies for only forty more days. That meant that on or about April 14 push would come to shove. Further, the Confederates had so enhanced their defenses that the major now believed that 20,000 troops would be needed to reinforce and supply the fort properly. He informed them that the Confederates surrounding Sumter had a new overall commander. Already the new Southern government was drawing order out of the chaotic profusion of volunteers. The new commander was Brigadier General Pierre G. T. Beauregard, only recently the newly appointed superintendent of the United States Military Academy at West Point, New York, and a noted engineer in what was coming to be called the "Old Army." "The presence here, as commander, of General Beauregard," warned Anderson, "insures, I think, in a great measure the exercise of skill and sound judgment in all operations of the South Carolinians in this harbor." This creole officer from New Orleans knew his business, and Anderson knew it, too. "God grant that our country may be saved from the horrors of a fratricidal war!" Anderson was almost closing his dispatches to Washington with prayers.[19]

Now Lincoln had Buchanan's problems tenfold, for the situation was much more tense than it had been even a few weeks before. He promised to hold all Federal property in the South, and that meant Sumter. He asked old General Scott for his opinion on ways to relieve the fortress, and less than a week later Scott told him frankly that it could not be done inside of six months. The garrison would have no choice but to surrender and probably sooner than later. At this point Lincoln's new secretary of state, William H. Seward of New York, stepped in to complicate matters. Prior to the inauguration, Seward had intimated to Senator William Gwin of California, a secessionist, that he did not favor secession but that, should it occur, then he would prefer that it be peaceable. Thereafter the North might use the gentle art of persuasion to show the South what it had given up and eventually win it back to the Union fold. On the basis of this, Gwin agreed to urge Seward upon Lincoln for the state appointment. Gwin's arguments bore little weight with the President-elect, Seward was so prominent in Republican counsels, and himself a narrow loser of the nomination, that a cabinet appointment was already assured him. But Gwin believed that he played an important part in getting the New Yorker his portfolio. Consequently, Gwin was flattered to be asked by Seward to act as an intermediary with Davis's commissioners in Washington, since Lincoln could not meet them personally without implying recognition of the Confederacy.

Seward told Gwin to assure the Confederates that Sumter's evacuation was inevitable, and for some days friendly messages passed back and forth. To others the secretary intimated that Lincoln had decided to withdraw Anderson. Yet in none of this had Seward consulted the new President. By the second week of March his maneuverings began to backfire on him when Montgomery Blair, the new postmaster general, brought his brother-in-law Gustavus V. Fox to the Executive Mansion to outline a plan for Sumter's relief. Lincoln liked the plan, which called for two ships, one troop transport, and some tugboats. They would anchor off the harbor at night and send in the tugboats loaded with soldiers and food under cover of darkness. "Uncle Abe Lincoln has taken a high esteem for me," Fox wrote to his wife, "and wishes me to take dispatches to Major Anderson." Something of an understatement.

Meanwhile Seward was still up to his peculiar game, working behind the President's back and without his knowledge. Gwin tired of the New Yorker and suspected duplicity, but another took his place as intermediary, and Seward now promised that Sumter would be evacuated by March 17, doing so on the expectation that Lincoln's cabinet would reject Fox's plan. But they accepted it or, more correctly, did not reject it. Rather than order evacuation, Lincoln sent Fox to Charleston simply to assess the situation. Fox went, found that Anderson's reports of his condition were not exaggerated, and that a major reinforcement would require an enormous fleet, and reported back to Lincoln. The hesitation on the part of men in Washington was getting to young Fox. He complained that "the whole thing is child's play. I feel like abandoning my country, moving off somewhere. I am sick down to my heel."

Meanwhile, Davis's commissioners repeatedly asked Seward when the President would order Sumter abandoned. It had not come on March 17 as promised. They, also, were guilty of dissembling, for at Davis's orders they led Seward to believe that if Anderson moved out of the fort, the seceded states might peaceably return to the Union. It was a case of each desperately wanting to believe the other's lies.

By March 29 Lincoln finally made his decision, the first major one of his administration. He would resupply Sumter. So long as the Confederates did not interfere, he would land only food and other supplies. If Beauregard did try to stop them, then he would land soldiers and weapons as well. The cabinet, except for a much embarrassed Seward, approved. As Lincoln tried to implement the movement, his secretary of state interfered with Fox's preparations in order to delay his relief plan, and then associated himself with Captain Montgomery C. Meigs in laying similar plans for the less threatened Fort Pickens.

Now Seward had to confess that Lincoln would not abandon Sumter, but that he would give Governor Pickens fair warning before trying to resupply. The Confederates realized they had been betrayed, or thought they had, but Seward mollified them for a few more days. Then on April 1, All Fools' Day, he diplomatically suggested to Lincoln that North and South could be reunited if war were declared on Spain or France, both of them now adventuring in the American hemisphere. An outside conflict like this would stir the Union sentiment in the Confederate states and result in their return to the fold. Meanwhile, Sumter should be abandoned, and Lincoln might do well to

turn the actual prosecution of affairs over to Seward. All in all, a remarkable proposal. Thanks to Lincoln's enduring patience, and his
ability to see through his associates' petty personality faults and ambitions to their real worth, Seward was not summarily dismissed from
the cabinet. He would have been by most Presidents, but this one saw
better things in the secretary of state.

There followed a comedy of errors in which Meigs and Fox's agent
battled over the use of a ship intended for the Sumter expedition, and
once more Seward's meddling backfired. It was April 8 before Fox
finally steamed his little flotilla out of New York. At the same time
Lincoln notified Pickens of his intentions. Hopefully, by alerting the
Confederates, they would hold their fire. It was a hollow wish, for
events were now out of control.[20]

Jefferson Davis had decided that Fort Sumter must be taken. On
April 2 his secretary of war, Leroy P. Walker, wrote to Beauregard
that "The Government has at no time placed any reliance on assurances by the Government at Washington in respect to the evacuation
of Fort Sumter." On April 9, upon learning of Lincoln's communication with Pickens about supplying Anderson, Walker instructed Beauregard to stop Sumter's mail. "The fort must be completely isolated," he said. Obviously, the situation was racing to a
resolution. For over a week the Confederates in Charleston had been
ready and awaiting an order to themselves attack. Also on April 9 the
Confederate commissioners in Washington finally gave up, believing
themselves betrayed and Seward dishonest. Lincoln's move in sending
Fox made further negotiations fruitless they felt. "Diplomacy has
failed," one wrote to Beauregard. "The sword must now preserve our
independence."

Walker ordered Beauregard to demand Sumter's surrender. If refused, he was to open fire and reduce the fort to submission. On April
11 Beauregard sent his demand to Anderson, giving him four hours to
consider.

Anderson did consider. The message came to him in the hands of
Stephen D. Lee, Alexander Chisolm, and James Chesnut, all of whom
would be heard from in the years ahead. Beauregard promised the
peaceful removal of the garrison and no dishonor to the flag. "The flag
which you have upheld so long and with so much fortitude . . . may
be saluted by you on taking it down." Anderson very politely refused.
Just as courteously, Beauregard's aides left, but not before assuring
the major that they would not open fire without further notice. Hoping still to avert calamity, Anderson then gave them a hint of a way
out. "Gentlemen," he said, "if you do not batter the fort to pieces
about us, we shall be starved out in a few days." Better to have to
leave because of exhausted rations, than be evicted in the first battle
of a long war. The message was not lost on Beauregard or the Confederate authorities in Montgomery. "Do not desire needlessly to

bombard Fort Sumter," Walker telegraphed. If Anderson would state the time of his evacuation, they would hold their guns.

It was after midnight, April 12, when Beauregard's three emissaries again docked at Sumter's wharf and asked to see Major Anderson. They delivered their commander's request that he be given a date and time for the evacuation. If so "we will abstain from opening fire on you." Anderson spent the next two hours with his officers, and they unanimously rejected surrender. Even Lieutenant R. K. Meade of Virginia, who will later become an officer in the Confederate Army after resigning his commission, even he advised resistance. Sense of duty led men to do seemingly illogical things in this war.

Anderson hedged. He would leave by noon on April 15 unless he earlier received supplies or other instructions from Washington. The Confederates would not accept his response, and before leaving gave him a note stating that Beauregard would open fire at 4:20 A.M. Anderson was deeply moved. The moment he had so long sought to avert, and at such painful strife within himself, had come. "If we never meet in this world again," he said, "God grant that we may meet in the next."[21]

Now it must come, and there was someone among the Palmetto Guard now manning the Stevens Iron-Clad Battery who thought it was past time. Old Edmund Ruffin was here in Charleston to witness the fruits of his handiwork at fomenting rebellion. He had been welcomed as a volunteer and honorary member of the Guard on April 9. "Three cheers for Mr. Ruffin," cried its commander George Cuthbert. The Virginian was looked upon as a hero, a pioneer, a prophet of secession, and they honored him as such. Beauregard personally gave him a tour of the defenses around the harbor. He was feted and entertained in the city. Different officers vied with each other to have him in their companies. Ruffin hardly ignored the display on his behalf, but he was far more interested in Fort Sumter. He positively champed for the attack.

At 4 A.M. on April 12 his waiting was almost done. Drums summoned the men from their sleep and marched them to the batteries. Meanwhile a strange scene took place at Fort Johnson. Beauregard's emissaries landed there first and ordered Captain George S. James to fire the signal gun that would open the barrage, the "first shot" of the war. James offered the honor of pulling the lanyard to Roger Pryor of Virginia, a prominent secessionist, but he declined. "I could not fire the first gun of the war," he said. And so Lieutenant Henry S. Farley fired it instead. The war was begun.

For Edmund Ruffin it was a proud moment. Captain Cuthbert had told him that he was to fire the first gun from the Iron Battery in the coming bombardment. "I was highly gratified by the compliment, & delighted to perform the service." He set off a sixty-four pound columbiad and sent its shell rocketing toward Sumter's parapet. Ruffin

believed that he fired the first hostile shot, but it was hard to tell just
which battery actually opened first after the signal shot. Cuthbert reported that two other batteries preceded his in firing. Nevertheless, it
was symbolic that old Ruffin should be here now, doing with the
sword what he had sought for so long to do with the pen.[22]

A chorus of cannon fire erupted in a ring around Charleston Harbor, the muzzle flashes illuminating the waterfront, their reflections
dancing across the water while their deadly missiles sped to crash
against the masonry of Sumter's parapet. Strangely, the fort seemed to
ignore their fire. It did not answer. In fact, Anderson fully intended to
respond with iron of his own, but not until after daylight. Meanwhile,
men like Doubleday unconcernedly stayed in bed. Others simply sat
in the safety of the fort's interior casemates and talked or prepared
their breakfasts. Only after assembly at 6 A.M. did they man their
posts and prepare to return fire. Anderson offered the fiery Captain
Doubleday the honor of firing the first cannon and, unlike the queasy
Pryor, Doubleday accepted with glee. "I had no feeling of self-
reproach," he would recall. It was simply a matter of good fighting
back against evil. Before 7 A.M. he gave the order and his thirty-two
pound smoothbore spat its ball against the roof of Ruffin's Iron Battery. How much simpler it would have been to put Ruffin and
Doubleday against each other in a pit. Far too many men this April
were going to war—and taking their brethren with them—to battle
out their personal spites.[23]

For the next thirty-three hours the firing continued. Sumter, under-
manned and short of powder, used only six cannon during most of the
fighting. Charleston threw everything at the Federals. As April 12
wore on, Beauregard's fire became gradually more accurate. Soon it
was too dangerous for Anderson's men to venture onto the fort's parade ground, and incendiary shells set fire to the wooden barracks.
Evening rain smothered the blaze, and Anderson halted his fire at
sundown to conserve ammunition. The Confederates, however, fired
sporadically throughout the night.

The next morning the battle resumed, and again the Sumter barracks went to flame. Soon the fire got out of control, threatening to
reach the powder magazine, the smoke choking the men who often
had to cling to the floor of the casemates to breathe. The fort, said
Doubleday, became a "pandemonium." Meanwhile, lying off Charleston Harbor, Fox and his relief expedition sat and watched what was
happening, realizing with anguish that they were just hours too late.
Furthermore, bureaucracy had defeated him, denying him his tugboats or the warship that was to meet him here to provide covering
fire. Fox must be only a spectator.

Anderson's situation rapidly became hopeless. Shortly after noon on
April 13 a shell cut Sumter's flag down, and Senator Wigfall who was
in Charleston for the fun, decided that it meant Anderson was ready

to quit. He had himself rowed out to the fort, a handkerchief tied to the end of his sword, and stepped in through an embrasure. "Let us stop this firing," he cried. "You are on fire and your flag is down. Let us quit." When Anderson appeared, Wigfall continued his entreaty. "Major Anderson, you have defended your flag nobly, Sir. You have done all that is possible for men to do, and Gen. Beauregard wishes to stop the fight." Faced with a hopeless situation, and having done all he could to defend his country's honor and do his duty, the major was forced to agree. He would surrender at once. It was 1:30 P.M., and with a white flag shown, Beauregard stopped his firing. He knew nothing of Wigfall's visit, and had not authorized it. He sent his own emissaries out to the fort and, after some confusion as to just who did represent Beauregard, the same result was achieved. The next afternoon, to the tune of "Yankee Doodle," Anderson paraded his men and marched them out of the fort. They boarded Fox's ships for the return North. In a final irony, Anderson was allowed to fire a salute to his flag. During the firing a cartridge bag exploded accidentally and killed Private Daniel Hough. He was the first man, arguably, to die in the American Civil War. He would not be the last.[24]

That night Governor Pickens made a speech extolling the victory. Yet he was not a fool. He warned that the danger to the Confederate cause was not ended by this one victory. "We, perhaps, may have just commenced the opening of events that may not end in our day and generation." The prominent South Carolina Unionist James L. Petigru saw it even better. He was convinced, he said, "that we are on the road to ruin." He sensed what the next four years of blood and toil would prove, that the Confederacy never had a chance of success from the moment of its inception. Not once during those years did the government of Davis have any possibility of winning, not so long as Abraham Lincoln was President in Washington. In making the ultimate expression of its nationalistic compulsion by firing on Sumter, the South sealed its own doom as a nation.[25]

CHAPTER 4

"THE GOVERNMENT MUST BE SUSTAINED"

Old Ruffin's shot from the Iron-Clad Battery helped open a conflict for which neither North nor South stood ready. But then, America has never been "ready" for a war. There was always in the American character an aversion to large standing armies, to a professional military, and to all the machinery that both require. The roots of the aversion went back to the Old World where enormous armies were kept largely to suit the whims of leaders who onerously taxed their subjects to support them. It went to the early frontier experience in the New World, where self-reliance counted for so much, where men and women defended their own interests without the aid of professional armed minions of government. It went back to that early established notion of state responsibility for internal affairs. Military appropriations, except in time of war, always met stiff opposition in the Federal Congress. Even Washington during the Revolution had to battle Congress nearly as much as the British. It is hardly a surprise, then, that as 1861 dawned, the entire United States Army numbered only 14,663 present for duty, most of them scattered across the country among a hundred frontier posts and eastern barracks. By the summer of 1861 that would make only a fair-sized division.

And until March 4, 1861, even this pitiful force had no one to give it direction. Old General Scott could not act without a President to take the lead, and Buchanan led in nothing but indecision.

Then comes the Rail Splitter, the American Abraham. He is of the soil and blood of Kentucky, a man of the West, matured in the Illinois prairies, hardened in character by the toil of the frontier, softened in spirit by a mother's memory and the gentle angels of his own soul. He is commanding, and ugly. He has wit and craft, patience to rival Job, the subtlety of a diplomat. His crow's voice utters the eloquence of a poet. He will dissemble and deceive to achieve just ends. His ambition is great, though reined by the humility of his low birth. Indecisive and vacillating in youth, he comes to Washington a man of unyielding iron resolve. The least imperious of men, he will become a master of power. No American President will ever use men and machines and money and the Constitution, bending each to his mighty purpose, with such relentless skill as Abraham Lincoln. He is the essential man.

Not many people thought so in 1861, even among his own party. Lincoln was largely an unknown quantity, even to himself. Just turned fifty-two, he had only a few terms in the Illinois legislature and a single term in Congress to his credit. He lost to Stephen Douglas the Senate seat he sought in 1858, but the campaign made him what even a victory could not—a national figure. He identified early with the Republican party. Though once a Whig, he like many others was so incensed by the repeal of the Missouri Compromise that the new party seemed his natural place. Whereas Seward was the ideological leader of the Republicans in the years prior to 1860, still he was too ultra, too *Northern* for many. Lincoln, taking his stand against Douglas on the further extension of slavery yet declining to attack it where it already existed, spoke for the more moderate majority in the party. Lincoln abhorred slavery by 1860, but his ideas were slow in maturing on the subject. Certainly he did not regard Negroes as the intellectual equals of their masters, but neither did he see that as justification for their being slaves.

His party had flirted briefly in 1856 with making Lincoln its vice-presidential candidate, but turned finally to another. Still, even at that date, Lincoln was already regarded as a leading party spokesman. His campaign against Douglas two years later, his declaration that "A house divided against itself cannot stand," and that the Union could not exist permanently half slave and half free, drew to him the popularity coveted by Seward and others. And Lincoln was no fool. He was a self-made politician. He started at the bottom and worked up the hard way. He knew how politics worked, and knew how to work politicians. Sensing the possibility of his own destiny, he quietly prepared his way for 1860. Still, Seward remained the leading contender even going into the Chicago convention in June 1860, followed by several other hopefuls like Simon Cameron, Salmon P. Chase, Edward Bates, and more. Lincoln was not given much chance. Yet when the balloting began, Lincoln ran second to Seward. As votes *against* Seward, the supporters of the other candidates began turning their eyes to Lincoln, and on the third ballot he won the nomination.

And of course he won the election in November, with only 40 percent of the popular vote. The majority of Americans said at the polls that they did not want him. A month later Lincoln saw in the secession of South Carolina just what it was that victory brought him. He had won a "house divided."

What he would do to set that house in order remained a mystery, and even many prominent Republicans felt little confidence. Lincoln made no statements of policy prior to his inauguration, which left most wondering. Further, the circumstances of his journey to Washington in February 1861, with rumors of an assassination plot and Lincoln coming into the capital disguised, did not help. Charles Francis Adams commented acidly that instead of reassuring the country, Lincoln was "perambulating the country, kissing little girls, and growing whiskers."[1]

But when the man from Illinois stepped out onto the platform on the Capitol steps on March 4, 1861, he finally made his policy clear and unequivocal. He told the South that "In your hands, my dissatisfied fellow countrymen, and not in mine, is the momentous issue of civil war." He would not attack them. "You can have no conflict without being yourselves the aggressors. *You* have no oath registered in Heaven to destroy the government, while I shall have the most solemn one to 'preserve, protect, and defend' it." They were friends, not enemies. Surely, the "better angels of our nature" would prevail to reunite the Union.

Hoping for the best, and fearing worse, Lincoln began preparing himself for war from the very day of his election. His first task was the selection of his cabinet, men to run the nation, and perhaps a civil conflict as well. There were political debts to pay, injuries to assuage, and office seemed the currency and medicine for both. Yet first in his mind was strength, of character, loyalty, and devotion to the Union. The Republican party was not so united as its victory implied, either. To cement it together—to forge a party whose strength could uphold a consistent domestic policy while also maintaining itself in power— was a formidable task. Lincoln the great President would always remain a dedicated party leader.

All of these influences so pulled at the President-elect that his cabinet was not in fact complete even at his inauguration. He changed his mind repeatedly, but in the end appointed most of the same men that he originally thought of the previous November.

Secretary of state: William H. Seward. The narrow loser of the nomination and thereby the election, a national leader for twenty years. An experienced if Machiavellian politician, who scarcely concealed his belief that Lincoln was not competent for his office. His seniority and contribution to the party demanded a high position, and the state portfolio was the highest.

Secretary of treasury: Salmon P. Chase. An extreme antislavery spokesman, also a contestant for the presidency. Just as Seward represented the old Whig element of the party, so Chase spoke for the abolitionists. He would never lose his disdain for the seemingly unpolished Lincoln, but his loyalty to party and Union were above question.

Attorney general: Edward P. Bates of Missouri. Not even a Republican! First a Whig, then a Know-Nothing, he refused to join the party of Seward. He was soft on the slavery issue, but enjoyed a reputation as the leading statesman of the border West. He too sought nomination in 1860 as a compromise candidate. It was imperative that the crucial border states of Missouri and Kentucky not join the South in secession, and Bates's influence in his home state was powerful.

Secretary of the navy: Gideon Welles of Connecticut. A former Democrat. Vain. An ill-fitting wig makes all the more obvious his baldness. Dour and fault-finding. A newspaperman, he had served briefly in the navy department. He brought New England and the loyal Democrats into the cabinet. And hidden talents as well.

Secretary of the interior: Caleb Smith of Indiana. Lincoln did not want him, but he had brought Indiana's vote to the Rail Splitter in the Chicago convention and Lincoln's managers, without his knowledge, promised something in return. Unlike Lincoln, also an unknown quantity, Smith will remain one.

Postmaster general: Montgomery Blair of Maryland. Member of one of the country's most influential political families, equally powerful in Maryland and Missouri, two of the border states that Lincoln must keep in the Union. Though Lincoln knew the family could be troublesome, and self-serving, he also knew that an alliance with them would buy him—with some qualifications—considerable support among the loyal Democrats, until recently the Blair family party. The insignificant portfolio of postmaster was little enough price to pay.

Secretary of war: Simon Cameron of Pennsylvania. A simple political bargain, and one that Lincoln did not approve and did not want. With a conflict more than a possibility, this could be the most important post in his executive family. It should not go to a party hack, a man of repeatedly proven low character. Even the inordinately imperceptive Buchanan took him for "an unprincipled rascal." A Democrat until 1856, he had disappointed no less than three Presidents. Andrew Jackson declared that he "was not to be trusted." James K. Polk was appalled at his "coarseness and vulgarity," adding that the Pennsylvanian served only "his own personal and sinister purposes." Buchanan's opinion is already known. So undisguised is Cameron's na-

ture that it is almost a matter of prideful boast and jest. Many will
claim that he defined honesty in a public man as being one who "once
bought, stays bought." Yet at Chicago two of Lincoln's managers, in
defiance of their candidate's explicit order to make no bargains,
traded Cameron a cabinet post in return for the vote of the Pennsylvania delegation. Lincoln was trapped, but probably from the first he
expected to divest himself of this corrupting influence as soon as the
Pennsylvanian provided an excuse. Undoubtedly he would.[2]

There, then, was the new Republican regime. It represented, bargains aside, an attempt to bring most factions in the nation into the
government. It was a moderate, a compromise cabinet. Lincoln had
even wanted to include a Southerner, but the North Carolinian he
approached would not accept. Few really appreciated what the President was trying to do with his choice of secretaries. Instead many
read weakness and indecision into his patchwork advisers. Some expected, and many feared, that Seward would in fact run the nation
for Lincoln.

Lincoln, too, had to face a new Congress, and one hardly unani-
mous in his support. Indeed, the irony of the case is that, had the
Southern states not seceded and their representatives remained in
Congress, they would have prevented a Republican majority in either
Senate or House and could have blocked any feared legislation. Their
best hope of preserving Southern institutions lay within the Union,
not out of it. By abandoning the Federal compact they risked leaving
the Republicans the majority party, and should events one day force
the South back into the Union, it would thus be on Republican terms.
Yet it could not be. Though Lincoln and the bulk of his party repeatedly promised noninterference, the South could hardly know for sure
that the pledge would be honored. Still, the new Confederate states
were surely guilty of myopia, even without the benefit of hindsight.
By staying in the Union, they could have made the Lincoln administration a virtual shambles, and if protecting their cherished institutions was their only motive, this they would have done. But their real
impulse was nationhood.

So Lincoln did have a majority in Congress. But it was flawed and
fragmented. In the Senate he could count on Lyman Trumbull of Illinois, Charles Sumner and Henry Wilson of Massachusetts, William P.
Fessenden of Maine, Zachariah Chandler of Michigan and John Sherman—brother of William Tecumseh Sherman—of Ohio, and Edward
Baker of Oregon. Yet even among these, particularly Chandler and
Sumner, there were men who had trouble with compromise. And in
the House it was worse. Owen Lovejoy and Elihu Washburne were
good men, Schuyler Colfax of Indiana, Roscoe Conkling of New
York, and Thaddeus Stevens of Pennsylvania, all commanded great
influence, which they could use for the President if they would. Fortunately, loyal Democrats like Douglas seemed disposed to work with

Lincoln, and even a few from the South, such as Senator Andrew Johnson of Tennessee. Lincoln would need them to forge his majority, for besides dissidents in his own party, the President also still faced several representatives from Southern states not seceded, Virginia, Tennessee, North Carolina. And in Missouri, Kentucky, and Maryland's delegations he had powerful opponents. Breckinridge now sat as a Senator, the leader of the most vocal "loyal" opposition. Such men were dangerous, for they inflamed passions in the always fragile border; and should they be able to take their states out of the Union, the game was lost.

Lincoln's first test awaited him, his legacy from Buchanan. Fort Sumter. He met with his cabinet repeatedly and, surprisingly, encountered some unanimity of feeling in support of his intended course, excepting of course the enterprising Secretary Seward. He also dealt effectively with the Confederate commissioners by refusing to deal with them at all, thus denying any claim of recognition of the Confederacy. Much of his time these first days—too much said his advisers—went to the horde of office seekers who thronged the Executive Mansion. He also had the foreign service to think of. Almost certainly the Confederates would turn to Britain and France, looking for formal recognition of their claim to sovereign status. If granted it would bring world disfavor on Lincoln's attempt to bring the South back into the Union, particularly if it came to war. And if war came, such recognition might also garner military aid for the Confederacy. Lincoln selected two good men, then, for those diplomatic posts. Charles Francis Adams, father of the man who disapproved the President's kissing girls and growing a beard, he sent to London as minister to Great Britain. It was to prove the wisest diplomatic appointment he would ever make. To France he sent William L. Dayton, Frémont's running mate in 1856.

Daily cabinet meetings and Lincoln's own resolve eventually resulted in the attempt to succor Sumter, but too late. Even as Anderson was surrendering, Lincoln, trying desperately to woo Virginia into remaining with the Union, told the Old Dominion's representatives that he had no wish to invade the South, only to hold Federal property. Yet he did say as well that "I shall hold myself at liberty to repossess, if I can." Obviously that meant Fort Sumter. But on April 14 came the definite news of the fortress's fall. Now he faced armed rebellion.

Lincoln met with his cabinet. Events forced them to take strong measures, and his advisers concurred in a proclamation which the President issued the next day, April 15. "The present condition of public affairs presents an extraordinary occasion," he said. Therefore he called for an "extraordinary" session of Congress to meet on July 4. The outrage to the flag allied many Northern Democrats behind him now, including Douglas, who that day promised his support.

But it would take more than an extra Congress. The seceded states were in a state of insurrection "too powerful to be suppressed by the ordinary course of judicial proceedings." He must resort to arms. He issued the call for 75,000 volunteers, to be raised proportionately from the states remaining in the Union. They would be used, he said, first to repossess the forts and other Federal property seized by the Rebels, and by peaceful means if possible. He called on Southerners then under arms to disperse and return to their homes within twenty days. It was a hollow hope.[3]

The reaction came swiftly, and predictably. Every Northern state vocally approved, and the work of raising the militia began at once. "This rebellion has wantonly and without provocation, inaugurated civil war, and its first blow has been successful," said the press; "but even its victory will bring down on its head a signal defeat and terrible retribution in the end." "The Government must be sustained," cried the New York *Herald*. "This inglorious success will cost them dear," said another New York paper. "Take your places in line," the Philadelphia press told its readers. Yet there was opposition. Editorials in Bangor, Maine, Hartford, Providence, and elsewhere decried the move. "Could this war policy possibly save the Union and promote the welfare of the people, we could look upon it with more complacency," said the Hartford *Times*. The Bangor *Union* likened Beauregard's Confederates to "your fathers of old gathered about Boston in defense of the same sacred principles of liberty."

And from certain states the response came even more melancholy. Despite all his efforts to hold Virginia to the Union, the Old Dominion, so often in the middle, so often torn, so different from the rest of the South yet so much a part of it—Virginia would secede. A state convention had been meeting in Richmond, and now it immediately took up the question of Lincoln's proclamation. Governor John Letcher refused to provide any troops for the purpose of, as he put it, the subjugation of the seceded states. Indeed, during its last session Virginia's general assembly had declared that any exertion of force against her sister states would be considered an act of war "to be resisted by all the power at the command of Virginia." Consequently, on April 17 Letcher issued the call for all of the state's volunteer forces to assemble ready for duty to defend the Commonwealth. It was merely a preliminary to what the governor knew was happening in the state convention. That same day it passed its ordinance of secession, setting May 4 as the day when Virginians would vote on its acceptance or rejection. There was little doubt.[4]

The reaction elsewhere in the South proved equally predictable. Jefferson Davis issued his own proclamation asking for applications for letters of marque authorizing privateers to attack Union shipping. He overstepped his constitutional bounds a bit, and the ever ready Rhett challenged him on it, calling the proclamation merely a suggestion of what Davis would propose to Congress. But Rhett did not quibble with its intent. "The South does not want war. We stand on the defensive. But if the Northern government choose to have war, they can and will have it, they may rest assured."[5]

North Carolina, too, refused to answer Lincoln's call, and so did Governor Beriah Magoffin of Kentucky. It was a "wicked purpose," he said. Missouri and Tennessee refused as well. Yet if these states would not contribute—and most of them, excepting perhaps Kentucky and Missouri, would surely secede instead—the rest of the Union responded willingly. The first troops arrived in Washington on April 18, and they were a welcome sight. With Virginia now joined in the rebellion, nothing separated the nation's capital from the Confederacy but the Potomac River. Flags of revolution could be seen on the rooftops of Alexandria, Virginia, and though the possibility was slim, there were many in Washington who feared for the safety of the city. It did not help when, the next day, the 6th Massachusetts tried to pass through Baltimore on its way to Washington and was mobbed. Several soldiers and civilians lay dead in the city's streets before the Bay Staters got safely away. Baltimore would be secured shortly, but meanwhile the capital felt uncomfortably isolated from the rest of the North.

With the situation escalating seemingly out of control, Lincoln struggled to stay ahead. In response to Davis's call for privateers, Lincoln on April 19 declared a blockade of Southern ports. It was lenient, to be sure. Any vessel attempting to pass in or go out in violation of the blockade would not be captured. Instead, an endorsement on the episode would be placed on its ship's register. However, a second offense would forfeit ship and cargo. The blockade was intended more as a deterrent than a genuine attempt to capture shipping. Foreign powers would be hesitant to risk violation of the blockade, recognized as it was by international common law.[6]

There seemed for Lincoln no controlling of events now. The day after his blockade decree Federals started evacuating the Gosport Navy Yard at Norfolk, Virginia, an important station for the maintenance of the Union fleet. Virginia state troops threatened to capture the valuable machinery and drydock and, rather than see it used against the Union, the yard's commander torched everything, including nine vessels. Among them was the USS *Merrimack*, which sank after burning almost to the waterline. The next day when the Confederates moved in, however, they found much of the machinery not destroyed or seriously damaged, and parts of some of the ships salvageable, including the *Merrimack*. Futhermore, they found over one thousand pieces of naval artillery of various types, most reusable. The capture of Norfolk was a major loss to the Union, assuaged only by the fact that Fort Monroe across Hampton Roads still remained in Federal hands. It gave Lincoln command of the entrance to the James

River and a strong base deep within the Confederacy. With Maryland strongly secessionist in temper, Lincoln also feared for the safety of the United States Naval Academy at Annapolis. Shortly afterward, it would be moved temporarily to Newport, Rhode Island. Along with it would go the venerable symbol of United States victory over the British, the USS *Constitution*. Her sister ship USS *United States* was lost at Norfolk.

The toll of these April days was already telling on Lincoln. It was a species of pressure he had never known, unrelenting, unforgiving. It required an enormous adjustment to go from small-town lawyer and politician to leader of a nation at war. He was making that adjustment, but slowly and at great mental pain. It did not help that there was a perceived threat to the capital. Lincoln worried constantly about Baltimore, talked with its mayor, even its Young Mens Christian Association. "Keep your rowdies in Baltimore, and there will be no bloodshed," he told them. He must defend the capital, however, and any attempt to prevent its reinforcement would be resisted. The anxious days waiting for those reinforcements left a frustrated President saying to his aides, "Why don't they come! Why don't they come!" On April 24, in the closest thing to an expression of absolute despair that he would utter, he said to the few troops then in the city that "I don't believe there is any North. The Seventh Regiment is a myth. . . . *You* are the only realities." But then the next day the 7th New York arrived, and following it in the next days came several more units, and the immediate threat to Washington abated. The relief to Lincoln was enormous, and showed. With renewed confidence, he continued his policy of peacefully putting down the rebellion.[7]

He extended the blockade from South Carolina to include the coasts of North Carolina and Virginia, even though the former had not yet left the Union. It seemed certain that it would. On May 3 he issued a call for another 42,000 volunteers. His first call had been for men to serve three months. Now however, apprehending more clearly that a war, if any, would likely be more than a summer's affair, he wanted men for three years. He authorized increasing the strength of the Regular Army to 22,000 and called for enlistment of 18,000 seamen to serve the blockade squadrons then forming under Welles. He and Scott organized the North and the border areas into military departments to facilitate the administration of the armies that would soon spring from the paper to the field. And he decided not to attempt to prevent the Maryland legislature from meeting to consider secession. It was a diplomatic move, and a perceptive one, for the Marylanders were ever so slowly turning toward the Union on their own. Any show of force would have injured that delicate shift disastrously.

In fact, to a much greater extent than even Lincoln believed, he had most of the remaining Union behind him, and even before the guns of Sumter. Many in the North had been weary of the repeated concessions made to the slave states during the last decades, and equally weary of the bellicose rhetoric and saber rattling so beloved of the fire-eaters. Many more—Lincoln among them—looked upon the Union as a spiritual being, something greater than the women and men who composed it, a compact for the common weal that, like John Winthrop's Massachusetts Bay Colony, sat like "a city on a hill" for others to follow. Destruction of the Union was very nearly a crime against the Almighty. The struggle between the sections reduced in their minds to a medieval morality play, a simple tug between good and evil. Some, like the abolitionist Horace Greeley, advised that Lincoln "let the erring sisters go," that the South be allowed to secede so they might not further spread their taint within the nation. But most favored resistance, even to war. Old John Brown of Harpers Ferry had declared on his dying day that the land would have to be purged "with blood" to eradicate the foul odor of slavery. Thousands in the North agreed and accepted war as the emetic.

There were hard political considerations too, and Lincoln was a distinctly political creature despite his much cultivated homely manner. Compromise with the slave states destroyed the Whig party in 1850 and similar compromise on the issue of Union now would likely drive the radical elements of the Republican party to bolt. As its leader, Lincoln had to hold his party together if he hoped to sustain the Union. The South must return to the fold on the Union's terms.

Business, too, stood increasingly on the side of asserting Federal authority without compromise. At first many Northern manufacturers and trades people feared that the sectional split, and any conflict that might follow, would seriously depress business and profits. Indeed, some like Samuel Colt were doing a thriving business just now in selling war matériel to the South, unconcerned that it might all be thrown back at them in battle. Hostilities would end those sales. Yet before long they also came to the realization that permanent disunion would likely have a malicious effect on credit, on government bonds, and on their sales to the Confederacy. Favoring free trade, the South would likely buy most of its manufactures from Europe rather than pay Northern tariffs. Worse, the debts they owed their Yankee suppliers might well be paid in Southern currency. Though none could say for certain that it would be worthless, many suspected as much.[8]

Thus most segments of the North favored a hard stand against secession, even to war if it became necessary. The motives ranged from good to greed, but Lincoln and public events forged a majority for the Union that would become a mighty resolve.

By the middle of May Washington began to look like an armed camp, the hills all around it topped with rows of white tents, and even the public buildings billeted volunteers. Scott sent men across the Potomac to occupy Alexandria. They met with no real resistance,

and almost at once the Virginia heights overlooking the Potomac also
sprouted campfires. Still the capital was cut off by water, for the Confederates had batteries below the city at Aquia Creek, overlooking the
Potomac. At the end of the month Federal gunboats began shelling
the batteries, but without immediate effect. Still, with a secure land
and rail route through Maryland, Lincoln could now turn his attention to offense. A Rebel army was gathering at Manassas Junction,
less than thirty miles southwest of Washington, and another was
aborning at Harpers Ferry, abandoned by Scott after Virginia's secession. Here were clear threats to the security of Washington, despite
any Confederate claims that they wished merely to defend Southern
soil. Since Lincoln did not recognize the right of secession, then logi-
cally, the South was still in the Union. These armies, therefore, were
insurrectionary, and it was his duty to put down rebellion.

To do so, to send Federal soldiers into Virginia, would make certain
that Sumter had not been an isolated incident of hostility. The contemplated invasion would mean certain warfare. Lincoln was ready
for it, and his moral ground was well prepared. He had done everything possible, without actually recognizing the new Confederacy as a
separate nation, to avert conflict in his handling of the Sumter crisis.
He did not rattle the saber. He had not called for volunteers or marshaled his small existing armed forces. Even in his announced intent
to resupply the fort, he was only sending food. His opponents in the
North soon accused him of feinting the Confederacy into firing first,
so that he could go to war without being the aggressor. Not so. But
admitting that war was a possibility, and having done everything but
surrender the Union to avoid it, the President still determined that
any first shot fired would be Southern. He told them as much in his
inaugural. And to Fox he wrote this May that "You and I both anticipated that the cause of the country would be advanced by making the
attempt to provision Fort Sumpter [sic], even if it should fail; and it
is no small consolation now to feel that our anticipation is justified by
the result." He had made the peaceful attempt to maintain the authority of the Union and the South spurned it with iron. The Confederacy's own act, thus, helped cement the North against it, and gave to
Lincoln in the eyes of his country and much of the world the aspect
of one fighting, not for conquest, but in defense of a moral right.[9]

To make that defense, Lincoln and Scott had almost to rebuild the
United States Army. Resignations among Southern-born officers ran
high. Long-respected senior officers like Robert E. Lee, Joseph E.
Johnston, Albert S. Johnston, Daniel Twiggs, William J. Hardee, and
a host of men of lesser reputation, left the service that had been their
lives rather than join in taking arms against their native South. A surprising number of Northern-born officers also "went South," either out
of sentiment with its cause, marriage into Southern families, or the
opportunity for speedier advancement in rank.

Yet most officers remained. Scott led the list, one of many officers from seceded states who put their loyalty to the Union above their local attachments. Army men like George H. Thomas and naval officers like David G. Farragut of Tennessee, stayed with their oaths of allegiance, frequently in the face of family obloquy and the rejection of friends. To augment the officer corps remaining, Scott called in almost all officers of any worth from the far-flung posts and garrisons from Maine to California. The United States Military Academy began to graduate its 1861 class early, and meanwhile the various state governors commissioned hundreds of officers for the militia regiments they were raising. Few remained, however, who had taken active part in the nation's last war, against Mexico; and most of those who did had not experienced actual field or battle command of anything larger than a company. The whole army being raised was green from top to bottom.

With the army growing, a general plan, an attitude toward the probable war seemed needed. Obviously Lincoln turned to Scott, and the old general showed that he still deserved the respect and deference of his subordinates and the nation. On May 3 he put into words the concept that, with some modification, would be the essential Union war strategy for the next four years. The blockade, he believed, would be effective in closing the Confederate coastline to shipping. Then, if the Federals could move down the Mississippi to its mouth, establishing forts along the way at proper intervals, it would isolate Texas—and Arkansas, sure to secede—from the rest of the South. More important, this serpentine encirclement by water would allow the North to slowly squeeze the Confederacy into submission by starving it. Not surprisingly, Scott's concept came to be called the "Anaconda Plan." It misjudged the will of the South to resist, and the length of time the Rebels could hold out, but the plan was sound nevertheless.

On May 6 Tennessee and Arkansas seceded, bringing to ten the number of states in rebellion. Certainly North Carolina would join them as well, but Maryland looked more and more secure, as did Missouri. Kentucky remained a troublesome matter for Lincoln, and one of many reasons why he did not do what would have seemed obvious and issue a declaration of war. The most he would do was a declaration of insurrection. War was fought between nations, and the South was still part of the Union. For him to declare actual war would only have aggravated the situation. For Kentucky, particularly tender on the subject of "the wicked purpose" of subjugating her sister states of the South, a war declaration might well have tipped the balance for secession. Jefferson Davis, however, had no such dilemma facing him. The same day that the two new states took cause with the Confederacy, he declared a state of war. And across the ocean in London's

Whitehall, the British accorded to the South a recognition of belligerence.

The terms differed only semantically. Their real meaning in the spring of 1861 was much the same. And if anyone, anywhere in the world, doubted that North and South were truly at war, then the coming summer of discontent would put those doubts to rest. Abraham Lincoln had put the "momentous issue of civil war" in the hands of his "dissatisfied fellow-countrymen" of the South. They were not long in giving it to him.

CHAPTER 5

"THE BATTLE IS THERE"

Joseph E. Johnston was a Virginian, small, slight frame, wisps of hair topping a rodential face that was bottomed by a tiny goatee. Yet his diminutive appearance belied one of the foremost soldiers of the old prewar army. He and Robert E. Lee attended classes together at the United States Military Academy at West Point. He fought the Seminoles in Florida and the Mexicans in the Mexican War of 1846–48. His wiry frame attracted bullets the way handsomer men lured women. He was wounded repeatedly, though after one such injury his friend Lee commented that "Joe Johnston is fat ready & hearty. I think a little lead, properly taken, is good for a man."[1]

Johnston won the repeated plaudits of his superiors during his career and rose steadily in rank and position. By 1861 he outranked even Lee, wearing the single star of a brigadier general and quartermaster general of the United States Army. Yet as soon as the Old Dominion took its stand with the Confederacy, so did Joseph Eggleston Johnston. He resigned his commission and took in its place a major generalacy in the state troops, followed by appointment as brigadier in the Confederate service. He was a man in his prime, fifty-four years old, proud—probably too proud—and confident. A kindly and consid-

erate superior, he had not the temperament to make a good subordinate, particularly to younger and less experienced men. He would not
take it well.

Subordination seemed far from his mind, however, as he built his
army at Harpers Ferry, Virginia, in May 1861. Now that his state had
left the Union, she must be defended, for with the Confederate capital moved to Richmond, and with Washington just across the Potomac, it looked plain to most that Virginia would be the scene of the
conflict's first major actions in the East. And many on both sides of
that river confidently expected that the first fight would also be the
last.

Harpers Ferry lay at the confluence of the Shenandoah and Potomac rivers, sixty miles northwest of Washington. It was, in American terms, an "ancient" place, selected by Washington as a site for an
armory in the late 1700s, and occupied since as an arsenal and manufactory for government weapons. Even more important than its guns
—which evacuating Federals tried to destroy on April 18 after Virginia's secession—was the position Harpers Ferry occupied at the
head of the Shenandoah Valley.

The great valley fed the Commonwealth, and could go a long way
toward feeding the armies of the infant Confederacy. Its fields provided some of the most fertile ground in all the South, a virtual
granary. More important, running as it did for one hundred fifty miles
from north to south, the valley provided a natural pathway for invasion, screened from the rest of Virginia by the Blue Ridge Mountains.
Armies, North or South, could move behind that screen and, by closing off a few mountain gaps, march unseen into the heart of Virginia
or Maryland, to strike an unsuspecting enemy flank. Control of this
valley meant control of Virginia, and Harpers Ferry was its key.
Peculiarly, though the ferry lay at the valley's northern end, it was
said to be "down" the valley, since the valley floor sloped downward
from south to north. One went south "up" the valley.

Before the coming of Johnston, the Richmond authorities, with Lee
nominally in charge, sent another Virginian to Harpers Ferry to organize its defense and train the companies of raw recruits there gathering. This man was as unorthodox as Johnston was conventional, a
genuine eccentric called Tom Fool and Old Blue Light by his onetime cadet students at Lexington's Virginia Military Institute at the
other end of the valley. Colonel Thomas Jonathan Jackson left everyone baffled except his God. His laugh was explosive silence. His food
he consumed unseasoned for fear that pepper would make his left leg
ache. He sucked lemons habitually when he could get them, and
barked his orders in a high-pitched voice that seemed out of keeping
with his robust frame and patriarchal bearded visage. He passed
among the men on Sundays distributing religious tracts, and his blue
eyes—the "Blue Light"—missed nothing.

By the time Johnston relieved Jackson at Harpers Ferry, Tom Fool had several regiments organized out of companies with colorful sobriquets like "Grayson Daredevils," "Ready Rifles," "Montgomery Fencibles," and such. They became the 2nd, 4th, 5th, 27th, and 33rd Virginia Infantries, but never lost their penchant for nicknames, like all soldiers in both armies in this war. "The Innocent Second," the "Harmless Fourth," the "Fighting Fifth" and "Fighting Twenty-Seventh," they became. And when the other unit suffered an infestation of body lice, they quickly metamorphosed into "The Lousy Thirty-Third." Jackson did not mind. "I am very thankful to our Heavenly Father for having given me such a fine brigade," he wrote to his wife. In time he would believe his brigade to be an instrument of the Almighty himself.[2]

Johnston relieved Jackson on May 15, 1861, and the work of drilling and equipping the new soldiers continued. Meanwhile regiments from other states came into his camp as well, and soon Johnston was organizing an army, albeit a small one. They came from Mississippi, Kentucky, Louisiana, Arkansas, Tennessee, Alabama, Georgia, and South Carolina. Most were raised by their states, but at least one was entirely a personal affair. The Hampton Legion was the private army and pet of its commander and benefactor, Colonel Wade Hampton.

He was perhaps the largest landowner in all of South Carolina, the grandson of reputedly the richest planter in the nation. Luxury and privilege were to him commonplace, power and influence taken for granted. Not surprisingly, he early espoused an ardent Southern nationalism, carrying his views into the state legislature. And like many who believed so fervidly in a distinctive Southern identity—and the need for a nation to encompass it—he immediately put his all at the Confederacy's disposal. The Confederacy became his adopted child. He gave his fortune in cotton to trade in Europe for guns and equipment. From his purse he raised, trained, and armed his own little army, his Hampton Legion. It contained its own infantry, artillery, and cavalry, and some of the cream of Palmetto society. Four of its officers would one day become generals. The men found Hampton "a young man, fully grown up, to be sure, but still young. His bearing was distinctly military, but without pompousness or egotism." His dark hair and beard matched his eyes, which flashed nervously to all sides. He personally led his legion as perhaps the South's foremost example of the military dilettante, playing soldier and destined to become remarkably good at it.[3]

Yet play or not, this was serious business in Virginia. As soon as the Commonwealth seceded, the immediate threat to Washington became apparent to Federal authorities. With Maryland strongly secessionist as well, the capital was threatened with isolation until Brigadier General Benjamin F. Butler secured a route for relief through Baltimore and other Union men took firm hold in the Chesapeake Bay state.

Even this proved costly, as evidenced by the secessionists in Baltimore who mobbed the first Union troops to pass through their city on April 19.

The protection of Washington as well as the suppression of the rebellion lay for now in the hands of yet another Virginian, old General Scott, hero of several wars, now seventy-four. "I have served my country, under the flag of the Union, for more than fifty years," he declared. "I will defend that flag with my sword, even if my native State assails it."[4]

He took immediate pressure to devise a plan to defend that flag, not only in the nation as a whole, but more particularly on the front between Washington and Richmond. He put an old friend, Major General Robert Patterson, in charge of raising troops in Maryland, Delaware, and Pennsylvania. Meanwhile, with the route through Baltimore secure, volunteer regiments from states farther north poured into the city by the Potomac. As soon as Scott felt sufficiently reinforced, he sent troops across the river to occupy Arlington and Alexandria, thus providing a foothold in the Confederacy. At Alexandria one of Lincoln's favorites, young Colonel Elmer Ellsworth, lost his life lowering a Rebel flag from a rooftop, the first officer to die in the war that no one believed would last out the year. Legions would follow in Ellsworth's mournful path. On June 1, at Fairfax Court House, the first Virginian fell in a skirmish, Lieutenant John Quincy Marr. Only the day before, he and his men had sung a hymn, "Joyfully, joyfully, onward we go."

Now Scott had breathing space and a place for staging the army being raised. That army needed a field commander. Too old himself, Scott appointed instead a man who had never led so much as a company in battle, a man who had been two weeks before a mere major doing staff duty, forty-two-year-old Irvin McDowell. The appointment surprised no one more than the appointee. An Ohioan, a man of increasing girth and rapacious appetite, he had spent his entire career to date in staff work. His manner impressed many as cold and aloof, indifferent, while his temper proved sufficiently volatile that he alienated many who he might better have kept as friends. Yet he possessed considerable organizational talent, patience, and an unswerving loyalty to the Union. Scott believed that he could keep the younger man under his thumb, but McDowell quickly showed an independence that rankled his superior yet boded well for the coming campaign.

McDowell was jumped three grades to brigadier general on May 14, and two weeks later took command of the newly created Department of Northeastern Virginia. At once he went to work on his burgeoning army, making his own headquarters in Arlington House, the columned mansion occupied until a month before by Robert E. Lee. As he forged his command, McDowell also came under considerable pressure to prepare a plan for invading Virginia and defeating the enemy and, after putting them to rout, going on to capture Richmond. Somehow the notion of possessing the enemy capital loomed far more important in Washington's eyes than destroying the Confederate armies. The lesson of their own Revolution of eighty years before seemed lost on both sides in this contest. Capitals did not wage and win wars, armies did. Loss of the capital at Philadelphia hardly crippled George Washington's army. So long as it remained in the field, the Revolution was alive. Men North and South might have profited by that example. But instead the North for far too long would aim at Richmond, just as the South would cling to it much too long for its own good. Indeed, by moving its capital to Richmond in the first place, the Confederacy committed itself more to the doctrine of holding supposed strategic positions than of maintaining a strong opposition to the Federals. It was a costly policy, even if it did help cement Virginia to the Confederacy. Yet there was little other choice they could make. The idea of a Southern nation demanded the protection and maintenance of all Southern territory. To do less would have been to deny the right of Southern nationhood.

On June 3 Scott asked McDowell to prepare a plan for an advance on Manassas Junction, Virginia, some twenty-five miles southwest of Washington. A Confederate army was organizing there under the command of the hero of Fort Sumter, Brigadier General P. G. T. Beauregard. This, plus Johnston's army abuilding at Harpers Ferry, posed a considerable threat. Even though Jefferson Davis avowed that the Confederacy's intentions were purely defensive, the Union could take no chance. And it and Lincoln were committed to putting down the rebellion. They must invade Virginia. Scott wanted Patterson to move against Johnston while McDowell occupied Beauregard. The problem was that the two Confederate armies were tied together by the Manassas Gap Railroad running directly west from Manassas to Strasburg in the Shenandoah, forty-five miles south of Harpers Ferry. By using this umbilical, the Confederates might easily and quickly move an army from one place to the other to combine against a single enemy. Thus, if Patterson was to engage Johnston, McDowell must completely occupy Beauregard, otherwise the creole might slip away from the junction and join Johnston within hours, with disastrous results for Patterson. And vice versa.

Scott's initial idea came to naught when his friend Patterson proved too slow and inept to wage an offensive. McDowell seemed more aggressive, and on June 21 he was asked to submit another plan, this one for him to make the primary move, into Virginia, while Patterson supported him in the valley. McDowell worked quickly, and he delivered a scheme whereby he would take 30,000 men in three columns and move south toward Manassas and the enemy positions along the south bank of Bull Run. Knowing that Beauregard had strong defenses, McDowell did not propose to attack them directly. Rather, he wished to cross Bull Run east of Beauregard's position and move against the Orange and Alexandria Railroad, which connected Manassas with Richmond. It was the Confederates' only link with their capital, and its separation by the Federals would force Beauregard to abandon his Bull Run line. Of course, the enemy might fight, McDowell warned Scott, saying that "the consequences of that battle will be of the greatest importance to the country, as establishing the prestige in this contest on the one side or the other."[5]

Scott and Lincoln accepted the plan and rightly so. It was a good one, far better than they should have expected from one of McDowell's limited experience. Yet even he saw its potentially fatal flaw and warned against it. If Patterson failed to hold Johnston in the valley, there could be disaster. Scott assured everyone that Patterson would do his part.

For a plodder like Patterson to fulfill his assignment, however, required that Johnston do absolutely nothing, and that was not in the nature of the feisty Virginian. Overall operations in the Old Dominion were being directed by Davis and Lee, and both expected Harpers Ferry to be held against all hazards. Johnston did not agree. "Harper's Ferry is untenable," he told them, and he was right. Thanks to the heights commanding it from across the Potomac, the position could easily be taken by Patterson's artillery alone. Johnston saw this and persuaded Richmond of it, but when Davis and Lee granted that he could give up the arsenal town if he felt it necessary, and on his own initiative, Johnston waffled. He wanted a specific order to evacuate, or at least a stated permission that would absolve him of responsibility should it prove to be the wrong move. Here was the problem with all too many professional soldiers, of whom Johnston was a type. "General Johnson [sic] has real active talent," thought the usually acerbic Francis W. Pickens. "He has boldly maneuvered in the face of an enemy far his superior in numbers. . . . I like his game." Yet so enamored was Johnston of his reputation that he feared at times to take risks that might blot his record. When Wade Hampton went hunting with Johnston earlier that year he noted that, though regarded an excellent marksman, the Virginian never fired his rifle. The birds were always too high or too low, flying too fast. "Things never did suit exactly. He was too fussy, too hard to please, too cautious, too much afraid to miss and risk his fine reputation for a crack shot."[6]

But on June 15, even while the order he wanted was on its way from Richmond, Johnston finally took a shot. He evacuated Harpers Ferry for Winchester with his ten-thousand-man army. It was the first real move of the campaign. Johnston felt much more secure in Winchester. It gave him speedier access to the Manassas Gap Railroad, and still controlled all approaches into the heart of the Shenandoah. And in the face of his withdrawal, Patterson had pulled away from Harpers Ferry! So confident did the Virginian become that he advised Richmond to send the bulk of its reinforcements to Beauregard. By the end of June, nevertheless, Johnston's little army numbered 10,654. He reorganized it into four brigades commanded by Jackson, Colonel Francis S. Bartow of Georgia, Brigadier General Bernard E. Bee of South Carolina, and Colonel Arnold Elzey from Maryland. In addition Johnston had the 1st Virginia Cavalry led by J. E. B. Stuart, and in the days that followed he sent Stuart and Jackson back down the valley to watch the Potomac crossings. Sure enough, on July 2 his scouts sent back word that Patterson was crossing the river. Jackson skirmished with him at Falling Waters, then fell back to Martinsburg. By the next day, Johnston brought the rest of his army to Darkesville to join Jackson and prepare to meet and defeat Patterson. Yet when the Federals did not advance further, Johnston pulled back to Winchester once more. Each feared the other and years later Johnston would admit that they "overrated each other's strength greatly." It would be a common failing in this war.[7]

Certainly, Johnston need not have worried about his opponent. Patterson was raising caution and sloth to an art, if not a science. After crossing the Potomac he waited nearly a full week before continuing his advance, giving Johnston plenty of time to prepare for him. Patterson knew that McDowell would march against Beauregard soon and that he must at all events hold Johnston in the valley. On July 9 he met in council of war with his officers. Almost to a man they advised against further advance, and Patterson was only too happy to listen. Guided by their counsel and his own fears, he decided to do nothing. He would wait.

By July 15, however, events forced him to move. The Federals had achieved a heartening, though hardly significant, victory at Rich Mountain in western Virginia a few days before. Morale soared, the little fight created a new hero in an obscure engineer from Ohio, George B. McClellan, and on this wave, borne by more reinforcements, Patterson could hardly stay put. That afternoon his advance came within five miles of Winchester. There was skirmishing all day and it looked like the Confederates were going to make a stand in the town. Patterson told his officers that the morrow would bring decisive results. He may also have told them of other events to take place on July 16. McDowell would march out of Alexandria toward Bull Run. At last a time of reckoning for the rebellious Confederacy seemed near at hand.

McDowell had, by the end of June, something less than the 30,000 soldiers he felt he needed, but he set about reorganizing his army for the coming campaign anyhow. He made five divisions, the first commanded by Colonel Daniel Tyler, the second by Colonel David Hunter, the third by Samuel P. Heintzelman, a fourth reserve division under Theodore Runyon, and the fifth led by Colonel Dixon Miles. Many of them will be heard from in the years to come, yet they

will be outstripped by some of their own subordinates who commanded brigades under them. Colonels like Oliver O. Howard, William B. Franklin, Orlando B. Willcox, Andrew Porter, and Israel B.
Richardson, will rise in this war. So will two other brigade commanders, Colonels Ambrose Burnside and William T. Sherman. This
first campaign will be a training ground for many of the men who will
dominate the war in later years.

McDowell had hoped to move on July 8, but delays prevented an
actual start for another week. McDowell, too, had fears. "I wanted
very much a little time," he complained, "all of us wanted it. We did
not have a bit of it. The answer was: 'You are green, it is true; but
they are green, also; you are all green alike.'" Hardly disquieting. Particularly when his own commanders like Tyler expressed a lack of
confidence in Patterson. Tyler bluntly asked Scott, "Suppose Jo. Johnson should reinforce Beauregard, what result should you expect then,
General?" Scott replied gruffly that "Patterson will take care of Jo.
Johnson." Tyler knew them both. Considering the abilities of the two,
he said frankly that he would be much surprised if "we did not have
to contend with Jo. Johnson's army in the approaching battle."[8]

Finally, on the morning of July 16, McDowell's columns packed
their baggage and marched out of Alexandria toward Manassas. Now
at last the Union would avenge Fort Sumter, avenge the dead hero
Ellsworth, erase the stain on the Federal banner. Rebellion would be
crushed and Federal authority once more installed in Richmond, with
the rest of the South soon to follow. This campaign would send a message to all in the Confederacy that judgment was at hand.

The Confederates got another message six days before. It came
rolled in the long dark hair of a heroine of Southern sympathies who
rode into Beauregard's lines on July 10. The dramatic scene as she unfolded her tresses gave way to even greater drama when the message
she bore was read. McDowell would advance on July 16 it said. Obviously, the Confederate spy system was working well in Washington,
filled as it was with hundreds of sympathizers, many with access to
high places.[9]

As McDowell was moving, Patterson was not, and it created an
anxious time for Johnston. He organized a fifth brigade for his army,
giving it to Brigadier General Edmund Kirby Smith, but it hardly
eased the anxiety. Word came on July 16 and 17 of a movement by
the enemy in his front but not toward him. Then on the afternoon of
July 17 came word from Beauregard that Richmond had ordered
Johnston to join him to meet McDowell; "do so immediately, if possible," it said, "and we will crush the enemy." Johnston chose not to
rely entirely upon Beauregard's word, and instead wired back to ask
the creole "Is the enemy upon you in force?" Johnston spent an anxious day and evening, but about 1 A.M. on July 18 came a telegram
from Richmond. "General Beauregard is attacked," it said. "To strike

the enemy a decisive blow a junction of your effective force will be needed. If practicable, make the movement." Now Johnston had real orders. He had always approved the doctrine of combination of his army with Beauregard's, and now he went to work speedily to accomplish that result.[10]

Patterson remained a problem, more potential than present however. By 9 A.M. of July 18, when Stuart's scouts reported that the Federals were not moving, Johnston decided to attempt escaping the valley unnoticed. "In an instant a thrill pervaded everything," wrote a Marylander in the army. "Not a word had been said; not a trumpet sounded, not a drum beat, but every one felt that something had happened." Johnston met with his brigade commanders and informed them of the intended move, and an expectant atmosphere spread through the camps. But when bugles called them to assembly, they believed it would be to march north to meet Patterson. Instead, Jackson and the others turned them south, and it puzzled the men. Were they retreating? Johnston anticipated that fears of this might depress the soldiers, so after an hour and one half he halted the column and ordered read an announcement that "General Beauregard is being attacked by overwhelming forces. Every moment now is precious, and the general hopes that his soldiers will *step out* and keep closed, for this march is a forced march to save the country." The message brought cheers. Then on they marched.[11]

Johnston now rode well ahead of the army in order to arrange their transportation at the Piedmont Station of the Manassas Gap line. He arrived probably before midnight, July 18, and soon thereafter Colonel Alexander R. Chisolm pounded into the hamlet on a badly winded horse. He came from Beauregard, having left Manassas that morning, riding over thirty miles. Out of breath, he gave Johnston Beauregard's message, probably imparting as well his general's pessimism that the reinforcements could arrive in time. When Chisolm had left the Bull Run lines, the enemy was already advancing against them. By now the battle could already be done. In the creole's message he proposed strategy to Johnston, his superior in seniority, and the latter wisely ignored the grandiose plan suggested. It was typical of Beauregard. At once Johnston sent Chisolm back on the road to take the news that the Shenandoah army would start arriving at Manassas late on July 19 or early the next day. By dawn the colonel had rejoined Beauregard, and the news he brought was delightful. Unless McDowell launched his main attack on July 20, it looked like the Confederates would be joined in time to defend themselves.[12]

But first Johnston must get there. Jackson brought his brigade into Piedmont Station by dawn, but their train had not yet arrived. When finally it appeared, the Virginians loaded and went on their way by noon. It was painfully slow. This was the only engine on the railroad at the moment. It would have to go to Manassas, deliver Jackson, then

come back for the next load. Any breakdown would mean disaster, so
the engineer took his time. It was eight hours before they saw the
campfires around Manassas in the distance. Disgorging its load, the
train, now empty, made the run back to Piedmont in half the time,
but could not get all of Bartow's brigade aboard, and then took another eight hours to reach Manassas once more, around 8 A.M., July
20. Then it was back for Bee's command. Meanwhile, Johnston somehow got another train into service, put Bee and himself aboard, and
forced it at a faster pace. They reached Manassas by noon, then sent
the cars back to bring Elzey's brigade, now temporarily commanded
by General Kirby Smith, whose own brigade remained in the valley.
It was a great feat so far, yet by the middle of July 20 nearly half of
Johnston's army still awaited transportation at Piedmont Station. It
was 3 A.M., July 21, before Kirby Smith got Elzey's men and another
regiment aboard and on the way. Their engine broke down repeatedly, but they kept it going somehow. It was well into midday July 21
before they approached Manassas, and ahead of them they could hear
the sounds of battle.[13]

Already, even if they did not achieve a victory over McDowell, still
Johnston and Beauregard could claim a significant feat of arms. Making strategic use of railroads for the first time in the annals of warfare,
each general, outnumbered in his own front, yet managed to combine
to face a single opponent. The two Confederate armies totaled together about 35,000. McDowell faced them with something under
37,000. The odds were even, despite the fact that two days before
over sixty miles separated the two Southern forces.

Almost at their first meeting, Johnston and Beauregard compared
rank, and the former won. He had just been promoted full general,
three grades ahead of the brigadier Beauregard. Johnston would command. Then the creole brought him up to date on what had happened
in the last four days. McDowell had marched out of Alexandria on
July 16, and two days later was in Centreville, north of Bull Run, the
Confederates having evacuated their works in the town. That same
day McDowell sent Tyler forward to make a reconnaissance near
Blackburn's Ford on Bull Run but, instead, Tyler brought on a small
engagement and got well pummeled for it. Learning little from the
action, McDowell remained in Centreville the next two days and,
even as the Confederate generals spoke, was still there.

Beauregard, full of Napoleonic aspirations, had already prepared a
battle plan, and now he proposed it to his new superior. Johnston, too,
believed it imperative that they attack the enemy on July 21, for fear
that any delay would allow Patterson to follow him from the valley
and hit their flank. He need not have worried, for Patterson did nothing, and will not be heard of or from again in this war.

The Louisiana general showed Johnston a map of the area. Bull
Run meandered roughly from southeast to northwest, and was crossed

at several places along the nearly six-mile front occupied by the Confederates. Sudley's Ford was at their far left. Below it a stone bridge marked the crossing of the turnpike connecting Centreville with Warrenton a few miles to the southwest. Immediately below the bridge was Lewis's Ford, then Ball's Ford, and then a mile further came Mitchell's, Blackburn's, and McLean's fords. The Orange and Alexandria Railroad crossed the stream a few thousand feet beyond, near Union Mills Ford. Beauregard had brigades or portions of brigades from his army guarding almost every crossing. Richard S. Ewell commanded at the railroad crossing. Acerbic, bald, cantankerous, he was supported by the command of Theophilus H. Holmes. David R. Jones guarded at McLean's, named after Wilmer McLean, whose nearby home served as Beauregard's headquarters. Jubal A. Early's Virginia brigade supported Jones. At Blackburn's Ford James Longstreet's brigade sat, the veterans of the first fighting on July 18, and to their left, guarding Mitchell's, Beauregard placed Milledge L. Bonham. At the stone bridge he put Nathan G. "Shanks" Evans and his half-brigade, and other scattered units covered Lewis's and Ball's fords.

Beauregard's plan was to mass the bulk of his army on his right and, certain that McDowell intended to attack his center at Mitchell's Ford, he would cross his brigades, cut off the enemy's line of retreat, and generally assail McDowell's left flank. It was not much of a plan, for the dictates of terrain had already forced McDowell to determine to attack Beauregard's left, the Sudley and stone bridge area. If McDowell saw this, surely Beauregard should have as well. Instead, now to protect that three miles of his line from Ball's Ford northward he had only Evans and another brigade under Philip St. George Cocke. And his battle order proved to be so lengthy and confused that many of his brigade commanders would not understand the parts they were to play. Beauregard was a good engineer but, Fort Sumter not to the contrary, he had a lot to learn about being a general.

At 4:30 A.M. on July 21 Beauregard awoke Johnston to have him sign the orders. Johnston's brigades from the valley were to support Mitchell's Ford where McDowell surely would attack. The signing done, Johnston remained awake and awaited what the dawn would bring. He did not like the confused and contradictory nature of the battle orders, but it was too late to alter them. They must strike now. Fortunately for the Confederates, McDowell proceeded to make their battle plan inoperative. He struck first.[14]

Following Tyler's botched reconnaissance at Blackburn's Ford on July 18, McDowell received further bad word that the ground leading to Union Mills Ford, beyond Beauregard's right and the place where he hoped to cross Bull Run and cut off the enemy from Richmond, was too rough to allow troop movement. As a result, his own plan of attack was rendered void and he had to form a new one tailored to the situation. Believing that Tyler's action would lead to Rebel reinforc-

ing of their center—which Beauregard did—McDowell now saw his
only option for a turning movement as being against the enemy left,
by way of Sudley's Ford. Two days spent in further reconnaissance
and bringing up supplies led to a new plan for attack, and it was a
sound one. Tyler would demonstrate against the stone bridge and
nearby fords, holding the Confederates there in place. Hunter would
march overland to Sudley's and cross, turn left, and move down the
south bank of Bull Run. Heintzelman would follow him, cross, and
head for the Manassas Gap line in hopes of cutting it before Johnston
could arrive. Tyler once more expressed his conviction that Johnston
would already be with Beauregard. They had heard train engine
whistles for two days, and it was an ominous sound. They might be
trains from Richmond. They might be from the Shenandoah.[15]

That night of July 20, the men in the Federal camps sensed something mighty was coming with the dawn. Sherman wrote to his wife,
"I know tomorrow and next day we shall have hard work, and I will
acquit myself as well as I can." Howard, ever religious, wished the
army was not so wicked, but believed "The Lord will take care of us."
Meanwhile, around the campfires that sent shadows dancing up the
trees, the men talked in low tones. A band played patriotic airs, someone sang the "Star-Spangled Banner," and cows in the meadows
lowed their mournful song. It was the final night of an America that
had lasted for two and one-half centuries. The dawn would bring a
new world, North and South.[16]

Reveille sounded in the Federal camps at 2 A.M., but it took an
hour for the first brigades to be ready to march. Once they started
down the road, their progress was slow and tortuous through dense
woods and thickets in the dark. It took an hour for the advance to
cover one-half mile, slowed even more by the folly of putting a pon-
derous three-ton cannon in the lead. It nearly collapsed the bridge
over Cub Run, barely a mile from the stone bridge. Nevertheless
Tyler continued his march, and by 5 A.M. could see the bridge in the
distance, and Bull Run flowing beneath.

Across the stream awaited Shanks Evans, a genuine eccentric in an
army that boasted a legion of characters. He was rude, insubordinate,
gruff, and no saint. An orderly followed him everywhere carrying a
wooden keg on his back. Evans called it his "barrelita," and kept it
filled with whiskey. A man in his headquarters said that Evans might
be the bravest man in the world, and "he is at the same time about
the best drinker, the most eloquent swearer . . . and the most
magnificent bragger I ever saw." He was also one of the best fighters.
Evans had just one regiment, a small Louisiana battalion, some cavalry, and two pieces of artillery, but during the rest of the morning he
would hold off whole divisions of Federals before relief.[17]

When Tyler got in position he signaled McDowell to start crossing
Hunter and Heintzelman. They took their time, but soon Evans re-

ceived word that the enemy was crossing at Sudley's Ford. He left just four companies to face Tyler's division at the bridge and took the rest of his command off to the left to meet Hunter. By 9 A.M. Burnside's brigade was across and beginning to engage Evans's little command. The battle was beginning in earnest.

Beauregard and Johnston were a bit surprised to arise to the sound of the enemy's guns. It severely disarrayed their plan to attack. Now they must defend instead. Yet the creole failed to cancel his order of the night before, so that many of his brigades on the right had no idea what was happening. Further, to some he still intimated an intention to attack, despite McDowell's stealing his initiative. As a result, when they should have been racing to the endangered left, some of the Confederate brigades were crossing and recrossing Bull Run with little or no idea of what they were to do. Already Beauregard had lost control of his battle.

The appearance of Federals on his left, and on his side of Bull Run, ended further thought of an offensive. At once Beauregard ordered Bee, Bartow, and Jackson to support Evans, and he could use the help. Moving north of the Warrenton Turnpike, Evans met and stopped Hunter's two brigades under Burnside and Porter, soon sending Hunter from the field with a neck wound. It was his birthday. Slowly the Federals pushed Evans back, however, and he withdrew just as Bee's brigade came up. Shortly, Bartow too was present, and they soon established a fairly secure line on Matthews Hill. A charge to stop the Federal advance failed, however, and the Rebels had to pull back south of the Warrenton road so that by 11:30 they were taking a new position on Henry Hill, awaiting a counterattack not only from Hunter's brigades, but also from Heintzelman's as well, the latter now reaching the battle line. Nearly half of McDowell's army sat perched on the Confederate left flank, with less than a third of Johnston's army there to meet them.

Beauregard and Johnston monitored the fight thus far from a position near Mitchell's Ford. Besides the sounds of more fighting than he expected coming from his left, the creole heard no firing at all on his right, where he wanted Ewell to advance against McDowell's left flank. Everything seemed to go wrong. All morning, furthermore, Johnston had been urging him to send available reinforcements to Evans. The fight would be decided there, said the Virginian, but Beauregard declined. Worse, word now came that a cloud of dust to the northwest had been seen from a signal tower. They feared it was Patterson, though in fact Johnston's own baggage trains stirred up the cloud. This new threat was more than enough to force Johnston to take a shot once more. "The battle is there," he said pointing toward the left. "I am going." Now at last he took direction of the battle. It was nearly too late.[18]

Beauregard, too, realized the obvious. He started sending Holmes,

Early, and Bonham toward the Henry Hill line. Ever the actor, he would later declare that "My heart for a moment failed me! I felt as though all was lost. I wished I had fallen in the battle of the 18th; but I soon rallied, and I then solemnly pledged my life that I would that day conquer or die!" Then he rode toward the left to join Johnston.[19]

The Federals believed that Beauregard had lost, too. Evans was being pushed back, and Sherman's and Erasmus D. Keyes's brigades of Tyler's division had crossed Bull Run and linked with Hunter's command. The Confederates seemed outnumbered and retreating. McDowell's adjutant raced along the battle line shouting, "Victory! Victory! We have done it! We have done it!" He was a bit premature.[20]

Hampton and his legion joined Evans on Henry Hill along with Bee and Bartow. In the wake of their unsuccessful attack of a half hour before, the Confederates were in a shaky condition. Bee, senior officer present on the line, tried as best he could to establish control over his restive command, but the advancing enemy pressed him too hotly. Looking back toward Henry's crest he saw Jackson and his Virginia brigade. Jackson was now a brigadier, too, and Bee rode to him. "General, they are beating us back," he cried.

"Sir, we'll give them the bayonet."

Bee rode back to his regiment but, seeing no officers he recognized, he asked "What regiment is this?" It was his own 4th Alabama. "This is all of my brigade that I can find," he told them, "will you follow me back to where the firing is going on?" They answered, "To the death."

Yet certainly Bee said something more before he led his men into the fight once again. Within a day one of the men would tell a newspaper correspondent that the general concluded by saying, "There is Jackson standing like a stone wall. Let us determine to die here, and we will conquer. Follow me." Three days later, in Richmond, the word will be about that Jackson's men "stood so stock still under fire that they are called a stone wall." Whatever the case—and at least some claimed that Bee's comment was derogatory—a legendary name was born. He would be Stonewall Jackson to posterity, and his command, the Stonewall Brigade.[21]

Within minutes Bee took a mortal wound. Bartow, too, would be killed by the time Johnston arrived on the line. The situation was bad, and feverishly Johnston and Beauregard worked to establish order. Johnston personally led the remnant of the 4th Alabama into the line, and his display of coolness helped rally the men. Then Johnston left the line to Beauregard's management while he returned to the rear to undertake the delicate management of feeding more reinforcements forward to their proper places. He now effectively directed the course of the battle, and by 1 P.M. the line was stable. When McDowell sent two powerful batteries to attack, they were demolished, and one almost entirely captured. When the Federals tried to use their advan-

1. The men who could not prevent secession. President James Buchanan stands at the center with his cabinet. They are from the left, Jacob Thompson, Lewis Cass, John B. Floyd, Buchanan, Howell Cobb, Isaac Toucey, Joseph Holt, and Jeremiah Black. Thompson, Floyd, and Cobb will become Confederates. (Library of Congress)

2. *The man in the middle: John C. Breck-inridge as a presidential candidate in 1860.* (Author's collection)

3. *The "Little Giant," Senator Stephen A. Douglas, whose ambition helped destroy his party and whose loyalty helped save the Union.* (Library of Congress)

*4. Edmund Ruffin, the firebrand, welcomer of secession, a man con-
sumed with hatred of the North, and a fanatical espouser of Southern
nationalism.* (Library of Congress)

5. *The officers of Fort Sumter. Seated are, from the left, Abner Double-day, Robert Anderson, Samuel Crawford, and John G. Foster. Standing are G. Seymour, G. W. Snyder, Jefferson C. Davis, R. K. Mead, and T. Talbot. Photographer George Cook captured their likeness inside the fort in January 1861.* (U. S. Army Military History Institute)

6. *The aged general who tried to hold Sumter without war, Winfield Scott. The war would pass him by, but this Virginian's loyalty never faltered for a moment.* (Author's collection)

7. *The Ironclad Battery at Morris Island, Charleston. From one of these cannon, Ruffin jerked his lanyard, thereby firing his famous "first" shot at Sumter.* (South Carolina Historical Society)

8. The other President, Jefferson Davis, a man unfitted for executive office in almost every arena but fierce devotion to the South. He will learn little. (National Archives)

9. Almost boyish in stature and aspect, Confederate Vice President Alexander H. Stephens, a Southern constitutionalist uninclined toward compromise. (Library of Congress)

10. *Success came to Brigadier General P.G.T. Beauregard at Sumter. So, too, at First Manassas; but from Shiloh onward his star will slowly descend, victim of his own contentiousness.* (U. S. Army Military History Institute)

11. *Gustavus Vasa Fox, a great schemer, was an able administrator whose efforts to succor Sumter failed by only hours. His work with the Union Navy, however, would rarely fail.* (U. S. Army Military History Institute)

12. The face of Fort Sumter on April 17, 1861, after the siege. (U. S. Army Military History Institute)

tage of numbers by extending their lines beyond the Confederate left on Henry Hill, Stuart's cavalry, which had come overland from the valley, routed them with a surprise flank attack. For two more hours the battle raged indecisively on Henry Hill. Hampton took a bad wound. McDowell sent in his attacks only a regiment at a time, and all were turned back. Jackson counterattacked. Jackson and Hampton's men stopped an assault by Sherman. The Federal line became more and more confused, the green soldiers more and more demoralized by seeing their piecemeal attacks thrown back. Then, at last, Howard's brigade came on the field and Heintzelman sent him to the far right to turn the Confederate flank. The enemy repulsed Howard and, instead of retiring in an orderly manner, his men began to panic and run away, disrupting the commands next to them and threatening to start a rout.

Suddenly, as black as it had looked for the Confederates that morning, it now looked bright indeed. Johnston was skillfully sending the reinforcements to precisely the right spots in the line to stop the Federal attempt to turn his left. Further, the unexpected appearance of new Confederates on the field had a demoralizing effect on the Federals. Among those reinforcements was the 2nd South Carolina, and who should be marching with them but old Edmund Ruffin. And then, at precisely the moment when McDowell was on the verge of breaking up, Kirby Smith appeared on the field. His train had made it to Manassas in time.

In fact, they arrived some time after noon, but it took another three hours to reach the front, guided by instructions from Johnston. Smith left behind as rearguard the 13th Virginia. Its colonel, A. P. Hill, was disgusted, certain that now he would never get to see action in this war. Smith himself saw little enough of it today. A bullet felled him before he reached the battle line, and Elzey resumed command of the brigade. Then Early came on the field as well, though not before Beauregard mistook the dust cloud created by Early's Virginians as being that of Patterson. Finally, with Confederates crumpling the enemy right flank, Beauregard ordered a general assault along his line. It worked, and soon the Union Army was not only retreating, but in a mushrooming panic, dropping weapons, and abandoning equipment, all in the frenzied rush to get away from the enemy to safety. Johnston ordered a pursuit, but his own army was too badly battered to follow effectively on the success thus far gained. Only the 2nd South Carolina and a battery of artillery, along with the Hampton Legion, managed to cross Bull Run at the stone bridge and go after McDowell. They came upon the bluecoats as they were crossing the fragile bridge over Cub Run. Kershaw had the artillery unlimber, and then once more a "first shot" was offered to Edmund Ruffin. He took it, and sent a shell crashing into the bridge, upsetting a wagon, and effectively blocking the span. That completed the Federal panic.

Lincoln took the news of the defeat in silence, but later whispered into a Congressman's ear that "It's damned bad." No one except Tyler, jealous as always, blamed McDowell for the defeat. He had planned a good battle and, but for using his regiments one at a time instead of massing attacks, he fought well. Sherman felt humiliated. "I am sufficiantly disgraced now," he wrote his wife. Losses were high, almost 3,000 killed, wounded, and missing. The greatest casualty was Union morale, but with the rout came also a resolution to return again. Lincoln would not accept defeat.

As for Davis, he was happy to accept another victory. First Sumter and now Manassas, or Bull Run, as some would call it. No matter the 2,000 casualties that the Confederates suffered. The South was obviously next to invincible. That militant heritage of which "Southrons" were so proud had been demonstrated once more. Certainly it was for Shanks Evans, who proudly boasted that the victory was due entirely to himself, "God Almighty and a few private gentlemen."[22] Beauregard will get the bulk of the credit for the victory. Johnston will deserve it. The laurels came at a cost. His army lay nearly as battered as McDowell's, and the disruption in Southern ranks lasted longer. "This victory disorganized our volunteers as utterly as a defeat could do in an army of regulars," said Johnston. "Everybody, officers and privates, seemed to think that he had fulfilled all his obligations to country—& that before attending to any further call of duty, it was his privilege to look after his friends, procure trophies, or amuse himself." And thinking men in the South realized that, beyond their own demoralization after the battle, they would have to face the enemy again. This would not be the last battle. The North's defeat, wrote a clerk in Richmond, would stimulate "renewed preparations on a scale of greater magnitude than ever." He was right. The Union had lost a battle, but not a war. A disgruntled Federal soldier spoke well for his nation when he wrote home that "I shall see the thing played out, or die in the attempt."[23]

CHAPTER 6

"THE MAN AND THE HOUR HAVE MET"

Jefferson Davis was ecstatic. In five months' existence, his infant nation won two significant victories over its enemy, was in the process of establishing its own internal government, including even its own postage and currency, and had work in motion to begin relations with foreign powers looking hopefully toward formal recognition and military aid. He and the Confederacy had come a long way since that sunny February morning in Montgomery when delegates of several states met to make a little treason.

Montgomery had rarely hosted such an assemblage since the commercial convention of several years before. Many of the foremost political leaders in the South were here gathered, and they all knew why they were there. With seven states seceded and more surely to follow, there must be a new government for the new Southern nation. As they assembled in their meeting hall more than one of them heard echoes of Franklin and Madison and Adams. They were repeating history. Or so they hoped.

There was little to do that first day except set the stage. As director, they selected Georgia's Howell Cobb, once an outspoken Union man, for president of the convention. He had been Buchanan's treasury secretary and before that governor of Georgia. Then they appointed a rules committee and adjourned. No hurry.

The next day proved a bit more full. They must decide what they were authorized to do here, though of course the matter had been discussed at length informally before the meeting convened. They must have a new constitution for their new nation. More specifically, it must be a *provisional* constitution, pending formal adoption. And they must select a provisional President and Vice-President. They appointed Christopher G. Memminger of South Carolina to head a committee charged with drafting the new document. Working with the United States Constitution as his model, Memminger spent two days trying constantly to adapt that charter to the specific needs and beliefs of Southerners.

It did not commence with "We the People." Rather, "We, the deputies of the sovereign and independent States," were meeting in assembly. The articles did not materially differ in other respects on most points, though the document was generally not as well organized as the Federal Constitution. Article I alone became a catchall, even including the Confederate "Bill of Rights." Interestingly, it also outlawed the foreign slave trade, sought to control domestic trading in Negroes, and devoted some time to tariffs, long a touchy subject between North and South. Article II provided for the presidency, giving the office a one-year term until a regularly elected President should take power. A rude act of succession was included, and the new Chief Executive was to be paid $25,000 per year. His oath was simple: "I do solemnly swear (or affirm) that I will faithfully execute the office of President of the Confederate States of America, and will, to the best of my ability, preserve, protect, and defend the Constitution thereof."[1]

The convention adopted Memminger's product late on February 8, then adjourned, leaving for the next day the most important work of all. A Constitution was important, to be sure, but this gesture of Southern nationhood, this secession supposedly on principle, was deeply symbolic. Equally symbolic must be their choice of a leader. Not only must he represent the new Confederacy, but also he must hold it together in the face of many divisive elements. It was a position that would require as much from its incumbent as the Union was even now preparing to require from Lincoln. The convention did not choose well.

Indeed, in their defense, their choices were in fact severely limited. One of the many reasons for the coming of this crisis in the first place was the lack, North and South, of truly great statesmen, men of the stripe of Clay and Webster. Statecraft had broken down in the country and of what little there was, most remained with the North. Nowhere in the recently seceded states was there a truly towering intellect and character, the mixture of patience, diplomacy, firmness, and flexibility, that must all reside in a single man to make the President this nation had to have. Indeed, it would be some time before even the people in the North realized that they had elected such a figure.

The best choice that the Montgomery convention could have made was a man not yet available, that man in the middle, John C. Breckinridge. He had served in the House of Representatives. Even now, after stepping down as Vice-President, he served Kentucky as a United States Senator. And most Southerners had looked upon him as the representative of their interests in 1860. He was widely popular and had carried every one of the states here represented. Furthermore, he had dignity, the presence of a President, the patience, tact, the firmness of resolve yet willingness to compromise, that any Chief Executive must possess. And as much as any man had demonstrated, he had the ability. But he was not available. He still maintained his allegiance to the Union, still sat in its Congress, even though he was speaking increasingly in defense of the South. Finally, the fact that his natal state, Kentucky, remained in the Union made his selection impossible. It was too bad. Breckinridge would not have made a great President. Just a better one.

No one that this convention might select could have altered the inevitable destination the Confederacy would start toward at Fort Sumter. Surely the delegates tried, however, but their alternatives were few.

Cobb himself was favored by many, but he made it clear from the first that he did not wish the office. Robert B. Rhett seemed to believe that, as the acknowledged "father of secession," he deserved the nod. But he was too ultra, and even South Carolina's delegates did not propose him. Toombs wanted the post avidly, convinced that he was the best man for it. But few others agreed. He was too erratic. He drank too much. Alex Stephens wrote a few days later that "drinking to excess" ruined Toombs's chances. "One day in particular about two days before the election he got tight at dinner and went to a party in town *tighter* than I ever saw him—too tight for his character and reputation by far. I think that evening's exhibition settled the Presidency where it fell."[2] Stephens, too, seemed a good candidate, but he had many enemies and was too contentious to make a leader.

Increasingly, thoughts turned to Jefferson Davis. He was a bona fide hero from the war with Mexico, son-in-law of President Zachary Taylor in his first marriage, Pierce's secretary of war, Congressman, Senator. He was fifty-three, a native of Kentucky but always identified with his home state Mississippi. From his first day in Washington, he stood for Southern rights and extension of slavery into the new territories. Never an ardent proponent of secession, still he believed in the right of a state to do so. Even with the election of Lincoln in 1860 he did not completely despair for the Union, but when Mississippi seceded Davis left his Senate seat and returned home. He knew that he would be considered for the new presidency. He was one of the

relatively few Southern politicians who enjoyed a substantial reputation, and outside Mississippi he had few enemies, yet. Thus it was no
surprise to him that the Montgomery convention finally settled on him
as its nominee when it voted on February 9. But he was "disappointed." "I had not believed myself as well suited to the office as
some others," he would say. He thought he would have been better
used as a general, yet he only had one year of active service in a war,
and one brief moment of glory at Buena Vista. That was enough to
convince him of his military competence.

In fact, Davis was suited neither for the Executive Mansion nor the
battlefield. There were character traits in the man that disqualified
him for both uses. His reserve and self-control would become legendary. Yet he lacked tact, did not listen well, and lectured overmuch. He
was a petty man, not in human terms—for his heart was warm and
large—but in the transaction of his business. When priorities demanded that he devote his time to matters of great state, he would
often as not mire himself in endless debate on inconsequent details.
He had a compulsion not only to be right but to convince others that
he and not they was right. He never learned to compromise. His loyalty to old friends was so great that, admirable in most men, it led
him to overlook their repeated failures, and even treachery.

Against this, Davis did look the part of a President. Tall, graceful,
dignified, he had the courtly manners of the Old South, the air of one
born to lead. Measured against Lincoln in February 1861 he looked
decidedly the more presidential. Since few knew him intimately—he
was not an intimate man—few suspected his inner weaknesses. Besides, he represented the middle ground. Repeatedly in this conflict,
North and South, men will seek the center, the median, anything but
the extreme. Neither side and neither President enjoyed a true unanimity of feeling in his domain. Their chief hopes for success lay in
unification by compromise. Davis had been an early—but not too
early or too strident—spokesman for Southern rights. He had become
a secessionist late—but not too late. He represented the average of
Rhett, the extremist, and Stephens, the near-Unionist. It was to be
hoped that the journey to a single mind and purpose would not be too
long if the men from each extreme had to go no farther than the middle.

Davis accepted and immediately left for Montgomery to be inaugurated. Even then he hoped that he would return to Mississippi when
his one-year term expired and take charge of its military forces. On
the journey he told a companion that, in his opinion, "there *would* be
war, long and bloody." He reached Montgomery, now to be the capital of the new Confederate States of America, on February 16. There
Yancey was present to meet him. The occasion called for eloquence,
of which Davis had little, but the old fire-eater was not wanting. To

those in hearing Yancey proclaimed that "the man and the hour have met!"[3]

Davis began his "hour" two days later with his inauguration on the steps of the Alabama state Capitol. Ten thousand spectators gathered, most of them entirely unable to hear what he was saying. Montgomery's photographer A. C. McIntyre brought his camera out of his studio and set it up opposite the state house portico. The hands on the clock above the doorway said 1 P.M. Davis and Cobb stood and listened as a band played "Dixie," the composition of a Northern writer. "The audience was large and brilliant," Davis would write to his wife. "Upon my weary heart was showered smiles, plaudits, and flowers; but, beyond them, I saw troubles and thorns innumerable."

He spoke before taking the oath. He felt himself unequal to the task allotted, yet he would try. He hoped that the South would be allowed to choose its course without molestation from the North. "Our true policy is peace," he told them. Yet they must be prepared to defend "by the final arbitrament of the sword, the position which we have assumed among the nations of the earth. We have entered upon the career of independence, and it must be inflexibly pursued." He cited the Revolution as their justification and example. Yet he had to calm fears of radical change, for this after all was a conservative movement. So he asserted that any reference to the Confederacy as a revolution was a semantic error. "We have changed the constituent parts, but not the system of government," he assured them. There was still continuity. Their constitution differed from that of the Founding Fathers only "as it is explanatory of their well-known intent." In other words, it was they who guarded the flame of 1787 and kept it burning. The Yankees were the real revolutionaries. That there might be war, he admitted. That they could ever reunite with the Union, he denied. And that "toil and care and disappointment" would accompany his term in office, he was certain. "You will see many errors to forgive, many deficiencies to tolerate." Indeed they would. Yet rarely again would President Jefferson Davis so readily confess his fallibility.[4]

The inauguration done, the convention went on to frame a permanent Constitution and establish itself as a provisional Congress. There were laws to enact, departments to create, virtually an entire government to conceive. They did it in a month. The new Constitution passed unanimously on March 11. Significantly this new document, itself the product of secession, avoided specifically recognizing the right of a state to do so. Already synergism was at work. The framers sensed something potentially greater in the whole than the mere sum of its parts. They even referred to "permanent federal government." Men like Rhett nearly choked on that phrase, as indeed they did on most of the compact. It was too conservative, too near the United States Constitution in intent and even wording. Rhett saw in it "the dread spirit of reconstruction." He and others like him believed that the South had thrown away the yoke of the Union, only to replace it with one of its own. During the debate over the Constitution, the ardent Southern rights extremists also argued against the admission of any new states to the Confederacy unless those states embraced slavery. There was talk abroad that some of the northwestern states of the old Union, Indiana and Ohio for instance, might someday wish to ally themselves with the South. Rhett denounced any thought of admitting them, for they would begin a free-state minority in the new government that might one day grow to a majority, as it had in the old Union. They were all protective of this new government. Having lost control—so they thought—of one Federal Union, they did not want to risk forfeiting this new one as well. There was finally a compromise, as on so many issues in this convention dominated by moderates. Free states could be admitted, but only after a two-thirds majority vote in the Congress.[5]

The work was done, the Confederacy born, and now President Jefferson Davis, like Lincoln, had to form a government. Unlike the Rail Splitter, Davis had no convention bargains to honor, but there were regional and ideological factions to appease aplenty. Indeed, more. Unable to please everyone, Davis was the loser before he began. In a revolution, everyone involved imagines himself a prime mover, deserving of recognition. The trouble is that revolutionaries are rarely able statesmen. Worse yet, extremists make rebellion; governments are made of moderates. Jefferson Davis was not a fool, and he knew that to work at all, his administration must be one of moderate men, if not conservatives. The old leaders of the movement for so many years, the true revolutionaries, would as soon bring down their new regime as they discarded the old. The first instinct of a new form of government is self-preservation. Davis must preserve the Confederacy.

He turned first to Robert Toombs. Though erratic and egotistical, and given overmuch to drink, Toombs was a commanding presence, and a popular conservative leader in the South. However much Toombs may not have been suited to cabinet work, he represented the proper interests in the new country. Three Georgians, Toombs, Cobb, and Stephens, had been considered for the presidency. Even though the last was now Vice-President, still that state was entitled to another post of importance. Davis wanted to make Toombs his treasury secretary, but other pressures made that impossible. And so the President offered him the traditional premier portfolio, state. Toombs declined at first. He did not much like Davis, and was still aggrieved that he was not made President himself. Stephens persuaded him to change his mind, however, and on February 24 the towering Georgian took his oath of office.[6]

The reason Davis could not offer Toombs the treasury job was that he had to use it to pay a debt to South Carolina. He first asked Robert

Barnwell to act as secretary of state in reward for leading the Palmetto State's vote for Davis rather than Rhett. Barnwell declined, but suggested instead that his friend Memminger of South Carolina be given the treasury post. Davis could not refuse. Memminger, fifty-eight, born in Germany, served for years as chairman of the finance committee in the legislature, and there acquired what reputation he enjoyed as a good man with money. There were some who questioned his sagacity. Edward A. Pollard of the Richmond *Examiner* would call the secretary's mind "juvenile in financial matters," and assert that Memminger never understood the need for a sound basis for a currency. Yet Davis had enough reason to trust him in Barnwell's recommendation.[7]

There must be a navy, and Florida must have a seat in the cabinet. Thus Stephen R. Mallory came quickly to mind. He had never been an ardent separationist, and not exactly a standout in his service in the United States Senate. He was accused of questionable morals, and even of disloyalty to the Southern interest, but he also had some experience with naval administration, having served as chairman of the Senate Committee on Naval Affairs. Thus secretary of the navy was a safe enough post for him. No one expected that the Confederacy would put fleets on the oceans. It merely had to protect its rivers and harbors and administer those commerce raiders granted letters of marque under Davis's proclamation. Mallory would surprise everyone.[8]

There must be an army, and there must be an Alabamian. But here Davis did not look too hard for a man of talent, for in his mind, Davis himself possessed all the military sagacity necessary. In a war secretary he needed little more than a factotum, for he would run any war from the Executive Mansion. As a result, the man tapped for this portfolio had nothing at all to recommend him except industry. Leroy Pope Walker of Alabama was just forty-four, and a secessionist only since 1860. Yancey liked him and made the suggestion to Davis. He knew not the first thing about an army.[9]

This left two posts to fill. While the United States Post Office continued in operation in much of the South, its postage remaining in use there for several weeks, yet the Confederacy must have its own mail delivery system, and its own postmaster general. What made Davis think of John H. Reagan for the portfolio is a mystery, but it was a happy thought. Indeed, Reagan frankly told Davis in Montgomery that, given the choice, he would not have voted for the Mississippian for President! Yet surely Davis took it as a compliment, for Reagan went on to say that he preferred Davis as general-in-chief. Whether intended as flattery or not, Reagan had undoubtedly touched deeply the President's military conceit. Indeed, Davis told Reagan that a general's uniform "would have been more agreeable" to him. On March 6, then, "much to my surprise," the Texan received Davis's tender of the postmaster's portfolio. He twice declined it, and explained in person to the President his reasons. For the present, the South was enjoying excellent mail service. But cease the United States system and start a new one, and delays and inadequacies would be inevitable for months, perhaps years. The Constitution expected the department to return a profit after two years. Everything would be blamed on the cabinet minister responsible. Reagan would be happy to serve the cause, he said, but "I did not desire to become a martyr." Davis persuaded him to reconsider, but Reagan left uneasy. "Instead of feeling proud of the honor conferred on me, I felt that I was to be condemned by the public for incapacity."[10]

One portfolio remained. Attorney general. All of the Deep South states were represented now. Mississippi had the President; Texas, Reagan; Alabama, Walker; Georgia, Toombs; Florida, Mallory; South Carolina, Memminger. One state remained. Louisiana. Davis first offered the inconsequential cabinet seat to Yancey, who refused. That left the President free to turn to Louisiana, and Judah P. Benjamin. The two once nearly came to a duel, until Davis apologized. Benjamin was a Sephardic Jew, born in Saint-Croix, fifty years old, enormously ambitious, and equally talented. He had been a United States Senator, a lawyer, a planter, a Yale dropout, and a past master in the art of adaptability. Davis selected him, he said, because of Benjamin's reputation as a lawyer and for "the lucidity of his intellect." Perhaps. The real reasons are difficult to fathom. Probably they were purely political. In any case, Davis, in assigning the least important cabinet post, had accidentally brought into his official family the greatest talent of the lot.[11]

The cabinet was done, like Lincoln's a patchwork affair, but with rather less talent on the whole, yet with more honesty. Now they must build their government. As each went to work they suffered almost precisely the same difficulties. Whereas Lincoln's ministers moved into established organizations with bureaucracies in place, Davis's secretaries each started with an empty room in "A great, red brick pile, originally built for warehouses and countingrooms" called the Government House. It was the best that Montgomery, as the capital of the new Confederacy, could offer. Benjamin and Mallory each had a room on the second floor. Toombs and the others quartered on the first story. They all had to build from almost nothing.[12]

Reagan was the most fortunate, perhaps, for mail routes and post offices were already established throughout the South. Even as he returned to the Exchange Hotel after accepting his appointment, the Texan began thinking of how he was to learn all that he needed to know. The answer came to him before he reached the hotel. It was simple. Ask the Yankees. He sent a friend to Washington with letters to the heads of the United States Post Office's chief clerk's office, bond division, dead letter office, finance bureau, and even to the third assistant postmaster. He asked them to come and take positions with his new department and to bring with them copies of their departmental forms, maps, and annual reports. All except one or two accepted! "They brought to me all the information necessary to enable me to organize the postal service of the Confederacy," he later boasted. Reagan, in effect, had stolen the U. S. Post Office. Then he organized a school for clerks and officers, systematized the mail routes, put out a request for bids for contractors, and codified all the various arrangements with railroads and steamboat lines for carrying the mails. He even had to look for furniture for the offices, and find more room for his expanding staff. By late April, when Davis asked each minister for a report on the readiness of his department, Reagan answered with pardonable pride. His report showed the phenomenal industry he bent to his task, covering in detail every matter from form blanks to new rates for periodicals and to the results of a convention he called of railroad representatives. They proved very cooperative. Indeed, Reagan reported that his department, on April 29, 1861, after just six weeks' existence, "was as completely organized as that at Washington." He was ready to commence operations. Davis admitted his amazement.[13]

None of the others could compete with Reagan, except perhaps Benjamin, who in fact had little to do. His function, besides appointing judges, consisted chiefly in offering legal counsel to Davis and others, and initiation of some legislation in legal matters such as patents. "He is a short, stout man, with a full face, olive-coloured, and most decidedly Jewish features," wrote an English correspondent who visited Montgomery. "Mr. Benjamin is the most open, frank, and cordial of the Confederates whom I have yet met." The Englishman found Benjamin most inclined to talk about international affairs, and his belief that Great Britain and the Confederacy would soon become bedfellows.[14]

And whereas Benjamin had little to do, Toombs was simply not inclined to do much. His office, like all the others, opened off a central platform on his floor, each door proclaiming its occupant by a simple piece of paper tacked to it. "Secretary of State" said the handwritten note on Toombs's door. As if that were not deflating enough an introduction to a supposedly august cabinet department, the incumbent was even more condescending. Toombs declared repeatedly that he carried the business of the state department in his hat. Instead of showing real interest in his office, Toombs "had nothing to do but talk politics, tell stories and say some very clever things." The English correspondent, William H. Russell, found the secretary "unquestionably one of the most original, quaint, and earnest of the Southern leaders," while yet noting inconsistency in his character.

Without consulting Toombs, Davis had already taken the Confederacy's first diplomatic steps when on February 27 he appointed commissioners to go to Washington to try and establish friendly relations. They failed, but Toombs and Davis entertained greater hopes for another trio, this one on its way to Europe even as the guns battered Fort Sumter. Pierre Rost, Ambrose Dudley Mann, and Yancey were dispatched to England and France to secure recognition of the South's belligerent status and hold the lure of cotton as an inducement for foreign aid.

The Confederate Constitution prohibited the taking or granting of titles of nobility. But there was one such title in the realm which no one questioned. King Cotton. The textile mills in Great Britain had relied for more than a generation on Southern cotton, and were wedded inextricably to them now, or so Toombs and Davis believed. Should the blockade cut off King Cotton, the secretary estimated, then England's industry would suffer to the sum of $600 million or more. This appeal to British self-interest alone was expected to bring formal recognition of the Confederacy as a nation, and hopefully alliance and military aid if needed.[15]

Toombs also sent envoys to Mexico, the West Indies, and even to the Indian nations in the territory beyond Arkansas. Yet he had little taste for his work, and even less for working under the thumb of the meddling Davis, a perfectionist who interfered in the workings of every one of his secretaries except Reagan. Memminger, on the other hand, took to his work with some will, and some talent. It helped that he commenced his office with a real treasury, albeit not a large one. He started with little else, his department's first order being written on a dry goods box, announcing office hours as 9 A.M. to 3 P.M.

When Louisiana seceded her officials seized $500,000 in hard money from the U. S. Customs Office and the New Orleans mint. The state immediately put these funds, in the form of a loan, at the disposal of the new Confederate government. Yet this was hardly enough to begin a new nation. Operating from the Louisiana precedent, however, Memminger speedily determined to attempt financing through several loans. Congress backed him wholeheartedly, for money from this source was far easier—and more politic—than heavy taxes. Memminger really preferred taxation, but the time needed to get the cumbersome bureaucracy and systems organized he simply did not have.

Speedily Memminger helped draft an act calling for $15 million in loans of specie from the South's banks. It would drain the hard cash then circulating in the Confederacy, forcing the treasury department, in turn, to resort to paper money with little backing in order to keep currency available. The seeds of grotesque inflation were thus planted, but the immediate need seemed to outweigh the longterm threat.[16]

One of the things that this specie was needed for was the financing of a Confederate Navy, and Secretary Mallory had considerable plans, but they would take time and a lot of money. During his first two months in office he could boast barely a handful of ships in the "fleet," most of them captured. At Pensacola Confederates took the steamship *Fulton,* but it was in the process of major overhaul when taken, and the Confederates would never, in fact, complete the job. Of course there were the ships abandoned by the Federals at Norfolk, but there was little to be done with them, either. Or so thought everyone but Mallory. Within days of the fall of Norfolk he wrote to Davis that "I regard the possession of an iron-armored ship as a matter of the first necessity. Such a vessel at this time could traverse the entire coast of the United States, prevent all blockades, and encounter, with a fair prospect of success, their entire Navy." The South could never hope to match the North ship for ship on the sea. It must instead turn to innovation. "Inequality of numbers may be compensated by invulnerability," he advised, "and thus not only does economy but naval success dictate the wisdom and expediency of fighting with iron against wood." Already Mallory was seeking designs for such a warship, as yet unaware that lying in the mud off Gosport there sat the remnant of a warship that he would use to make legend.[17]

Yet already overshadowing all other cabinet departments stood that of war. There must be armies to defend against Yankee aggression, and large armies at that. Leroy P. Walker began his task with some advantage in that every one of the seceded states had numbers, indeed scores, of active volunteer militia companies already armed and equipped. They would form the nucleus of his armies, but they lacked any sort of uniformity or consistent training, and often as not were led by complete amateurs whose only qualification was that they donated the money for uniforms. The men forming the companies, too, were all too frequently the town dandies, planters' sons, Sunday soldiers who had never really endured the hardships of camp and field and were not now so inclined.

Still, this is where Walker would have to start. He asked Congress to authorize an army of 100,000. That done, he then petitioned the governors of the several states to raise and forward regiments. The soldiers would be equipped, armed, and paid at Confederate expense, to become part of a national army, no longer subject to directions from the governors. The response from those state leaders varied, the ultra state rights men raising more objections. But very quickly Walker had more men on his department rolls than he could handle. By the time the guns opened fire on Fort Sumter, more than 60,000 soldiers waited at his disposal. They were not all at one place, but some here, some there, some on their way from their states, and a few existed only on paper. Still it was a good beginning. To Walker fell the task of providing officers to command these troops. Each regiment generally elected its company officers, and even its colonel. But the regiments would be joined into brigades, brigades into divisions, divisions into armies, and to command all those larger organizations

would take generals. Promotion to general was a right reserved
strictly to the war department, with the concurrence of Davis and
Congress. Many of the states had already their own militia generals.
Virginia appointed Lee major general as soon as he resigned his
United States commission. Now Walker and Davis made appointments of their own. And this was the way it quickly came to be in
most facets of the War portfolio—Walker and Davis. The President
wasted little time in asserting his own influence in managing the armies, which by his own admission he would rather lead as commander than as commander-in-chief. And Walker, a poor choice from
the start, did not help. He was soon almost lost in the mountain of detail, and confided to Davis his own sense of inadequacy. Soon
Congress, too, saw Walker's limitations. He would not last long, but
his tenure had a lasting impact on the Confederacy. It helped raise
the first armies—regardless of how efficiently—and it established
Davis as the dominant force in the war department, a situation that
would not change for nearly four years, and too late.[18]

The Confederate Constitution also provided for a Supreme Court,
but it never came to be. Yet there was another branch of government
besides the Executive. Congress. Every President in the old Union at
one time in his administration would have liked to forget that contentious assembly of men, and Davis would be no exception. Yet President and Congress here at Montgomery began with a happy relationship, both still high on the euphoria of new nationhood.

They met in the hall of the Alabama legislature in the state Capitol,
and enjoyed in their first weeks two tables kept piled high with fruit
and meat and bread by patriotic ladies of the city. When loungers
and vagrants started wandering into the building solely for the free
lunch, however, the ladies quickly stopped and the members of
Congress had to provide their own meals. The hotel lobbies thronged
with the members and their families, smoke filled every room in town,
and very quickly the special interests grouped together, and the lobbyists converged. The latter, it was said, chewed their cigars, which
distinguished them from the Congressmen, who smoked theirs. The
members of the Montgomery convention made up the Provisional
Congress. Their terms would expire within a year, when a new permanent, popularly elected assembly would take their place. The majority of them had been secessionists for some time, though the compromise men made a significant minority. With the Constitution
framed and sent to the various states for ratification, the chief work of
the body was routine, enacting the laws and measures requested by
Davis and his cabinet to implement the government. Very soon those
who had been members of the Federal Congress in Washington
would see little difference between that service and this.[19]

Fort Sumter took the routine out of the Capitol, and the Capitol out
of Montgomery. From the first the Alabama city proved too small and

backward to suit a rapidly expanding government and its bureaucracy. The climate and its mosquitoes ill-suited any of the delegates,
except the Alabamians. Most important of all, with Virginia's secession the Old Dominion became automatically far and away the premier state of the Confederacy. It grew more agricultural necessities
than any of the other states. It could feed armies. It produced more
manufactured goods. It could supply armies. It would be obviously
the major battleground of the coming war, so dictated by its geography and proximity to Washington. It would need armies.

And the state had Richmond, one of the major cities of the South.
Yet secession had not been for Virginia an easy matter. Many of her
leaders felt strong sympathy for the old Union. In 1860 her vote went,
not to Breckinridge or Lincoln, but to John Bell, a status quo candidate whose platform called, essentially, for people to ignore the sectional crisis, hoping it would thus go away. In 1861, as the state's convention met in Richmond to decide its course, the avowed
secessionists were outnumbered two-to-one. The majority hoped for
peace and another compromise. Even while Jeremiah Martin stood
making a "very fierce fire-eating speech," John Echols of Staunton sat
just two steps away writing a letter to his friend, Francis H. Smith,
superintendent of the Virginia Military Institute. "I really believe if
this State was taken out of the Union before the people were satisfied
that all fair and honorable means were exhausted to avoid this step,"
wrote Echols, "that we would have a revolution in our midst." The
state must be slowly prepared for the crisis. "I am sure if you knew
the feelings and sentiments of a large majority of the people of the
State that you would agree with me that it would not now be proper
to pass an ordinance of secession." Whatever the state did, he concluded, whether they went "either to the North or South, we have a
dark future in view."[20]

Sumter and Lincoln's call for 75,000 volunteers changed the situation radically. It took only days for a secession ordinance to pass. A
few days later, sensing the importance of Virginia to the Confederacy,
as well as the necessity for the new government to have an unshakable commitment to the Old Dominion's defense, Governor John
Letcher and the legislature sent the Congress an invitation to move
the capital to Richmond. Davis had been considering a move anyhow,
and a few days prior to Letcher's invitation he had sent Vice-President Alex Stephens to Richmond to negotiate an alliance between Virginia and the Confederacy. The problem was that Virginia had sched-
uled a referendum on secession for May 17. Between now and then
the Federals might invade the state and the Confederacy would be
powerless to resist. Rather than wait until May 17, Davis sought a
"temporary" association. Stephens went immediately, spoke with Lee
and other prominent Virginians, and met with the secession convention. "The Virginians *will* debate and speak, though war be at the

gates of their city," he complained privately. Finally on April 25 the convention agreed to place control of all military operations in the state under Confederate authority. In speaking he had hinted that the Confederate capital need not be Montgomery. It could just as well be Richmond, he said, suggesting strongly that this would be the immediate result "within a few weeks" of the alliance. It was.[21]

Even before the referendum, the Montgomery Congress accepted Virginia into the Confederacy on May 7. Four days later it voted to hold its next session in Richmond but, since this did not specifically include all of the government, another vote was needed to move the entire machinery of Confederate nationhood. It passed, only poor Alabama putting up a real fight. Four years later it would be thankful.

There was wisdom, and folly, in the change of capital, both obvious yet obscure at the same moment. The gesture proclaimed the Confederacy's commitment to defend Virginia, thus winning the support of a state whose people were not unqualified secessionists. It would enable Davis to protect the vital industrial resources at Richmond, and the fertile valley of the Shenandoah. At the same time, however, the move also began an inevitable shift of Confederate attention to the Virginia theater, sometimes to the exclusion of the rest of the vast Southern territory. The constant threat always gets the most attention, and for four years to come Virginia will be threatened long and repeatedly. Being only one hundred miles from Washington, it could not have been otherwise. This they should have foreseen. In fact, both sides will become too conscious of Richmond, but for the South it was natural. This was a war based largely on symbols. Slavery, state rights, the Old South, were all a part of the symbolic heraldry of the new Southern nation. In the days ahead this new capital, Richmond, will come to symbolize for North and South the Confederacy itself. It will be a costly image for both.

CHAPTER 7

"THIS MEANS WAR"

In December 1860 a leather salesman asked an acquaintance "How do you all feel on the subject of Secession in St. Louis?" As a Western man himself the writer felt a keen interest in the sectional crisis that, from the first, grew largely because of disagreement over slavery in the Western territories. "It is hard to realize that a State or States should commit so suicidal an act as to secede from the Union," he continued. Buchanan, "the present granny of an executive," was much of the cause, he felt, adding that "It does seem as if just a few men have produced all the present difficulty." It would certainly take more than a few men to solve that "difficulty." Many of them would be men of the West, and one of them would be the writer himself, Ulysses S. Grant.[1]

Grant was the quintessential Westerner, that "West" in the mid-nineteenth-century sense being the region between the Appalachians and the Great Plains. These were rugged, hard-scrabble men with grizzled beards and determined eyes, rawboned and rough-edged. They knew hard times and hard drinking and felt closer both to life and death than their Eastern brethren. The land made it so. Chicago and Kansas City and St. Louis were thriving cities to be sure, but most Westerners lived on the prairies or in small towns like Galena and Cairo, Carondelet and Belmont. There was much success and much money to be had, but it came more from hard work than high birth. Most everyone had known failure.

That was Grant. He was nearly thirty-nine when 1861 dawned, and a man of many ups and downs. He stood medium high, of lean but sturdy frame, with a handsome face in the Western way—high, wide forehead, well set eyes, and a jaw firm and resolute. He spoke softly and was of gentle manner, a manner bred of humility, and a humility spawned in failure. He was born in Point Pleasant, Ohio, son of a father who never seemed to approve. Jesse Root Grant, a tanner, named his son Hiram Ulysses. In 1839 he secured the boy an appointment to West Point where, in an administrative error, his name became altered to Ulysses Simpson Grant on the records. Rather than fight, young Grant bent with the officials and eventually adopted the name change himself. "Hiram" was hardly worth fighting for anyhow.

He was an excellent draftsman, talented with the sketch pad and imaginative. He loved horses and won standing as the finest horseman in the academy. Mathematics, too, he loved, but not so some of the other subjects taught. Classmate Rufus Ingalls found Grant "rather slouchy and unmilitary at infantry drills." His real reputation among his fellow cadets was for "common sense, good judgment, entire unselfishness, and absolute fairness in everything he did." When there was a dispute between classmates, it was common to hear "Well, suppose we see what Sam Grant has to say about it and leave it to his decision." Thanks to his altered initials, U. S. was often called "Uncle Sam," or just "Sam."

He married Julia Dent, not at all a handsome woman, but one in whom he sensed constancy and depth of feeling. Even as a young man Grant was unmindful of the appearance of things—himself included, as his demerits at West Point showed—but saw through the surface to what lay beneath. His judgment of character in military men and his perceptions of a military problem were almost childish in their simplistic intuition. But he could not judge a businessman and was a sucker for a good salesman. He warred in Mexico, returned a modest hero to claim his bride, then went west to Fort Vancouver on the Pacific coast. It proved a lonely life. Julia stayed in the East. There was little to do, and too little money to do anything. Rumors would later circulate that he passed the weary hours at the bottle. Perhaps. Perhaps not. But in 1854, tired of army life, he resigned and returned home. He worked cutting firewood. He built his own log house named, appropriately, "Hardscrabble." He tried farming and failed. He tried real estate and did not succeed. He applied for a county office and was turned down. Finally, though hating the business, he sought a position with his father's leather concern. Then came the war.

"In all this I can but see the doom of slavery," he wrote after the secession of Virginia. "I tell you there is no mistaking the feelings of the people." The North would fight to protect the Union. As for Virginia, he said prophetically, "she should be made to bear a heavy portion of the burden of the war for her guilt." He would have something to do with that.[2]

At the outbreak of hostilities, Grant offered his services to the war department but received no response and instead took the temporary task of organizing and mustering new state regiments from Illinois. On June 21, however, Governor Richard Yates issued an appointment for Grant to command the newly raised 21st Illinois Infantry. They were tough, rebellious Westerners, but Grant soon brought them to order. By August they were in Missouri, and the war.

It was here in this West that the war really began, said some, and they dated it from the days of Bleeding Kansas. The declared state of war was mostly a formality here where sporadic guerrilla fighting and bushwhacking had been going on for years. Missouri was the troubled stage for the first acts of 1861. Her governor, Claiborne Jackson, avowed secession openly, as did many in the state senate. After all, the state was settled chiefly within the last two generations by people from Virginia and Tennessee and North Carolina. Their ties to the South were strong, even though economically Missouri was part of a new region yet to be identified as the Midwest. It was agricultural, but not in cotton. It had 115,000 slaves, but still far fewer than any other Southern state except Arkansas—its neighbor—and Florida. Yet its total population exceeded that of every state in the Confederacy except Virginia. It was, in short, more Northern than Southern in temperament and values, and more Western than either. But the family and sentimental ties to homes in the South left within living memory were strong, and the state's leaders like Jackson felt particularly close attachments to the Old South. And so Missouri would be torn by the conflict as no other state. As a battleground-to-be, she will become the Virginia of the West.

By the time Sam Grant crossed the Mississippi with his regiment to bivouac at Mexico, Missouri, a good deal had already happened. Indeed there had been chaos. On January 5 the state senate called for a state convention, obviously to consider secession. They met first in Jefferson City, then moved to St. Louis the same day that Lincoln took his oath of office. Yet as the debating commenced, it became evident that a considerable Union feeling animated many of the delegates. Secession would not be as easy as Governor Jackson had hoped, though Grant at the time feared that "I don't see why . . . a few hundred men could not carry Missouri out of the Union." On March 9 the convention committee charged with deciding upon "Federal relations" reported that it found no cause for the state to leave the Union.

This hardly ended the matter. Jackson, like his counterpart in Kentucky, refused to answer Lincoln's call for volunteers after the firing on Sumter. Meanwhile, militia formed of men with secessionist intent gathered in several counties, and on May 6 they combined at Camp Jackson outside St. Louis. There under the command of Brigadier General Daniel M. Frost, they drilled and made ominous threats toward the city and its arsenal. Union sympathizers in St. Louis answered to Captain Nathaniel Lyon, a redheaded, bearded, little firebrand with a tinder temper and an inclination toward immediate action. When the city's police asked him to remove his soldiers from public buildings, he refused, and four days later he took St. Louis into his own hands.

Lyon, in command of the arsenal, organized between May 8 and 10 a small army of almost 7,000, mostly Unionist civilians, some home guards, even political clubs. He had intercepted a shipment of arms being sent to Camp Jackson, and that only seemed to confirm his belief that Frost intended taking the arsenal. With the urging of Francis Preston Blair, Jr., brother of Postmaster General Montgomery Blair, Lyon decided to capture Frost and Camp Jackson first. On May 10 he led his army to the camp where Frost's 700 men hardly expected them. It was bloodless. Lyon surrounded the secessionists, disarmed them, and took them back to the city to be kept under guard. St. Louis boasted a large German population, all of them fiercely pro-Union, and many were with Lyon. He set them the task of guarding Frost's men, with dire results. It was not so many years since the old Know-Nothing, native American, surge through the country. Many still resented foreigners, and now they screamed "Hessians" as Lyon's men marched Frost into town. Someone threw a brickbat, someone fired a shot, and the slender hold on peace broke. When the firing was done nearly thirty lay dead from the indiscriminate firing. Two that escaped the storm were a man just recently superintendent of a military school in Baton Rouge, Louisiana: William T. Sherman and his son. Within a few days he would be taking a commission as colonel of the 13th United States Infantry and journeying to Washington to join McDowell's growing army.

The mob ruled St. Louis that night and much of the next day before Lyon's superior arrived and restored order. There had been another man in St. Louis watching these events, U. S. Grant. Writing to Julia on May 10 he told her of seeing "Union troops marching out to the secession encampment to break it up." "I very much fear bloodshed," he wrote. That morning Grant had visited the arsenal and spoken with Blair and probably Lyon. This same afternoon he, like Sherman, watched the procession as the prisoners returned. Already, it seemed, Grant would be present when something happened in the West.[3]

Hard on this Union success, however, came what many regarded as a betrayal. Lyon's superior, Brigadier General William Harney, signed a compact with Sterling Price, former governor and president of the recent state convention. A moderate, Price was driven to the secessionist cause in reaction to the threats of men like Blair and Lyon. Now, by appointment from Jackson, he commanded the state guard. His agreement with Harney left military control of the state in his hands so long as peace was maintained. Harney promised not to introduce Federal soldiers into Missouri so long as Price kept his word. Blair and Lyon were incensed, and the former loudly questioned Harney's loyalty. On June 11 the two Union leaders met with Price and Jackson at the Planters' House in St. Louis. Relationships now were changed. Harney, viewed with suspicion by Washington, was removed from command and Lyon was in his place, a brigadier. He, unlike his predecessor, would not stand state authorities dictating to the Federals in Missouri. Already he had taken possession of secession centers like Potosi, and now he told Jackson that he would see Missourians "under the sod" before he compromised Union rule. When Jackson and Price attempted to hold their position, Lyon told them flatly that "This means war."

The next several days saw hurried activity. Jackson asked for 50,000 militia to assert state authority, but on June 15 Lyon marched on Jefferson City and took possession of the capital. Jackson and his sympathizers abandoned the place for Boonville, and Lyon followed them. They met on June 17, in the first real fight of the war in Missouri. Lyon put 1,700 of his men on three steamers and left Jefferson City on June 16, moving up the Missouri River to a point just below Boonville, where they disembarked. Lyon moved directly toward the town and soon encountered the enemy's skirmishers. A correspondent along for the show expressed his contempt for these first Rebels met in battle, saying that even though they had the advantage of better ground, "it has been clearly demonstrated that one secessionist is hardly superior to many more than his equal number."

Lyon opened the main fight with his little artillery. It was not much of a battle that followed, barely a skirmish by later standards, and the Federals hardly displayed a great deal of finesse. Price had gone to Lexington, leaving Jackson with only 500 men. Accounts of the actual fight varied, but Lyon's men advanced steadily, easily driving Jackson's little force out of its pitiful defenses. The Confederates attempted to reform several times, but resistance was useless. Lyon had his men fire from prone positions on the ground to evade enemy fire, and this considerably agitated his opponents. After the brief fight one of the score of prisoners taken complained that "This yeah business of a-firin' an' a-loadin' while a-layin' on the ground—that's what whupped us!"

The press greatly inflated the little Boonville fight, the North particularly, since it needed any sort of victory to counter the humiliation of Fort Sumter. Yes, Federal soldiers could fight and win, and this mighty battle in Missouri had created in Lyon a new national hero.

He could not pursue Jackson due to inclement weather, but he could issue a proclamation the day after the fight promising that he did not intend to use his army to maintain Federal authority any longer than was necessary. He asked all then holding arms in rebellion to turn them in and go home unmolested. As for his prisoners taken at Boonville, he found most of them "young and of immature age." He let them go.[4]

Jackson and his little command retreated south, but met at Carthage on July 5 with a Federal command led by Colonel Franz Sigel, one of those St. Louis Germans. The Rebel forces were augmented after Boonville to nearly 4,000, while Sigel's numbered barely one fourth that. Yet Sigel attacked, the first sign of what he would repeatedly demonstrate in this war to be a singular unfitness for command. Jackson's forces repelled the Federals handily, and continued their retreat toward the southwest corner of the state. There they would recruit and reorganize their army. They would come back again.

And then U. S. Grant returned to Missouri. On July 13 he had his regiment camped at West Quincy on the Mississippi. "Secessionists are thick through this part of Missouri," he found, "but so far they show themselves very scary about attacking." His first assignment was to track down a notorious guerrilla named Tom Harris who had been burning bridges and attacking small parties of Federals. It was about all that a secessionist could do in northeastern Missouri, for Jackson and Price had almost no strength there. Harris was said to be around Florida, a little town about twenty miles from West Quincy. On July 17 Grant took six companies of his regiment on the march to find Harris. He was depressed by the lack of inhabitants on the way, everyone fleeing before his column passed. Every house sat deserted. The next morning they reached the vicinity of Harris's camp. Grant led his party quietly up a hill beyond which they would meet their first battle. "My heart kept getting higher and higher until it felt to me as though it was in my throat," he remembered. "I would have given anything then to have been back in Illinois, but I had not the moral courage to halt and consider what to do; I kept right on." Topping the hill, he discovered to his great relief that Harris had left shortly before, obviously on word of Grant's coming. "It occurred to me at once that Harris had been as much afraid of me as I had been of him." This had not appeared to him before. Now, however, he knew the measure of fear. "I never forgot that he had as much reason to fear my forces as I had his. The lesson was valuable." Grant never feared again.[5]

He watched the events of the next few weeks in Missouri with great interest. On July 22 the state convention, now meeting at Jefferson City, decided permanently for the Union, declared Jackson and his government evicted from office, and elected Hamilton Gamble as the new governor. For safety they also moved the capital to St. Louis. Yet a month later, August 19, the Confederate Congress in Richmond "admitted" Missouri to the Confederacy, and Jackson maintained that *his* was the lawful government of the state. Thus Missouri found herself in the peculiar position of being in two nations at once, though her participation with the Confederacy was always to be more on paper than anything else unless Jackson and Price wrested the state from Union control. Certainly they would try.

Indeed, the admission to statehood was in part a result of the most recent try. On July 25 Major General John C. Frémont, the pathmarker of the Far West and internationally known explorer, assumed command of the newly created Western Department with headquarters at St. Louis. His command included Illinois and all the states and territory between the Mississippi and the Rocky Mountains. He was a genuine autocrat, a man who believed most if not all of the inflated accounts of his life published in the press, a man of small military judgment and, as a general, of petty nature. The powerful Blair family wanted Lyon for the command, but he was too extreme for the President's Missourian attorney general, Edward Bates. Scott and Bates desired someone more conservative, less likely to arouse by his own personality a major rebellion in the state. They finally settled on Frémont, which made no one but the explorer happy. Certainly Grant was not impressed with the new general.

The new commander rented a personal headquarters for $6,000 a month, enlisted a personal bodyguard of some three hundred, and erected such an intricate wall of aides around him that it became virtually impossible for his subordinates in the field to deal directly with him. Thus much pertinent information never reached him, and that which did often did not penetrate his imperceptive mind. Lyon and his command were by now at Springfield, considerably exposed in the western part of the state, and very undermanned. Yet Frémont devoted his attention to Cairo on the Mississippi, since he hoped to advance by this route into the heart of the Confederacy. Lyon would have to wait, the commanding general entirely missing the point that if Lyon were forced out of western Missouri, Sterling Price would have the country wide open for his own advance into the state's heartland, to the Missouri River and beyond. Control of the river would cut off water transportation and communications with Nebraska, much of Kansas and Iowa, and Fort Leavenworth, not to mention forsaking Kansas City and several other pro-Union communities in the northwestern part of the state. In effect, Frémont had abandoned Lyon.

If his own superior ignored the fiery redhead, his enemies did not. Sterling Price, now an army commander of sorts, had been organizing his command at Cowskin Prairie in the southwestern part of the state. By the end of July he felt ready to take the war to the enemy and reclaim Missouri. Indeed, he had to do something, for his ragtag command threatened to disintegrate if he did not take the field. This man Price, called "Old Pap" by his men, was a Virginian by birth, a lawyer and farmer before he entered public life. Vain, a bit prone to drink, he still had good judgment, though often slow to think. He was not slow now.

His army left Cowskin Prairie on July 25 and by August 10 he had confronted Lyon near Wilson's Creek southwest of Springfield. Price was not alone either, for he was joined on the route by Brigadier General Ben McCulloch commanding Confederate troops in Arkansas. McCulloch brought 5,700 men north with him. Combined with Price's command, this gave them a total of over 11,000 effective troops, and several more unarmed that Price brought along. The two commanders did not like each other, and quickly a dispute arose over who should command. McCulloch regarded Price as "nothing but an old militia general," while "Old Pap" chaffed that a soldier who was only a captain when he was a brigadier during the Mexican War, should now outrank him. For several days the two operated independently until circumstances forced them to reach an accommodation. McCulloch took command.

It was Lyon who made the first move, however. Frémont had told him to retire before the enemy, but Lyon thought little of the effectiveness of most of the advancing Confederates, and the enlistments of some of his own regiments were almost expired. If he did not stop the enemy now, he would not have an army at all to stop them later. Consequently, on August 10 he took McCulloch and Price by surprise when his army, divided into two columns, struck the Confederate camps. Lyon led the majority of his army and steadily drove back the disorganized enemy until McCulloch restored order. The Federals then withstood two heavy Confederate attacks, all the while waiting for the other column, 1,000 men led by Sigel, to strike the enemy rear. But here Sigel showed his true stripes. After an initially successful assault, his command was put to complete rout by a volley and fire from artillery. Sigel himself completely abandoned Lyon, failing to inform him of what had happened, and ran with an aide back to Springfield to hide.

Left to himself now, Lyon faced a bitter contest. During a lull in the fight, he thought he saw Price astride his horse in advance of the enemy line. Lyon tried to ride out and engage the Confederate in personal combat before an aide stopped him. Then while attempting to rally his men, Lyon lost his horse and was himself wounded slightly in the head and leg. "I fear the day is lost," he said to Major Samuel Sturgis. The major gave Lyon his horse and the general mounted, waved his hat in the air, and called for the 2nd Kansas to rally. A regiment appeared on their flank. Many thought it was Sigel arrived at last. Lyon knew better. "Shoot them! Shoot them!" he cried, but the first volley came from the enemy and a bullet struck the general in the chest. Caught as he fell, he whispered "I am killed; take care of my body."

Soon after Lyon's death the Federals repulsed a third assault, after which Lyon's successor Sturgis withdrew the army from the fight, leaving Lyon's body behind in the rush. It was a sad defeat at bitter cost. Federal casualties totaled fully one fourth of the army, while the Confederates lost 1,200. The tenor of the fighting was unbelievable, far more vicious and brutal than Manassas of the month before. This was a Western fight, and Western men fought like no others. There will be many more battles in Missouri during the war, many with greater numbers engaged, but none to equal the frenzy of Wilson's Creek. Its effects, too, were brutal. Sigel, with characteristic fearfulness, resumed command of the army when it joined him in Springfield, then withdrew it one hundred miles to Rolla, halfway to St. Louis. This left the entire western half of the state open to the enemy. For the second time in three weeks, the South had a major victory. Southern morale soared, and for Missouri Confederates it looked as though the state was destined to be theirs.[6]

Grant, of course, was not encouraged by the defeat. The Northern press, in fact, tried mightily to prove that Wilson's Creek had been a victory, and Grant believed it in part when his scouts reported that the Confederates had themselves been in the act of retreating when they discovered that Sturgis, too, was abandoning the field. They moved back, took the empty battlefield, and now declared victory. Perhaps this in part gave him the confidence to tell his sister that, though he had changed his mind several times on the subject already, "the Rebels will be so badly whipped by April next that they cannot make a stand anywhere." The next April that view would change a bit as a Confederate Army almost destroyed him in Tennessee, but that lay in the future. As for the present, Grant was getting a new uniform. He needed one, for he had a new rank to go with it. On August 3 he read in the *Missouri Democrat* that "my name has been sent in for Brigadier Gen.!" He had done nothing himself to effect this, being repelled by the "pulling and hauling for favors" that he saw back in Springfield, Illinois, a few weeks before. But Congressman Elihu B. Washburne and others knew Grant and took it on themselves to recommend him to Lincoln for promotion. Even before certain of the elevation, he wrote to his father Jesse, the father who rarely approved of anything Ulysses had done. Then Grant wrote to his wife. The appointment came on August 7, and now he needed a new uniform.[7]

But it would take more than a suit of clothes to retrieve what had been lost at Wilson's Creek. Fresh from their victory against Lyon, the Confederates quarreled once more. McCulloch did not want to advance farther for the moment. Price, the Missourian, sought to capitalize on their advantage and drive north to the Missouri River. They finally split, and Price resumed direct command of his own little army and moved north. By September 12 Price had reached Lexington, on the river, and went to work to drive out the 3,500 Federals there entrenched. In the first real siege of the war—Sumter excluded—the Confederates spent eight days closing around Lexington and battering its garrison before the commander, Colonel James A. Mulligan, surrendered. Governor Claiborne Jackson was along for the campaign, and when the Federals lined up to take their parole, he subjected them to a speech. Now "Old Pap" stood doubly a hero. Here was absolute victory, not just the capture of a paltry garrison like Sumter, but the defeat and surrender of an "army." And Missouri was more than ever ready for absolute domination by the Confederacy. The whole business made Price inordinately proud of himself.[8]

"The news from Lexington to-day is bad," Grant wrote to Julia. Missouri was still uncertain for the Union. Frémont was barely hanging on to the state. Yet this same week events in another Western state took a different turn, with profound results for Grant and the Union. Kentucky came off the fence.[9]

Here was the state that Lincoln regarded as the key to the whole Union war effort, and an odd state it was, a mix of the old Tidewater and the new West. Virginians settled it, Virginians like the grandfather of John C. Breckinridge, who brought much of their civilization with them. Education, enlightenment, art, culture, all were dear to places like Lexington and Frankfort and Louisville. "Athens of the West," Lexington called itself. Yet the frontier experience made these Kentuckians rugged as well. Those rawboned men of Tennessee and Georgia mingled their blood here with the sons of aristocrats and produced a remarkable blend of gentility and ferocity. They bred arguably the finest horses in the country and undeniably the best whiskey in the world. A "de luxe edition" of Virginia, some called the state. It fathered Clay and Lincoln and Davis, and Breckinridge and a score and more of the most prominent leaders of the century.[10]

It bred as well a dichotomy in outlook toward the Union and its nature. During the early decades of the century, left mostly alone by Washington, Kentucky defended itself against Indians and the British and developed a hearty self-reliance. That tended many toward a state rights posture already their inheritance from their parents in Virginia and the Deep South. Yet others in the state could almost outdo any in the East for their ardent support of the Union. The common ground was trod by the middle men, the compromisers, the Clays and Breckinridges, though even they could be sometimes uncertain of their course if forced to make a choice. Philip Lightfoot Lee spoke well for Kentucky's attitude toward the sectional crisis when talking of his home town of Shepherdsville and Bullitt County. If the Union dissolved, he said, then he would stand by Kentucky. Should the state disintegrate, then he would fight for Bullitt County. The county disrupted, he would defend Shepherdsville. And if Shepherdsville be torn asunder, then he was for his side of the street![11]

The crisis of 1861 forced a lot of Kentuckians to choose which side of the street they stood for. In the election they took the middle of the road, voting for John Bell even over their own enormously popular Breckinridge. Fearful of what was going to happen to the country, Governor Magoffin began raising his own army that same summer, placing the Kentucky State Guard under the command of Brigadier General Simon B. Buckner. The impulse was chiefly defensive, for Magoffin knew that if war came, both sides would regard Kentucky as vital, commanding as it did hundreds of miles of the Ohio, Mississippi, Tennessee, and Cumberland rivers, and Cumberland Gap in the Appalachians. It was vital to Confederate defense; equally vital to Federal offense. The State Guard, however, took a distinctly Southern bent from the first, and after the firing on Sumter, the Union men in the legislature authorized a separate Home Guard which quickly attracted young men of Union inclinations. Thus the state had two armies, antagonistic to each other. After Magoffin's refusal to furnish volunteers for Lincoln, a special Congressional election went overwhelmingly for the Union candidates, the first sure sign that, in a final crisis, the commonwealth would probably stand by the Federal government. In June both Union and Confederacy were operating recruiting camps just outside Kentucky's borders, and the young men picked their sides of the street and flocked to enlist. On May 16 the legislature had adopted an official position of neutrality, but it could not last. Both sides violated that neutrality throughout the summer, sending agents into the state to encourage recruits surreptitiously. Finally Lincoln established a camp within the state and refused to remove it. A growing Union majority in the legislature forced Confederate sympathizers to cling hopelessly to neutrality as their only recourse to seeing the South lose Kentucky to the North.

Finally, seeing that a peaceful melding of the state with the Confederacy was hopeless, on September 3 Brigadier General Gideon J. Pillow, acting on orders from Major General Leonidas Polk, moved his Confederate command from Tennessee into Kentucky and occupied Columbus. The excuse cited was that the Federals had been recruiting for some time in the state, and were then marshaling their forces in Missouri with the intent of taking Columbus themselves. The explanation hardly mattered now. Neutrality was ended. A week later the legislature ordered all Confederates out of the state. Kentucky would side with the Union. For the next three years, however, Jefferson Davis would try to coax her to cross the street.

Pillow's move demanded an immediate Federal response. The man who was in place and ready to make it was Brigadier General U. S. Grant. He had in fact advised the occupation of Columbus himself, almost at the instant that Pillow moved into the little river town.

Columbus commanded the Mississippi at a point just south of its confluence with the Ohio River at Cairo. Batteries at Columbus and New Madrid thirty miles downriver could interdict Federal shipping and gunboat movement on the water. Since Frémont intended to move down the Mississippi to invade the Confederacy, control of the stream was vital. In response to Pillow's move, Grant left his headquarters at Cairo late on the evening of September 5 with two regiments and a battery aboard three steamboats. Covered by the cannon of the gunboats *Tyler* and *Conestoga*, they steamed overnight up the Ohio to Paducah, Kentucky, at the mouth of the Tennessee River. Confederate sympathizers there abandoned the town at his coming, and the next afternoon Grant could report to Frémont the successful taking of a Union foothold in Kentucky. More than that, the Tennessee would provide a natural path of invasion into the very heartland of the Confederacy.[12]

For the next two months little happened. Grant returned to Cairo while his onetime mentor Brigadier General Charles F. Smith assumed the Kentucky command. Smith had been superintendent at West Point when Grant was a cadet. The main action in the West was political. Grant's superior Frémont, after months of antagonizing every interest in the state, and Lincoln as well, finally outstayed his welcome. He had abandoned Lyon, forsook Mulligan to his fate at Lexington, arrested Francis Blair on charges of insubordination, and even issued an emancipation proclamation declaring free the slaves of anyone in Missouri in rebellion against the Union. Frémont was not only an embarrassment, but a positive danger. With Missouri sensibilities tender, his foolish acts might upset the delicate Federal sentiment, not only there but in Kentucky as well. Should it appear that this war was going to be waged against slavery rather than disunion, these two slaveholding states could easily be lost. Despite the general's powerful influence in political circles, Lincoln could keep him no more. On October 24 the President ordered him removed from command, but it took until November 2 for the message to get through Frémont's elaborate bodyguard. Major General David Hunter, recovered from his Manassas wound and now promoted, temporarily replaced him, followed a few days later by Major General Henry W. Halleck.

While Hunter was still in his brief tenure, Grant acted on his own initiative and conducted his first offensive of the war. It was a small one, to be sure, but not unimportant. On November 6 he put 2,850 men aboard five steamers and moved down the Mississippi toward Columbus, intending not to attack but only to demonstrate and thereby prevent Confederate reinforcements from crossing the river from Kentucky to go to Price. However, en route he learned from scouts that the enemy had already crossed a few thousand men then camped opposite Columbus at Belmont, Missouri. He had no orders to attack, nor any intention of doing so when he first left Cairo. But the men were anxious to fight. It was what they had volunteered to do. Grant had built up an army totaling nearly 20,000, but none of them had yet met the enemy in battle. The situation at Belmont gave him an opportunity to fulfill his orders, strike a blow at the Confederates, and boost the morale of his command. He would attack.[13]

His intent was to break up the camps at Belmont, destroy any supplies held there, and return. The Federals landed after dawn on November 7, climbing off the steamers and marching through a cornfield before Grant halted them. After posting a regiment as a guard against surprise and to protect the transports, Grant led the remainder of his blue-clad soldiers toward Belmont. Going but a mile, he formed his men into two lines and sent out skirmishers. Within minutes the Confederates discovered what was coming toward them and opened fire. "The *Ball* may be said to have fairly opened," he wrote his father the next day. For the next four hours Grant slowly pushed them back toward Belmont, the men fighting almost from tree to tree in the woods. "I feel truly proud to command such men," he crowed. Finally the Confederates turned and ran, abandoning their camps to the Federals. Then Grant's men showed their greenness. Reaching the camps, they discarded their arms and began sacking the tents for trophies. Meanwhile the Confederates, first surprised that they had not been pursued, slowly recovered and began working their way along the riverbank until they got between Grant and his transports. Then Grant saw two steamers loaded with Rebels coming toward him from Columbus, and soon thereafter discovered that he was cut off from his route of escape. The alarm cry "surrounded" brought his men back to their senses at last. Some officers wanted to surrender, but Grant calmly said they would cut their way back to their boats.

The Confederates offered a feeble resistance when Grant attacked again, and then his little army raced for the transports. The Rebels from Columbus landed meanwhile, posing a new threat. The guard regiment he had left had retreated without orders, and Grant himself rode alone through the tall corn to see if the enemy was getting close. In fact, they were in the corn too, not fifty yards away. By now all of the rest of his command were boarded and the transports were pulling away from the bank, oblivious of the fact that Grant was not aboard. As he quietly rode back to the water's edge, the captain of one boat put in toward the bank and ran out a plank for him. Safely aboard, Grant went to the pilot house, lay down on a sofa to rest, then jumped up again as fire from the shore started pelting the boats. An instant later a Confederate bullet tore through the cabin and struck the head of the sofa, the first narrow escape for one whose life would seem charmed in years to come.

Grant accomplished all that he wished at Belmont, even though it was hardly an unqualified success. He utterly destroyed the Confederate camps. The attack discouraged General Polk from further attempts to put Confederates across the river from Columbus. Best of all, felt Grant, "the National troops acquired a confidence in themselves at Belmont that did not desert them throughout the war."[14]

The Northern press was highly critical of the Belmont operation, regarding it as an unnecessary battle at high cost. Grant did lose about 607 in killed, wounded, and missing, over 20 percent of his command, but it bought his men an ardor and élan that no other Federals in Missouri—or the West for that matter—enjoyed. They were the first victorious Union Army in the West. Though he could not anticipate it then, the battle also bought for U. S. Grant a little more valuable experience. Yet the aftermath of the fight seemed an anticlimax, for Grant, like Federals throughout the West, was given little more to do. He could see nothing ahead, and only years later in retrospect would he know that "from the battle of Belmont until early in February, 1862, the troops under my command did little except prepare for the long struggle which proved to be before them."[15]

CHAPTER 8

"THIS DAY WILL LONG BE REMEMBERED"

How did it happen that a man who had been Vice-President of the United States and a candidate for the presidency, would become a brigadier general in the Confederate Army? Even John C. Breckinridge did not know exactly; but it had happened, and to him.

Even his defeat by Lincoln in 1860 had not really destroyed the Kentuckian's political fortunes. Several months before, the legislature in Kentucky had elected him to the Senate, and his conduct as presiding officer of the Senate during his last months as Vice-President enhanced his reputation among most of his colleagues. With threats of attempts to disrupt the counting of the electoral ballots in the Senate, Breckinridge presided with an iron hand, allowing nothing to interfere with the democratic process. When he stepped down in March 1861, however, he was deeply troubled, and Fort Sumter made it worse. Never in favor of secession, he still somewhat believed in the abstract right to do so, though regarding any attempt to break up the Union as absolute folly. Yet as soon as he took his Senate seat, Breckinridge spoke for moderation, even defending Lincoln's appointment of Montgomery Blair to the cabinet against charges from Senator James Mason of Virginia that no man of Southern birth—Blair was born in Kentucky—should hold office under the Rail Splitter. Breckinridge favored withdrawing Federal soldiers from the South via negotiation, to avoid bloodletting, but added in a speech that in the last extremity he believed Kentucky would unite with the Confederate states to preserve the old constitutional liberties that the Republicans were seeking to subvert. He did not say publicly, however, that he saw Kentucky's secession only as a means, not an end. A solid, united Southern front, he believed, would force concessions and guarantees from Washington, another compromise after which the South would rejoin the Union. He never looked to a permanent Confederacy.

That summer he returned to Kentucky and stumped the state in favor of neutrality, though still preferring the gesture of Kentucky's secession. When he returned to Washington for the July 4 special session of the Senate, the Northern press had so exaggerated his position that he was already regarded a dangerous man. For the Lincoln government he was indeed dangerous. Given his popularity and sway with Kentuckians, it was not unlikely that his unbridled speechmaking could persuade them to make cause with the South, and the Union could not afford to lose Kentucky. Even while he was making his lonely stand in the Senate that summer, often the sole voice of opposition to the war policy of Lincoln, Breckinridge was being watched. When the session ended in August, he returned home, fully intending to be back for the winter convening. But events moved too rapidly. He was barely home a month before Federal authorities in Kentucky, violating neutrality flagrantly, attempted to arrest him. He escaped and spent several more days unmolested, staying with friends in Frankfort. He confided to them a conviction. The Confederacy could not survive. Ultimately it had to fall. And should he, like other Democrats, take the side of Lincoln and loyally support him, then certainly he would be able to obtain high rank in the army then forming like several other generals appointed for political expedience. He could even get back on the road to the White House. But principle would not allow this. He would stand for his beliefs. He was being forced at last into the moderate's purgatory. He must choose a side of the street. While neutrality lasted, he would support it. When Kentucky inevitably embraced the Union, he would go South. Friends begged him to reconsider, but he was, he said, "already over the dam." Two days after neutrality was declared at an end, the Federals formally ordered Breckinridge's arrest. Warned by friends, he and William Preston escaped first. "I go where my duty calls me," he told friends in farewell. "It is a hopeless cause." Riding in a buggy with an associate and his slave boy, the onetime Vice-President made his way to Tennessee. Behind him his enemies gloated over his flight, claiming their accusations that he was a secessionist had been right all along.

"John C. Breckinridge escaped from Lexington," they said, "by skulking in a buggy behind a small nigger."[1]

He claimed that he was giving up his seat in the Senate for "the musket of a soldier," but no one really supposed that he would be allowed to serve as a private in the ranks. Jefferson Davis and his government dreamed of Kentucky from the first, and Breckinridge, the most popular Kentuckian of his time, would be instrumental in realizing that dream. Davis at first thought of making him secretary of war, Leroy P. Walker having resigned. But it was obvious that he would be more useful if made a general in the field with the Western army that would try to retake Kentucky. There the Confederacy could capitalize on Breckinridge instantaneously. No one supposed, or expected, that he would make a good general. It was to be a war of the unexpected.

The army that the new Brigadier General John C. Breckinridge joined in November faced an almost impossible task. It was an army still abuilding, yet it had to cover a front hundreds of miles long, from Cumberland Gap at the southwest corner of Virginia, all through Tennessee, and up to Columbus, Kentucky. Thinly manned in most places, the line was not entirely well selected. It reflected, however, Davis's policy at this stage of the war of holding onto every single acre of Confederate territory. Further, it represented the Kentucky dream. Indeed, immediately after the state declared neutrality at an end, Buckner, now a Confederate brigadier general, led a small army of Confederate Kentuckians back into the state to occupy Bowling Green. Here he hoped to rally more men to his banners, as well as cover and protect valuable recruiting camps and planted fields in Tennessee from enemy assault.

This Western army had a new commander, General Albert Sidney Johnston. He was himself a Kentuckian, a man of West Point, a brigadier in the revolutionary Texas army in 1837, a colonel in the Mexican War, and until recently, commander of the Union Department of the Pacific. Jefferson Davis came as close to idolizing Johnston as he ever would any general, and most military men, North and South, regarded him as a premier soldier. He was fifty-eight now, but still vigorous. Everyone looked to him to drive the enemy from Kentucky and take Kentucky from the Union.

Yet when Johnston assumed his new command he came with no clearly defined plan of what he wished to do, no strategy either for attack or defense. As a result, he reacted to events rather than shaping them. The Federal commander in Kentucky in the fall of 1861 was a man not unfamiliar to Kentuckians, and now to the nation, Brigadier General Robert Anderson. His second officer was another new brigadier, William T. Sherman. These men from the war's first two actions will seem to appear everywhere in the years ahead

For Johnston, their presence was a threat and, having barely 27,000

troops at his disposal, and those widely dispersed, he set about at
once to confuse the enemy as to his numbers. He sent feinting attacks
into Kentucky, cavalry raids, and a buildup of forces under Buckner
at Bowling Green, where Breckinridge joined the army and took command of a new brigade. When Anderson was relieved by Sherman,
and Sherman in turn replaced by Brigadier General Don Carlos Buell
in November, Johnston continued his ruse, all the while desperately
trying to augment his army.

The Kentucky dream captured Johnston as it did so many others.
He made his growing encampment at Bowling Green the center of his
attention, burying himself in little details instead of formulating a
genuine broad strategy. And he held to the Bowling Green salient
long after prudence dictated that it was untenable. Johnston convinced himself that the enemy would attack by way of Bowling Green
in order to invade Kentucky, almost ignoring the fact that Grant was
building a sizable army in the western part of the state.[2]

Where he could, Johnston fortified his long and tenuous line. His
left flank threatened by Grant and C. F. Smith, he built fortifications
overlooking the Tennessee and Cumberland rivers. Fort Henry
guarded the former, and Fort Donelson the latter. They were earth-
work forts mounting cannon that could command the water and, it
was hoped, prevent any Federal fleet from passing. The rivers led into
the very heart of the Confederacy. Their possession by the enemy
would threaten Nashville and all of western and central Tennessee, as
well as making any position in Kentucky impossible. The right flank
of the line rested at Mill Springs, Kentucky, another advance position
which protected Cumberland Gap, many miles to the southeast.

But not for long. Buell's people in Kentucky were ready to move
before Johnston's. Brigadier General George H. Thomas, a Virginian
who braved absolute obloquy from his family to remain loyal to the
Union, had been gathering forces in southeastern Kentucky during
December and early January 1862, intent upon striking Johnston's
Mill Springs command. The Confederates there looked to Major Gen-
eral George B. Crittenden for command. The son of Senator John J.
Crittenden of Kentucky, he was a long-time friend of Breckinridge.
His brother Thomas, symbolizing the terrible divisions this war
inflicted upon Kentucky families, was even then a brigadier in the
Union Army.

When Crittenden discovered Thomas moving toward him, the Kentuckian seized the offensive first. On the dark, rainy morning of January 19, 1862, Crittenden led his little army of about 4,000 toward the
enemy. The Confederates first drove back the bluecoats, but then
Brigadier General Felix Zollicoffer fell killed and his command, demoralized by his loss, fell back. Thomas capitalized on the opportunity to counterattack. The fight raged hotly for several hours before
the Confederates simply fell apart. Crittenden lost hundreds in killed

and wounded, and many more captured or deserted. He had to abandon his camps and most of his equipment to Thomas, and left the Mill Springs flank of Johnston's line exposed. Here was another Confederate defeat in the West. Now, too, the Rebels had no organized troops left in the eastern end of their line except those at Cumberland Gap. There were one hundred and fifty miles between the gap and Bowling Green, and Crittenden's defeat left all of it open to the Federals as a pathway for invasion.

While this took place, the new General Breckinridge worked steadily away at the unfamiliar business of building a brigade at Bowling Green. Breckinridge went to Mexico as major of the 3rd Kentucky Infantry in 1847, but he saw no action and obtained little real experience. He was getting it now, earning while he was learning. Buckner had begun the work of raising Confederate Kentucky regiments several months before. When Johnston took command of the army, he organized these men into the 1st Kentucky Brigade and placed Breckinridge in charge. It was a remarkably happy melding of man and men, one from which legend would sprout. Their native state never seceding from the Union, and the repeated loss of commanders, would in time give them a name, the Orphan Brigade. Through war and into posterity their adopted father would be Breckinridge. He clothed them, armed them, trained them, kept them from drinking too much, saw to their medical needs, and aggressively protected their rights and dignity. When a captain arrested a private who refused to sweep his quarters, the general flew to the tent in a fury and confronted the officer. When a private refused voluntarily to sweep his tent, said Breckinridge, he would do it himself. "They are not menials in the Orphan brigade," he said. "They are all gentlemen, and you have no right to command one of them to do a menial service. Now go to the guardhouse and apologize to the soldier you have insulted and sweep about your own tent, or you will take his place." An unmilitary attitude to take, perhaps, but one that cemented to their general the affections of 4,000 Kentuckians who in time will fight and die for him.[3]

Christmas came, a dinner of turkey and biscuits, chickens, eggs, apples, butter, bread, cakes, and hams, all shipped by friends and relatives in Kentucky. They would never eat like this again. It was a day for reflection. There were mounting threats all along the Confederates' thin line in Kentucky, and a long new year lay ahead. One soldier of the brigade mused in the Clothing Account Book of the 4th Kentucky's Company C: "Dec 25th 1861, The birth day of Christ our redeemer finds our country Struggling in the holy cause of liberty with the vile horde of Robbers & assasins sent to burn and destroy by their master Abraham Lincoln." Where the next Christmas would find them was anyone's guess.[4]

The events of the next two months, however, assured that they would not be in Kentucky. The fall of Mill Springs in itself crippled Johnston's line. What happened two weeks later crushed it. The destroyer's hand belonged to Grant.

There is irony in the fact that, even though Grant's first tender of his services to the government was not deemed important enough even for an acknowledgment, the early date of his commission as a brigadier made him one of the senior officers in the volunteer service. Thus, by late 1861, he stood as the fourth ranking officer in the Department of the Missouri, which included Arkansas and west Kentucky. Already, though still largely unknown, he was wielding one of the most important commands in the West. Yet increasing importance also brought problems. Grant made enemies among contractors who, like camp followers, hungered for some of the money inevitably to be made when a government maintained large armies in the field. He refused to pay their inflated prices, buying his army's forage and other supplies from locals at better rates. In retaliation, the contractors apparently circulated rumors that the general was drinking heavily. It was a charge easily made, for many in the army recalled the faint echo of hints made about Grant when he was stationed on the Pacific coast several years before. Now, with grievances to revenge, several disappointed characters began a heavy campaign against him. "Gnl Grant is drinking very hard," came one report in December 1861, and the next month a disgruntled officer whom Grant placed in arrest sent a whole list of charges to the war department. Drunkenness—"beastly drunk" read the charge—drinking with enemy officers, "vomiting all over the floor" of a steamer, cavorting with a harlot, and gambling, were among the calumnies laid at his door. Congressman Washburne anxiously wrote to Grant's aide John A. Rawlins for a confidential report, and Rawlins, regarding himself as Grant's guardian angel, had been watching the general closely. He assured Washburne that the general was quite abstemious and had been for five or six years. Beyond an occasional social glass these days, Grant touched nothing. "No man can say that at any time since I have been with him has he drank liquor enough to in the slightest unfit him for business," said Rawlins. Grant would never entirely escape those old rumors, but there can be little doubt that he was faithful to his duty, not his thirst. Besides, there was too much to do.[5]

It was time for an offensive. The Confederates hardly expected one in the winter, and thus this was the best time for it. Buell was intended to move against Buckner at Bowling Green, and of course Thomas and his bluecoats began working their way toward clearing eastern Kentucky right after the New Year. Orders came from Washington to Halleck for Grant to make a demonstration against the enemy's western flank at Forts Henry and Donelson. This would prevent any reinforcements from those places being sent to Buckner. The command of General C. F. Smith had been placed under Grant, and early in January he sent the older officer up the west bank of the Tennessee to threaten Fort Henry and a lesser work nearby, Fort Heiman. Another column led by Brigadier General John McClernand, a loyal Democratic politician turned general, demonstrated against Columbus. Though the move by Buell against Buckner did not materialize, Grant's threat did prevent the reinforcement of Crittenden, with some influence on Thomas's victory at Mill Springs.[6]

The whole business reinforced an idea that originally occurred to Grant some time before. On January 6, before the recent expedition, he asked to see Halleck. Now that Smith's movement led him to believe that Forts Henry and Heiman could be taken from the land, Grant renewed his request for an audience. Halleck did not like Grant, though he hardly knew him. It went back probably to an exchange they had the previous fall when Grant implied a criticism of the security at department headquarters. Now, when the commanding general received Grant, the man called "Old Brains" because of his bookish appearance and manner barely gave Grant a hearing. He should have listened, for his visitor was outlining the strategy that would win western Tennessee and Kentucky for the Union. "The true line of operations for us," he would write, "was up the Tennessee and Cumberland rivers. With us there, the enemy would be compelled to fall back on the east and west entirely out of the State of Kentucky." Yet when Grant spoke, Halleck was barely cordial, cut him off in midsentence, and dismissed him "as if my plan was preposterous." It was a crestfallen general who returned to Cairo. The day before, on January 23, he had written to his sister with pride that "I have now a larger force than General Scott ever commanded. . . . I do hope it will be my good fortune to retain so important a command for at least one battle." Now it looked as if there would be no battle.

Yet when Grant returned to Cairo, he discussed his plan with Flag Officer Andrew H. Foote, a naval officer commanding the gunboat flotilla at Cairo, though under orders from the army. Foote was a forty-year veteran of the naval service, and he agreed with Grant that the two rivers were the key to Tennessee and Kentucky. Encouraged, Grant laconically reiterated his request to Halleck. "With Permission I will take Fort McHenry [sic] on the Tennessee and hold & establish a large camp there." Foote wrote at a little more length, and Halleck agreed, but not before Grant telegraphed him again on January 29 stating that "The advantages of this move are as perceptible to the Gen. Comd.g. Dept. as to myself." Grant was showing the beginnings of a sense of literary persuasion. Plainly, if Halleck could not perceive what was obviously "perceptible," he was a fool.[7]

Grant and Foote planned for seven gunboats to steam up the river while 15,000 of Grant's men followed on transports. There were not enough boats for all of the men, however, so Grant sent McClernand ahead with one division on February 3. He followed the next morning and, aboard the ironclad *Essex,* steamed to within gunshot of Fort Henry to reconnoiter. That night, aboard his headquarters steamer *Uncle Sam*—the prophetic U. S. again—he wrote to Julia that he intended to attack on February 6. "I do not want to boast but I have a confidant feeling of success." The next day he had his entire army in place and ready. He sent Smith to take Fort Heiman, only to find it abandoned by the enemy. Grant did not know that his foe, Brigadier General Lloyd Tilghman, a onetime Kentuckian and not long ago the colonel of one of Breckinridge's Orphan regiments, had only 3,000 men in Fort Henry. Worse, it was unfinished, and thanks to high water in the river stood partly inundated.

The night before the fight Grant wrote again to Julia. "The sight of our camp fires on either side of the river is beautiful," he told her. "To-morrow will come the tug of war. One side or the other must to-morrow night rest in quiet possession of Fort Henry." "Kiss the children for me," he closed, and "Kisses for yourself."[8]

He would rest in Henry the next night, but without having fired a shot. The morning of February 6 Tilghman saw that any defense was hopeless. He sent the bulk of his men to the much stronger Fort Donelson, and kept only 115 men, some of them hospitalized, to work Henry's guns. According to plan, Foote's gunboats attacked first and for three hours battered the fort. At 2 P.M. Tilghman surrendered, while Grant's army was still marching to the battle. It had been intended that Foote would keep Henry's garrison occupied on the river side so Grant could attack from the rear. But it did not matter. Painless as it was, Grant had another victory, and the Tennessee was his.

At once he turned his mind toward continuing his offensive. From the moment he entered Fort Henry, Grant started writing to Halleck, McClernand, and others, making disposition of his captures. "Fort Henry is taken and I am not hurt," he wrote Julia that night. "This is news enough for to-night." His fingers ached from the pen, but as he rested his hand, he exercised his mind. That day he had sent Halleck a brief report of the action, adding that "I shall take and destroy Fort Donaldson on the 8th." Here was something not included in his orders from the department commander, yet it was perfectly obvious as the next logical move. Only about eleven miles separated the two forts and the rivers they guarded. Grant could easily dispatch Foote's flotilla back down the Tennessee to its mouth, up the Ohio to the Cumberland's mouth, and up it to Donelson. Meanwhile, in the same strategy intended for Henry, he would march overland and invest the Confederates from the land.

On February 7, Grant and his staff joined a few companies of cavalry in riding toward Fort Donelson to reconnoiter. He knew who the enemy commanders were there, and feared little from them. One was Pillow. Grant knew him and his unsavory reputation in Mexico. and believed, correctly, now that "I could march up to within gunshot of any intrenchments he was given to hold." Pillow would never think to post advance guards. The actual ranking officer in the fort Grant did not know except by his service as Buchanan's secretary of war, for now John B. Floyd wore the gray as a brigadier. He would prove to be no better at his new career than at his former. Grant's reconnaissance met with no opposition at all, and he easily secured sufficient information to plan his advance.

The weather did not cooperate, however, and the rising river delayed the start of his program. Grant was frustrated. "I was very impatient to get to Fort Donelson because I knew the importance of the place to the enemy." He feared heavy reinforcements coming to Pillow and Floyd. Yet all the time he received more men as well, for Halleck forwarded several regiments as soon as they became available. By February 11 Grant and the weather were ready. He sent 15,000 men out of the lines at Fort Henry. That same day reinforcements reached Pillow. It was Buckner with several regiments, among them the 2nd Kentucky from Breckinridge's Orphan Brigade. The next day the Federals arrived and formed their lines surrounding the fort, while Foote's fleet steamed into place. The fight would open on the morrow.[9]

At last Grant got a real fight, too. For three days the battle lasted, and during it the Confederates continued to receive reinforcements. Floyd, in fact, only arrived to supercede Pillow on the opening day of the siege. By then their garrison numbered 12,000 or more, quite enough to give the Federals something to conjure with. "We have a large force to condend [sic] against but I expect to accomplish their subjugation," Grant wrote Julia. With remarkable prescience, he added that she should "not look for it for three days yet."

It rained off and on, and turned bitterly cold. Snow and sleet alternately pelted the attackers. On Saint Valentine's Day it fell to a bone-chilling 12° F. Yet, Grant had driven the Confederates back to the shelter of their main works, and he could wire Halleck that "I feel every confidence of success." Privately to Julia he admitted that "The taking of Fort Donelson bids fair to be a long job." With a failing common to most generals in these early days of the war, Grant greatly overestimated the strength of Floyd and Pillow, putting it at double their real force. He did not despair.

That same day Foote's gunboats took the brunt of the fighting, severely battering Donelson's river face, but at high cost. Foote took a bad wound from a shell that killed the flagship's pilot, and two of his ironclads were rendered unmanageable when their steering gear was severed. This gave renewed hope to the Confederate defenders, who sent word to Richmond that night that they had won a signal victory. The next morning, while Grant was downriver conferring with the wounded Foote, Floyd launched an attack against the Federals. Pillow and Buckner did the fighting, and that Orphan regiment of

Breckinridge's, the rowdy 2nd Kentucky led by Colonel Roger W. Hanson, spearheaded an assault that actually cut through McClernand's lines, opening a route of escape toward Nashville. Instead of taking the advantage, Pillow ordered the men to retire. By early evening Grant had reestablished his line around the fort.[10]

That night there was genuine consternation inside Donelson. Meeting at an inn at Dover, within the lines, Floyd and Pillow determined that all was lost. Worse, Floyd now showed the white feather. Fearing no doubt that his life would be forfeit if captured, since he had been accused of using his position as Buchanan's secretary of war to scatter the army prior to Sumter, as well as misdirecting arms to the South, he decided to escape. This left Pillow in command. While he suffered less from a guilty conscience than Floyd, he was at the same time a simple coward. He, too, would flee. And that left Buckner, "who was third in rank in the garrison," said Grant, "but much the most capable soldier." He might have added that Buckner was the only real man of the three. The Kentuckian knew the situation. Completely surrounded, with no hope of help from Johnston, his eventual capture was inevitable. Better to surrender honorably and save further loss of life.

Before dawn on February 16 he sent A. C. Montgomery, one of Hanson's Orphans of the 2nd Kentucky, to the lines of General C. F. Smith with a message. He asked for terms upon which to negotiate surrender. Grant's reply was swift and brief. "No terms except an unconditional and immediate surrender can be accepted. I propose to move immediately upon your works." Buckner had no choice. Failure to comply would not only have been suicidal, but also it would have stood in the way of a legend. U. S. for United States; U. S. for U. S. Grant; U. S. for the good steamer *Uncle Sam*. And now U. S. for "Unconditional Surrender." Confronted unknowingly by something larger than his army, in the face of the demands of symbols for posterity, Buckner could not but give in. He called Grant's terms "unchivalrous," but he surrendered just the same. Thus Grant's place as the premier hero of the West stood secured.[11]

And there was a quiet human side to the official doings of the next several days. Grant and Buckner chummed together in happier days at West Point and in the Old Army. Sometime later when the forever impecunious Grant fell on hard times, Buckner lent him money. Now, as they met in friendly conversation with the formalities done, Grant took his old friend aside. Knowing him to be separated from home, and probably short of funds, he placed his own purse at Buckner's disposal. It was probably the first time in his life that U. S. Grant was in a position to loan money to someone else.

"The war is about over for us," lamented Hanson's Kentuckians as they learned the news of the surrender. For many in the West it looked the same. In the space of less than a month Johnston's line had crumbled entirely. Mill Springs in the east and now the twin losses at Forts Henry and Donelson. Indeed, even before Donelson fell, the day after the capture of Fort Henry, the Confederate general decided that Donelson could not hold. That doomed his Kentucky line, and forced him to order the evacuation of Bowling Green and the abandonment of Kentucky. Breckinridge got his orders on February 11. The next day, the birthday as it happened of yet another Kentuckian now sitting in the White House, Breckinridge led his men south. The column looked gloomy from front to back. An icy north wind seemed trying to push them out of their homeland. Two days later they reached the state border. "Everything which could contribute to crush the spirits and weaken the nerves of men, seemed to have combined," wrote an Orphan on that march. In a symbolic act, Breckinridge and his staff dismounted and, leading their horses, walked across the border. Breckinridge was the first to cross. Ironically, he would be the last of them ever to return. He was quiet and reflective for the next two days' march, as they passed through Nashville and toward Murfreesboro. To one of his officers he confided that "there was no hope for the Confederacy . . . there was nothing before us but to do our duty to the end, and make any sacrifice for our convictions which honor and manhood demanded."[12]

Those demands would come soon, for U. S. Grant had tasted victory and wanted more. "This is the largest capture I believe ever made on the continent," he boasted to Julia. It was a heady feeling being able to crow, for a man who had eaten so much of it before. Lincoln made him a major general, and Grant, never able to shake the feeling that he did not live up to his father's expectations, asked "Is father afraid yet that I will not be able to sustain myself?" Since he believed that his family must be growing weary of the newspaper coverage of the Donelson victory, he promised Julia that he would "make a new subject soon." There would soon be easy sailing, he said. "My impression is that I shall have one hard battle more to fight." He had told her before that the war would fizzle out in the West in the spring, and April was coming.[13]

So were the Confederates. Johnston withdrew deep within Tennessee to consolidate his battered forces, while Buell's small army pursued as far as Nashville. Richmond sent assistance in the person of the Confederacy's only hero to match Grant to date, P. G. T. Beauregard. There was uneasiness in Richmond on Johnston's management in the West. Some Congressmen were already clamoring for his removal, even suggesting the utterly inexperienced Breckinridge as a replacement, so disenchanted were they with the current commander. Beauregard went instead, not to replace Johnston, but to be his second officer and to lend the aura of a winner to the battered Western army. Also Davis wanted him out of the way. The President was al-

ready starting to feud with his generals, and none could be as infuriat-
ingly contentious as this young Napoleon from Louisiana.

Beauregard went to Jackson, Tennessee, and there brought together
10,000 men from Mobile led by Major General Braxton Bragg, a favorite of the President's, 5,000 from Louisiana, and eventually Polk's
command from Columbus. Johnston, meanwhile, continued his withdrawal from Nashville, and by the end of March joined Beauregard at
Corinth, Mississippi. Here they combined their forces and built a new
army, the Army of Mississippi. Johnston was beginning to lose control
of affairs to the more vigorous Beauregard and deferred to him more
and more. Major General William J. Hardee came from Arkansas with
a small command, too. He was the author of *Hardee's Tactics,* one of
the standard military text books at West Point, a book that Grant
would boast that he had not read carefully.

Beauregard organized the army anew into four corps. Polk commanded the first. Bragg took the second, and Hardee the third. The
fourth, reserve corps, belonged at first to General Crittenden, the loser
at Mill Springs. Then he was arrested and charged with drunkenness,
and the command of the corps devolved upon the next ranking officer,
John C. Breckinridge. Thus, on March 31, 1862, a man who had never
led troops in battle commanded nearly one fourth of the 40,000-man
Army of Mississippi. All of his superiors had implicit faith in his bravery and manliness, but that had little to do with the instincts that
made a man a good fighter and leader. Much remained to be discovered, and little time for it. Johnston was going to attack.

Beauregard and Johnston vacillated from offense to defense repeatedly during the month of March. The creole loved to formulate grandiose plans, generally quite impractical, but then lost heart in them.
When the two generals met in Corinth late in the month, they finally
decided for good to steal a march on the enemy. The war in the West
was going terribly, and only a bold stroke could redeem it. The Union
command, for a change, also suffered much from divided counsels.
Halleck barely acknowledged Grant's part in the captures at Forts
Henry and Donelson, and on March 3 relieved him of his command
for what he termed misconduct. It was a sorry business, partly the
outgrowth of the drinking rumors, partly Grant's inability to supply
figures on his strength which Halleck wanted but apparently never
directly asked for. Then, too, Charles F. Smith was very highly
regarded and conducted himself ably in the attacks on Donelson.
Grant himself believed that Halleck thought Smith more fit to command this army than Grant. "I was rather inclined to this opinion myself at that time." Halleck, in fact, hoped to make personal capital on
Grant's victories, expecting to deliver a final blow to the Confederates
under his personal command. Having a subordinate who upstaged
him was a considerable embarrassment.[14]

Given his head, Grant wanted to move up the Tennessee River at once, and the Cumberland as well. Under a unified command, a Federal army could have taken Vicksburg, Corinth, Chattanooga, and all of the territory in between with little resistance. Johnston's Confederates were simply too scattered during March to resist. He told Julia on March 11 that "I believe that I have the whole Tennessee river." "We have such an inside track of the enemy that by following up our success we can go anywhere." Finally on March 15 Halleck reinstated Grant in command of his army. C. F. Smith had taken over when Grant stepped down, and now "he was delighted to see me and was unhesitating in his denunciation of the treatment I had received." Denounce was all poor Smith could do, for he was bedridden. He had abrased his shin jumping into a rowboat several days before. This combined with dysentery to so attack his system that, before April was done, he was dead. Many, Grant included, believed that the Union thus lost one of its best generals in the West.[15]

There would be more losses in the West before April waned. When Grant resumed command of his army he found it spread along the Tennessee River in the vicinity of Pittsburg Landing and Savannah, one hundred miles directly south of Henry and Donelson near the Mississippi border, and just twenty-five miles from Corinth. Buell, commanding his small army at Nashville, was ordered to join Grant here, and together they intended to march on Corinth, defeat Johnston, and destroy that important rail and supply center. While awaiting Buell's arrival, Grant consolidated his army around the landing. His six divisions totaling about 42,000 men were spread out chiefly with a view to favorable camp sites. "I regarded the campaign we were engaged in as an offensive one and had no idea that the enemy . . . would take the initiative." He told Julia that "A big fight may be looked for someplace before a great while." It would be the last one in the West he believed. By April 5, as the first of Buell's divisions arrived, he wrote to Halleck to report that his outposts had been attacked by the Confederates "apparently in conciderable force." He went to the front in person but found all quiet. He calmed any fears his superiors might have. "I have scarsely the faintest idea of an attack . . . being made upon us." He hoped not, certainly. He did not feel well. Diarrhea had been bothering him for several days.[16]

Another general did not feel well that evening, and he was closer than Grant thought. At a crossroad just a few miles south of Pittsburg Landing John C. Breckinridge spread his blanket on the ground beside a small fire. Already seated were Johnston, Bragg, Beauregard, and Polk. Two days before Johnston ordered the army out of Corinth to march against Grant. Delay followed delay so that they had already postponed the attack twice. Now the generals debated whether to make it at all. Bragg and Beauregard had lost their confidence. Surely after the clash of their outposts that day Grant must know he was being threatened. But Johnston and Polk still favored attack.

Breckinridge sided with them, sitting up from time to time in his discomfort to add his counsel. Defeat of the Federals here would be the first step on the road back to Kentucky. The final decision was Johnston's and he made it. Attack at dawn, April 6.[17]

"This day will long be remembered," one of Breckinridge's Kentuckians wrote in his diary the next evening. At 3 A.M. he roused his men from sleep. The fires were lit and water for coffee began to bubble in the pots. Some salt pork was fried over the flames, but before the men could eat Breckinridge came riding along the line. "Boys, fall in. You have better work before you than eating." Minutes later the Orphans heard the roar of cannon as Hardee's guns signaled the opening of the Battle of Shiloh. Grant had been almost completely surprised. Indeed, he was several miles away from his army at the time and now feverishly rushing to rejoin it. Ordering Buell to hurry with the remainder of his army, Grant said that "I have been looking for this" but did not expect it until the next day. Not likely. He was surprised, rendered a bit careless by his string of victories and, perhaps, by his tendency to mind-read his opponents. He had judged rightly about Floyd and Pillow at Donelson, but he reckoned without Albert Sidney Johnston, a man desperately clinging to his command while it threatened to go to another if he did not show a success. "I anticipate victory," President Davis had wired Johnston. Grant did not consider the boldness a man can find when pushed from above.[18]

"To-night we will water our horses in the Tennessee River," Johnston told his men that morning. They very nearly did. Grant's army lay spread out in camps by division in the rough wooded country that led down to the river. In the center of the field stood Shiloh Church, with McClernand nearby and, on the right a new division commander who was hardly new to the war. Sherman. He had briefly been Grant's senior before Grant's promotion to major general. Yet Sherman gladly deferred to him. They were not well acquainted. They would be. To the left the division of Brigadier General Benjamin Prentiss sat most in advance, while Stephen Hurlbut's division was some distance in the rear. The division that had been Smith's now looked to W. H. L. Wallace as its leader, while another Wallace, Lew, commanded a division several miles away at Crump's Landing.

Johnston's attack disrupted his own army nearly as much as Grant's. Corps, brigades, and regiments quickly lost all unity and became frequently just a mass of men answering to the nearest officer. Yet they pushed Sherman and the others back from the outset. Only Prentiss made a stand, holding out all morning and well into the afternoon though nearly surrounded. He was buying time, for Johnston became so occupied with this one pocket of resistance that he failed fully to pursue his advantage along the rest of the line. During all of this, General Breckinridge was learning his business in the hardest school of all. His so-called Reserve Corps went into the fight almost from the first. Johnston wanted him to go to the extreme right of the line, find the Tennessee, then move along it to help drive Grant away from the landing, isolating him from Buell's marching reinforcements. With no knowledge of the terrain and no good maps, Breckinridge like most other generals this day almost wandered blindly in groping toward the river. The informality with which the American landscape was cartographically rendered in the days before this war would have a significant impact upon its course. Some of the best maps yet made were produced during the conflict, but all too often *after* the battle in which they were needed.

Noon came before the Kentuckian found approximately his place in line. Johnston joined him and ordered an attack on Prentiss. Before the order was given Breckinridge and his generals waited on their horses under a great oak. Like so many in the Confederacy at this stage of the war, he honored uniform regulations chiefly in the breach. His uniform, not gray, was made of blue Kentucky "jeans." He was growing a mustache. "His dark eyes seemed to illuminate his swarthy, regular features," said Johnston's adjutant, "and as he sat in the saddle he seemed to me altogether the most impressive-looking man I had ever seen." Then an enemy shell struck the oak, and Breckinridge and companions dashed out in a rain of splinters. It was time to attack.[19]

For the next hour Breckinridge and others made repeated attacks against Prentiss's sternly held position. It is to be a war of sobriquets, and before the day is out this place will be called the Hornets' Nest for the ferocity of the fire and the buzzing sounds of the bullets with their deadly sting. As so many did, Breckinridge failed to coordinate his attacks, using the full might of his command. Rather he wasted their strength a brigade at a time, and failed to maintain control of what happened all along his line. After another hour of fighting he was tired, and some of his regiments stopped answering the call to renew the battle. Johnston joined him personally to steady the men and lead the next attack. It was his last. Struck in the leg by one of those hornets, he bled to death in his boot while bravely waving a tin cup captured in an abandoned Federal camp. Now Beauregard commanded.

There followed a lull, then the attack renewed, and finally by 5 P.M. Prentiss was forced to surrender after one of the most heroic and self-sacrificing acts of the war. Very probably he saved Grant's army from being pushed into the Tennessee. Now with the Hornets' Nest in Confederate hands, there was nothing to prevent Beauregard from continuing that drive. Breckinridge pursued the enemy toward Pittsburg Landing and got to within less than a mile of it, the most advanced position taken by any Southern command. Bragg was being resisted well on the right while Polk and Hardee were slowing down on the left. The whole Confederate Army was disorganized. Thousands had broken ranks to plunder the Federal camps. Others simply felt too exhausted to continue. Now Beauregard received a report that Buell would not reach Grant in time to help on the morrow and this, together with the condition of his army, decided him. He would stop for today. They could at least see the Tennessee. Tomorrow they would water in it. To Breckinridge, just readying another attack on the new Federal defenses, the order to retire was a disappointment. "It is clearly a mistake," he said, but the mistake was his. Grant was on the field now, Buell was arriving, disorganization had been replaced by determination, and the Federal Army stood now in a position from which they could withstand more than Beauregard had left to give them. With the aid of the gunboats *Tyler* and *Lexington* firing from the river, Grant would not budge.[20]

That night Buell crossed the river with most of his army, and the next morning Grant was ready to seize the offensive. In spirited attacks he drove his divisions back over most of the ground they lost the day before. By 1 P.M. they had regained the Hornets' Nest, and delivered Breckinridge in particular some telling blows. They were symbolic as well, and tragic. The first Federals to attack him that morning followed his old friend from Kentucky Major General William Nelson. Four regiments of Federal Kentuckians battled against his own Orphans for a time. "Wherever Kentucky met Kentucky, it was horrible," wrote an artilleryman. In a later attack a Union division struck Breckinridge, the Federals commanded by his dear boyhood friend Thomas L. Crittenden, brother of George.[21]

"It was a case of Southern dash against Northern pluck and endurance," Grant said of the battle. Despite a gallant and bloody resistance, Beauregard could not withstand him on April 7, and was compelled to withdraw from the battle. Back toward Corinth they went, leaving Breckinridge and his little corps to act as rearguard. Grant would always feel defensive about Shiloh, as it came to be called. Surprised, he was human enough not to want to admit it. The armies had been evenly matched at about 40,000 apiece before Buell added 20,000 more to the beleagured Grant. The ferocity of the fighting was perhaps the hottest ever seen in the West during the war, the fighting not of disciplined units and experienced commanders, but of desperate men at the edge of panic. Grant lost nearly 35 percent of his army in casualties, hundreds of them men who ran from the fight to huddle at the riverbank, only to return sheepishly to their regiments in the days that followed. Johnston lost more than 25 percent of his command, and himself in the bargain. He will be the only Confederate Army commander to be killed in the war. Nearly 3,500 other Americans went to the sod with him.[22]

"I saw an open field, in our possession on the second day, over which the Confederates had made repeated charges the day before, so covered with dead that it would have been possible to walk across the clearing, in any direction, stepping on dead bodies." Grant felt heartily glad the battle was done. His army had performed about as one made of volunteers should have in its first great battle, with untested leaders. Some men stood out. Sherman, accused months before in Kentucky of instability, stood firm. Grant could count on him he now knew. There would be a promotion coming for him. Prentiss had proved a hero, as did Hurlbut. McClernand stood well, and Grant would ever be grateful to Buell, whatever his later failings, for his alacrity in coming to the rescue. Yet he would never forgive Lew Wallace for being slow to the field on April 6, despite the fact that Grant gave him confused orders. Even "Unconditional Surrender" Grant had much yet to learn. Even he was human enough to hold a petty feeling. But now he wanted to move again and quickly. "I am looking for a speedy move, one more fight and then easy sailing to the close of the war," he wrote Julia. "I really will feel glad when this thing is over."[23]

The day after the battle ended Grant received word that a prominent Confederate general, not Johnston, had been killed and left on the field. He went to see the body in person, only to discover that it was not the man he was led to believe it was. In fact, the dead Confederate was George W. Johnson, governor of the shadowy Confederate state of Kentucky, who took his mortal wound while carrying the musket of a private with the Orphan Brigade. Grant and others at first thought he was another Kentuckian. John C. Breckinridge. And so the two would not meet at Shiloh, but there were other opportunities ahead.

CHAPTER 9

"THE GOVERNMENT IS CONSTRUCTING A MONSTER"

Shiloh was a long way from Washington and Richmond, and yet the three were bound by one unseverable tie that even disunion and war could not break. Water. The rivers measured the land, dividing and binding, and joined with the salt sea to surround the whole. From the Great Lakes, down the St. Lawrence, into the Atlantic and on to the Gulf of Mexico, then up the Mississippi and Ohio, it was possible nearly to circumnavigate the entire scene of the war without stepping foot on land. Water and war called for navies, and navies meant ships and seamen. It would need years yet for the issue of "sea power" to grow into enunciated doctrine, but North and South understood it well enough in the days of '61.

It was an acquired understanding. The first attempt at nautical action failed signally for the Union when Charleston's guns bloodlessly turned back the *Star of the West* in its attempt to succor Sumter. Thanks to bureaucratic politicking and interdepartmental interference, Fox's planned naval expedition did no better. Indeed, the first decisive naval steps waited until Sumter's guns were being used by victorious Confederates as still props for their photographers. On April 19, 1861, Lincoln declared the blockade of Southern ports. The next day the Confederates seized the abandoned Norfolk and its Gosport Navy Yard. Each act was symbolic of the next four years' commitment of North and South. The Union would try to squeeze and starve the enemy by the sea. The Confederacy would seek to defend its rivers and harbors using a new class of warship, the nucleus of which lay in the mud at Gosport.

The real battleground was to be men and ideas as much as ships. Men like Gustavus Fox, like Stephen R. Mallory and Gideon Welles, and men like David G. Farragut and John Taylor Wood, James B. Eads and John Ericsson and John Mercer Brooke. There was naval revolution incipient in their brains, yet the naval war began, as all wars do, in conventional mind.

Old tight-wigged Gideon Welles, happily, was too untutored in seamen's ways to bind himself to conventionality, but he was executive enough to feel uttery dismay when he assumed his portfolio in March 1861. The United States Navy and the department that ran it were a mess. Almost as soon as Welles took over the chief of his ordnance bureau resigned, taking all his staff with him to Virginia. Old Franklin Buchanan, commanding the Washington Navy Yard, left as well, as did scores of officers of the line, and even midshipmen from the Naval Academy. Many of the remaining department clerks had been in their posts for two decades, and a distressing number of the captains commanding on the water were older than any of the ships in the Navy. Conservatism found great soil to root in this service, and even the few inclined toward innovation saw with limited vision. The whole thrust of the Navy from its inception had been defensive. Now with a new war a new mind-set had to come forth. Welles must build a Navy that would take the war to the enemy. It all required great organization. Of all the attributes that Welles might boast, organization stood at the head.

He came from New England, from the world of business and the fiercely independent press. A "nutmeg" from Connecticut, he attended university for three years before taking the editorship of the Hartford *Times* when only twenty-four years old. Even while he spent a decade at the ink he took as well a Democratic seat in the state assembly, espousing what were, for his time, liberal causes. It won him recognition from Andrew Jackson, some spoils appointments, and of course his three-year term as chief of the Navy's Bureau of Provisions and Clothing in the same building where now he sat as secretary. There had been no little indecision on Lincoln's part over what to do with Welles. He wanted him in his cabinet, both as a New England man, and as a gesture to the more radical wing of the Republican party. But for which post—postmaster, navy, something else? Pressures and political fighting prevented his offering Welles the navy post definitely until March 5. The appointment immediately made Welles an object of some curiosity. He confided to his wife that "I shall be glad as soon as this novelty is over."[1]

It would not end soon. His first month in office consumed itself almost entirely in the Fort Sumter situation and the resolution of that problem led directly to his next. The declaration of Lincoln's blockade gave him a nightmare. The Confederacy's coastline stretched for over three thousand five hundred miles, including hundreds of inlets and bays, sand bars and outer banks, and an inland waterway that ran inside those banks from North Carolina to Florida with little interruption. To patrol all this, he had barely fifty ships fit for service. Indeed, Welles initially opposed the blockade on philosophical grounds. Lincoln was putting down rebellion, not engaging a foreign power in war. To declare a blockade, by internationally accepted law, European nations could recognize the Confederacy as a belligerent and commence military trade with it. Foreign powers would not do so, however, so long as Lincoln acted as if this uprising was purely an internal affair, as indeed it was. Furthermore, law required that a blockade be effective before those powers would honor it. How, Welles asked, could he blockade all that coastline with only one ship for every seventy miles? Yet the President persisted, and Welles obeyed. Now he must begin.

Within six weeks Welles made a good start. At least one and sometimes more vessels stood off the mouths of every Southern port from the James River to the Mississippi. They were too pitifully few to interdict sea traffic seriously, their presence being more symbolic than threatening. But while they sailed and steamed back and forth at their appointed stations, their master in Washington quickly augmented their numbers by purchasing and commandeering vessels of every description for conversion to his great purpose. Merchantmen and old retired warships echoed to the tread of martial feet. Pleasure yachts like that of Cornelius Vanderbilt took naval commission. Even New York ferry boats groaned under cannon instead of commuters. Vessels too old or too outmoded for active service became recruiting stations and billeting ships. And new vessels went on the ways as quickly as facilities could handle them. The loss of the navy yards at Norfolk and Pensacola proved major setbacks until Northern yards could be enhanced to fill the gap.

Lincoln expected Welles to produce a comprehensive plan for the blockade, and Welles in turn called on Benjamin Franklin's great-grandson, Alexander D. Bache, superintendent of the Coast Survey. Together they and the members of a special board created for the purpose produced that plan in a month. They called for two blockading squadrons, dividing the Atlantic coast at the border of the two Carolinas. Further they suggested selective invasions to establish bases on the Confederate shore to act as staging areas for future military operations, and for supply bases for the blockade. Then each port of major importance would be assaulted and captured when a sufficient buildup had been achieved. Welles's advisers produced an excellent plan, tailored to start immediately with limited immediate results, and then to escalate gradually as more and more sea power became available. As their first targets they recommended Port Royal, South Carolina, and Fernandina, Florida. The plan delighted Lincoln, and within two weeks it was approved and in progress.[2]

As a prelude to the Port Royal expedition, Welles almost literally had to force Captain Silas Stringham, recently commanding the fleet off Pensacola, to attack Confederate forts on Cape Hatteras, North Carolina. On August 28 Stringham led his fleet of eight ships against Fort Clark, at Hatteras Inlet. This fort and Fort Hatteras nearby protected the inlet, a chief outlet for blockade runners from New Bern, Beaufort, and Plymouth. Clark fell without opposition that day, and the next morning Stringham sent his fleet against Fort Hatteras, firing his ships' 143 guns while they moved, thus presenting a difficult target for the Confederates. Hatteras, too, surrendered, and Welles had his first victory, insignificant as it was. After Bull Run just a month before, any Union success was a triumph.

Yet Stringham remained slow, and Welles had to replace him with Louis M. Goldsborough, who would continue in the newly designated North Atlantic Blockading Squadron. Captain Samuel F. Du Pont took over the South Atlantic Blockading Squadron, both departments being created on September 19. Thus to Du Pont fell the task of taking Port Royal and Forts Beauregard and Walker protecting it. On November 7 he led his squadron of seventeen ships directly into Port Royal Sound, between the two forts, brushing aside a pitiful Confederate defense by four tiny gunboats. Then Du Pont circled his ships and began the systematic reduction of both forts at once. Before long the Confederates were driven from their earthworks, and Du Pont landed without opposition the 12,000 men led by Brigadier General Thomas W. Sherman. Port Royal Sound, with Hilton Head, immediately became Union territory, much to the delight of Du Pont and one of his officers, Commander Percival Drayton. Not quite so elated was the luckless Confederate defender of Port Royal, Brigadier General Thomas Drayton. Brother against brother.

Welles's master plan bid fair to succeed, for now Port Royal would rapidly grow into a jumping-off place for assaults on Savannah and later Charleston. Meanwhile, his buildup of the Navy went well also. Within six months in office he had doubled the number of effective steam warships available. More came into service almost daily. His two foremost department chiefs, John Lenthall of Construction, Equipment, and Repair, and Benjamin Isherwood, Engineer in Chief, proved energetic, if conservative men, that he could depend on for results. Welles quickly put the two to work designing a new class of gunboats for the blockade, vessels combining speed, armament, and light draft for the shallow coastal waters. It took them a short time to complete the specifications and get twenty-three gunboats contracted. This done, and before actual construction began, Welles set them the task of designing another class of even shallower draft vessels that could operate up the rivers as well as in the sounds and off harbors. Lenthall and Isherwood produced a design for a double-ended ship with two engines, one operating each end so that, without turning around in narrow streams, the ships could go forward or backward.[3]

Thus before the summer of 1861 was done, the Union Navy was well on its way to becoming a major sea power, even if most of its contemplated vessels were for specialized use along its own waters. Some forty-seven ships were under construction by August along the Northeast coast. But of course, this was only half the Navy, for these boats abuilding were designed for salt water blockade duty and for the Southern streams and channels that fed into the Atlantic. They did nothing for that other sort of water war, the one in the West where the mighty rivers held the key to the Confederate heartland. The Mississippi and her tributaries were great rivers. They called for a great navy of their own.

If the Navy on the oceans was depleted when war came, that on the Mississippi simply did not exist. It was the Army that first proposed that there be one. In May General George B. McClellan, commanding the militia in Ohio, suggested to Winfield Scott that three gunboats ought to be put into service in support of Federal troops at Cairo, Illinois. Situated where it was at the confluence of the Ohio and the Mississippi and close to the mouths of the Tennessee and Cumberland, Cairo occupied a desirable strategic position. Very soon thereafter Attorney General Bates, concerned for his beloved Missouri, arranged for a brilliant engineer from St. Louis, James B. Eads, to present some ideas for river defense—and offense—to the President and cabinet. Eads was only forty, yet already widely noted for his innovative sense of design in river vessels, and he understood the value of Cairo better than any. Lincoln was impressed, as was Welles. Yet, with a surprising indifference to his territory, which would not have been found in a career naval officer, Welles judged that gunboat operations on those Western waters would better be left to the management of the Army, since any action must necessarily be in support of a much larger land movement. Therefore Welles turned the matter over to the war department and Simon Cameron. The Navy would supply men and ordnance and officers to command the dreamed of gunboat fleet, but they would answer to the Army.

Welles sent Commander John Rodgers west to consult with Eads and McClellan, and late in May they were well at work. Rodgers was a Marylander, like Franklin Buchanan, but when the war came his loyalty to the old flag did not waver. His father had been a commodore in the Revolution, and he himself had served in the Seminole War and surveyed in the waters off Japan. When Norfolk fell he had been unable to escape capture. Governor Letcher treated him cordially, however, and shortly released him, since Virginia had not yet formally joined the Confederacy.

As soon as he was back Welles sent him West. Rodgers enjoyed a fine reputation, knew steam well, and had good personal connections with men in the Army. All this would be necessary. Best of all, he had a single-minded devotion to duty.[4]

Rodgers and McClellan adopted Eads's suggestion to convert old salvage boats into gunboats, but the commander was not enthusiastic. Eads offered one of his own salvage vessels, the *Submarine No. 7* for conversion, but Rodgers found it "old and rotten." At first he vetoed the idea and went instead to Pittsburgh and Cincinnati to look for himself. He was assisted by naval constructor Samuel Pook, and together they selected three wooden steamers, the *Lexington, Conestoga,* and *Tyler.* "Considerable alterations are necessary to fit them for use," Rodgers reported to Welles, and they were vulnerable in their boilers. He was not overly optimistic. "We must take our chance." McClellan approved their purchase and soon Rodgers was at work arming them. The boats themselves went to Cairo for their conversion, the adding of extra layers of oak on the bulwarks.[5]

While these three gunboats would be vulnerable to small-arms fire from shore, not to mention cannon, Rodgers next turned to creating a new class of river gunboat that would withstand anything the enemy could send. These must be entirely different vessels, built specifically to carry a heavy weight in guns and iron armor and yet able to operate in the shallows and shoals of these changeable rivers. Lenthall had not been optimistic. "It does not seem to be practical to make an armed steam vessel for the 'Mississippi' that will be very efficient," he complained. Nevertheless, he recommended that Pook, now at Cairo, be directed to prepare a plan for consideration. Lenthall submitted some basic outline. Pook, Eads, and Rodgers himself would refine it into the new ship.

They were called "Pook Turtles" after their constructor and their decidedly tortoiselike appearance. Pook submitted his basic plan on July 2, calling for boats fifty feet wide and one hundred seventy-five feet long. They would draw just five feet of water and be propelled by a paddle wheel mounted in the center. The Army quickly approved and gave Eads a contract for building seven of them. Working in shipyards at St. Louis and Mound City, Illinois, Eads organized his workmen to work around the clock. Thanks to the war department's sloth in paying for materials, Eads had to finance some of the work from his own pocket, delaying their completion. Still on October 12, 1861, forty-five days after laying its keel, the *St. Louis* slid into the Mississippi at Carondelet, Missouri. She and the six other "city" class gunboats that would follow—*Cairo, Carondelet, Cincinnati, Louis-ville, Mound City, Pittsburgh*—were formidable vessels, with limita-tions. They did not carry full armor. Only two and one half inches of iron protected the forward end of the slab-sided casemate, and a sec-tion amidships where the boilers and engines sat. The casemate sides rose at a 45° angle from the deck and there was little difference be-tween the stubby bow and stern. But for the thirteen rifled and smoothbore cannon inside their casemates, these ungainly vessels might have been mistaken for coal barges. Yet they would be the backbone of the Mississippi fleet.[6]

This put ten river gunboats under construction or conversion, and General John C. Frémont interceded early in August to get another. Counter to Rodgers's opinion, Frémont wanted the *Submarine No. 7* purchased and converted, probably in part from a desire to have his own "navy," since the other ships would not come under his juris-diction. The salvage barge was bought and then turned over to Eads to be made into a namesake of Frémont's father-in-law, Senator Thomas Hart Benton. The *Benton* would be the most powerful vessel on the Mississippi, with three and one half inches of iron and sixteen big guns. The cost proved enormous, the boat slow and unwieldy, but she would become the flagship for most of the remainder of the war on the rivers. Later in November another mammoth salvage barge, the *New Era*, would undergo rebuilding under the eye of her com-mander, William D. Porter, son of Commodore David Porter. He would name her after his father's famous wooden ship *Essex*. By Jan-uary 1862 all nine of the ironclad gunboats were ready for duty and Andrew Foote, who replaced Rodgers in September, took them into service. There were thirty-eight small mortar boats nearly ready as well, and the three old "woodclads" *Tyler, Lexington,* and *Conestoga*. More warships would be coming to the Western waters in 1862 and the years to follow, most of them unconventional, some revolutionary, a few utter folly, but by the time Grant was ready to start his con-quest of the South along its waterways, Foote had enough muscle to help him. In barely nine months the Union had marshaled and built the most powerful inland navy in the world. The debt was owed to Eads, Rodgers, Pook, the war department's purse, and the Yankee practicality of Gideon Welles.[7]

And practicality, to say the least, was what was needed to face a whole new, and to many terrifying, threat. Not long after the fall of the Gosport Navy Yard disturbing rumors reached Washington that the Confederates were doing something formidable with the remains of the *Merrimack*. Union sympathizers who remained in Norfolk filtered reports through the lines from time to time on what happened there. Indeed, Welles had one informant working right in the shops at Gosport. On June 25, 1861, came word that the *Merrimack* had been raised and brought into the dry dock. At first Welles was told that the

Confederates decided the hulk was worthless, but in the months to follow the prognosis changed. By November a Union man sent news that a casemate was being fitted onto the deck, and on December 18 Welles's navy yard informant sent him a detailed account of all construction and specifications of armor and armament. He estimated that the converted ironclad would be ready for duty by February 1, 1862. Later warnings came of a terrible underwater ram being fixed to the bow. In January the rumor spread that the ironclad, now called CSS *Virginia,* had left dry dock. A black woman from Norfolk personally visited Welles. Concealed in her bosom she carried a letter which told that the vessel was being armed at that moment. Welles's fears were confirmed when the Norfolk *Day Book* published an account in January that the ironclad had been proved an utter failure. The ruse was so obvious that Welles now knew that only days separated the ship from her first voyage.[8]

What the Confederates had, in fact, was like unto everything that Mallory would attempt in his program of river and harbor defense. He had too much to do, and too little with which to do it. On May 30 he received word that the *Merrimack* was up and in the dry dock. The raised ship looked terrible. Charred timbers arched grotesquely out of the waterline, all the metal fittings twisted, the deck destroyed and the iron beginning to rust as soon as it hit the atmosphere. "She was nothing but a burned and blackened hulk," complained an engineer.[9]

Nevertheless, it was a hull and relatively good machinery. The former would take weeks—more likely months—to build from the keel in a shipyard; the latter could not be manufactured in the Confederacy at all in 1861. Charred and blackened as it was, then, the *Merrimack*'s remains looked in fact like an enormous head start. Already Mallory advised Davis of his belief that an ironclad warship would be of inestimable value. It was not entirely a new idea. The notion of ironclads went back centuries. The king of Syracuse in the third century B.C. supposedly built a ship sheathed in lead. The Norsemen inadvertently made ironclads of their longships when they placed their shields along the bulwarks for defense. In 1592 a Korean admiral Yi-sun repelled a Japanese naval attack with a "tortoise-ship" covered with iron plate. Even then the comparison with a turtle seemed natural. The Spanish built floating batteries protected with iron in the 1700s, and in the 1840s both Britain and America built iron-hulled ships, though not with the intent of repelling enemy fire. Then in 1859 France built the *Gloire,* a conventional steamer with four and one half inches of iron plate on her sides. At the same time England built the *Warrior* and the *Black Prince* entirely of iron. By 1861 John Bull had ten ironclads finished or under construction, some with nearly seven inches of armor.[10]

These were vessels designed for offense. Even though the United

States was slow to get involved in ironclad building, it too would look to its ironclads as attack ships. So did the Confederacy, though both sides in fact built ships suitable only for defense. It was not until August 1861 that the Union Congress appropriated $1.5 million for experimentation and development of three prototype ironclads. Curiously, one Senator voting in favor of the measure was a Kentuckian who had not yet "gone South," Breckinridge.[11]

But the Confederates were well into it when Congress gave Welles its approval to go ahead with an ironclad program. The Confederate Congress readily agreed to give Mallory the mere $172,523 needed for the *Merrimack*'s conversion, and work commenced at once. Naval Constructor John L. Porter was assigned the task of doing the work, while John Mercer Brooke, once John Rodgers's closest friend and subordinate, oversaw the weaponry and armor. Brooke and Porter despised each other and their relationship quickly degenerated. Both claimed credit for the design of the new ironclad, and spent the rest of their lives making their case, yet Brooke's claim is the better. At least three others also said the ironclad was their brainchild, one accusing Brooke of stealing his idea through an unexplained maneuver he called "jeremy diddling."

Porter cut away all the charred timbers and reduced the superstructure down to three feet above the waterline. Then they laid the new deck. Porter had as many as fifteen hundred men working at one time, Sundays and nights not excepted. Quickly rumors spread in the new capital at Richmond of what was happening at Gosport. "The government is constructing a monster at Norfolk," said a war department clerk. Another engineer devoted himself almost exclusively to repairing the damaged engines, while Brooke designed and tested the armor and guns that would go aboard. The Tredegar Iron Works in Richmond, the Confederacy's only substantial manufactory of iron, contracted to make the guns and plate. Scrap iron came from all over the South, and from rails removed from portions of Yankee railroads briefly captured.

The result was a long casemate atop the *Merrimack*'s deck. Overall the ship measured 262 feet from bow to stern. The casemate itself took up just over 178 feet of that deck. Its sides sloped upward at about 36° and carried four inches of crudely laminated wrought iron bolted to two solid feet of oak and pine. The top of the casemate was fourteen feet wide and 168 feet long, an iron grate of two-inch bars making a topdeck. At its forward end Porter placed a conical pilot house with slits cut for sight. The ship was to carry ten heavy guns, four in each broadside, and a pivot gun at each end which could swivel and fire through any of three ports. Just under the waterline at the bow Porter installed a fifteen-hundred pound cast iron beak or ram.

All in all it was a fearsome war machine, but in no way did it represent an advance in naval design or technology. It simply fit the need, the materials at hand, and the very limited manufacturing facilities available. It was slow, heavy, cumbersome, and crude. It leaked, was underpowered, inadequately ventilated, and worst of all, drew so much water that it stood at once unfitted for part of Mallory's purpose. He hoped that such a machine could break the blockade, even steam into Northern ports and disrupt them. There was talk of taking the ship to New York, even to Washington. In fact, so heavy was she that she could barely maneuver in her own waters. Never could the vessel have met blockaders on the open sea. Even a heavy swell would have sent her to the bottom. Considering the time and man hours, the effort and money, and the precious iron and ordnance that went into her, the *Virginia* was a bad investment. The fault lies chiefly with her builders, who failed to fit their craft to Mallory's wants, and gave him a vessel useful only for defense, and not too suitable even for that. The brief success she achieved might well have been accomplished by an armored vessel half her size. Her usefulness in defending the Elizabeth River, where she berthed, might have been equaled by a good shore battery. But Porter and Brooke should not be blamed overmuch. They were working quickly, in to them a new field, and with limited means. There was not time to do better.[12]

Gideon Welles had even less time, but better men and materials. Once the congressional appropriation passed in August 1861 he appointed a board to examine the plans submitted for ironclad designs. Commodores Joseph Smith, Hiram Paulding, and Captain Charles H. Davis were to pass judgment on the designs, which Welles advertised should be submitted within twenty-five days. None of them knew anything of ironclad design. They soon did. Seventeen proposals came in quickly, some absolutely outrageous. Still the board found two of merit, two that were recognizable enough to conventional seamen that the old salts did not feel ill at ease contemplating them. One came from C. S. Bushnell of New Haven, Connecticut, a speculator, businessman, and old friend of Welles. He offered a vessel 180 feet long, built entirely like the usual wooden steamer except that its sides were to be protected with iron applied in overlapping layers, like clapboard siding. His cost was only $235,000, and the work could be done quickly, which made the proposal very attractive. They did not know at the time, however, that it also made a very ineffective ironclad.

The other plan the board liked called for a much larger ship, 3,486 tons, built more along the lines of the British ironclad warships. It would carry eighteen heavy caliber cannon, its wooden sides protected by four-and-one-half-inch iron siding mounted tongue and groove like flooring. She should do nearly ten knots and cost $780,000. She would be called *New Ironsides*. It would take a year from submission of the plans for her to launch, but she would go on to be

the most reliable and most battle-used ironclad of the war, unsung
and largely unappreciated by all but her commander and crew.

In large part the reason why the *New Ironsides* would not receive
her due rests with the third design which Welles's board finally accepted. Whereas Bushnell's ship, the *Galena,* and the *New Ironsides*
were very conventional, this third one was so unusual to the layman
and even most seamen that it at once captured the imagination of the
Northern press and public. Indeed, it even swept the navy department with a malady that some would call "monitor fever."

The designer was an eccentric mechanical genius, John Ericsson.
Bushnell knew him well—though Ericsson's personality denied him
many real friends—and went to him with a problem of his own on the
Galena design. Ericsson solved it for him quickly. The fifty-eight-year-
old Swede boasted loudly of a long procession of novel inventions,
from the fire engine to the screw propeller now in use on virtually all
of the world's modern warships. He designed the USS *Princeton,* the
nation's first screw-propelled steam man of war, along with several
other steam engine improvements. He was not always successful, as
his attempt to promote his own ship *Ericsson* demonstrated. She was
propelled by hot air, and many thought Ericsson was too. In 1854 he
tried to sell France an idea for an ironclad with a revolving turret
centered on a flat deck, but Napoleon III was not buying. Ericsson
shelved the idea until his visit from Bushnell.

Ericsson showed Bushnell his plans and his friend immediately saw
not only the novelty of the inventor's ideas, but also some tidy personal advantage if the Navy should adopt Ericsson's design. Acting as
go-between, he brought Welles and Ericsson and the ironclad board
together in a tense series of meetings in which more than once the
Swede's enormous ego and fragile pride almost eliminated him from
consideration. At last the board agreed, and now they had their third
ironclad.

It was most unusual. Ericsson wanted a vessel 172 feet long and 41
feet in the beam, tapered to a point fore and aft. In fact, it was to be
a wooden hull, 122 feet in length, with an iron raft laid on top. The
effect was an armored overhang of three and one half feet on either
side, and twenty-five feet at bow and stern. Thus an enemy might ram
from any direction without piercing the ironclad's vital submerged
hull. Of course, the dominant feature of the ship was the cylindrical
turret that sat in the middle of the otherwise flat deck. In fact at least
six plans for turreted ironclads had been submitted. It was not a new
idea, and certainly not original to Ericsson. One enterprising inventor
showed a model with no less than four turrets, and another suggested
that his design had three revolving towers that could disappear into
the deck when not firing.

Yet Ericsson took an existing idea and made it more simple, more
attainable than the rest. There lies his genius in the overall design of

his new ship, his *Monitor*. His turret revolved on a central shaft, operated by an engine in the bowels of the hull. It was to carry two cannon, protected by eight one-inch layers of wrought iron plate. Iron port stoppers closed the gunports when the cannon were being loaded. Meanwhile, the low deck would be almost awash and, perfectly flat, offered no target at all. Thus, only the turret, and a small rectangular pilot house gave an enemy anything at all to shoot at, and the turret's armor and curved sides made it almost impregnable.

The ship could be built speedily and quickly, said Ericsson, and it offered the advantage of maneuverability. In battle in a narrow channel, the ship did not have to turn to fire as would the *Galena* and *New Ironsides*—and the *Virginia*. Only the turret need revolve. With Bushnell's backing, the design was approved. Ericsson said it would cost $275,000 to build. He gave contracts to several firms for different parts of the vessel in order to save time. To help finance the project while awaiting government funds, Bushnell and others advanced money for shares in the enterprise, and here Bushnell's motivation becomes evident. The final contract was signed early in October 1861, and called for completion within less than six months. Ericsson took exactly four months from the day he laid the keel until the ship was officially commissioned into the United States Navy.[13]

Welles did not suspect it yet, but certainly the experienced officers on his ironclad board should have realized that this new creation offered only very limited potential for this war. True, it could withstand fire from almost any shore battery, and be impervious to shot and shell from other ships, even the powerful *Virginia*. True again, her own guns would be formidable against any wooden antagonist, and could probably do severe damage to the inferior armor on any Confederate ironclad likely to appear. But the *Monitor*'s firepower was woefully inadequate for any offensive purpose. Indeed, a fleet of twenty of them, if built, would only offer the attacker forty guns, less than the firepower of two front line sloops of war. With her low deck, the *Monitor* would be awash in even a light sea, making her easily vulnerable to swamping. In sum, much like Mallory, Welles was authorizing a class of warship that he expected would not only meet the enemy's vessels on more than even terms, but also fight successfully against Confederate coastal fortifications as well. In fact, the ironclads both North and South would prove suited only for river and harbor defense.

While this ironclad fever swept both Union and Confederacy, the two chief antagonists, the *Monitor* and the *Virginia*, seemed destined for each other. In the North, Ericsson's ship came to be regarded as the only hope of checking the enemy leviathan, and its builders rushed the ship accordingly. At Norfolk, meanwhile, news of the Federal ironclad abuilding filtered through from time to time, but the Confederates really knew little of the new design or its capabilities.

Their main concern was the Federal fleet of wooden ships in Hampton Roads, chiefly the *Minnesota, Congress, Cumblerland,* and *Roanoke.* If these could be eliminated, the James River would be opened to Confederate traffic and European blockade runners should they be able to slip into the Chesapeake. Then, Mallory hoped unrealistically, the *Virginia* might slip out and take the war to Northern ports.

Even while the *Virginia* took on crew and ammunition for her first sortie against that fleet in March 1862, the Confederate Navy had already been bringing the war to the North for nearly nine months. When Mallory first took office he saw plainly that the South did not have the facilities to build seagoing warships. Barely could it manage to construct its unruly and unreliable ironclads. Consequently he would look to purchase abroad as his main source of ocean vessels and chiefly from Great Britain. Yet one or two ships could be found in the early days of the war in waters closer to home. Back in April 1861, when the Confederate capital still sat in Montgomery, Secretary Mallory received a visit from newly commissioned Commander Raphael Semmes. He was a Marylander, like so many officers in the new Southern Navy, now fifty-two years old. He began his career before there was a Naval Academy for him to attend, going from midshipman up through the officer ranks as he served aboard the old *Lexington,* the *Constellation,* and other ships before obtaining his own command during the Mexican War. The late 1850s found him an inspector of lighthouses, but shortly after secession Jefferson Davis sent him north on a purchasing trip. There being no hostilities yet, Semmes went unmolested and bought munitions for the coming conflict, and looked without success for two light draft steamers to buy. Then he returned to Montgomery, having resigned his United States commission on February 15, 1861.

Mallory at first appointed him to the Confederate lighthouse bureau, but soon realized that Semmes had other uses. Even before the firing at Sumter Semmes proposed to friends that the Confederacy should operate on the seas against Union merchant shipping. Then he made his call on Mallory and advanced the same position. The secretary received the idea readily, and showed Semmes a list of vessels then in New Orleans which the department was considering for purchase and conversion to warships. Semmes saw one that he liked, the *Havana,* a little steam packet. Two weeks later he was in New Orleans inspecting his new ship, renamed CSS *Sumter.* "I found her only a dismantled packet-ship," he wrote, "full of upper cabins, and other top-hamper, furniture, and crockery, but as unlike a ship of war as possible." Still he saw something in her. "Her lines were easy and graceful, and she had a sort of saucy air about her, which seemed to say, that she was not averse to the service on which she was about to be employed." Indeed, she was not.[14]

Six weeks later Semmes had her commissioned, a completely

different vessel than the *Havana*, and now mounting five guns instead of passenger cabins. On June 30 he steamed out of New Orleans, evaded the blockade, and set out on Mallory's bidding "to do the enemy's commerce the greatest injury in the shortest time." Three days later she took her first prize. Six months later, when Semmes ended the cruise thanks to being blockaded at Gibraltar by Federal cruisers, the little *Sumter* had taken eighteen such prizes and left the bulk of the Northern merchant fleet in near terror, at the same time drawing several great war sloops like the *Kearsarge*, the *Tuscarora* and the *Chippewa*, away from blockade duty to track her down. It set the pattern for Confederate commerce raiding for the rest of the war, and several ships would follow in *Sumter's* wake. Indeed, as Semmes was returning to the Confederacy from Gibraltar he met with orders sending him to England to assume his next command. The Confederacy was more than satisfied with the benefits of commerce raiding, and would field as large a fleet as possible in the years ahead. Names like *Florida, Rappahannock, Georgia, Chickamauga, Tallahassee,* and *Shenandoah,* would come to be internationally known. Though their actual captures would barely be felt in the flow of Northern merchant goods in the oceans of the world, still their threat was enormous, and the Union reacted accordingly. Only nineteen commerce raiders would actually take the sea and prizes, but Gideon Welles would have over eighty warships plying the oceans in their wake. The cost was enormous, and over 800 guns were thus removed from the blockade, though not all at the same time. Northern insurance rates went up for maritime ventures, and many merchants declined to risk shipping in United States hulls.[15]

In fact, however, the South would derive little benefit from all this, little that is in terms measurable within the borders of the Confederacy. But this American conflict was having global impact and while the commerce raiders themselves little affected the war, the impact of their image in the North and across the Atlantic was more powerful than Mallory ever imagined. Gideon Welles took a beating in the Yankee press for his seeming inability to stop Semmes and other raiders. The trading community even suggested that Welles himself license privateers to chase them down. The ever crafty Seward began to meddle in the business, and across the ocean in British shipyards lay the catalysts for an explosion that some feared would offer the Confederacy the only frail opportunity it would ever have of actually winning this war. Symbolic of the whole was the new command that called to Semmes after he abandoned the *Sumter*. Her registered name was hardly threatening—*No. 290*. But Semmes would shortly christen her anew after his adopted state: CSS *Alabama*.

CHAPTER 10

"I DON'T KNOW ANYTHING ABOUT DIPLOMACY"

It was of course inevitable that, just as they had since the founding of the Union, the Adams family must contribute to a position of importance in the present difficulty. After all, two of the Adamses had served as Presidents. Both as well acted as diplomats. What then could be more natural than that a current member of the Massachusetts dynasty be offered a post in the foreign service. Of the several available, Secretary of State William H. Seward chose Charles Francis Adams, Sr., son of President John Quincy Adams, a Harvard graduate, lawyer, an old-time Whig turned Republican, noted in Congress and at home as a moderate. Like all the Adams men he seemed dour at first encounter, but there was spine and nerve, and some wit beneath the scowl. It was a happy appointment. Adams would go to Great Britain to represent the Union. He would be instrumental in averting war.

The surgeon handling instruments like Adams was Seward, a crafty, ambitious, meddlesome, and supremely overconfident career politician with few attributes to recommend him except extraordinary skill at his work. He would scheme against his fellow cabinet ministers, and even against his President. He will lie and connive and even forge orders over the President's name, but none of Lincoln's secretaries would more ably accomplish his assigned tasks.

The challenge facing Seward immediately upon taking his portfolio was simple. America's foreign relations were remarkably pacific in 1861. She had no real enemies. The old differences of two wars with England lay half a century behind, and only France posed any threat as Napoleon III seemed intent upon adventuring in Mexico. Thus the Union as a whole need feel little threat. But divided, North and South looked toward the old powers of continental Europe in a different light. Should England or France, even Spain, see its interest strengthened by an alliance with the Confederacy, and a military assistance, then Seward had a problem. Such a wedding of the South and Europe would not result in the subjugation of the North. But they believed it could well enable the Confederacy to defend successfully its bid for nationhood. For Seward, then, what the Europeans called "the American question" offered a major problem. By the 1860s the major Old World powers looked upon intervention into the affairs of other nations as a right of might. Britain was expanding still her Empire. Napoleon III was trying to match English colonial power with his own. An opportunity to intervene and perhaps regain some of what both had lost in the New World must offer a considerable temptation.

Lincoln himself was not encouraging. "I don't know anything about diplomacy," he claimed. "I will be very apt to make blunders." Yet to Seward it seemed certain that there would be foreign meddling in "the American question." Either Europe would intervene in behalf of the Confederacy, or it would remain neutral. Wholly aside from their impulses toward empire, both Britain and France were monarchies, and an opportunity to defeat the notion of democracy would be most attractive to them. In May 1861, when news of Fort Sumter and the coming conflict reached Parliament, one member declared that they were "now witnessing the bursting of the great republican bubble which had been so often held up to us as the model on which to recast our own English Constitution." His fellow members in the Commons responded with a rousing "Hear! Hear!" The temptation was sore to take a hand at pricking that bubble themselves. It was not only on ideological grounds, either. America stood midway between England and the Orient, commanded much of two oceans, and thus threatened Europe's perceived corner on world trade and balance of power. To weaken the Union would be to strengthen themselves, as well as vindicate the notion of monarchy as a more stable form of government than democratic mob rule.[1]

It did not help Seward's cause that much of England's influential upper class favored the South, partly out of a natural affinity for a society that attempted to ape its aristocracy, but as well because the chief organ of public opinion, the *Times* of London, was ardently pro-Confederate. At the same time, however, the majority of the British public—those who had an opinion or even cared—sided with the Union. Most of Britain's commercial community had profitable mone-tary ties, almost exclusively with the North. The large antislavery or-ganizations were naturally appalled at the South's adherence to the peculiar institution. And having themselves come through a period when "the condition of England" was a topic hotly debated and defended by the growing body of humanitarians and social reformers, the general public leaned far more toward the democracy of the North than the elitism of the South. Just which segments of the nation would decide its policy would also decide Seward's success in keeping England out of the war.

Certainly the secretary of state did not advance his cause when on April 1, 1861, he sent Lincoln his proposal to "Change the question before the Public from one upon Slavery, or about Slavery, for a ques-tion upon Union or Disunion." Spain had invaded San Domingo. The French were in Haiti and looking covetously at Mexico. France had also received advice from its Washington minister that the Confed-eracy should be recognized, and a Russian diplomat promised much the same. Britain, of course, held the top hand. Others would follow where John Bull led, and Lord Lyons, minister in Washington, seemed decidedly unfriendly. Thus in Seward's recommendation on April 1 about the tenor of the war, he added as well that Lincoln should demand categorical explanations of their intentions from France and Spain at once, and "ask" for declarations of intent in the secession crisis from England and Russia. Unsatisfactory answers should be met with a declaration of war. Word of this suggestion eventually reached Europe, causing the United States some little em-barrassment. Yet it served a useful purpose as well, for it gave notice to the powers that the Union—or at least Seward—did not fear to combat with them.[2]

Neither did Charles Francis Adams. He did not care for Lincoln. That business of the kissing and whiskers bothered his chilly Yankee sensibility, yet he took the post offered and left for London. He ar-rived on May 13, a bad day to start his mission for on that same day Queen Victoria announced that Britain would recognize a state of bel-ligerence in America, and remain neutral. This according of belligerent rights to the South could easily be a first step to formal recognition. It granted that a genuine government was operating in the Confederacy, one entitled to the internationally recognized rights of a nation at war, not just a section in uprising against its own government. Adams at once set about acting calmly and judiciously in his initial meetings with Britain's foreign secretary Lord John Russell, and even more so in brief encounters with the decidedly anti-American prime minister,

Lord Palmerston. It did not help him that the Confederates enjoyed a head start. Their envoys had been in Britain for some time before him, and now Seward further complicated matters by sending Adams instructions that he was not to have any dealings with Russell or others so long as the British continued to meet with Confederate diplomats, thus interfering in and encouraging a distinctly internal American matter. Seward also gave notice that he would maintain the blockade and that foreign shipping that attempted to violate it would be seized, a particularly sore point to British shippers. Should Britain formally recognize the Confederacy, it would be looked upon as "intervention to create within our own territory a hostile state by overthrowing this Republic itself." Should that intervention be performed, he said, "we from that hour, shall cease to be friends." And should Britain give harbor and shelter to Confederate privateers, in violation of her own signing of an 1856 international compact outlawing privateering "everywhere in all cases and forever," it would be tantamount to intervention.[3]

The British, meanwhile, stood nearly convinced that Seward actually intended to make war upon them. Their minister in Washington decried what he saw as blatant attempts by the press—which he suspected of doing Seward's bidding—to prepare the public mind for war with England. Further, assuming that the North finally acquiesced and acknowledged the South's independence, the humiliation would be so great that Lincoln and his government would "divert the popular wrath from themselves to a Foreign Foe," namely Great Britain. This made Palmerston and his administration hesitant about the safety of Canada, for a large Northern army would be ready at hours' notice to launch an attack. Consequently, Palmerston decided that 10,000 soldiers should be sent to Canada at once. With classical unilateral misunderstanding, Seward in turn interpreted this as a warning of impending war. As each side misread the other's signs, the declaration of belligerence further complicated matters, and gave Charles Francis Adams a problem.[4]

Not only did Victoria admit this status to the Confederates. The declaration also mentioned "further questions" arising from that belligerence about which the government was still in doubt. To Adams that meant that Britain might actually be considering formal recognition, and much sooner than anyone anticipated. Adams found the move premature at best, "raising the disaffected States up to the level of a belligerent power, before it had developed a single one of the real elements which constitute military efficiency outside of its geographical limits." The South did not have a navy in international waters even, though the little *Sumter* would carry its banner out to sea within a few weeks.[5]

Yet as time went on, Adams found Lord Russell a reasonable man and discovered that British public opinion was largely in favor of the

Union. A motion to grant formal recognition to the Confederacy was quashed before it got to Parliament's floor. Then Adams received Seward's May 21 dispatch, which threatened war. "I believe that our Government means to have a war with England," wrote his son Henry. "I believe that England knows it and is preparing for it; and I believe it will come within two months." Some interpreted Seward's message as moderate in tone, but the man charged with representing the United States in Great Britain felt almost betrayed.[6]

Adams spent the next months trying to calm the troubled relations between the two countries, helped little at all by the widespread feeling that Seward hated England, and by bitter attacks on Seward in his own country from Charles Sumner and others. Here is where the wisdom shown by Lincoln in making this appointment became apparent. Adams did not fluster. Possessed of enormous patience, calm, and, most of all, tact, he was the perfect diplomat, not only carrying forth his superiors' instructions, but tempering them with his own conscience as well. He was not an exciting man. He was a near-perfect diplomat.

He had to be, for the British and French invariably misinterpreted almost every act of William H. Seward as warlike when, in fact, his principal aim was always to keep foreign powers out of the American war. When Seward attempted to have the United States adopt the 1856 Declaration of Paris, which outlawed privateering and recognized the legitimacy of an effective blockade, the negotiations became so embroiled and his motives so suspect that the whole affair had to be abandoned. The issue of the blockade itself remained volatile, for Europe wanted Southern cotton. When Lincoln threatened to close officially Southern ports, Russell brought the matter to the British cabinet, and they spoke of war. The defeat at Bull Run further weakened Union support in Whitehall, and when Seward discovered that a British consul at Charleston was issuing English passports to men going North to buy arms for the Confederacy, he became enraged. Further, British diplomatic officials were carrying correspondence for Confederates. That was bad enough in itself. What so aroused Washington, however, was that such activity encouraged a public notion that the British were having diplomatic dealings with the Rebels, an intimation of recognition. Seward's jailing of British subjects suspected of aiding the enemy only aggravated the situation further.

Compounding matters was the widespread feeling, even among Britons who supported the Union, that the division between North and South was permanent. What scared them, then, was the fear that the continued blockade would starve England's cotton mills. It was commonly believed that the island kingdom had only enough cotton on hand to last out 1861. In fact, there was much more, but still the government began cultivating other markets in Africa and India just in case. In time this would work to Adams's benefit, considerably weakening the Confederate state department's cornerstone "King Cotton" diplomacy. But for now Russell foresaw a severe shortage, and in October it prompted him to speak out in terms strongly hinting at intervention in favor of the Confederacy and sooner than later. France, too, feared the continued loss of cotton due to the blockade. The national interest of the two major European powers seemed linked with Southern independence.

Seward was no fool and quickly he strove to diffuse the cotton situation. "We ask nothing of you save moral support," he told a French envoy. "Have confidence in the reestablishment of the Union, and let this be well enough known, so that the South is convinced of it, and for our part we shall find a way to supply your industry with cotton." By the end of the month, through such pacific efforts by Seward and Adams, the situation cooled, and Adams felt secure that Whitehall would remain neutral. Among other things, Britain's need for Yankee grain was as great as that for Confederate cotton. Intervention for either side would cost her from the other. "My fears of foreign intervention are subsiding," Seward wrote to his wife. "The prestige of secession is evidently wearing off in Europe." And Adams could now predict that "we shall be suffered to pursue our course in America without molestation to the end." Only in the event of a major military disaster to the Union did he believe Britain and France would step in on behalf of the South. Further, Seward eased cotton shortage fears by promising that the Union would shortly seize a Southern port from which cotton could be exported to England and France. The promise came in October 1861, and the capture of Port Royal came in November—certainly no mere coincidence. France agitated for intervention, trying to persuade Britain to join with her in common policy, but to no avail.[7]

Yet Napoleon did not abandon his plans to interfere with affairs in North America. Mexico had been in revolution for some time, an attractive opportunity for foreign powers to step in but for the threat of a united nation to the north and its Monroe Doctrine. With the Union sundered the way seemed clear for some adventuring in Mexico, and rumors quickly reached Seward that one or more European nations were conspiring to attack the land of Montezuma. Not only did it violate long-standing American policy in the hemisphere but, worse yet, in tandem with any foreign recognition of the Confederacy it would unite a vast territory against the Union, perhaps ensuring Southern independence. Adams met with Russell asking the postponement of any intended action. He agreed, but on October 31 Britain, France, and Spain agreed upon a joint Mexican expedition in "defense" of their citizens and financial interests there. On December 17 the Spanish landed first at Veracruz. British forces came ashore soon thereafter, and the French began an expedition to Mexico City. By January 1862 the combined European forces in Mexico totaled over 10,000. England

and Spain withdrew four months later after satisfying their claims against the revolutionary regime of Benito Juarez, but France had come to stay. A year later they will capture the capital and install Maximilian, archduke of Austria, as Napoleon's puppet ruler. The whole episode only exacerbated the unstable relations between the United States and Europe. Then on November 8, 1861, Captain Charles Wilkes stepped onto the scene and did his best to precipitate war.

The Confederacy's diplomatic efforts toward Great Britain and France in 1861 were amateurish at best. They began with the appointment of three men of little diplomatic ability to a combined mission for dealing with all of Europe. Here is where Davis paid his debt to William L. Yancey, and incurred a liability for the South by sending the least diplomatic of men abroad. With him went Pierre Rost, a Frenchman by birth with absolutely no qualifications except a knowledge of the French language, and that imperfect from long absence. A fellow Confederate in Paris, where Rost made his headquarters, found his appointment "a very serious political fault." Frenchmen wondered if the Confederacy had so few native men of talent that it had to send a foreigner, even if he were of their blood. For the most part Rost lived in style and spent his time being agreeable, accomplishing nothing. The third member of the party was Ambrose Dudley Mann, a well-meaning windbag with little political acumen, remarkable gullibility, and only unswerving loyalty to Davis and the Confederacy to recommend him. He found great things in nothing and stretched the patience of his fellow commissioners and everyone they met, despite his social charm.[8]

The commissioners reached London in April 1861 and first met with Lord Russell on May 3. He warned them at once that he would hear them out but could say little in return since they were not recognized plenipotentiaries as yet, and might never be. They argued the right of secession, the ability of the South to maintain itself in the present war, and then closed with King Cotton. Britain would suffer with cotton from the South cut off, they implied. Russell needed little more than the hint. Yancey, Rost, and Mann came away from the interview believing that the South only needed one good victory in the field to convince the British to recognize the Confederacy.[9]

Then came the belligerency declaration, and the Confederates were certain that their mission would prove a success. Rost went to France, followed by Yancey, and there received assurances that Napoleon III would repudiate the blockade. By June the commissioners reported to Secretary of State Toombs that England and France need only be "satisfied as to our ability to maintain our position, and that when the cotton crop is ready for market, their necessities will force them to conclusions favorable to the South." King Cotton would rule in Europe.[10]

Then came word of the great victory at Manassas, and the commissioners jubilantly asked Russell once more for discussions that might lead to recognition. Yet Victoria's government was not convinced by one victory. It would remain neutral until the arbitration of the sword, or more peaceful means, indicated which side was likely to prevail. Dedicated entirely to its own interests, Great Britain would not risk war with the North until assured of the South's success. Behind the scenes, too, the subtle persuasion of Charles Francis Adams kept planting doubts about the Confederacy. Russell found himself squarely in the middle.

Meanwhile, Robert Toombs had tired of a cabinet post that he could carry in his hat. He resigned in July and in his place Davis appointed Virginian R. M. T. Hunter. Here was a man more in keeping with the portfolio of secretary of state. To be sure, he had no foreign service experience, but he had been a Congressman and Senator, a conservative man of mature judgment. He approached the position with less condescension than Toombs, and more ability. To him, on October 5, the commissioners could report the growing desperation for cotton, with supplies due to exhaust by December. The resultant threat, not only to manufacturers, but also to the thousands of laborers who would be put out of work, seemed certain to drive England to recognition. In France they believed the situation was even worse. As a result, they advised Hunter that prospects looked better than ever for recognition. The Confederate government also imposed an embargo on foreign shipment of cotton. Along with Reagan's profit-making post office, it was the most successful single enterprise to which the Confederate leaders put their talents. No embargo in history proved more effective. England and France, expecting a steady flow of cotton through the easily penetrated blockade, instead found Southern supply cut entirely. Davis and Hunter used their weapon of persuasion with a heavy hand. It was all they had, all that is, until the unwitting assistance of Captain Wilkes.[11]

Mann and Yancey did not get along, and Rost was spending all too much time enjoying the high life of Paris. By the late fall of 1861 Davis and Hunter could see that their triumvirate had outlived its usefulness. Yancey despaired of ever accomplishing anything and sent in his resignation, anxious to return to his natural element, Southern politics. On September 23 Hunter officially dissolved the commission. Henceforth Mann would use his efforts in Brussels, and Rost would try Spain. New commissioners to England and France had been appointed in their place, men of more experience and ability, men whose appointment represented Davis's awareness that recognition might take more time, and more talent. To England he would send James M. Mason of Virginia; to France, John Slidell of Louisiana. They would leave for their new posts on October 11, aboard the *Gordon*, for Havana. There, on November 7, they would leave for England aboard the British mail steamer *Trent.* Captain Wilkes was waiting.[12]

Motives are an absolute morass, and nowhere more so than in diplomatic matters. First there is the case of Captain Wilkes. He is sixty-two, a forty-three-year veteran of the sea, a noted explorer of the Antarctic coastline, the famous Wilkes Expedition. His temper and difficulty as a subordinate stood in the way of his career, but his loyalty to the Union was never in question despite his sons' well known Confederate sympathies. In 1861 he, like Semmes, served on the lighthouse board, but he anxiously sought Union command. He was sent to Africa to bring the *San Jacinto* back to Philadelphia, his instructions including no leeway for stops or destinations other than that city.

Yet now Confederate policy unwittingly worked against Davis and Hunter, for Wilkes chose to delay in returning to Philadelphia. He cruised instead in search of the *Sumter,* from Africa to the West Indies. He stopped in many ports, and at Cienfuegos, Cuba, he learned that Mason and Slidell were in Havana awaiting passage to England. Perhaps the Confederate envoys wanted him to know.

Wilkes went on to Havana himself, arriving on October 30, 1861. There he found that Mason and Slidell were speaking freely of their intention to go to Europe on November 7 aboard the *Trent.* Further came the word that the captain of the British steamer had personally booked their passage and was even then presenting them to Cuban officials as recognized diplomats. The implied status accorded Mason and Slidell was not lost on Wilkes, nor was the notion that this was beyond the bounds of British neutrality.

There was some fraternization between Wilkes's officers and the two envoys. Two of his officers dined with Mason and Slidell at their invitation. The Confederates spoke freely of their trip plans, adding that by sailing on a British ship "they were free from any worries about arriving at their destination." Others soon claimed that Wilkes himself entertained the envoys aboard the *San Jacinto,* and that there a strange pact was agreed. Wilkes, the story went, promised to intercept the *Trent* and take them prisoner![13]

Why would either side seemingly conspire to have Mason and Slidell captured from a British ship? It must be admitted first that neither North nor South *probably* did so conspire. Rumors would fly that Seward secretly ordered Wilkes to arrest the two. Yet Wilkes was on the African coast just taking over the *San Jacinto* when Davis appointed his new commissioners. Thus he could not have received word from Seward or anyone of the appointments until he touched port in the Indies in October. Even assuming that Seward had the remarkable prescience to expect that Mason and Slidell would be ready to leave Havana just when Wilkes was there, the fact was that the Confederates' original announced route was not by way of Cuba at all. Further, Seward had no way of knowing that Wilkes was disobeying his orders, nor any reason to think him bound for the Indies instead of Philadelphia.

For the Confederates, however, there is a much better case to be made for some scheming. Jefferson Davis wanted Great Britain in the war against the Union. Mason and Slidell were charged to accomplish that end. If it occurred to either of them that their seizure forcibly from a British ship by an American warship would produce a major international incident, then a plan to arrange that confrontation made good sense. After all, in 1812 the United States and England went to war in part over the issue of unlawful search and seizure on the seas. Might it not happen again? That these thoughts animated Mason and Slidell, no one can say, and they never said so themselves. But neither did they make any attempt to keep their sailing date a secret. Captain Wilkes made good use of the information.

Some time during the first week of November Wilkes decided to lay a trap for the *Trent,* halt her, and seize the two emissaries. His executive officer opposed the plan, fearing that the insult to England and the violation of neutral rights might lead to war, but the captain would not relent. He told the United States consul in Havana of his plans and enlisted his aid in notifying Wilkes of the exact time when the *Trent* left harbor. Late on the morning of November 8, then, the *San Jacinto* sat abroad the Bahama Channel when the *Trent* came into view. Some time after 1 P.M. the British steamer approached within a few hundred yards of Wilkes. He sent a shot across her bow. When the startled British captain failed to stop in response to the threat, Wilkes sent another shell close to the *Trent.* The steamer stopped at once.

Wilkes sent his executive officer aboard the *Trent* with written orders to take Mason, Slidell, and members of their official entourage. When he stepped aboard and made his mission known, Mason and Slidell readily came forward and identified themselves. Indeed, it may even appear that they were anxious for the capture to take place. When Slidell's daughter placed herself between Wilkes's armed men and the door to her father's cabin, he obligingly climbed out a window to be captured instead. Later in London Slidell's daughters left the impression "that the catching was voluntary." When Slidell's wife asked who commanded the *San Jacinto,* she exclaimed "Really. Captain Wilkes is playing into our hands!" Mason interrupted her immediately and changed the subject, perhaps because she unwittingly spoke the truth. The whole scene elsewhere was ugly, British and Southern passengers angrily crowding the Yankee sailors while the *Trent's* captain shouted promises that England would avenge the insult by destroying the Union blockade. A false step would certainly start shooting, but Wilkes eventually got the captives aboard the *San Jacinto* without violence. He could barely contain his elation at his prizes. That day, he would write in his diary, "has been one of the most important in my naval life."[14]

It nearly ended his naval life as well. The uproar in the international community was immediate and predictable. Certainly the news of it perturbed Charles Francis Adams. While he cared little for the legal niceties of the incident, he knew that he faced an enormous task in preventing it from bringing war. Almost at once Lord Russell summoned him to an interview, and Adams could predict what he would hear. Russell wanted to bring the matter to a head at once, for Americans "are very dangerous people to run away from," he said. Palmerston began preparations to increase British military strength. He believed that they should send a demand that Mason and Slidell be released at once, allowed to complete their journey, and that the United States should issue a formal apology. Otherwise they should break diplomatic relations. The British press expressed outrage, demanding apology or vengeance. "Englishmen can put up with bluster, but not with blows," said the Birmingham *Daily Post;* "A challenge has therefore deliberately been thrown down to this country."[15]

In the North, meanwhile, Wilkes received a hero's welcome, banquets feting him and even Congress approving his blow at the rebellion. Gideon Welles applauded the move, though lamenting that Wilkes had not taken the *Trent* in tow and brought it into a Northern port for a prize court's ruling on ship and passengers. That would have adhered more strictly to international law. Seward rejoiced, first in the move made against the Confederacy, and second that the matter of tacit British support of the South could be brought out in the open. Yet from the first he sought to avoid war and communicated that desire to Adams as well. For the Federal diplomat in London, by the end of November his hopes for averting conflict were dim. The press in England escalated in its outrage. Palmerston sent 8,000 soldiers to Canada and readied a fleet of warships. "This nation means to make war," wrote Adams's son. In December he found the air around the legation "would have gorged a glutton of gloom." Charles Francis Adams wrote to Seward frankly expecting that his mission soon would end.[16]

A few influential Britons defended the North against the storm. Others looked to France to mediate the difficulty, though few trusted Napoleon III to act selflessly. There was talk in the British cabinet of issuing an ultimatum to Lincoln and Seward. Release the commissioners or else, everyone feared it would say. Finally on December 21 Seward received the official British response. It was much less an ultimatum than feared, though Lord Lyons, British minister in Washington, preferred giving Seward that option of "surrender or war." "Unless we give our friends here a good lesson this time," he wrote to Russell, "we shall have the same trouble with them again very soon." Lincoln, who at first approved Wilkes's action, began to come under

13. *The essential man, Abraham Lincoln, a crafty, homespun, Machiavellian politician gifted with a limitless capacity to learn and grow. Taken May 20, 1860.* (U.S. Army Military History Institute)

14. *Wig in place, Gideon Welles of Connecticut ran Lincoln's navy department with imagination and resourcefulness, if a bit in conflict with some of the other cabinet officials. He was ever loyal to his President.* (Library of Congress)

15. *Lincoln's ablest diplomat, Charles Francis Adams, minister to Great Britain, the man who for two solid years tenderly tried to keep the Confederacy—and Seward—from forcing England and the Union to be enemies.* (Library of Congress)

16. *Confederate soldiers in camp. Men of the 9th Mississippi at Pensacola, Florida, early in 1861.* (State Photographic Archives, Strozier Library, Florida State University)

17. *General Joseph E. Johnston, gamecock Virginian who earned the lion's share of victory at First Manassas. First a bullet on the Peninsula and then his temperament would put him out of the war effectively until 1864.* (Author's collection)

18. *In the wake of Sumter, the North looked to new men to win the war. Some of them pose here in Washington late in 1861. From the left they are: Daniel Butterfield, William H. French, Samuel P. Heintzel-* *man, Andrew Porter, Irvin McDowell, George B. McClellan, George W. Morell, Don C. Buell, Louis Blenker, Silas Casey, and Fitz John Porter.* (Library of Congress)

19. *Part of the battlefield at Manassas, the first soil of Virginia to be nurtured with blood in the Civil War.* (Western Reserve Historical Society)

20. *Howell Cobb of Georgia, who declined ambitions for the Confederate presidency, gave Davis the oath of office, then took arms in Congress and on the battlefield.* (U. S. Army Military History Institute)

21. *The energetic and resourceful Confederate postmaster general, John H. Reagan of Texas. He built his department by stealing it almost intact from the Union and ran it at a profit.* (National Archives)

22. Richmond, Confederate capital, like Rome, a city on hills. And in Federal thinking, all roads must lead eventually to Richmond. (Kean

23. *Ulysses S. Grant as a major general. Here is the archetypical Westerner, tough, self-effacing, accustomed to failure, and more accustomed to not quitting. Belmont, Henry, Donelson, and Shiloh leave him, preparing him for the great work of opening the Mississippi.* (National Archives)

24. *The magnificent Western firebrand for union, Nathaniel Lyon. Ungiven to talk and diplomacy, he understood only action, and gave it to the Confederates until they killed him at Wilson's Creek.* (Library of Congress)

25. *The man who gave Lincoln only trouble, Major General John C. Frémont, once the Pathfinder, but in Missouri in 1861 an imperious and ineffective administrator.* (Library of Congress)

26. *Lincoln's Navy moved west with the building of gunboats and river ironclads. Here the converted steamer USS* Tyler *lies tied at the bank for repairs. Not very well protected these ships still gave Grant good aid in 1862.* (U. S. Naval Historical Center)

27. *A Pook "turtle," the USS* Mound City, *built in St. Louis by James B. Eads.* (U. S. Naval Historical Center)

28. *An ironclad fleet on the Mississippi. From the left, the Baron De Kalb, the Cincinnati, and the Mound City, "city" class gunboats that did the bulk of the river fighting.* (U. S. Army Military History Institute)

29. A man who helped cause a diplomatic storm, Raphael Semmes of the Confederate commerce raiders Sumter *and* Alabama. *His skill—and British assistance—embarrassed Union captains and strained relations between England and the North.* (Library of Congress)

Semmes's superior, Confederate Secre-
y of the Navy Stephen R. Mallory, an
ovative administrator who early rec-
ized the value of privateers and of
nclads. (U. S. Army Military History
titute)

31. *Union Secretary of State William H. Seward, acting the diplomat. He stands at far right, in company with several ministers from Great Britain, Russia, Nicaragua, France, Italy, and Sweden.* (National Archives)

32. *Mallory put the mighty new ironclad* Virginia *in the hands of a lifetime seaman of the old Navy, Admiral Franklin Buchanan. Buchanan's brother was paymaster aboard the* Congress, *which was sunk by the* Virginia. (Museum of the City of Mobile)

33. *Two of her officers survey the turret of the original* Monitor *in the summer of 1862. Dents from the* Virginia's *shot show clearly.* (U. S. Army Military History Institute)

34. *A very unlikable man, Secretary o_
*War Edwin M. Stanton replaced the co-
rupt and incompetent Simon Cameron.
Indefatigable, contentious, humorless,
Stanton is Lincoln's ablest administrato_*
(National Archives)

35. *Captain, later Admiral, David G. Farragut, the Tennesseean who, seemingly too
old for service, became Lincoln's most
loyal and effective seaman. His foster
brother David Porter constantly con-
spires against him.* (Library of Congress)

36. Farragut's mighty ship, the USS Hartford. Much of the naval tradition of the Civil War will be made by this ship. (Naval Photographic Center)

37. *General Mansfield Lovell, ill-fated de fender of New Orleans. Richmond left him too little to hold the city, then never trusted him again after its loss.* (Library of Congress)

38. *Commander George N. Hollins, who tried his best to save New Orleans, gave the South its first naval victory and was removed from command for his trouble.* (U. S. Army Military History Institute)

heavy pressure to release Mason and Slidell. Yet to do so, as he and Seward realized, would be to admit that the United States had been in the wrong. That they could not do. Lyons thought he detected in Seward an anxiety to give up the Confederates "if he can manage to do so without injury to his personal reputation in the Country."

There was tremendous suspense on both sides of the Atlantic awaiting Seward's response to the ultimatum. Lincoln and his cabinet met on Christmas day to decide the matter, and a solution was reached that it was hoped would soothe British pride and end the confrontation without a consequent loss of face for the Union. Russell wanted an apology from the North, along with the release of Mason and Slidell. Would the British settle for a statement that Wilkes acted without authority from his government? That would dissociate Seward and Lincoln from the act altogether, and make the surrender of the Confederates not a defeat for the nation, but rather merely the setting right of a wrong done by a subordinate. The British would accept that posture. And so on December 26 Seward notified Lyons that Mason and Slidell would be released. They even, thanks to a suggestion from Adams, managed to make it appear that the release in fact had its origins in an American policy of long standing. Thus Seward did not give in to Russell, but rather to his own law that not Wilkes, but a prize tribunal, should judge the legality of his seizure of the envoys. They were thin straws to cling to, but they helped save face, particularly at home where Northern public opinion was decidedly against releasing the captives.[17]

Fortunately, the North reacted well to the release on the grounds Seward quoted to Lyons. "The great principles of maritime law to which the United States has always adhered," said the New York Times, "are worth to us a thousand-fold more than the persons of Mason and Slidell." The diplomatic community in Washington applauded the release. Poor Captain Wilkes, vehement to the end, felt betrayed. He would do it all again, he declared, for he seemed to believe that bringing war with Great Britain would not ensure the Confederacy's survival but, rather, would call upon the old ties of blood and sentiment to unite the South with the North in defense of the American continent. As for the Confederates, they were depressed, for almost to a man they looked upon the episode as their certain route to recognition and intervention. Now it was all gone and in a surprisingly brief time the whole matter was nearly forgotten as Anglo-American relations resumed their normal stable, if distant, tenor. A clerk in the Richmond war department lamented that "now we must depend upon our own strong arms." Poor Slidell, while appreciating the small French influence in bringing about his release, still would say that "I had always regretted it, because if we had not been given up, it would have caused a war with England."

Captain Wilkes never got another significant command, but he con-

tinued to be a troublesome subordinate. Finally in 1864 he would be
court martialed for, among other things, further violations of neutrality. He had promised to do the same thing all over again, and apparently he tried.

The lesson of the *Trent* affair was lost at the time on both antagonists, North and South. Each believed in large part that Great Britain
really wanted to go to war with the Union. There could hardly have
been a better excuse to do so than Wilkes's provocation, yet during
the month-long crisis that followed, and despite heated passions in the
country and even in the government, Palmerston's administration
relied on diplomacy. They did not have to give Seward and Adams a
chance to relieve the situation. That they did shows what Davis could
not see, and what Seward only partially suspected. Despite King Cotton, despite interrupted merchant trade, despite the *Trent* problem,
Great Britain did not *want* to go to war with the North. It was that
simple. Such a conflict stood to gain her nothing, and the effort
required would have been enormous, something that no Confederate
seems ever to have thought through carefully. Any Anglo-American
war would not be fought in Britain. It would come either in Canada
or on the sea, and chiefly at first along the blockaded Southern coast.
That meant a supply line three thousand miles long. The mere movement of men and equipment in numbers sufficient to combat the
Union posed daunting logistical problems. The Union, despite its
heavy involvement in the war by late 1861, did not have half of its actual resources committed. There was more than enough reserve in
Northern manpower, industry, and determination, to field an army of
100,000 or more to defend itself against Britain. Yet for that nation to
send a like force to America was practically impossible with her other
commitments of empire around the globe. England could not win in
America. She had lost once before, admitted a status quo defeat in
1814, and to renew another American war would risk losing Canada if
Northern arms proved victorious. Even had the Palmerston government
gone to war over the *Trent* affair, it is still no guarantee that Britain
would at the same time have made common cause with the Confederacy. Britain acted solely in self-interest. Protest over the seizure of
Mason and Slidell did not at all involve the fact that they were taken,
only that they were taken from a British ship by force. The Confederate States had yet to prove that it could sustain its existence on its
own, and until it did England would not intervene. In short, the *Trent*
affair may have strained relations between the North and England but
at no time did it in fact improve chances of Confederate recognition. It
was a situation symptomatic of the entire course of the Union's relationship with John Bull. Many times he and America would heat each
other's passions, yet in every case the issue was only war between the
two, not alliance with the South. Davis would never understand.[18]

But though this crisis calmed through diplomacy, through the pacificating influence of Adams and Seward, more problems would come to replace it. Just as Seward could proudly proclaim the matter of the *Trent* done, Gideon Welles discovered the matter of the *Oreto*, then abuilding in a Liverpool shipyard. She had been contracted by the Confederate purchasing agents in England, and she was destined to be another commerce raider in the mold of the *Sumter*. That would mean more ships withdrawn from his blockade, more Northern commerce gone to the bottom, and more cause for friction with Great Britain. The *Oreto* would excite few passions in the months to come, but renamed the CSS *Florida* she would ignite the Atlantic, and set new flame to the ever smoldering relations between the two great English-speaking nations.

CHAPTER 11

"I CAN DO IT ALL"

Old soldiers pretended little understanding of diplomacy, particularly when the issues related to their webfooted friends in the navy. Joseph E. Johnston, certainly, showed small interest in the efforts of Mason and Slidell. As 1862 came into bloom he looked far more to divine the intentions of Lincoln and McClellan. The months after Manassas had been a peculiar time, a season of waiting, of change and maturing, and of grueling uncertainty.

For one thing, the Virginian felt very unsure about the President of the Confederacy, Jefferson Davis. The man was meddlesome, prone to lecture and interfere, at times frankly insulting. And there was discontent in the army. "Mr. Davis and the peculiar people he trusts have given cause for every gentleman in the army to mutiny," complained a Georgian. Johnston shared the restive feeling.[1]

He argued with Davis over rank. In the Old Army he had outranked in grade and seniority Samuel Cooper, A. S. Johnston, and Robert E. Lee. However, on August 31, Davis sent Congress recommendations proposing all four gentlemen plus Beauregard for the rank of full general, yet dating them such that Johnston stood fourth in seniority behind men he had commanded in previous days. He protested vigorously to the President. "It is plain," he wrote, "that this is a blow aimed at me only." His "fair fame as a soldier and as a man" was tarnished. Worse, he was reduced in seniority from first general to fourth "for the benefit of persons neither of whom has yet struck a blow for the Confederacy." True. Cooper would never lead in battle. As senior officer of the Confederate service this sixty-three-year-old New Yorker, brother-in-law of James M. Mason, would serve out the war as adjutant and inspector general in Richmond. A. S. Johnston had only Davis's high regard as a recommendation. Kentucky and Shiloh all lay months in the future. As for Lee, he remained an unknown.

Johnston's protest hardly endeared him to Davis. The President pronounced the general's complaints "utterly one-sided" and "as unfounded as they are unbecoming." Criticism was no way to win Johnston's affection. The correspondence ended on that note and Johnston remained the fourth ranking general, third after the death of the other Johnston at Shiloh. He never forgave Davis; Davis never forgave Johnston—and may have disliked him even before the war began—and the pettiness of both men cost the Confederacy dearly in divided counsels. Their time spent fighting each other were better directed at their enemies.[2]

Those enemies had been busy since Manassas. The Union Army that retreated in rout from Bull Run carried more than a tale of defeat. It brought the breath of change to the whole attitude of the North toward this war. In the wake of the demoralization came insight. This would be no summer's conflict. Out of the panic and humiliation of defeat came resolve. McDowell, an unfortunate man forced by expedience to start too soon with too little, had to be replaced, not as a punishment, but to remove the stigma of the battle lost from the high command. Unsuccessful generals in this war will not last long unless they have powerful political connections or, like some in the South, are close friends of Jefferson Davis. McDowell met neither test. Sherman had predicted before Bull Run that it would not do to receive too high a place too soon, for the early commanders were destined to fall by the way as new armies tried new kinds of warfare on what was to Americans a new scale. There would be a second level of men, however, who would rise in their place. That was where he expected to be. As a member of that second echelon he served first McDowell and then for a time in Kentucky the man who would come to take McDowell's place, another hero from the West. George Brinton McClellan.

He made a baffling hero, for he had done nothing, or very little, to earn such a reputation except violate Kentucky's neutrality and take credit for a battle won by another. Some cited his refusal to acknowledge Magoffin's neutrality decree in the Bluegrass State as a major factor in holding Kentucky in the Union. In fact it meant little. The voters decided the matter some time before when they elected a Union majority to the assembly. McClellan's action in sending soldiers from Ohio into the state was more provocation than preservation. And in western Virginia, largely Unionist in sentiment, his subordinate

William S. Rosecrans won a little battle at Rich Mountain on July 11, 1861, that drove the Confederates out of the area and protected the vital East-West link of the Baltimore and Ohio Railroad. McClellan took the credit for the victory and when, ten days later, McDowell met defeat, McClellan was the only "hero" the Union war department had at hand to replace him. He proved a mixed blessing.

It is undeniable that McClellan was a remarkable man, the Northern counterpart of Beauregard in many ways, and certainly in flair, élan, and ego. He came from Philadelphia, thirty-four years old, short, dark, of genuine military bearing, a man in many fields of true genius. He matriculated second in his class at West Point in 1846, some distance ahead of classmates Thomas J. Jackson and George E. Pickett. Assigned to the elite engineers, he won promotion and plaudits for bravery in Mexico. He taught at the Military Academy, turned Western explorer, observed the Crimean War for the war department, and designed the standard cavalry saddle. Yet in 1857 he tired of army life when just thirty and became chief engineer of an Illinois railroad. In the rush for volunteers following Sumter, he was living in Ohio and immediately obtained a commission as major general of state militia. Then came Kentucky, Rich Mountain, and a summons from Lincoln.

There were deep personality defects in McClellan that no one could yet see, and which he certainly did not acknowledge himself. Above all was his towering conceit. It was said of him that he "would have been a better man had he encountered some humbling reverses in his early years." Grant knew humility and humiliation. So did Sherman. Truly to understand and cope with success and use it well, a man first must understand failure. Yet McClellan never suffered a setback from childhood, was rather the darling of every situation. His brief campaign in western Virginia, with Rosecrans actually commanding on the field, brought an easy victory. Everything came easily to him, too easily. By the time he received Lincoln's summons to Washington, McClellan took his lifelong success for granted as his due. He was hardly surprised, then, to be offered command of the Division of the Potomac in McDowell's place. Nor was he surprised, as he wrote his wife, to find that "By some strange operation of magic I seem to have become the power of the land." So insensible was he to his own outrageously egotistical posturings that years after the war he published his wartime letters to his wife, braggadocio and all. When critics found him vainglorious he was truly bewildered.[3]

Beneath his pomp and show, however, McClellan possessed the one trait that Lincoln needed most in the fall of 1861. He was confident. Supremely so. McClellan could not lose. It was simply unthinkable. He instilled that same spirit in the demoralized remnants of the Bull Run army. He labored incessantly to reorganize, retrain, remold. Volunteers were a special sort of soldier, and McClellan understood them far better than most of the old Regular Army men. Their confidence had to be won, their loyalty earned, their obedience and discipline built by example, not simply by orders. Here was his genius. No one, not Scott, nor McDowell, nor Lincoln, not even Grant or Sherman, understood the American volunteer as did "Little Mac." It enabled him to build of this oft-troublesome stuff the remarkable Army of the Potomac, an army created almost in his image, yet as unlike him as night from day. It would know defeat and failure and humiliation. But never again would it know panic. It had hard years ahead that would mature it in the blood of loss after loss before its time came for victory. It learned to accept defeat as part of war. McClellan would not. His losses must be the losses of others. His defeats the responsibility of his superiors. He, like Joseph E. Johnston, would get in the way of his own reputation. Nurtured in fame and success, he, too, would rather do nothing than risk taking "a shot" and missing.

Johnston knew McClellan well from Old Army days. They had been close friends despite the disparity in their ages. "Beloved Mc" Johnston called him. The two had even talked of a filibustering expedition to Mexico in the late 1850s. They hardly ever expected to be antagonists. But when Lincoln brought Little Mac to the East, he wanted nothing else.

McClellan immediately clashed with old General Scott, and finally maneuvered him out of the picture entirely. Lincoln allowed Scott to retire gracefully, and on November 1, 1861, McClellan became general-in-chief. That same day the President visited the new commander and spoke with him about the enormous responsibility placed with him. "I can do it all," said McClellan. Lincoln visited him almost daily, urging planning and action, sometimes himself suggesting strategy for an offensive against Johnston's Confederates around Centreville. Once old General Heintzelman met with them while Lincoln pored over a map of the Old Dominion. When the President left, his contemptuous little gamecock general said to Heintzelman, "Isn't he a rare bird?"[4]

The "rare bird" was a good deal more intelligent than McClellan suspected. He knew for one thing that an enemy had to be met to be defeated, yet now the general took a genuine dislike to him. "The original gorrilla," he called Lincoln in letters to his wife. He quarreled with the President's making civil policy that he did not care for. He actually snubbed Lincoln on at least one visit the President made to his headquarters, and even as he assumed supreme command of the Union armies he was already allowing Democratic politicians to court him for their presidential nomination for 1864. Being hailed as the David who would lead the Union to victory against the philistine Confederates, McClellan seemed already captured by the comparison. David, after all, had become king.

Repeatedly Lincoln pressed for action, as well as for a coordinated

plan for the whole war effort. He wanted the Mississippi seized, first
New Orleans, then Vicksburg. That would divide the South. He
wanted an advance on Nashville by the army in Kentucky now under
Buell. And he wanted McClellan to move against his old friend Johnston. Little Mac, however, consistently raised demurs. He was too
weak. His army was not ready. Johnston was too strong, too well entrenched. The Army of the Potomac must be bigger, stronger. His intelligence reported Johnston as having up to 100,000 men to McClellan's 75,000. The coming of winter made movements difficult. Soon,
instead of looking toward a direct advance against Centreville,
McClellan turned his thoughts to putting his army on ships, taking it
to Fort Monroe, then up the Rappahannock to a point below Richmond, and marching on and bloodlessly capturing the Confederate
capital. As the winter progressed, and as Lincoln's puzzlement with
his general's sloth mounted, McClellan further refined his ideas, but
failed intentionally to take the President into his confidence, thinking
him a fool. At the same time he was already showing a trait that
would mark his generalship. He consistently and grossly exaggerated
the numbers of the enemy in his front. Increasingly he showed a
reluctance to advance, to take a risk. Instead, he planned, and begged
for more, and believed increasingly that powers in Washington deliberately withheld from him the numbers that he needed to win. Ever
mindful of his reputation, he built the case for his own exoneration
from defeat long before he ever moved toward a battle. "I have a set
of men to deal with unscrupulous and false," he told his wife; "if possible they will throw whatever blame there is on my shoulders, and I
do not intend to be sacrificed by such people."[5]

Meanwhile he planned, and showed his innovative sense in the nature of his grand plan for all Union armies. He proposed the most
comprehensive combined operation of land and naval forces that this
war would produce, calling for Foote and Halleck to move south from
Cairo to take Memphis and Corinth, while Butler and Farragut took
New Orleans and moved up the Mississippi to join the others in
pinching Vicksburg. Buell was to advance against Nashville and
Knoxville, on to Chattanooga, then take Atlanta, being joined there by
the forces of Thomas W. Sherman to advance on Montgomery. In the
East he would send a corps under Burnside by sea to Roanoke Island,
then to New Bern, and on to Raleigh. There were some novel ideas
here. First, he avoided meeting in battle the Confederacy's principal
army in Virginia. Rather, the plan separated the rest of the South
from the Old Dominion. McClellan would always believe that a war
could be won by maneuver without risking pitched battle. It may
have stemmed in part from the fact that he loved the army he had
raised too much to send it to death. Second, his plan recognized the
importance of railroads and provided for the disruption of all of the
South's major lines, not just by seizing their termini, but by cutting
them at the middle.[6]

The problem with the strategy, as with all of McClellan's thinking, is that he based it on a desire to win easily, as he had always won things before, without risking his army and his reputation. Unfortunately, Lincoln forced him to risk both, and McClellan never forgave him.

The pressure for McClellan to move against the enemy became intense by January 1862. First there were political factors. This would be an election year. The Republican party needed a victory to lend prestige to its administration. The stain of Bull Run had to be erased. Too, the populace was becoming restive. The continuing presence of an enemy army within miles of the Federal capital was an insult. And there were those with fears that if the Union Army did not soon move against the Rebels, its commander might instead lead it against Washington. McClellan was a Democrat, a loud one, and intemperately declared more than once his lack of sympathy with the administration on political matters. The radical Republicans, the more extreme fringe of the party, feared that Little Mac coveted dictatorship. "I would cheerfully take the dictatorship," he wrote to his wife in August 1861 in response to such talk. To a subordinate he confided that "I understand there is a good deal of talk of making a dictatorship." "It's me they're talking of," he added. In fact, as life had made him an elitist, so now that elitism made him a potential demagogue. He developed a genuine contempt for democracy and for the constitutional authority that gave civil government power over the military. It made him the most dangerous man in America. He stood at the head of the largest army on the continent, its men as loyal to him as to the Union, and his officers more so. His personal dislike for Lincoln, and his contempt for the Republicans then in power, offered powerful goads to his burgeoning megalomania. George McClellan was not a bad man, not a man of ill will or malevolent motive. The welfare of the country as *he* saw it impelled him in his course. Nevertheless, in the year that he held supreme command in the North, the future and very existence of democratic constitutional government in the United States faced the greatest peril of its career.[7]

Finally Lincoln could wait no more. On January 10, 1862, with McClellan ailing, Lincoln met with other generals asking for a plan of action, stating that as Little Mac did not seem intent on using this mighty army, he would like to borrow it. The news healed McClellan in a hurry, further strained relations, but got some armies moving. Buell set afoot the Mill Springs operation, and Halleck let Grant move against Fort Henry. That left only the Army of the Potomac inactive. On January 27 Lincoln gave McClellan a direct order. On Washington's birthday next the army must advance, and he wanted McClellan to move overland against Manassas. This stirred the general to action at last. He declined the President's suggested operation, and finally revealed his amphibious plan instead. Lincoln, not entirely convinced, still approved it. Any action was better than none. All at once the general's attitude toward the President changed or seemed to. He became almost obsequious. "Your confidence has upheld me when I should otherwise have felt weak," lied McClellan. He was playing a game. Now that his pet idea was going ahead, he needed Lincoln's friendship in order to get cooperation in building his army even larger. Too, he may have seen in the Rail Splitter a useful ally against the Republicans now talking openly of replacing him. It is doubtful that Lincoln was fooled by his duplicity, but one of the President's greatest strengths was his willingness to overlook personal indignities, even insults, from people of whom he expected great ends. Even then in March, with the general on the eve of embarking for the great campaign, Lincoln still had to ask him personally for an assurance of his loyalty in the face of repeated rumors of dictatorship and treason.[8]

Of course, the whole problem may simply have been that McClellan did not want to go into battle against his oldest and dearest friend, Joe Johnston. Certainly Johnston did not want to meet McClellan, at least on the Potomac line around Centreville. He had barely 47,000 soldiers—not the 100,000 and more believed by Little Mac— and of those he had sent 6,000 to the Shenandoah under Jackson to threaten the enemy and attract troops away from the main Federal Army. Five thousand other Confederates were on the lower Potomac. Johnston, commanding 36,000 around Centreville, knew he could not resist an attack. It took powerful argument to persuade President Davis, but late in February Johnston won approval to withdraw his army south to the Rappahannock River near Fredericksburg. This put him midway between Washington and Richmond, in good position to attack the one and protect the other, and the river itself made an excellent line of defense. Johnston anticipated four avenues of possible Federal movement against him, two of them by way of the Chesapeake and the Rappahannock, almost exactly McClellan's planned route. Consequently, Johnston soon moved south yet one river more, to the Rapidan. Without the Confederate's knowing it, this move thwarted McClellan's original intent to invade by the Rappahannock, since Johnston would now be between him and Richmond. Instead McClellan had to adapt his plan one river to the south as well, to the York. The upset only compounded an already bad situation for Little Mac. On March 11 Lincoln relieved him as general-in-chief, leaving him only the command of the Army of the Potomac. Lincoln did so to make sure that the general's only concern would be the army he led, not affairs elsewhere. McClellan pretended to understand, and renewed his hollow-sounding pledge of fealty.[9]

On March 17 the Army of the Potomac began leaving Alexandria aboard the steamers and transports that would take it to Fort Monroe and on up the James and York rivers. The fort would be his base. He would move his army by river to West Point on the York and, using that as his land base of operations, move against Richmond. However, to reach West Point he must first take control of the York, and that meant capturing or destroying the powerful Confederate water batteries on the river's mouth at Yorktown. He proposed to move his army from Fort Monroe overland to take Yorktown from the rear while naval support battered the water defenses. It could be done quickly, in less than a day he thought. It took a month.

Simply, the operation was far more complex than the general believed. No one had experience with a combined movement of this magnitude. The Port Royal attack was small in comparison, and Grant's attacks at Henry and Donelson were of a different character entirely. McClellan was making new military history here, and it was not as easy as inventing a saddle.

Little Mac landed his first divisions at Fort Monroe on March 23, but delays commenced at once. First and most galling was more interference from Lincoln. The President only agreed to this move up what was called the Peninsula in Virginia, on the condition that McClellan leave a sufficient force in Washington to defend against Johnston. With most of the Army of the Potomac marching along the York, the capital stood virtually open to attack by the enemy. McClellan promised, but only to quiet the President. When Lincoln learned that far fewer soldiers were left than he was led to believe, he arbitrarily withheld McDowell's army corps from sailing for Fort Monroe. In fact, McClellan did leave Washington secure from any threat that Johnston could mount. Little Mac correctly divined that as soon as he landed on the Peninsula, all thought of a Confederate attack would be lost in the rush to defend Richmond instead. Even without McDowell, McClellan still had 100,000 troops, yet at once he began crying that he was outnumbered, laying the groundwork for his exculpation should he meet with reverse.

Logistical problems further delayed the advance on Yorktown. Finally, on April 4 McClellan began to approach the little town, defended by a bare 15,000 Confederates under the splendiferous Major General John Bankhead "Prince John" Magruder. He would turn fifty-five in the next month's operations, tall and handsome, more talented than most gave him due, hampered chiefly by his own towering conceit. Yet he gave McClellan his match and more. On March 27, with the threat of a Peninsular movement evident, Davis ordered Johnston to leave the Rapidan line and come to Yorktown to reinforce Magruder. It would be April 12 before real reinforcements began reaching Yorktown. Until then Magruder brilliantly feinted McClellan into thinking that his 15,000 men were in fact more like 50,000. Magruder planted imitation cannon, "Quaker guns," logs painted black and intended to exaggerate the Federals' idea of his armament. He paraded his little brigades back and forth to give the image of more numbers than he really had, and the ever timid McClellan was only too ready to believe him. As soon as he reached the vicinity of

Magruder's outer defenses on April 5, McClellan decided that he could not assault. Instead he must lay siege. With at least 75,000 of his army at or near the front, he could have walked over Yorktown in an afternoon. Rather, he sacrificed the surprise he had gained on the enemy and the momentum of his own campaign. Without even a sortie to test the depth or resilience of Magruder's pitiful defenses, Little Mac decided they were too strong. Instead of seeking weaknesses in the Yorktown line, he began at once to look for excuses.

One came immediately to mind, and it was the only justifiable explanation he could offer. The navy did not do its part at Yorktown. Well before he set the campaign in motion, McClellan got an assurance from the navy that he would have the cooperation of a fleet on the York River to reduce Yorktown's water batteries and provide a diversion for his land attack. Such a fleet was now denied him thanks to an ironclad monster that sent the same sort of paranoid chills through Lincoln in Washington that Magruder's wooden smoothbores did to McClellan on the Peninsula. The USS *Merrimack* had metamorphosed into the CSS *Virginia*, and she was loose in Hampton Roads.

Mallory's ironclad ship rushed to completion despite a host of unfinished tasks aboard her. On February 24, 1862, old Franklin Buchanan took command of the ship. "The *Virginia* is a novelty in naval construction," he admitted, but Mallory pressed him to be bold with her. "Action, prompt and successful action," said the secretary, "now would be of serious importance to our cause."[10]

By March 4 most of the ship was ready, and three days later her magazine finally lay filled. Buchanan planned his attack. The Federal naval forces out in Hampton Roads numbered several substantial ships, chiefly the *Cumberland, Congress, Roanoke, Minnesota,* and *St. Lawrence.* He intended to steam out into the Roads at dawn on March 8, attack and sink the first two, anchored well inside the Roads, and then shell Federal shore batteries above Fort Monroe. Even as he awaited the dawn, a more ambitious suggestion came from Mallory. Destroy the fleet in Hampton Roads, it said, then slip out of the Chesapeake and up the coastline to New York Harbor, there to "shell and burn the city and the shipping." The utter folly of such a suggestion escaped Mallory, and perhaps even Buchanan.[11]

With the dawn, March 8, 1862, Buchanan and crew raised steam, and at 11 A.M. cast off and moved slowly down the Elizabeth River toward the enemy fleet. Workmen tinkered right to the final minute, the last of them jumping off only as the ironclad cleared the dock. The people of Norfolk lined the banks to watch the monster move toward her destiny. The day's fight was expected to be a spectator event, and small boats loaded with civilians armed with binoculars and picnic hampers followed in the *Virginia's* wash. "Go on with your old metallic coffin!" shouted one bystander. "She will never amount to anything else!"[12]

She amounted to something that day. The men aboard thought they were off on a mere shakedown cruise. None but Buchanan and his first officer, Catesby ap Roger Jones, knew that they were to attack the Federal fleet. As soon as the ironclad entered the main channel leading into Hampton Roads and could see the enemy ships, Buchanan saw signal flags running up the masts of the frigates and sloops. Soon black clouds of smoke erupted from their funnels as the steamships began the slow task of firing their boilers. Buchanan stepped down to the gun deck, called all hands, and spoke to them. "In a few minutes you will have the long-expected opportunity to show your devotion to your country and our cause. Remember that you are about to strike for your country and your homes, your wives and your children." The world was watching, he said. "Beat to quarters."[13]

What followed shocked Hampton Roads, and Washington. The *Virginia* moved first toward the *Cumberland,* and her opening shot found its mark. The second shot destroyed an entire Federal gun crew. As the ironclad continued steaming straight toward the *Cumberland,* her course brought her abreast of the *Congress.* Glowing red hot shot went screaming from the *Virginia's* starboard battery, immediately starting several fires aboard the *Congress.* Even as her crew tried to save the severely damaged ship, the *Virginia's* crew maintained their course toward the *Cumberland,* finally driving the crude iron ram at her bow straight into the wooden ship's side below the waterline. When the ram struck the *Cumberland* at once began to sink, almost taking the ironclad down with her. Buchanan got his ship out, but left the ram in the bowels of his victim. For the next half hour he battered the sinking ship with his guns, while the Federals fought until the water reached the muzzles of their cannon. "She went down bravely, with her colors flying," said Jones. As the *Cumberland* settled on the bottom, her masts still protruded from the water, and those colors continued to fly throughout the day.[14]

The Confederates turned now to the injured *Congress.* While Lieutenant Joseph Smith, Jr., son of Commodore Smith of Welles's ironclad committee, attempted to get his ship to shoal water out of range of the *Virginia's* guns, an enemy shell fragment took off his head and shoulder. Within ten minutes Buchanan demolished the stern of the Federal frigate. His own brother McKean Buchanan was a paymaster aboard the blazing ship. Finally the *Congress* did run aground, but still within Buchanan's range, and finally her officers surrendered. But while Confederate officers were alongside the ship receiving the capitulation, shore batteries opened on them, and an enraged Buchanan ordered his gun crews to "Destroy that——ship!" They did. All that saved the *Minnesota* from a similar fate was the fact that she had run aground in shallow water in the Roads and Buchanan could not safely get to her in the dimming light of evening. He broke off the engagement, intending to return on the morrow and finish destroying the fleet.

But the morrow brought another monster. With incredible timing, the recently completed USS *Monitor* was just arriving under tow as the engagement finished. Still it was 9 P.M. when the ironclad entered Hampton Roads. Ahead she could see the burning *Congress.* "Our hearts were so very full," wrote the executive officer aboard, "and we vowed vengeance on the *Merrimac.*"[15]

Buchanan was not aboard the *Virginia* the next day. He took a painful wound on March 8, and now Jones commanded the ship. Neither expected what they found on returning to Hampton Roads. At first they did not know what the *Monitor* was. Some believed it to be a raft with a ship's boiler aboard. "An immense shingle floating in the water, with a gigantic cheese box rising from its center," thought one Confederate. Yet they soon saw steam and smoke escaping from her decks and knew that it was a ship. "She could not possibly have made her appearance at a more inopportune time," wrote Lieutenant John Taylor Wood, commanding one of the *Virginia's* guns.[16]

The *Monitor's* commander, John L. Worden, put his ironclad between the grounded *Minnesota* and the enemy. Jones still intended to battle the frigate but, finding that he could not get close enough in the shallow water, decided instead to give his undivided attention to the *Monitor.*

Theirs was a curious battle, lasting over two hours and accomplishing nothing. The turret on the Federal ironclad soon caused problems, being difficult to control in its turning. Finally they simply let it keep revolving slowly, and fired their guns "on the fly" as they came to bear on the *Virginia.* The Confederates' shot bounced harmlessly from the turret's rounded sides, causing nothing more than dents. Meanwhile, the *Monitor's* fire cracked several plates on the enemy's casemate. Then the *Virginia* ran aground and for several minutes the *Monitor* battered her from a position in which the enemy guns could not reply. Only getting the Rebel ironclad free and slowly moving again saved it from certain slow demolishment. With headway regained, Jones determined to ram the *Monitor,* not knowing that his ram was aboard the sunken *Cumberland.* The attempt failed, and fortunately, for crashing the *Virginia's* wooden bow against the iron sides of the *Monitor* might have been fatal for the wrong party. Worden's own attempt at ramming proved no more successful, and then he was injured when a shell struck the pilot house. The *Monitor* went out of action for half an hour and Jones, interpreting this as victory, steamed away to get back to Norfolk before the tide went out. Seeing the *Virginia* return up the Elizabeth River, the Federals believed that *they* had driven her away. Neither ship suffered serious damage, and both claimed the victory.

The repercussions North and South were phenomenal. Ironclad

fever swept the Union Navy with even greater virulence. The *Monitor* design had been proved, and many more were ordered from delighted contractors. Mallory, too, felt his vision vindicated. More Confederate ironclads would be built and, though their hulls varied greatly, most adopted the casemate design of the *Virginia*. Later in the war Mallory would even order a turreted vessel, recognizing the superiority of the *Monitor's* concept. Yet neither side learned the real lesson of Hampton Roads. The heavy, lumbering ironclads were useful only for defense and in coastal waters and harbors. The *Monitor's* voyage to Hampton Roads was almost a disaster in a moderate storm. In December of 1862 she was so unmanageable in more severe weather that she sank. The *Virginia*, meanwhile, drew so much water that she could barely maneuver in the Roads. The shallows and sandbars at the mouths of most of the Eastern rivers would certainly deny her access to the Northern ports she hoped to ravage. Should she get to sea, her erratic engine could hardly give her enough headway to maintain a course in any sort of foul weather. For purposes of offensive strategy, she was as useful as a battery on a barge. It did not require hindsight for her builders and officers to recognize these shortcomings, but the events of the next two months would make them plain. Unable to sortie into the Roads again with the *Monitor* there, Buchanan could not react to McClellan's movement to the Peninsula by taking his ship to the York to disrupt the Federal transports and support vessels there. The *Monitor*, too, did not again risk battle. The very fact of each knowing its inability to defeat the other kept them apart. And in May, when the *Virginia* had to get into the Roads to escape the Federals, who were retaking Norfolk, she encountered her greatest enemy, the mud, once more. In hopes of retreating up the James, her men had to lighten the ship for her to cross the sandbar at the river's mouth. It did not work, but the lightening exposed her wooden understructure. No longer an ironclad, and vulnerable to the advancing enemy, the *Virginia* ran aground and her crew destroyed her.

Yet however ineffectual the *Virginia* was as an offensive weapon, the imagined threat of her proved powerful indeed, and it kept the Union Navy from cooperating with McClellan in his Yorktown operation. Not until the Confederate ironclad lay on the bottom would the Navy risk its wooden ships. What happened to the *Congress* and *Cumberland* in the wide and generally maneuverable waters of Hampton Roads, could happen to many more vessels in the more constricted waters of the York. Denied his webfoot cooperation, McClellan had no choice but to make a land offensive against Magruder, an offensive that became a siege.

The siege lasted until May 4. Little Mac sent north for siege guns and began the laborious process of planting batteries and building earthworks, slowly extending his lines so that they might eventually completely encircle Magruder with his back to the York. Johnston meanwhile finally began sending his reinforcements into "Prince John's" lines and by mid-April Magruder was relatively secure. In fact, McClellan's sloth in trying to win a victory by the spade worked much to the enemy's advantage. It gave Johnston vital time to rear-range his forces in Virginia, bring all but a few to the Peninsula, and prepare for a defensive campaign on his own ground and his own terms. One fear Johnston had, and would always have, and that was losing an army by clinging too long to an untenable position. He would prefer always to give up ground and withdraw to better scenes. He wanted to abandon Yorktown early in the siege, but Davis and Lee persuaded him otherwise, and well so.

As the siege wore on, Johnston reinforced Magruder to the point that they combined about 53,000 men to face McClellan. They used local slaves in gangs to finish the earthworks, while Johnston attended the issues of feeding and clothing and reorganizing his army in the face of the enemy. By April 27, however, he had to tell Richmond that the Federals' preparations looked complete, and that Little Mac might attack at any time. Too, the Federal Navy had finally been willing to risk ships on the York, with the *Virginia* still effectively bottled in Hampton Roads. But the Union's heavy siege guns were to Johnston the deciding factor. "The fight for Yorktown, as I said in Richmond, must be one of artillery, in which we cannot win." It was time to pull out.[17]

Johnston began the movement late on May 3, under cover of a stiff artillery fire. Miraculously, he got his entire army and much of its equipment and supplies out without the enemy detecting the move-ment. Only the heaviest naval guns in the water batteries had to be abandoned. The next morning, when McClellan was finally ready to launch his much vaunted attack, there was no one there to meet him. Instead, in the wake of the enemy, the Federals found a new terror of war, land mines, called torpedoes and "infernal machines." Containers of gunpowder buried in the roads and earthworks, set to explode by trip wires. Even most Confederates found these hidden tools of death repugnant. Johnston did not know they had been planted, and when he learned of it immediately launched an investigation. He ordered that they not be used again, and they were not. For a time.

Time was the all-important matter to Johnston here on the Penin-sula. Magruder and McClellan bought him time at Yorktown. A rear-guard action at Williamsburg, the old colonial capital, on May 5 won more, though at the price of heavy casualties. As Johnston continued his retreat up the Peninsula in the face of an army that outnumbered him two-to-one by now, anything that gained him an extra week, an extra day, was a godsend. Now God sent him Stonewall Jackson, and Jackson sent him time. Both worked in mysterious ways.

CHAPTER 12

"GOD CROWNED OUR ARMS"

However brilliantly "Tom Fool" began the war at Manassas, it appeared by early 1862 to have gone a bit sour for him, more sour than the lemons he constantly chewed. After months of inactivity with the army camped around Centreville, Johnston had ordered Jackson to return to the Shenandoah. It had been designated a separate military district, a part of Johnston's overall Virginia command, and Jackson would command its nonexistent army. While Johnston remained nominally Jackson's superior, in fact "Old Blue Light" would be largely left to his own devices. He must raise an army, protect the valley from enemy invasion, and provide a diversion to keep McClellan from concentrating his entire army on Johnston. On November 5, 1861, Jackson formally assumed his new command of the Shenandoah Valley District at Winchester, and he embarked upon what only he and the Almighty could achieve.

The Shenandoah faced immediate and considerable threat as the general took over. In the northwest part of the state, outside the valley proper, some 4,000 Federals operating around Romney posed an easy threat to Winchester. Worse, Major General Nathaniel Banks, one of those fortunate politicians that Lincoln would make unfortunate generals, held a much larger Federal command in western Maryland, poised to strike at any time up the valley. Should the two enemy forces act in concert, the Shenandoah could not stand. Jackson had to keep them apart if he would save the valley, yet on taking command he found only 1,600 militia, widely scattered, and of dubious worth. Happily the war department anticipated his first request for reinforcements by sending him his old brigade, now called officially the Stonewall Brigade in honor of Manassas. Despite furious protests from Johnston, who regarded them as his best soldiers, the brigade left Centreville early in November to rejoin its beloved, if peculiar, commander.

Facing his military situation, Jackson decided to assume the offensive as soon as his strength warranted. Despite the obvious risk, it seemed the only sure way of keeping the Federals north and west of him from combining. In his first real expressed strategic thinking, Jackson told Richmond of a plan that marked well his insight. He would move on Romney and take it. This would first neutralize the smaller of the forces confronting him. It would give him control of the Baltimore and Ohio Railroad, which ran nearby, as well as two major roads. It would deceive McClellan into thinking that Johnston had weakened his army at Centreville more than he had in fact, and that deception could lure Little Mac into an early attack before his army grew too big. When the Federals did attack, then Jackson would be ready to repeat the glorious maneuver of July and race by train to Manassas to reinforce. "I deem it of very great importance that Northwestern Virginia be occupied by Confederate troops this winter," said Stonewall. "I know that what I have proposed will be an arduous undertaking," he said, but he and his little army were ready to make the sacrifice and take the risk.[1]

The Romney campaign did not turn out to be as great a risk as Jackson feared, but neither did he find there the success he hoped to achieve. By the end of 1861 Jackson had added another small "army" of 6,000 Confederates to his command led by General William W. Loring, a one-armed hero of the Mexican War called mysteriously "Old Blizzards." It may have indicated his temperament, which would soon clash with Stonewall's.

On New Year's Day, 1862, Jackson put his army of about 8,000 on the road to Romney. Almost at once contention erupted. Loring declined to have his three brigades made a part of Jackson's army. Rather, he insisted that orders from Richmond told him to cooperate with the Valley Army, not become a portion of it. Jackson reluctantly agreed, allowing the seeds of discord to be planted early. Worse, several days of warm weather lulled Jackson into leaving his heavy weather equipment behind in their slow wagons. Without overcoats, the men felt the returning cold bitterly. Jackson himself, growing chilly, turned to a bottle, the gift of an admirer in Winchester.

Though an abstainer, he believed that the bottle contained wine, which would drive away the chill. He put it to his lips and drank deeply, his staff watching him take great swallows without tasting. It was whiskey. Soon the general complained of being warm, then started talking with unwonted effusion on the fickle temperature in the valley. Probably for the only time in his life, he was nearly drunk.[2]

On January 4 Jackson took Bath, directly north of Winchester, and pushed its defenders back across the Potomac to Hancock, Maryland, where he shelled them for the next two days. It was a spearhead driven directly between the two enemy forces confronting him, a move designed to confuse them as to his intentions. Then on January 7 he turned southwest and moved directly for Romney. Three days later its defenders gave it up without a fight in the face of Jackson's advance. It was a case of mutual misunderstanding. The Federals, counting about 5,000 by now, believed Jackson terribly outnumbered them, and never intended to fight him. Stonewall, his army reduced to less than 7,000 effectives by the cold and sickness and rigors of the march, had himself just decided that he could not attack the town. With great relief he took the gift.

The ensuing winter spent in Romney was one of discontent. Loring protested Jackson's handling of his army to Richmond, and Jackson promptly sent forward his resignation. Richmond persuaded him to reconsider. Still Loring's command almost mutinied when Jackson himself returned to Winchester, and later the war department ordered Loring's men back into the valley as well, negating what Stonewall had won after three months' hard work. He wanted to return to his professorship at the Virginia Military Institute and leave the army to others. Richmond would not let him. Still, even though his first campaign proved bittersweet, and unhappy officers would continue to give him trouble for some time as a result, Jackson had accomplished much of what he sought. Already the enemy was reinforcing Banks at the expense of the Army of the Potomac, convinced that this valley army was a great host. Spring brought better days.

Yet it did not seem so at first. When Johnston retired from Manassas to the Rappahannock, Jackson had no choice but to withdraw from Winchester as well, falling back forty miles to Mount Jackson. Soon, however, he learned that the enemy had marched into the Shenandoah in his place and were shifting their forces east to Manassas. Intent on stopping this threat to Johnston's Rappahannock line, Jackson marched his army north thirty-five miles in a single day and a half and attacked Major General James Shields at Kernstown on March 23. Thanks to bad intelligence reports, Jackson thought he outnumbered the enemy. In fact they had him by almost three-to-one. Despite the odds Jackson gave Shields a severe testing before Federal strength took the day, forcing the Confederates to retire. Yet this tac-

tical defeat proved an enormous strategic victory. Shields believed a
huge enemy force had attacked him. So did Washington. Only days
later Lincoln decided to hold McDowell's corps around Washington
for fear of an attack from the valley. Reinforcements slated for
McClellan began going to Banks instead, and Banks was ordered to
pursue. Thus, even in a defeat and while retreating up the valley,
Jackson had begun his most brilliant season of the war.

In response to Kernstown Banks, instead of going to McClellan,
began a slow pursuit of Jackson, while Washington created two more
independent Federal commands to operate in the valley. One was
McDowell's corps, now the Department of the Rappahannock, and
the other the Mountain Department, once commanded by Rosecrans,
but now led by the troublesome alumnus of Missouri, John C.
Frémont. Already it becomes evident in the war that no matter how
incompetent or repeatedly beaten in the field, politicos with powerful
friends would continue turning up in new commands.

Banks, Frémont, and McDowell, all had but one task. Find and
stop Jackson. Stonewall, too, was reinforced with Richard S. Ewell's
division, giving him in all about 17,000 to confront well above 60,000
Federals whose purpose was his destruction. Audacious beyond belief,
and brilliant in his design, Stonewall chose to make an offensive campaign against the separate elements of the divided Union command
before they could combine against him. His first move was to stop
Frémont. The Pathfinder had sent a division toward Staunton, hoping
to link with Banks, who was still slowly advancing. Jackson left Ewell
to hold Banks in the lower valley, and with one division raced south
to Staunton, then east to McDowell, Virginia, where, with 10,000 Confederates, he repulsed an attack by about 6,000 of the enemy on May
8. With Frémont's people retreating back into western Virginia, Jackson turned once more to Banks. Using his cavalry under Turner
Ashby to screen his movements, Stonewall managed to combine almost 16,000 against a little post of barely 1,000 at Front Royal, destroying them on May 23. Since Front Royal controlled the principal
route up and down the valley, and since Banks was retreating down
the valley toward Winchester, Jackson now had a chance to cut him
off. Banks reached Winchester first, however, and on May 25 Jackson
attacked him. Outnumbering Banks two-to-one, Jackson put the
enemy to rout that Sunday, costing the Federals one fourth of their
army.

Now Frémont and McDowell began moving to converge in the valley south of Winchester to catch Jackson, while Banks, when he
stopped running, turned to move south again. Jackson was caught in
the middle between three forces totaling over 40,000. On May 30 he
left his old Stonewall Brigade facing Banks and moved south only to
find that the enemy pincers had almost cut off his line of retreat at

Strasburg. Calling in the Stonewall Brigade, Jackson barely escaped south of Strasburg before the road was cut.

Now the three enemy commanders followed Jackson up the valley, and in the sometimes heavy skirmishing the dashing Confederate cavalryman Ashby was killed. His mournful followers, when they had the chance, dressed the body in his best uniform, sat it in a chair, put flowers in Ashby's hands, and took his photograph. It was a sad moment for the Valley Army.

Yet two days later Jackson avenged Ashby's death when he caught Frémont at Cross Keys. The Federal attacked him. Though heavily outnumbered, Jackson's men held and forced the enemy to withdraw. The next day, June 9, Stonewall took Ewell's men to Port Republic to meet Shields's column. At first driven back, the Confederates finally held, then outflanked the enemy and defeated them.

With these two Federal setbacks, Frémont, Banks, and McDowell were called back, the former to Harrisonburg in the valley, and the others clear to Fredericksburg. The Union admitted its defeat in the Shenandoah. It was Stonewall's valley indisputably. In his thirty-eight-day campaign he fought five battles, marched roughly four hundred miles, and withheld four times his numbers from reinforcing McClellan on the Peninsula. In almost every engagement, though outnumbered overall, he managed to segment the enemy and attack on terms equal or advantageous to the South. "God crowned our arms with success," he reported to Richmond. It also helped immeasurably with the situation on the Peninsula, and Johnston expressed his gratitude. "I congratulate you upon your new victories and new titles to the thanks of the country and the army," he wrote to Jackson. That was a few days before Port Republic. Now Stonewall was needed on the Peninsula, and on June 11 came orders for him to leave the valley. They came from a new army commander, for Johnston lay in the painful bed of the wounded. Finally there had been battle on the Peninsula.[3]

In the days following the evacuation of Yorktown on May 4, Johnston pulled his army steadily back toward Richmond. He masked the movement as best he could with the army's cavalry, now commanded by Brigadier General J. E. B. Stuart. The battle, or heavy engagement, at Williamsburg was hailed North and South as a victory, but it accomplished little toward the goals of either side. Johnston bought time, but with substantial losses he could ill afford. It did, at least, give Confederate authorities some indication that Johnston was willing to fight, and at the same time it made an already excessively cautious McClellan even more timorous.

Yet Johnston too was fearful. With Yorktown gone, he dreaded the Federals moving troops up the York River by transport and landing them at any one of the several good places available in his flank and rear. That is what McClellan attempted to do on May 6, sending William B. Franklin's division upriver to land at Eltham's Landing,

which put them right on Johnston's vulnerable left flank. The next day
Johnston ordered Franklin attacked to hold him in place until the balance of the Confederate Army withdrew farther up the Peninsula,
between Franklin and Richmond. The maneuver worked, and a
delighted Johnston requested promotion for some of the men who
worked his will. Among them was Wade Hampton, well recovered
from his Manassas wound, and now a brigade commander. Johnston
saw in him a rising star, gave him a beautiful sword, and every
confidence. Accustomed to command as a planter, Hampton seemed
to make the transition to the military high echelon effortlessly. Yet already as well his boastful and sometimes superior manner cooled
those around him.[4]

No sooner did Johnston counter the threat to his left, however, than
his right presented an equal opportunity for trouble. The loss of Norfolk to the enemy on May 9 and the destruction of the *Virginia* on
May 11 opened the James River to Federal vessels as far north as
Drewry's Bluff, barely ten miles from Richmond, and well behind
Johnston's army. On May 15 the *Monitor,* the *Galena,* and several
other conventional vessels steamed up the James to the bluff and
there battled for four hours against the shore batteries. The *Galena*
was severely damaged, and the *Monitor,* because she could not elevate her guns sufficiently in the turret, proved ineffectual. The attack
failed and the Union flotilla retired. Yet it proved Johnston's point, repeatedly made, that his army was dangerously exposed by being on
the Peninsula at all. It should stand before Richmond, and there make
the battle on its own terms. Two days later most of Johnston's army
lay within three miles of the Confederate capital.

While panic spread through many homes in Richmond, Johnston
looked to concentrating his scattered commands in the rest of Virginia
here for the great effort to defeat McClellan. Richmond interfered, to
the point that Johnston actually asked to be relieved of his geographical command. Lee, now Davis's chief military adviser, managed
to calm Johnston's petulance, while the army commander himself
brought his forces even closer to the city and into a semicircle around
it. Thus he could meet an attack from the James, on the south,
McClellan advancing from the east, and McDowell should he come
south from Fredericksburg. Johnston intended from the first to fight a
defensive battle. He felt more comfortable doing so, and it helped
make up for the disparity in numbers with the enemy.

For the next two weeks Johnston waited, consulted reluctantly with
the President—whom he now despised—and with his onetime West
Point classmate Lee, whom he began to distrust. Johnston told them
as little as possible and resented any interference or even wise counsel. His similarities to the Union commander facing him on the Peninsula steadily mounted, though there is no indication that Johnston's
military conceit advanced to the point of flirtation with dictatorship.

Still his situation revealed, as did McClellan's, a major problem in these early days of the war. The Mexican War had been a small affair, pitiful by 1862 standards. This was the first major land war in America involving armies of great size and, more significantly, employing an officer corps composed of trained professional soldiers in high command. They were chiefly West Pointers, North and South. For the first time in a war, America had commanders who had made arms their careers for decades, men with a species of confidence in their own knowledge and ability and who resented interference from amateurs. Thus, for the first time too, the notion of a civilian commander-in-chief and civilian control of the armies, received its real tests. Men like McClellan, Johnston, Beauregard, Frémont, and others, clearly resented that restraint on their powers; and they posed serious challenges to the basic constitutional doctrine of both Union and Confederacy.

McClellan had cautiously followed Johnston as far as the Chickahominy River, which ran from a point several miles north of Richmond, in a southeasterly direction to flow into the James. Little Mac arrayed his army along the stream from Mechanicsville on the right to Bottom's Bridge on the left. Three corps occupied this line, while two other corps sat south of the river, separated from the rest of the army by the swollen stream. Johnston, despite his intention to act on the defensive, saw here an opportunity to attack the isolated corps of Heintzelman and Erasmus D. Keyes, barely 36,000 men. On May 31 Johnston launched a badly timed and poorly coordinated assault in the vicinity of Fair Oaks and Seven Pines. It was, in fact, the first major Confederate attack of the war in the East that involved real movement and coordination of large units. As a result, it was almost bound to be a learning affair for all concerned. Most of Johnston's brigade and division commanders had been mere regimental colonels at Manassas. For his part, Johnston gave unclear orders and, worse, failed to tell General Benjamin Huger that he was to take orders from General James Longstreet. Longstreet, meanwhile, a Georgian, was unfamiliar with this Virginia ground and, thanks to the added factor of miserable maps, easily got himself lost.

Keyes was in an exposed position between Seven Pines and Fair Oaks Station, inviting attack. Yet it was 1 P.M. before the division of Major General Daniel H. Hill struck Keyes's left. Longstreet, supposed to hit Keyes's center and right, wound up getting in Hill's way, and actually came partially into the battle on Hill's right, completely at the opposite end of the line from his assigned position. Ordered to assume overall guidance of the attack, Longstreet did not and further only used about half of his available strength and that in the same piecemeal fashion that had wastefully spent so many troops at Manassas. As a result, Keyes, though driven back, held long enough for Heintzelman to start getting reinforcements to him, as did Edwin

V. Sumner from across the Chickahominy. Keyes staved off rout, and by evening Johnston had lost any advantage. He lost more than that, too, for riding close to the firing line at Fair Oaks, he felt a bullet strike his right shoulder. Only moments later a shell fragment hit him in the chest and sent him reeling out of the saddle. President Davis was on the scene observing the battle, which people in Richmond could hear with considerable anxiety. He came to the wounded general. Johnston regained consciousness, smiled at Davis, then immediately sent an aide back to recover his horse. The animal carried his pistols and, more, the sword his father had worn through the Revolution. "I would not lose it for $10,000," said Johnston, and it was happily found. Across the lines private George Tainter of the 16th Massachusetts was less happy. He had two teeth pulled. Angered at the glee of his onlooking comrades, he rammed his molars down his rifle and fired them at the enemy.[5]

As Johnston was carried from the field, command of the army went temporarily to Major General Gustavus W. Smith, a Kentuckian, West Pointer, and next ranking officer. Smith and Davis took an almost immediate dislike to each other. Repeatedly the President asked Smith what his plans were. The general, who until that moment had no occasion to make any plans for an army he did not expect to be commanding, said that he must first find what had been happening at all points on the line. "Mr. Davis did not seem pleased with what I said," recalled Smith. Indeed, years later the President would give the indication that he in fact assumed direction of the Confederate Army.[6]

Smith's tenure was a brief one. The next morning, June 1, 1862, he resumed the offensive by ordering Longstreet to attack once more. With no more success than the day before, Longstreet met repulse by the now much strengthened Federals. Johnston would always later assert that only darkness the day before prevented victory, but that was nonsense. His own failings in improperly preparing for the attack stood chiefly at fault, but the Virginian could never admit that. He had taken "a shot," failed, and soon worked stealthily from his sickbed to lay the responsibility on others. Longstreet was most culpable, but as a favorite of Johnston's he was safe. Instead, they conspired together, along with Smith, to ignore misunderstandings of their own and put blame for the bungled attack on Huger. It was a harbinger of things to come from many commanders in this war. So enamored of their own reputations that they could not take responsibility for their own failures, these fell shepherds would create a veritable flock of scapegoats.

Poor Smith, it appears, could not handle his new responsibility. Already ill during much of the previous month, he found it difficult to think clearly on June 1 and did not manage his troops well. Under fire he was remarkably calm, but responsibility overwhelmed him. On June 2 his nerves began to shatter. Partial paralysis set in, and Smith's adjutant feared that "the case is critical and the danger imminent." Smith recovered when removed from the army in the field, but he would spend much of the rest of his life denying what had happened and the reasons for it.[7]

Davis already knew who his new commander would be for the army. He never intended Smith as more than a temporary leader. This Virginia army must be led by a Virginian. On May 31, as they left the battlefield, Davis confided to Lee that on the morrow he was to take the command. When Johnston heard the news he reportedly expressed the view that "The shot that struck me down is the very best that has been fired for the Southern cause yet. For I possess in no degree the confidence of our government, and now they have in my place one who does possess it." His sentiment appears to have been genuine. Certainly Lee's solicitation for his badly wounded friend was not feigned. Years before in Mexico he could write flippantly of how a bit of lead did his friend good. They were younger then. Now, he said, "I am so grieved at the general's wound." He feared that he would not live up to Johnston's leadership. "I wish I was able, or that his mantle had fallen on an abler man," wrote Lee on June 2. There were not a few in the Confederacy who felt the same way.[8]

Lee's reputation just then was not of the best. Indeed, at the very first of the war even his loyalty was seriously questioned, and by people in high places. Governor Francis Pickens of South Carolina declared in July 1861 that "Lee is not with us at heart, or he is a common man, with good looks, and too cautious for practical Revolution." Lee was not a slaveholder, having manumitted the blacks inherited from his family, and further he had strong ties to the Union. Never a secessionist, he left the Old Army only when Virginia seceded, and then with heartbreaking reluctance. He had played, from his post in Richmond, a major role in building the Confederate Army at Centreville and Manassas that defeated McDowell, then later went to the mountains of western Virginia after the defeat at Rich Mountain. His brief tenure there brought no glory. The heavy Union sentiment in the mountain counties of the state would ever foil Confederate commanders. Then the war department sent him south, to Charleston and elsewhere, inspecting coastal defenses along the South Atlantic. He won no renown and little respect. "Granny Lee" some of the soldiers called him. They accused him of fighting only with picks and shovels, not rifles.[9]

He was a life-long soldier, fifty-two years old, the son of a Revolutionary War hero Henry "Light-Horse Harry" Lee. He graduated second in his class at West Point in 1829 with a spotless record of conduct. His high standing got him automatically into the engineers, the army's smallest and most elite branch. Years spent at major coastal fortifications and as harbor engineer at St. Louis led into the Mexican War where he took a place on the staff of Generals John E. Wool and

Winfield Scott. The bond formed with Scott, a fellow Virginian, never parted until April 1861 when Scott offered Lee the command that finally went to McDowell. Lee won repeated promotion in Mexico, and came home to superintend the Military Academy for several years before going to Texas as second-in-command of A. S. Johnston's 2nd United States Cavalry. In 1859, of course, he commanded the marine detachment that captured John Brown at Harpers Ferry. In April 1861, faced with having to fight against Virginia if he kept his commission, Lee resigned.

In younger days Lee enjoyed a sparkling sense of humor. Indeed, his wit was so sharp and subtle that one letter he wrote to a friend in which he described his murdering a "viper" in a lighthouse, was misinterpreted for well over a century after as a literal, and disturbingly out of character, cold-blooded killing of a man. It caused his biographers considerable discomfort, and led to a lot of painful rationalization. In fact, Lee told the truth all along. He had killed a snake. By 1861, however, Lee stood tired from his long years of service, the slow promotion, the interminable absences from his family and home at Arlington. His wife's almost constant illness further sobered his personality. And the collapse of the Union completed the change. Lee was already a sad figure when he took command of Johnston's army. The cares of the next three years would age and sadden him even more. Yet, like Lincoln, his sadness, the physical and mental toll that his burden took upon him, worked to his advantage. It captured the sympathies of the people and the army that he served, and won from them more regard, perhaps, than even his victories. Lee, in person, temperament, and character, made an ideal symbol. To nations that win, and more to nations that lose, symbols are all important.

Lee made his presence felt with the army as soon as he took command. Long called the Army of the Potomac by Johnston, it thus carried the same name as the enemy facing it. From the time of Lee's assumption, it became the Army of Northern Virginia. In the ensuing three weeks, while the Chickahominy line remained relatively quiet, Lee steadily built the army up until it numbered perhaps 85,000. The soldiers did what they considered menial work by digging and building fortifications and resented it. But they did not resent the better food and clothing they received. It came in part because of better administration within the army but even more from an improved relationship of that army with *the* Administration. Lee knew precisely how to work with the markedly difficult personality of the President. It required enormous tact, straightforward honesty about his plans and resources, an absolute self-effacing humility on the part of the general, and not infrequently some base flattery. More than once Lee would imply to Davis that only the President knew best in what the army should do. Unlike other courtier-generals like John B. Hood who would flatter Davis for their personal benefit, Lee did it only to secure the betterment of his army. Because the general seemed obviously to place so much trust and confidence in him, Davis returned in kind. Lee might disappoint Davis by losing a battle, but he never failed to be—or seem to be—what the President wanted in a general. Theirs became a relationship between commander-in-chief and commander in the field never equaled excepting, perhaps, Lincoln and Grant.

While Lee molded his army, he detected Federal movement. McClellan saw the narrow escape he made when Johnston's attack failed to destroy his exposed corps south of the Chickahominy. To guard against another such move on his left flank, he moved all of his army except Major General Fitz John Porter's V Corps south of the river. The trouble was, that now left Porter just as exposed as Keyes and Heintzelman had been before. In fact more so, for McDowell would not be coming down from the Rappahannock to link with Porter. Who would be coming was Jackson.

Lee realized immediately the mistake McClellan made in leaving Porter north of the Chickahominy. Yet he needed more information. For intelligence a general turned to cavalry; in some cases it turned out to be an unfortunate choice in this war, for the mounted arm on both sides largely attracted would-be cavaliers whose West Point training was augmented by a bit too much Sir Walter Scott. So it was with the man Lee asked to reconnoiter Porter, J. E. B. Stuart. Handsome, dashing, youthful and flamboyant, Stuart possessed all the instincts of a true cavalryman, good and bad. He could pull great feats from his troopers, push them the extra miles, take them deeper into enemy territory, severely discomfit Federal communications and supply. But he could not resist the bold stroke, a flourish instead of subtlety. Now, when Lee asked him to reconnoiter Porter's flank, Stuart instead rode entirely around McClellan's army. Lee gained information, but so did Little Mac. It showed him that his base on the York was not at all secure, and he began preparations to shift his base to the James River instead. Thus, should Lee turn Porter's flank and manage to cut the Federals off from the York, they would not be trapped after all; instead they would withdraw directly to the south, with their new base waiting at their backs. Stuart's foolish bravado might well have cost Lee a crushing victory.

What Lee learned made him ready to move, too. He met with Davis and proposed an audacious plan to take most of his own army north of the Chickahominy, call Jackson from the Shenandoah Valley, and leaving only the divisions of Huger and Magruder to face the bulk of McClellan's army, deliver a smashing blow to Porter in his positions around Mechanicsville. It represented a brilliant assessment of the overall situation, the first mark that Lee possessed strategic genius. Heavily outnumbered, the Confederates could not sit and await McClellan's siege. Eventually sheer force of numbers and matériel must overcome them. McClellan had to be driven from the Peninsula

by a decisive blow, which could only be delivered to an isolated portion of the Federal Army. Little Mac provided the opportunity with
Porter. Further, Lee already showed some ability as well at a kind of
military clairvoyance. Having witnessed extensive demonstration of
McClellan's timidity, Lee predicted that Huger and Magruder would
in fact face little danger. His plan took the best of the situation.

Like most plans, it did not work quite as expected. Despite attempts to keep the movement a secret, word of Jackson's coming
leaked North and South. McClellan expected something but postponed taking action of his own. On June 25 he did send forward a
small probe from his left, accomplishing nothing, and doing nothing
to relieve the danger to Porter. The next day Lee's attack began, the
first battle of what would come to be called the Seven Days Battles.
Unaccountably Jackson did not arrive on time. The attack was
delayed and delayed, until 3 P.M., when A. P. Hill, now a major general, finally opened the assault on Porter. A year before Hill fretted at
being left out of the fight at Manassas. He got plenty of battle now.
Hill pushed Porter out of Mechanicsville and back to a line on Beaver
Dam Creek, where the Federals held. Now Jackson was supposed to
come around and envelop Porter's exposed right. But he was not
there. Instead, unaccountably, Jackson put his little army into bivouac
barely two miles from Porter's flank and did not advance further.

Nothing more was accomplished that day. Magruder and Huger
did their parts well and McClellan feared to attack on their front.
Porter, knowing himself outnumbered in his front, had to withdraw
that night. McClellan finally ordered his change of base from the York
to the James River, and once more exaggerated the number of Confederates in his front. He immediately assumed the defensive. The
next day, June 27, Lee tried the same maneuver, striking Porter in his
new position near Gaines' Mill. Porter had to hold out there to buy
time for McClellan to effect his change of base. He did, all day,
against heavy assaults in which, once more, Jackson performed badly.
By nightfall Porter could stand no longer and his line broke to retreat
across the Chickahominy. McClellan had done little for him for two
days, keeping the bulk of the army idle south of the river. Now Little
Mac, though a brave man personally in the face of danger, exhibited
the moral cowardice that marked his whole tenure. He ordered a retreat to the James.

McClellan ordered Porter to move directly south to Malvern Hill,
protecting the new base he would establish at Harrison's Landing.
Then McClellan himself left the field, leaving no one in command,
giving no adequate orders for the withdrawal of the rest of his army.
In short, abandoning his command. Though not paralyzed, yet still he
suffered much the same emotional instability as G. W. Smith a month
before. Though his defenders would claim that his transfer to the
James was a part of his strategic intent, McClellan showed clearly this

day that he felt his army was beaten, and he had to find someone for the blame. "I have lost this battle because my force was too small," he said. In fact, isolated as he was, Porter had still outnumbered the enemy at Mechanicsville, while McClellan's main line outnumbered Magruder and Huger by well over two-to-one south of the Chickahominy. But McClellan could not believe that and would not. Writing to Lincoln from Harrison's Landing, he declared that "If I save this army now, I tell you plainly that I owe no thanks to you or to any other persons in Washington. You have done your best to sacrifice this army." Drowning in his well of self-pity and petulance, even McClellan went too far in this letter. Clerks in the war department kept Lincoln from seeing its more offensive parts.[10]

The next day, June 28, Lee crossed the Chickahominy, joined with Magruder and Huger, and struck again at Savage's Station. Still Jackson was late, and only this perhaps saved the corps of Heintzelman, Sumner, and William B. Franklin, for they acted completely without concert or direction from McClellan. During the fight Heintzelman actually pulled his command out of the battle without consulting the embattled Sumner, while one of Franklin's division commanders did the same without the knowledge of Franklin. The Army of the Potomac was virtually wandering back toward the James while Little Mac sulked. There were still two days to go.

On June 30 Lee planned to crush the Federals with a massive assault as they sat strung out on a five-mile front and considerably disorganized by the passage over the difficult White Oak Swamp. Jackson, once again, was to deliver the telling blow to the enemy right flank while Longstreet drove against the center. Thanks to the inept staff work and poor communications that plagued the entire offensive, Lee's attack yet again failed. Worse, if local lore be believed, there were even semantic difficulties to overcome. Long before, in the mid-1700s, the daughter of a local man named Enroughty married well below her station, to a man named Darby. Her family ignored him for years, and when he died a widower with no issue, he left his then considerable estate to the Enroughtys on the condition that they change their name to Darby! His revenge was dampened somewhat when they complied. They changed their name but not its spelling. Henceforth the family pronounced Enroughty as Darby, and pocketed the fortune. Alas, it became a part of local topography. Everyone pronounced it the same way, and when maps were made of the Peninsula, the Darbytown Road was printed as it sounded. However, the landmark "Darby" house appeared "Enroughty." This day of June 30, Lee ordered Longstreet to move on the Darbytown Road to the Darby House. The poor Georgian, unfamiliar with local lore, saw an Enroughty house, but none for Darby. As a result, he did not push far enough that day, and with the rest of Lee's troubles, contributed to the Confederate failure. Jackson was late yet again, and the

Enroughty-Darbys were saved a battle in their yard. Instead it was fought in Frayser's Farm.[11]

The final battle came the next day, July 1, and there was little chance of victory for Lee even if all his commanders were on time and all the local landmarks pronounced as spelled. For a week the outnumbered Confederates had been pushing an offensive, taking greater losses than the Federals, and ever stretching their lines of communications while McClellan's—thanks to his shift to Harrison's Landing—shortened. On July 1, the Federals had all the advantage. McClellan positioned his army on the slopes of Malvern Hill, and Lee attacked, with little finesse, little coordination of his divisions. His assaults were senseless, wasteful, indicative mostly of his frustration at being repeatedly thwarted in six days of careful plan and maneuver. There was little left but the frontal assault, almost invariably doomed in this war thanks to improved firepower in artillery and small arms.

That night McClellan retreated yet again, this time to defenses at Harrison's Landing itself. Yet none of the Confederates but Jackson, now recovered from his lethargy of the past week, wanted to pursue further. Richmond was safe. Obviously McClellan was not a fighting general. Losses had been heavy, as much as 20,000 in killed, wounded, and missing. That was one fourth of Lee's army. He decided that it had done enough, particularly after another foolish raid by Stuart to White House on the York denied Lee the mounted arm that might have been used to provide timely information of McClellan's movements.

Lee could take considerable satisfaction in this, his first campaign. Within a month of assuming command he had ended the threat to the capital and effectively neutralized the enemy on the Peninsula. Given the odds against him, the fact that he and the army were new to each other, that the roads were bad and his subordinates as yet unreliable, this is his best campaign. He would plan and lead others against greater odds and with more spectacular results, but for sustained effort, for day after day of replanning and adaptation, of being checked yet coming back with renewed vigor, none of his later campaigns compares with the Peninsula. He emerged in crisis and saved the day. Of course, it must be admitted that he faced a distinctly inferior adversary. Never again would Lee battle a Federal commander as timid as Little Mac. Never, that is, except once. This gray fox and the young Napoleon would meet yet one time more.

CHAPTER 13

"MAY GOD SAVE THIS PEOPLE"

What was it exactly that Lee saved on the Peninsula? Richmond was more than a city in 1862, more even than a capital. Already it was the very symbol of the rebellion, of the Confederacy. Some might well argue that Lee actually saved the cause, for in this first year of the war that initial euphoria and enthusiasm had not yet been replaced by the iron resolve that would come to sustain the Confederacy. Federals like McClellan believed that capture of Richmond would symbolically end the war, robbing Confederates of the will to fight on. With the defeat and death of A. S. Johnston at Shiloh, the loss of New Orleans, Henry and Donelson, the winds of war would have appeared decidedly against the Confederacy. Negotiation, compromise would have looked very attractive to the South. Western Virginia was almost in rebellion against the rest of the state; northern Alabama and east Tennessee were Unionist in sentiment. The blockade was proving effective enough to drive up prices for most necessities and all luxuries, and foreign powers showed no inclination for an early recognition. The loss of the capital at a time like this could very well have taken the fight from the men who led the war and the people who had to support it. Lee saved a great deal.

Most of all, however, he saved Richmond.

"Richmond, as seen from the hill, with the James River flowing by, its broad, level streets, full foliaged trees, and spacious homes, is a beautiful city." So said the wife of Alabama Senator Clement C. Clay. "Never did it appear more attractive to Southern eyes than when, arriving in the late autumn of '61, we found our Confederate Government established there, and the air full of activity." Yet this genteel Virginia city was hardly ready for what becoming the capital of the Confederacy would do to it, and it would never be the same again.[1]

It was not exactly a Southern city. Its business was trade and manufacturing, industry, carrying. A Yankee could be nearly as much at home here as in Boston. To a planter from Alabama it would seem just as foreign as Boston but for the similarity of accent and people. Businesslike as it was, Richmond still boasted a distinctly Southern society. With 38,000 inhabitants in 1860, the city was less populous than New Orleans, though more so than Montgomery. Conservative in nature, and not rabidly secessionist, the city went for the John Bell ticket in the 1860 election. It was peaceful in the evenings, a bandstand providing music for nighttime strollers near the square by the state Capitol. It was the literary center of the South, its dailies ranking with the best Northern newspapers, and its *Southern Literary Messenger* boasting among other things its onetime editorship by Edgar Allan Poe. It had theaters and ballrooms, libraries, sumptuous hotels, counting houses, bordellos, and slums. The Tredegar Iron Works down by the James was the major iron producer in the South. The Gallego Flour Mills stood premier in their trade. The Richmond Arsenal was a chief manufacturer of small arms. It was a typically *American* city.

The government came with a rush. Jefferson Davis arrived on May 29 to a rousing salute of cannon and cheering. Without delay Davis and his party went to the Spotswood Hotel at the corner of 8th and Main streets. The President and his wife took rooms 121 and 122 and there made their "Executive Mansion" for the next two months. Their expenses came to $3,288.99, and though the city paid the bill for the Davises, there were those who questioned whether or not the proprietor of the hotel was profiteering a bit at government expense. After all, the President hardly drank any spirits, yet $1,800 of the bill was for wine and extra meals. Since wines were then going for $5 a bottle elsewhere, some doubted that Davis actually consumed 360 bottles in 60 days. It was a symptom of Richmond to come, however. Where government and power and money gather, so too do those who take advantage.[2]

On June 11 the city purchased the old Brockenbrough house on Clay Street and leased it to the Confederate government as a formal executive mansion. Davis and family moved in on August 1, but the rest of the government hardly matched their comforts. Nearly one thousand bureaucrats followed Davis from Montgomery, and office space came to those who got it first. Secretary of War Walker sent his clerk John B. Jones ahead to secure rooms for the department, and Jones lost no time. Meeting the manager of the new customs house, Jones "succeeded without difficulty in convincing him that the War Department was the most important one, and hence entitled to the first choice of rooms." He took the entire first floor, leaving the one above to be fought over by treasury, justice, navy, and even the President's executive office. The war department would later move to the Mechanics Institute Building on the Capitol square. Navy and justice would join it there for the remainder of the war.[3]

Lodgings for the hundreds of office-holders had to be found. Richmond's sixteen hotels and several more boarding houses filled quickly, and rates rose rapidly as the demand exceeded supply. Jones called his landlords at the Carleton House "blood-thirsty insects." By far the most prestigious hostelry was the Spotswood. Nearly half of the Confederate Congress lodged there, as did Attorney General Benjamin, and much of the President's staff. "This Spotswood is a miniature world," wrote the wife of Colonel James B. Chesnut. The gossip of the nation passed through its drawing rooms and parlors like the wind. Soldiers moved in and out, and even an occasional *vivandière*, a female mascot of a regiment, came in bright uniform and Turkish pantaloons to play the drum and sing war songs. It was a gay place, made the more attractive during the two months that Davis and his family lodged there. The string-pulling and politicking to be invited to dine at the President's table was shameless. Once he moved into the Brockenbrough house he was never again as readily accessible as here at the Spotswood.[4]

The Confederate Congress occupied, at the legislature's invitation, the Virginia State House, there to remain for the rest of the war. The lobbyists and profiteers, harlots, and street thugs followed in train. The business boom was prodigious. "Our City has already assumed an appearance of business activity quite cheering to see," the Richmond *Dispatch* commented on June 26, "while every day from every morn to sun down the pavements resound with tread of gathered thousands of all shades of complexion and degree in life." Within two years the population will soar to over two hundred thousand.

Quickly it became a city of rumor; military speculations dominate its parlor conversation for the next four years, and every wild flight of fancy escaped the citizens' lips. It was inevitable, with the major Eastern front never more than fifty miles away and frequently closer. The days of Manassas set the tone. "We have talked of battles, and said that they were fought here and there, or would be, but the 21st of July, 1861, made us realize for the first time what war means," wrote a Richmond lady. At first there was a feeling of confidence, thanks to Beauregard's army standing between the city and any enemy advance. "Here in Richmond we feel safe," said Mrs. Chesnut, "for we cannot be flanked!" Already the ladies spoke in terms more customary to the headquarters tent. Those close to officers and high politicos thrived on the bits of information they could obtain from their husbands or friends. Indeed, where in another time a woman's social standing often derived from her clothing, very soon now her place in society came instead from the veracity and timing of her war gossip. No one, of course, could compete with Mrs. Davis in that regard, but many would try.

Then, as the husbands left in mid-July to go to the army for the expected battle, a sober reality set in. "I wept my heart away today when my husband went off," wrote Mary Chesnut. "Things do look so black." By July 19, with the armies confronting each other along Bull Run, the city was riveted to news from the front. Though invited to examine a new ship in the James, several ladies declared that "wild horses could not drag us an inch from here now." They clustered at the Spotswood. "To this spot all telegrams tend," and Mrs. Davis was there. Then came July 21.

"The day dawned quietly, calmly, beautifully," wrote Mrs. Eugene McLean. Most people knew that the President had gone to Manassas, but few suspected his object. War clerk Jones was one who did, however. "I have always thought he would avail himself of his prerogative as commander-in-chief, and direct in person the most important operations in the field." Secretary of War Walker too wanted to be at the front. He paced to and fro in his office, damning his position, and wishing himself in the battle then raging, becoming "almost frantic with anxiety." Mrs. Davis, with the wives of General Johnston and McLean, went to a funeral in the late afternoon, returning toward the Spotswood shortly after 5 P.M. Mrs. McLean was struck by the activity and excitement in the streets, but the President's wife laughed at her and said that nothing had happened. Then Varina Davis asked a passerby if there was any news. "Yes, madam," came the reply, "they have been fighting at Manassas since six o'clock this morning."

The hotel was pandemonium. "There were ten of us whose husbands were known to be on that field," said Mrs. McLean. They passed a tense three hours awaiting more news before Mrs. Davis received a telegram from the President. It announced the victory, and the dead. Mrs. Bartow was already asleep, and Varina Davis delayed telling her the news of her husband's death until the morning. She did awake Mrs. Chesnut to say that Colonel Chesnut passed the battle safely. "I had no breath to speak," wrote the relieved wife. "Times were too wild with excitement to stay in bed." When Mrs. Davis finally went to Bartow's widow, she read the evil tidings in Varina's face. "It seemed as if a pall had fallen on every house," wrote Mrs. McLean, "and people spoke low to each other as they waited to learn with what price victory was bought." Almost every family in the city had some member with the army at Manassas. Women who a few weeks before proclaimed that they would willingly sacrifice their husband or son for the glorious cause now changed their songs when actual battle came. For the women at the Spotswood, with stricken Mrs. Bartow in their midst, there was no rejoicing. "God help us if this is what we have prayed for!" exclaimed one.[5]

Slowly the mood changed as more and more news arrived from the front. First came relief, then exultation over the victory. When Davis returned to the capital he made a stirring speech to a cheering multitude crowded in front of the Spotswood. Every parlor was ablaze with light. People in the avenues spoke jubilantly, congratulating themselves and each other on their loved ones spared. But during it all, behind the cries of "the President," "the Confederacy," and "the Generals," Mrs. McLean could hear the faint strains of the "Dead March" as the bodies of Bee and Bartow were brought to lie at the Capitol. "I left the parlor feeling that, let war bring what it would, I should always hear the accompaniment of that sad note." Richmond would come to know that sad note well.[6]

The city was more nearly ready for the even greater strains that the Peninsular Campaign placed upon it. In 1862, after a year of war and capitalhood, Richmond knew better what to expect. Still, McClellan brought a threat far more imminent and actually visible than McDowell. From church spires the people could see the tiny soldiers and cannon on the Chickahominy. Here was a real threat to the city.

The news of Yorktown's evacuation hit the city like a bolt of lightning. Near panic ensued at first. Parents began sending their children off to school in the interior, or to other states, but admitted that "it is in reality another flight from the enemy." War clerk Jones lamented that "No one, scarcely, supposes that Richmond will be defended. But it must be!" Davis declared martial law in the city some time before. The Congress discreetly adjourned. On May 10 the President sent his family to North Carolina and most of the cabinet did likewise. Discussions of destroying tobacco stores and other things that could not be evacuated occupied the time of the military authorities in the city. Secretary Memminger kept a special train ready with steam up to transport the treasury in case of evacuation, and the secretary of war had his department's records packed in cases to be ready. "Is there no turning point in this long lane of downward progress," lamented Jones; "our affairs at this moment are in a critical condition."[7]

News, any good news, greatly encouraged the inhabitants. Word of the repulse of the Federal ironclads at Drewry's Bluff gave cheer. "We breathe freely," said a Richmonder, and when McClellan began to entrench, the citizens took more heart, for this at least did not look like an attack was imminent, and any time gained favored the Confederates. Yet within the city the always latent Union sentiment began to appear. Anonymous graffiti appeared chalked and scratched on board walls and buildings. "Union Men to the Rescue," they said, and "God Bless the Stars and Stripes." One ardently loyal Union lady readied a guest room in her house for General McClellan's arrival.[8]

In the midst of this, on May 14, Virginia's legislature took assertive action. It called on the Confederate government to defend the city "at all hazards," and agreed to hold the national authorities harmless for damage done to the city in the process. The governor, John Letcher, organized militia from citizens to aid in the defense. Still many believed that Davis intended to abandon Richmond. Indeed, he had decided that, rather than submit his army to a siege, he would give up the capital. But of course, Lee could only be besieged if the city were surrounded, and for that to happen, McDowell would have to come overland from Fredericksburg as expected. He did not, and the repulse at Drewry's Bluff gave the President new heart. On May 20 he announced that Richmond would be defended. "A thrill of joy electrifies every heart," Jones wrote that day, "a smile of triumph is on every lip."[9]

Then came Seven Pines. The night before Johnston made known his plan to the war department. "Gen. Johnston has determined to attack . . . tomorrow," said Jones. "Thank God, we are strong enough to make the attack." On May 31 thousands of citizens flocked to the higher hills to listen to the battle and perhaps see it. They heard the heavy firing of cannon, followed by musketry, and then a pause. "We knew what this meant!" A battery had been taken, or so they thought. That night the ambulances streamed into the city, Johnston among the wounded. People in Richmond regarded the battle as a great victory and, coupled with the good news coming from Jackson in the Shenandoah Valley, they felt relatively safe once more. Lee inspired confidence when he took command of the army. Indeed, by June 24 people expressed a fear that the fighting before the city was done too soon. Better battle than allow McClellan to dig his way into the capital. They need not have worried. The next day Lee began the Seven Days, and Richmond was safe from McClellan. Archives were unpacked again, families returned, and spirits and confidence soared. "What genius! what audacity in Lee!" they exclaimed.[10]

Yet with McClellan safely out of the way at Harrison's Landing, life in Richmond did not exactly return to "normal." Indeed, normality's definition for Richmond remained cloudy for the rest of the war. Its population trebled overnight, its streets crowded with refugees, stragglers, and wounded, the comings and goings of regiments and officers, lent to the city's affairs an atmosphere of controlled confusion. The old time residents felt little at all comfortable. Those who left in the panic in May came back often to find refugees squatting in their homes, and surly at eviction. Many others could not be evicted, the wounded and dying. Richmond was becoming a vast hospital.[11]

The influx of injured and invalided soldiers began even before the fight at Manassas and continued almost unabated. If they did not bear battle-inflicted injuries, they more often bore the wounds of the camp: measles, dysentery, scarlet fever—the illnesses that always emerged when large numbers of men were brought together. In time, Richmond would sprout twenty-eight military hospitals, and unnumbered informal infirmaries. The largest took root on a hill east of the city, named Chimborazo after a mountain in the Andes. On October 17, 1861, the war department opened what would become one of the largest military hospitals in the hemisphere. When completed its 150 buildings would occupy over forty acres, with nearly as many more tents to handle the overflow patients. The hospital maintained its own cattle and goat herds. Its bakery produced every day up to ten thousand loaves of bread, and its beds handled up to three thousand patients at once. In the course of the war some seventy-six thousand men passed through the facility. Other hospitals abounded as well, many named for the states they served. Fourteen represented states from Alabama to Virginia, with even Kentucky, Missouri, and Maryland providing care for the wounded from those states. Richmond, said one citizen, became "one immense hospital."

The ladies of the city did what they could to assist the woefully insufficient number of doctors and nurses in tending the injured soldiers. It came often as not at the expense of a lifetime of carefully cultivated sensibilities. "Oh such a day!" exclaimed Mary Chesnut after her first visit to a hospital. "I can never again shut out of view the sights I saw of human misery. . . . Long rows of ill men on cots; ill of typhoid fever, of every human ailment; wounds being dressed; all horrors to be taken in at one glance." Local physicians and groups like the Sisters of Charity took service, but supplies were inadequate thanks to the blockade, and organization was often lacking due to simple ignorance. "Horrors upon horrors" met the visitor. Frequently the surgeons' attentions were needed for the well-meaning ladies who came to help but, like Mary Chesnut, fainted when confronted with the evil aspect of the carnage. "They were awfully smashed up objects of misery, wounded, maimed, diseased," but they became a permanent part of Richmond's population.[12]

There were other, less desirable, inhabitants as well. The proximity of the army, the large number of refugees disrupted from their homes by Federal advances, the possibility for easy money, and the deprivation caused by overcrowding and the blockade, all conspired to bring an epidemic of crime to Richmond, and criminals great and small flocked to the capital along with everyone else. Much of the crime was innocent enough. Drunken soldiers, bullies and braggarts, caused an unending parade of vandalism and civil disorder that, despite all of Lee's efforts, never abated. Petty theft, gambling, and whoring hurt relatively few except the participants. Professional card sharps fleeced the soldiers of their all-too-infrequent pay, and what was left went to liquor and tarts, the latter in turn helping promote a radical upswing of venereal disease.

The city augmented its police forces to combat crime, but never stopped it or even provided an effective curb. Extortioners and confidence men were even harder to catch, but when convicted, they were often dealt with summarily. John Richardson counterfeited Confederate bills. He was hanged, a large crowd gathering for the event. There was a city jail, but hardly large enough to accommodate the number of offenders. Soldiers caught were returned to their commanders for punishment or incarceration in military stockades.[13]

Yet these offenders paled when compared to the numbers of other prisoners that began flowing into Richmond after Manassas and never stopped. Men captured from McDowell were later joined by those taken from McClellan, as well as Federals captured in the Shenandoah Valley and a host of other places. The influx of great numbers of Federal prisoners after the Seven Days—over three thousand—created such an emergency that space had to be commandeered for them. The ship chandlery of Luther Libby became Libby Prison, most infamous of the capital's several hostelries for enemy soldiers. Eventually only officers would be held there. At Belle Isle, on the other hand, the war department sent its enlisted prisoners. It was an island in the James, in full view of the city, yet it eventually became the largest prison in the city. From 6,000 to 10,000 Federals languished there at the same time. Hundreds died. A barrel factory became Castle Thunder, for spies, political prisoners, and deserters, as well as unfortunate Federals. Castle Lightning, a tobacco warehouse, held Confederate soldiers convicted of offenses. Several other buildings found themselves converted to prison use by the government, and all became a commonplace sight to the people of the city. At first the citizens found captured Yankees a great novelty, their parading through the streets to prison a great spectator event. Then this, too, became nothing out of the ordinary. Richmond rapidly acclimated itself to all the discomforts and inconveniences, all the intrusions, and insults, of a capital at war.[14]

To their credit, the people strove mightily to maintain their old culture, their social life and civilization, in the face of a conflict that outraged all. The churches flourished and in all denominations. Thirty-two houses of worship served their congregations, the numbers attending their services rising steadily as the war's worries and hardships drove people closer to the Almighty. There were five Episcopal churches, eight Baptist—three of them for blacks—four Presbyterian, four Methodist, three Catholic, three synagogues, and a variety of other beliefs represented. Several of the churches operated and supplied their own hospitals for soldiers. The orphan asylums continued to take in the parentless, now much more numerous. Fraternal lodges like the Odd Fellows and Masons continued to meet, as did Powhatan

Tribe Number 15 of the Improved Order of Red Men, who gathered every Thursday night at the Corinthian Hall on Main Street. The YMCA on Clay Street carried on in the face of a bordello opening across the pavement, and the Confederate Reading Room on Main Street sold newspapers and books to soldiers on leave. In the Capitol itself the state library offered books to citizens, though they had to have a letter from a senator for every two books they borrowed![15]

Yet the theater provided the best entertainment of all, and the gayest. The people needed that gaiety as the months wore on, the hardships increased, and the casualty lists lengthened. At least three theaters operated in Richmond during the war, and several amateur theatricals took stage in improvised warehouses and meeting halls. The fare ran to farce and heroic drama, but none so memorable as a performance of Richard Sheridan's *The Rivals*. Indeed, in after years it would be remembered as the major social event of the war in the capital, perhaps the finest expression of the determination of Richmond's society to persevere despite the war. Few indeed were those of prominence who missed the performance. "That historic evening's pleasures crown all other recollections of social life in the Confederate capital," wrote Mrs. Clay.[16]

The affair was the concept of Cora Semmes Ives, sister-in-law of Captain Semmes, and one of the city's most popular hostesses. She rehearsed her cast mercilessly, even inviting a professional actress then appearing in Richmond to come and critique her players, themselves all members of Confederate society. Mrs. Ives chose the play by Sheridan specifically because she believed Virginia Clay could carry the show. Constance Cary, one of the city's most eligible young ladies, took Lydia Languish. Her brother Clarence, then a midshipman in the Confederate Navy, played Fag. Mrs. Ives herself had to take a part when one of her players opted out of the play in order to present a farce, "Bombasties Furioso," which was to follow. No expense was spared in preparing the costumes from such meager resources as could be had. Cora Ives borrowed her hat from Secretary Mallory's daughter. Mrs. Clay wore all her feathers and diamonds. Wigs not being available and a gargantuan hair arrangement being necessary for her part as Mrs. Malaprop, she put a pair of boots on her head and piled her hair over them.

Cora Ives staged the one and only performance in her own home. She placed her stage at the end of her long parlor where every one of the three hundred anticipated guests would have a fine view. "The fame of that entertainment, the excitement which the preparation for it caused, spread far beyond the picket lines," Virginia Clay recalled. They later heard that a dashing officer of the Federal Army actually planned to don the Confederate gray in order to cross the lines and "take a peep at the much-talked-of performance." Everyone in Richmond society attended. President and Mrs. Davis, the cabinet officials, many members of Congress, and the more prominent generals, including John B. Hood, and John C. Breckinridge, then visiting in the capital. Mary Chesnut sat in the crowd, next to Breckinridge. "Mrs. Clay as Mrs. Malaprop was beyond our wildest hopes," she wrote that night. "Even the back of Mrs. Clay's head was eloquent." Cora Ives showed even more enthusiasm for her star. "You carried the audience by storm," she told her Malaprop. "I can see you yet, in imagination, in your rich brocaded gown, antique laces and jewels, high puffed and curled hair, with nodding plumes which seemed to add expression to your amusing utterances!"

But Virginia Clay herself, like all stars, worried that the audience was not appreciating it enough, that they were too cold. Part of the problem was General Hood, handsome, a genuine war hero, and desperately taken with a young lady who ignored his attentions. A good many of the audience were watching him, not the play. Hood, when he did watch the actors, was so baffled by the subtlety and parody of the lines that his reactions alone attracted attention. "Watch Hood," Breckinridge whispered to Mrs. Chesnut. "That's better than the play." Finally Mrs. Clay sent word between acts she "wanted encouragement," more demonstrative appreciation of the play. "To that hint General Breckinridge responded like a man," said Mrs. Chesnut, "and after that, they followed his lead and she was fired by thunders of applause. Those mighty Kentuckians turned *claquers* were a host in themselves."

Afterward, during the farce, Mrs. Clay sat with Breckinridge, who said "What a splendid head of hair you have!" "And all my own," she replied, holding her head erect to prevent the boots falling out.

That performance gave Richmond food for conversation that lasted the rest of the war and long into posterity. But all too quickly the war intruded into the thoughts of the happy audience. The play done, many people adjourned to a hearty "Richmond supper" at the home of a war department official. Afterward, in the clear moonlit night, Breckinridge and Mary Chesnut walked back to her home. "You have spent a jolly evening," she said, thinking back to the sound of his roaring laughter during the play. "I do not know," he replied. "I have asked myself more than once tonight: 'Are you the same man who stood gazing down on the faces of the dead on that awful battlefield; the soldiers lying there, they stare at you with their eyes wide open. Is this the same world?' "[17]

Certainly it was the same world, and growing more so as the hardships of the war intruded increasingly into the life of the capital. Amateur theatricals and gay attempts to maintain the old social life and order could not disguise the shortages and inflated prices confronting everyone. Judge John A. Campbell advised his friends not to spend whatever gold or silver they had. Instead, they should buy

what they could with the notes being printed and issued by Memminger's treasury department. "In the event of the restoration of
Northern rule," he said, "Confederate money may be worthless. I pro-
ceed on that assumption." He was saving his hard money, for only it
would have value. "If the war should last another year," he told Virginia Clay in April 1862, "the embarrassments of everyone will be increased tenfold!"[18]

Prices escalated almost from the first days of the war. The costs of
butter, flour, whiskey, and coffee doubled between September 1861
and January 1862. A year later it had grown much worse; the Richmond *Dispatch* calculated that the weekly foodstuffs for an average
family had increased from a cost of $6.65 in 1860 to $68.25 in 1863.
Hoarding, both for personal use, and for exorbitant profits, compounded the problem. "Oh, the extortioners!" cried war clerk Jones.
"Meats of all kinds are selling at 50 cts. per pound; butter 75 cts.;
coffee $1.50; tea, $10; boots, $30 per pair; shoes, $18; Ladies' shoes,
$15; shirts, $6 each. Houses that rented for $500 last year, are $1000
now." That was in May 1862. Every month it grew worse, and particularly in the spring, when the last year's produce was exhausted and
the new year's crops not yet ready. "Our markets grew suddenly
poor," lamented Virginia Clay, "a stringency in every department of
life in the city was felt. The cost of living was doubled, and if, indeed,
any epicures remained, they were glad to put aside their fastidi-
ousness. Within a year our vermicelli, when we had it at all, would
have warranted an anglicising of its first two syllables, and our rice,
beans and peas, as well as our store of grains and meal, began to discover a lively interest in their wartime surroundings."

The story went round of a soldier who advocated eating green per-
simmons. The effect on his stomach was so radical that all hunger was
forgotten. The wife of Roger Pryor roasted a friend who complained
that a barrel of sorghum received was "Horrid stuff" and sent it back.
"Why! in these days, with our country in peril," she remonstrated, "I
am grateful when I am able to get a pitcher of sorghum, and I teach
my children to thank God for it!" At times there appeared to be
something of a surplus. In October 1862 Jones walked through the
city's markets and found all crammed with meat and vegetables, poul-
try, fruit, and dairy products. "But the prices are enormously high."
What hit many families the hardest was coffee. They could not get
through the day without it, yet the blockade effectively cut off all supply except to those who could pay enormous prices. Jones's wife
solved the problem for them by toasting corn meal and making a bev-
erage from that "which I like very well." Even soap approached $1
per pound. By the fall of 1862 Jones was genuinely worried. "How
shall we subsist this winter?" he asked himself. "There is not a supply
of wood or coal in the city. . . . Flour at $16 per barrel, and bacon at
75 cts. per pound, threaten a famine." The only solution was to field

an army of a million or more and drive the enemy from the South quickly. "Better die in battle than die of starvation produced by the enemy."[19]

Clothing, too, became a problem. Simple muslin and calico went up to $6 and $8 per yard. Most women began to resort to homespun, even those of the first families. They began knitting their own stockings, even caps, and sometimes shoes. Coloring offered a challenge, never entirely solved for the vegetable dyes used often washed out. Draperies and tablecloths became gowns, and everyone worked at home to augment what little was available—or affordable—in the stores. "I do not know when I have seen a woman without knitting in her hand," wrote Mary Chesnut. "It gives a quaint look, the twinkling of needles, and the ever-lasting sock dangling." As for living space, it decreased directly in proportion to the expanding population. When Mary Chesnut returned to the capital from a stay in South Carolina, she had to take dismal lodgings at "the most extravagant price," only to be treated scornfully by her landlord who, a scant two years before, stood considerably below her socially. Later she found a better place but still felt "We had no right to expect any better lodgings, for Richmond was crowded to suffocation, with hardly standing room left."

Not surprisingly, the people of the city, the wives and mothers and daughters, and the men too old or young to fight, or too important to running the government, found their chief entertainment in talking about the war, and often as not on the steps before their homes and lodgings. It got them out of their stuffy, cramped quarters, and on the street they could see and speak with passersby. There was news and gossip and rumor aplenty. Richmond fed on conversation. "On the front steps every evening we take our seats and discourse at our pleasure," wrote Mrs. Chesnut. First they spoke of Yancey and the foolishness of sending him to England. Then they turned to the navy, and how divided in loyalties were many of its officers. "No scandal today," she said, "no wrangling, all harmonious. Everybody was knitting; I dare say that soothing occupation helped our perturbed spirits to be calm."[20]

Of course, for the city's poor there was less of everything. While the society people maintained their morale and tried to support war and President against the increasing assaults of disenchanted editors and politicians, the poor folk thought little beyond survival. The war's shortages hit them the hardest, for workers' wages lagged far behind the increase in prices. And with the city largely competing with Lee's army for the supplies that had to be brought into Virginia, the poor somehow came last, after the soldiers and the upper class. What made things worse, in March 1863 the war department promulgated a policy of impressment of foodstuffs, taking produce from farmers and paying them what was regarded as a fair "market value." Since that value always fell way behind actual worth, merchants had to charge even higher prices for what they sold across the counter, virtually pricing the poor out of contention for the limited quantities available. The resentment was widespread, and by the end of March Richmond was at a crisis. A heavy snowfall closed the roads that would have brought produce in from the country. The government had just seized all reserves of flour from the local mills. And on March 27 Davis rather undiplomatically declared a day of fasting and prayer. "Fasting in the midst of famine," exclaimed Jones. "May God save this people." Three days later he added that "The gaunt form of wretched famine still approaches with rapid strides." The next day one of Letcher's aides cried that "We are on the eve of starvation."

The poor and lower-middle-class women of the city could take no more. On husbands' wages, or soldiers' pay sent from the front and always late, they had to care for families that were starving. There were stories of a "women's mob" raiding stores in Salisbury, North Carolina, and now a Mary Jackson, wife, mother, fruit seller, organized a protest meeting of women for April 1. She proposed to the crowd that they march to the produce stores and demand that food be sold to them at the same prices the merchants accepted from the government's impressment officers. If not, then they should take it by force.

The next day the women gathered, between two hundred and three hundred of them, many armed, and Mary Jackson herself carrying a knife. She would have "bread or blood" she told her companions. They went first to protest to Governor Letcher, but he offered no encouragement, so off they marched to Main and Cary streets. War clerk Jones watched them pass, asking where they were going. "They were going to find something to eat," came a reply. He wished them well. The merchants, however, met them with locked doors. Brandishing hatchets and axes, one party of the group attacked the grocery of Pollard and Walker, broke in, and quickly looted the place. The same fate befell other nearby establishments, many being "thoroughly eviscerated." Some men and loafers joined in the orgy. A shoe store was cleaned out, then another, and soon the mob forgot bread in the riot that ensued. A year of frustration and hardship found vent in mob rule, breaking and taking anything within reach. Women who needed food, took seven and eight pair of shoes or packages of sewing needles.

Letcher tried speaking to the mob then threatened to have the city's public guard open fire on them. One half of the mob dispersed, but the other had already moved to other markets, looting dry goods stores and even taking a wagonload of beef on its way to a hospital. Finally the mob gathered near the treasury building, and President Davis himself spoke to them. He tried to conciliate the crowd, told them how their acts would only drive prices even higher, pointed out that instead of taking bread they were in fact simply plundering, and then threatened to have them fired upon within five minutes if they did not disperse. The main bunch did break up and melt back to their homes, but a few, Mary Jackson among them, tried one or two more break-ins before police arrested them.

Further "bread riots" did not occur, but this one alone gave Davis great embarrassment. Desperately he asked the city press not to print accounts of the affair and had the war department order telegraphers not to allow passage of any information out of the capital that told of the mob. The news got out just the same, and the *Examiner*, the major anti-Davis paper in the Confederacy, printed highly colored accounts of the riots. Most of those arrested obtained release and only misdemeanor charges. Ironically, none of them actually got any bread, yet their march would remain the Bread Riot to posterity. The city itself responded in part to the need that started the disturbance by opening two "free markets" at which the poor could redeem coupons for food. In time the city would be giving foodstuffs at cost to about one thousand families a month. It did not prevent starving but was a significant step toward social welfare, a remarkable step for a city at war. As for the looted merchants, they submitted claims for their losses when the city offered to make restitution; but when the city council saw that those claims totaled in the tens of thousands, they promptly withdrew their promise.[21]

It had been a sobering episode. Just two years into the war and citizens in the very capital rioted in the streets. Their action embarrassed the government locally and obviously provided encouragement to the enemy and discouragement to foreign powers that might think of recognition of the Confederacy. Yet quickly the city returned to its wartime normal. However much the poor and hungry cared or did not care who won the war and when, the affluent still believed in victory and stood by the government. Their loyalty was to them a matter of pride, pride in themselves, their city, and their country. Such a brave people as those of Richmond could not be defeated. Virginia Clay walked down a busy city street one day and passed President Davis. On his left strode General Simon Buckner. On the President's right, John C. Breckinridge. "Three stalwart and gallant men as ever walked abreast," she thought. "As I watched them the thought came involuntarily, 'Can a cause fail with such men at the head?' "[22]

CHAPTER 14

"THE LUNATIC ASYLUM"

The success or failure of any cause, North or South, would depend not only upon the men at the head, but as well on their organization, their organization for victory. Those of vision quickly perceived that this was to be no war of Minute Men gathering briefly at the village green to put down a threat then return to their farms. Though many felt notions that it would be a quick and easy conflict, Manassas and Wilson's Creek made Northern men think otherwise, and Henry, Donelson, Shiloh, and foreign reluctance toward recognition, gave Confederates the same understanding. It would be long war calling for great armies on a scale never before seen in the Americas, and seldom if ever in the Old World. And the advent of recent technologies in arms, travel, and communications, required an organization and system on a scale never before seen in human history.

The organization began at the top, and the constitutions both North and South clearly indicated the commander-in-chief. The President. Other American Presidents had acted as commanders-in-chief during wars. James Madison did during the second war with Great Britain in 1812–1815. So did James K. Polk in the war with Mexico in 1846–1848. Yet neither really involved himself much with the actual operation of the war. For Polk the conflict was too distant, its outcome never in doubt. His chief contact with the armed forces was with his major generals, Winfield Scott and Zachary Taylor; and much of that took the direction of trying to prevent the presidential aspirations of both. Madison involved himself more with his war. Indeed, he had to flee it when the British captured Washington; yet he too left direction of military affairs primarily to his secretary of war and the generals.

War in the 1860s presented a different aspect. This war was not just armies. More than any conflict in human memory, it mobilized natural resources, industry, economy, and population. It was a war of nations. In time it would involve every ounce of every single resource in the Confederacy to the point that other customary benchmarks of a functioning nation halted or even retarded. And although the North experienced brisk growth in areas not directly related to the war, it too came to commit the majority of its energies to defeating the South.

The mobilization of the men and resources to accomplish their goals depended chiefly on Lincoln and Davis, the commanders-in-chief. Both, for their individual reasons, chose to use the powers their constitutions gave them to manage military affairs in a way not thought of by previous Presidents. Davis did so largely because it suited his natural inclination. His moment of glory in the Mexican War, when he formed his Mississippi regiment into an inverted V and repulsed an enemy charge at Buena Vista, gave Davis an idea of his own military prowess, which was augmented by his years as Pierce's secretary of war. By 1861 he fully believed that he was as well, if not better, qualified to command the Confederacy's troops in the field as any other man. Many, like war clerk Jones, fully expected that Davis would in fact interpret his commander-in-chief powers in such fashion that when battle was imminent at Manassas, Davis would go to the front to lead the army personally. Though he perhaps wished to, Davis did not, but he dominated the war department for all but the last few months of the war. Critics would later complain that the Confederacy perished because of a "V."[1]

Lincoln had no military pretense. His only service at arms had been as an officer, and then an enlisted man, briefly during the Black Hawk War. He cared little for things military, though somewhat fascinated by the workings of war's machines. But he did care for power. Like any great executive, he understood its use and its potential. The instinct came to him naturally, for his background gave him little encouragement for it to have been an acquired taste. His few ventures into business failed. His law practice did well enough, and as an attorney he enjoyed considerable regard, but his political career prior to 1861 certainly afforded no opportunity to feel the thrill of power. Somehow, Abraham Lincoln was simply born to it, ready to rise when occasion and opportunity came together. One of the great thinkers of military science, Karl von Clausewitz, declared that experience did not count in a war leader half so much as "a remarkable, superior mind and strength of character." That Lincoln had. Davis had only the strength of character, and that flawed by ambition and pride. Therein lay the essential difference between these two Kentuckians now Presidents.[2]

Lincoln began to exert his influence as commander-in-chief immediately upon taking office. The situation forced him to it. He took his inauguration with a major crisis already happening in Charleston, and the Union looked to him for policy and leadership as it never had before. His first and major concern was a military one. As a result, in his first months in office events demanded that he devote more time to the war department and the army, and once in the habit, he never stopped.

Those early weeks showed him the ineptitude of many in office and in uniform. They revealed the need for unified thought and policy that no one was providing. And they revealed something that probably surprised even Lincoln: His own military thinking, untutored and innocent, was nearly as good as theirs. Very quickly he acquired confidence in his own ideas, and soon even pride—or something similar, something as close to pride as Lincoln could come. By the end of the year he believed that his plans for the Army of the Potomac were more sound than McClellan's and diplomatically said so. Yet he was not doctrinaire. He would yield his own preference to a general who would act rather than talk, as he yielded to Little Mac for the Peninsular Campaign. At the same time, however, Lincoln by 1862 did not fear to take a matter entirely into his own hands. Indeed, where Davis never led Confederates in battle, Lincoln almost did personally command a Federal military maneuver. In May 1862 he came to Fort Monroe. While McClellan readied his intended assault on Johnston in Yorktown, Lincoln came to visit with him, but the general said he was too busy to speak with the President. Lincoln ignored the snub. Instead, he ordered navy gunboats sent up the James to assist McClellan's pursuit of the Confederates then turned his own attention to Norfolk. Lincoln and a few others personally made a reconnaissance to find a landing place for Federal soldiers and ordered General John Wool to attack. The enemy evacuated first, but treasury secretary Chase and others believed that Norfolk would not have been taken but for Lincoln's action.[3] They were mistaken, for the Confederates planned to abandon the place anyhow, but it is significant that Lincoln was perceived as not just a President by his people, but also as a war leader in the fullest definition. It was his assertion of his position, as well, that made his relations with the imperious McClellan inevitably cool.

Other circumstances forced the President to interfere. His secretary of war, the man customarily charged with oversight of the military establishment, was incompetent to the task and dishonest as well. Lincoln never wanted Simon Cameron, and he kept him no longer than he had to. Indeed, Cameron himself lacked interest in his office and actually asked Salmon Chase to handle many of his tasks. The ambitious Chase took them gladly, and Seward, too, stepped into Cameron's territory without reproach. "While he was Secretary of War, General Cameron conferred much with me," Chase would boast. The treasury secretary actually managed much of the war business in the West in 1861. Cameron oversaw almost nothing. Instead of coordinating and managing the efforts of the several states in recruiting volunteer regiments, he left the task to the governors, in fact abrogating most of his responsibility to them. Worse, he allowed the most gross frauds to be perpetrated against the war department and perhaps profited personally. Unsound horses were purchased at double the going price for good animals. Arms were bought at prices up to twice their market value, and contractors providing construction and other services sometimes got away with profits of 60 percent and more. The excesses of his administration finally came exposed in the Supreme Court, which condemned the manner in which government war contracts were distributed. By late 1861 the situation demanded a change, and Lincoln was happy to make it. Still, always a party man, the President did not risk alienation of all the old bosses who backed Cameron and helped elect him. Rather than dismiss the secretary, Lincoln persuaded him to resign in order to accept a diplomatic post. But even Lincoln could not keep Congress from formally condemning Cameron the following April in a House resolution.[4]

That called for a replacement, and Lincoln's decision had as great an impact upon the Union war effort as any action he would take during the conflict. He appointed Edwin M. Stanton, onetime attorney general under Buchanan, a Democrat who favored Breckinridge in 1860, yet a man of unswerving devotion to the Union. He was a bully yet lacked moral courage and frequently backed down when confronted face-to-face. He could lie and scheme shamelessly yet was otherwise an honest man whose basic instincts were unrelenting hard work. His single-minded goal was victory and the ascendance of the Republican party, and few means were too distasteful to achieve those just ends.

Lincoln's reasons for selecting Stanton are complex. In fact, the forty-seven-year-old Ohioan began the war as an ardent critic of the new administration. After Manassas he predicted that "as a result of Lincoln's 'running the machine,'" the whole war effort was lost, and expected Jefferson Davis to turn out "the whole concern" in a few months. Meanwhile Stanton was on good terms with Cameron and did some legal work for the war department. He and McClellan were friends as well, Stanton having supported the general's efforts in Ohio in the early months of the war. When Cameron was ready to resign, Chase and others began pushing for Stanton as his replacement. Stanton himself contributed to Cameron's ouster by writing for him in part a report advocating the use of Negro troops in the war. It seriously embarrassed the President, who still had to keep this from being a war over slavery or risk defection in Kentucky, Maryland, and Missouri. If Stanton divined what Lincoln's reaction would be, he may have used the unwitting Cameron for his own ends. Yet even Cameron supported Stanton as his successor, and on January 14, 1862, Lincoln made the appointment. It also put a loyal Democrat in the cabinet, as well as a man of proven administrative ability.[5]

Stanton's inheritance from Cameron was a cabinet department whose organization stood woefully below the level of the war it was waging. It consisted of eight bureaus, some of them staffed by officers whose service dated to the last war with Great Britain. Offices of the adjutant general, paymaster general, surgeon general, commissary general of subsistence, quartermaster general, engineer bureau, bureau of topographical engineers, and ordnance bureau, were barely able to handle their peacetime workload. Worse, at the outbreak of the war many of these operations had been eviscerated by resignations. Joseph E. Johnston and Samuel Cooper had headed the quartermaster and adjutant general's offices, and many lesser employees of those and other bureaus departed as well. This left the war department relying largely upon newly hired and inexperienced personnel. Montgomery C. Meigs, Lincoln's new quartermaster, actually had to hire staff without getting authorization to do so.

To add to the administrative load, Stanton soon recognized that other and more specialized bureaus were needed to administer the very special problems and challenges created by this war. A lawyer, and understanding the myriad legal difficulties and courts martial that an army of a million or more would create, he inaugurated the judge advocate general's office. To meet the difficulties of feeding and sheltering prisoners, and exchanging them back to the Confederates in return for captured Federals, he began the offices of the commissary general of prisoners and commissioner for exchange of prisoners. The new uses of rapid travel and communications required bureaus for the director and general manager of military railroads and the United States military telegraph. A war department telegraph office also operated as a separate function, working almost exclusively as a part of Stanton's own office.

In the days to come, even more specialized services demanded their own bureaus. It is a measure of Stanton's flexibility and vision as an administrator that he molded his department to the needs of the situation, rather than attempting to force to his rigid demands the operation of the war. In 1863 he instituted the cavalry bureau, to deal chiefly with the knotty problem of procuring good mounts. The provost marshal general's bureau appeared then, as policing military districts and handling unruly soldiers mounted. An office of the chief signal officer began, as did an inspector general. The two former engi-

neer bureaus united, and other reforms within the existing system
came about. Then came a bureau of refugees, freedmen, and abandoned lands to handle freed slaves and "liberated" Rebel property. An
office of the chief of ordnance administered the thousands of cannon
with the armies. And in 1864, well before the war was done, Stanton
commenced the war records office to manage the historical documents
accumulating in virtual trainloads, and to arrange for their publication for posterity—and undoubtedly for political use.[6]

When Stanton took office, he found stacks of unopened mail in the
war department, the building itself in need of much repair, officers
and civilians crowding the hallways seeking position and promotion.
Locals, and some employees, referred to the department as "the luna-
tic asylum." Stanton changed all that, not overnight, but with remarkable speed considering that he had a war to fight as well.

While setting his own house in order, the new war secretary had to
come to some understanding with Lincoln and McClellan and the
other generals, for the chain of command in the Union was uncertain
at best, and often counterproductive. Responsibilities and authority
became frightfully confused. Ideally Lincoln, as commander-in-chief,
should deal with his secretary of war, who should in turn deal with
the commanding general and/or the ranking commanders of each of
the armies, and largely through his bureau chiefs. Instead, Lincoln
bypassed Cameron all too frequently, planning directly with old General Scott and his staff. Cameron, of course, let Chase do much of his
military work, and for a time the generals in the field like McDowell
received little direction from anyone, or else too much from too many.
When McClellan came to Washington in August 1861, he worked at
first under Scott, but quickly engineered his superior's retirement by
circumventing him and dealing directly with Lincoln.

The appointment of McClellan as general-in-chief was in theory a
good move, but even here problems arose. When Stanton took office
he discovered soon that a mountain of important military telegrams
had not been shown to him. The reason was one of Cameron's rules
established to suit Little Mac that no one was to see this intelligence
before McClellan himself. Stanton soon changed that. His relationship
with McClellan quickly deteriorated, made the worse when all department commanders were ordered henceforth to report to Washington, not McClellan.

Yet still the organization did not work smoothly from top to bottom. When McClellan was relieved as general-in-chief, Lincoln appointed no one in his place, and then faced Jackson's Shenandoah
Valley Campaign and the Peninsula Campaign by trying to coordinate efforts himself. Stanton was doing more than his own job. Subordinate field generals were reporting to the war department rather
than their own army commanders. Lincoln was counseling with informal groups of generals on strategy, sometimes without McClellan

present, thus inviting military infighting. It was a bad situation, but in July 1862 the President took a great step toward alleviating the problem. Henry W. Halleck was no great field commander, but he was not called "Old Brains" for nothing. His mind thrived on order and system. Now Lincoln made him general-in-chief, largely as reward for Grant's victories. Halleck did not solve all of the problems in the chain of command, but he brought the situation under control. Stanton retreated from his personal involvement in strategic affairs and returned to his assigned duties of raising and equipping the armies. Lincoln also took a lesser role, though he would never entirely bow out. From March 11 to July 11, 1862, he had acted as commander-in-chief and general-in-chief, and he liked doing both. Though Lincoln would never lay claim to military brilliance, surely he believed in himself, that he was as capable as his generals—certainly as capable as those he relied upon in 1862.[7]

Within less than a month of taking office, Stanton had already alienated many, creating enemies who would dog him all his life. Indeed, he made enemies easily, being humorless, insulting, and tactless. Yet he won more than his share of admirers as well. He regarded Lincoln with contempt at times, tried even to scold and lecture him, but came in the end to feel a substantial regard and respect. Lincoln, master of men, knew how to handle the secretary for his own ends, and overlooked Stanton's cantankerous nature. Each served the other, each made and took the blame for decisions that the other preferred not to make. In the end Stanton always deferred to Lincoln. When the President, after exhausting all tact and diplomacy, told him directly "Mr. Secretary, it will have to be done," Stanton complied. He never loved Lincoln. But he came to respect him, and Stanton respected few men indeed.[8]

Stanton also respected the American volunteer soldier. Like many Americans, he distrusted most professional soldiers, but to him the volunteer was a special figure. Most of his efforts were spent in that soldier's behalf. By the time Stanton took office, the work of raising the armies was already begun, however inefficiently. From the paltry 14,000 men under arms in April 1861, the armies totaled 576,000 when he assumed his portfolio. Yet inequities plagued the system. Lincoln's calls for volunteers established quotas for each state, but some states overcontributed while others failed to meet their requirements. New Hampshire, Massachusetts, Connecticut, and New Jersey all produced fewer recruits than expected. Yet the states to the west, even slave state Missouri, considerably overcontributed men, revealing an interesting contradiction between New England and the Middle Atlantic and Western states. Part of the explanation was seasonal. After the autumn harvests, the West had a surplus of labor available, while the East suffered a shortage due in part to the increased employment in war industry. Cameron had compounded the confusion by accepting regiments not only from the state governors, but also from private individuals as well, men who financed and raised volunteers on their own. Stanton soon ordered that only governors were authorized to raise regiments.

The initial euphoria of enlisting of 1861 did not sustain itself, and this, too, Stanton had to combat. He and the governors soon resorted to offering enlistment bounties, cash rewards for those who took service for three years or the war. Sums of up to $500 lured men in ways that appeals to patriotism did not, yet even here problems arose. "Bounty jumpers" quickly made a practice of enlisting, taking the bonus, then deserting to reenlist elsewhere under another name and for another bounty.

Still this measure did not produce enough grist for Stanton's mill. This war required men in undreamed-of numbers. By the end of 1862 the Federal armies totaled nearly one million, almost twice their size when the secretary took office. For every man on the firing line, at least two others were needed in the support services. By this time the Union Army had become an enormous, highly organized machine, the largest "corporation" in the world. It fed on men, and its appetite seemed endless.

A draft was inevitable. On July 17, 1862, Lincoln signed a militia draft act, authorizing the conscription of men between eighteen and forty-five for nine months' service in state militia units. Though never used, the act opened the way for later moves to draft men to fill the regiments. Here was a touchy, indeed explosive, issue. Just as Americans never really trusted a professional standing army, so also did they resent any attempt at enforced service, or impressment. They rebelled against Great Britain over such issues, and when the Continental Army resorted to conscription during the Revolution, it met little encouragement or cooperation. For an American, the decision to take arms was a personal matter of conscience, not something for government to force upon him. Lincoln knew this well, and only under the force of necessity did he work toward a major conscription act. Again in August 1862 he signed another militia draft bill, this one also never put into effect. Yet even then he could see the reaction that a full-blown attempt at a draft would receive. At the mere threat of these militia drafts many men left the country for Canada to escape it, or else cut off fingers or toes to make themselves unfit for service. In October, when Pennsylvania tried to enforce the militia draft acts, violent opposition broke out in some counties. Then on February 25, 1863, Congress passed the Conscription Act, and on March 3 Lincoln signed it. The measure required service of all able-bodied males between twenty and forty-five. Excluded were the ill or unfit, felons, government officials, and those with large numbers of children or other dependents. The act set quotas for each state based on their population and number of soldiers already serving. The opposition was immediate, and would become violent in days ahead. Yet in sum the Conscription Act produced the desired results, though in a subtle way. Fear of conscription led tens of thousands to volunteer instead and receive the bounty. Futhermore, the act allowed a man to "hire" a substitute to go in his place if drafted, or else to buy his way out of the situation by paying $300. As a result, 116,118 men bought substitutes. Another 86,724 paid the fee for escaping the act, thus raising $26 million for the Federal war treasury. In fact, only 46,347 men actually allowed themselves to be drafted into the service, and the desertion rate among draftees ran high. Thus, the act brought many men into the armies yet allowed wide opportunities for evading that service. Like most conscription acts in most countries, it fell hardest on those too poor to pay for substitution or commutation. Still, Lincoln's draft was a comparatively gentle introduction to the subject. More conscription calls would follow, but none would elicit the reaction of this 1863 act. In days to come it would bring Northern men to battle against themselves.[9]

Once he had the men, Stanton must feed and clothe them, a gargantuan task for him and his commissary of subsistence. Under Cameron the system had been indescribably corrupt and inefficient. Cavalry horses, for instance, frequently proved to be unfit for any task after being purchased at prices well above market. Of 411 mounts bought at St. Louis in October 1861, five were actually dead! Of the remainder, 330 were undersized, underage or overage, "stifled, ringboned, spavined, and incurably unfit for any public service." Only 76 were fit, and the government lost over $40,000 on the transaction. The situation even brought parody in the popular press. A cartoon in *Harper's Weekly Illustrated* depicted a contractor exhibiting his wares and quoting the percentage of bribe he would pay. "There sir! examine that blanket Sir! What could be better than it to protect our volunteers.— It is 2 feet 4 inches Square.—I'll allow 20 per ct—if they are passed," said the contractor. His shoes, yes, they had a bit of wood instead of leather in the soles. But the inspector would take them. And his trousers, he admitted, were rather open at the seams. "Just the thing for our Volunteers. The sewing you observe is open—for the purpose of ventilation!!!" "Beautiful—how cool it will be for our brave fellows," said the inspector. "50 percent did you say?" said another inspector, "let 'em rip."[10]

Stanton investigated all contracts for food, clothing, animals, and weapons for the armies; and a commission he appointed saved the government millions of dollars on existing contracts, as well as new ones to come. That there was an incentive for the profiteers is undeniable. In the course of this war Stanton's department will spend over one billion dollars with contractors just on subsistence and quartermaster goods. In the first year of the war alone subsistence cost over $50 million. Quartermaster supplies cost the same. The administration of all this occupied more of the war department's time than any other task except the soldiers themselves, and it was the men in uniform who ultimately paid the price for the grafters and contract swindlers. Bad food, inadequate clothing, and defective arms and equipment all made their lives more difficult, and despite Stanton's best efforts, the problem was never entirely eradicated.[11]

By the coming of 1863, this colorless, humorless, largely petty and unlikable man, Edwin M. Stanton, managed to form a partnership of himself, Abraham Lincoln, and one million men. The President he regarded as a "giraffe." He looked down on most individuals. He developed a mistrust of many of his generals and almost all contractors. The rest of the cabinet disliked him, except for Chase, and some, including Welles, openly despised the man. He could be cowardly and prone to panic, as when he feared that the *Virginia* might steam up the Potomac and destroy Washington. Yet Stanton could also learn a prodigious amount about the workings of an army in the field, how to organize and follow an efficient chain of command, how to select officers for appointment on merit rather than political influence. He would reject his own nephew's commission, knowing him unsuited. And he understood as well as any, including Lincoln, that this war had to be won by civilian authority directing the military. The generals must hold themselves subservient to the government or else the Constitution was subverted as much by them as by the secessionists. There were dangers with a man like Stanton, and Lincoln knew it. The President likened his secretary to an old Methodist preacher who was so animated and active behind the pulpit that his congregation thought of putting bricks in his pockets to keep him down. "We may be obliged to serve Stanton the same way," said Lincoln, "but I guess we'll just let him jump a while first."[12]

Jefferson Davis might well have followed Lincoln's lead. He did not. While Lincoln learned about war from experience in office, Davis took office knowing all there was, or so he thought. His confidence in his own military prescience was such that he could tell his wife with perfect sincerity that "If I could take one wing and Lee the other, I think we could between us wrest a victory from those people." As a result, Jefferson Davis from the first impressed his personal stamp on the Confederate war effort in a way Lincoln never did. It became as much the President's war as the Confederacy's.[13]

Davis in fact brought to his position several attributes that Lincoln lacked. The trouble was, the Mississippian did not know how to use them. He had a long and wide acquaintance with military men. Unlike Lincoln, then, he stood in a position to judge the merits of the men who offered their services to the Confederacy. Officers like Lee, J. E. Johnston, Cooper, Braxton Bragg, A. S. Johnston, Beauregard, and scores of others, were well known to him. Unfortunately, however, Davis's judgments of men took their form not from dispassionate consideration of their merits but, rather, from the peculiarities of Davis's own personality. He judged men on how they related and reacted to him. Those who agreed with him, flattered his military vanities, or who lacked sufficient assertiveness to balk at his interference in their affairs, stood high in his judgment. In time even the most bald-faced obsequiousness from courtiers like John B. Hood was welcome. Davis came to Richmond intent upon running the war, and particularly the army, himself. It showed in his selection of men to administer the war department.

Leroy Pope Walker had politicked personally for his cabinet position, soliciting the support of friends of Davis. Without knowing Walker personally, still the President appointed him. Some thought it was because Walker in fact possessed talent at administration, but others saw more clearly the motivation. First Walker brought Alabama into the cabinet. Second, and more important said some, "he was only a man of straw whom Mr. Davis had offered the portfolio, simply that he might exercise his own well-known love for military affairs and be himself *de facto* Secretary of War." If Walker did not know it at the time, he soon would learn that much of his duty, particularly that relating to the appointment of officers and direction of the armies, would be usurped by the President.[14]

Walker was not a man of significant military perception. During the Fort Sumter crisis, in which his part was almost entirely that of transmitting Davis's instructions to Beauregard, he failed to appreciate the need for a major Confederate mobilization. Instead, he boasted that the flag of the South would float over Washington by May 1, thus seriously arousing Northern public opinion in the face of a threatened invasion.

On March 6, 1861, in fact, the Congress in Montgomery had authorized Davis to raise 100,000 soldiers, but chiefly to garrison existing forts and frontiers. It indicated a belief that the North would not carry the conflict into the South. Walker, however, suggested to Davis that the Regular Army also authorized by Congress could not be raised very quickly and proposed instead that state troops be assimilated into the national service. That became, in fact, the chief system of enlistment and recruiting for the rest of the war. A few Regular Confederate units were formed and put into the field, but they constituted less than one percent of the Confederate Army.

At once Walker ran headlong into a problem that plagued the nation throughout its existence, state prerogatives. Each state's militia system differed from the others, and from the army structure required by Montgomery. The result was a constant battle with the governors to subordinate their wants for their regiments with the organizational needs of the war department. Matters of length of service, commissioned officers, uniforms and equipment, pay, and even methods of recruiting all provided grounds for dissension. Walker could not solve the problem, nor did any of his successors. By September 1861 he raised about 200,000 troops in spite of these difficulties. Once raised, however, he proved woefully unable to arm and equip them. Weapons came either from the state militia or captured Federal armories. The two sources hardly provided enough, and immediately Walker had to look to foreign purchase, which the blockade made uncertain. Again the governors caused trouble, refusing in many cases to release their states' arms, and supported by the insistence of the Confederate Congress that nothing be taken from a state without its governor's permission. Worse, in the early days when shipping was still moving with little difficulty and before it was too late, Walker failed to act on importation of equipment for the Confederacy to manufacture its own arms.

Other forms of supplies hampered Johnston after the victory at Manassas. Walker and Davis were not sensitive to the organizational needs of the war department. There was no quartermaster general until late March, Walker handling it all himself until then. Indeed, at the outset of the conflict, Walker broke down the functions of his department into only engineer, ordnance, quartermaster, and commissary bureaus, and only one of them could boast a really efficient chief. Davis, not Walker, made the appointments, and they came from among old friends and cronies. Colonel Lucius B. Northrop, a man of unbounded incapacity, became commissary general solely on the basis of his friendship with Davis during their days together at West Point. He had spent twenty-two years on permanent sick furlough from the United States Army, and wore newspapers inside his shirt instead of undergarments. "The reason for his appointment," said an associate, "was a mystery." Unfitted either by experience or ability for his task, yet Northrop would hold his office for four years, so determined was Davis to keep his friend. Northrop never complained, never differed with his President, and to Davis that was the most efficient way to run the war department.[15]

Walker did not last long. His health, like that of a surprising number of Davis's appointees, was not good. Worse, the President made major military decisions and issued orders before even consulting the secretary. On top of all, the criticism of Walker in the Confederacy at large had mounted to a high pitch within only a few months of his appointment. The failure to pursue the Federals after Manassas was laid at his door. His conflicts with the governors led to widespread disapproval in the press of his administration. And Davis did little to defend him, having lost confidence in Walker by late summer. Accordingly, when war clerk Jones saw an envelope placed conspicuously on Walker's desk addressed to the President, he correctly surmised that it contained a resignation. The envelope sat on his desk for several days, and finally on September 10 Walker gave it to Davis.

The President accepted, and by way of consolation made Walker a brigadier general.[16]

The Confederate war machine demanded more attention, more experience at its head, than any other branch of the government. Yet Davis, rather than learn the lesson offered by Walker's poor showing, proceeded to compound the error by succeeding him with someone of even less experience or fitness for military affairs. Judah P. Benjamin, attorney general. Jones correctly surmised the real reason for Benjamin's appointment. "Mr. Benjamin will please him," Jones told his diary; "he knows how to do it."

Davis apparently never intended that Benjamin be more than a temporary occupant of the war office, yet even such a stopgap appointment of one manifestly unqualified for the task reflects on the President's unbalanced priorities. He felt comfortable with the unctuous Benjamin, but the critical timing of Walker's resignation demanded someone who could do more than massage the Chief Executive's ego. The Confederacy had seemingly exhausted its initially available resources of men and matériel. The war department was organized, but barely. Benjamin, for whatever military knowledge he lacked, knew at least that the nation needed more men under arms. Most of the regiments in service had enlisted for twelve months. He urged that new regiments be raised for three years only. He tried, without much success, to increase the importation of foreign arms. He contended, very diplomatically, with the inefficiencies of Northrop. Most of all, he managed to agree with the President. When Davis broke with Joseph E. Johnston, so did Benjamin. As a result, when the press and generals began complaining about Benjamin's administration, Davis took the criticism personally and backed his secretary. It drove the two closer together, for censure of Benjamin became censure of the President. It would be the same throughout the war with other Davis favorites like Northrop and Braxton Bragg. Instead of recognizing the substance behind the complaints, the President regarded such situations as a test of wills. By hanging onto his friends and outlasting the critics, he would prove that he had been right all along. Davis felt a positive compulsion to be right.[17]

"There could be no hope of success as long as Mr. Benjamin was Secretary of War," said Joe Johnston. Hardly an unbiased observer, still he was right. Benjamin almost caused the resignation of Stonewall Jackson. Worse, during his months in office the Confederacy lost Roanoke Island, North Carolina, and Forts Henry and Donelson. In the case of the first, at least, Benjamin stood culpable of neglect. The press now attacked him as well, calling him the "chief thief in a cabinet of liars." Indeed, one Congressman proposed that the office of secretary of war be abolished for the duration of the war. In every facet of his portfolio except the managerial administration of his office routine—at which Benjamin excelled—the Louisianian had failed. The army was no better fed or clothed or armed. The enlistment problem was no better than under Walker, and relations of the department with the generals in the field actually declined. Davis finally had no alternative but to relieve Benjamin, yet managed to keep him at his side by giving his friend the newly vacant post of secretary of state. On March 18, 1862, Benjamin changed offices.[18]

In fact, Confederate armed forces declined slightly during Benjamin's tenure. When Walker left office the army totaled almost 250,000 men present for duty. When his successor departed that had declined to about 225,000. At the same time the Union forces totaled 534,000 present, more than double Southern numbers. If the armies were not growing, however, the war department bureaucracy was, and much of this is due to the good points in both Walker and Benjamin, particularly the latter. When formed, the department had an adjutant and inspector general—old General Samuel Cooper, another Davis friend—a quartermaster general, Northrop's commissary department, and a medical department. Then came the engineer bureau, a bureau of Indian affairs, the bureau of ordnance, a signal bureau, the army intelligence office, a bureau of exchange, another for conscription, a niter and mining bureau, a bureau of foreign supplies, and a commissary general of prisoners.

As in Washington, and despite the lack of an administrator of Stanton's ability, the growing organization of the Confederate war department reflected in most ways an admirable flexibility in adapting to the peculiar needs and resources of the South. It is significant that Indian affairs became a war department office rather than part of interior, as in the North. The Davis government looked upon the Indians of the trans-Appalachian and trans-Mississippi West as potential military allies, as indeed many tribes became. The bureau of foreign supplies created a special machinery to deal with the necessity of acquiring arms and munitions abroad, and the niter and mining bureau equally sought to cope with the South's need to produce its own gunpowder and lead. It is unfortunate that, with such a malleable organization available, the men in charge of the war department, and the man who controlled them, were not themselves more flexible.[19]

In one branch of the department, the Confederacy found that it could not differ from the Union. Conscription. Indeed, the South led the way, for the Congress passed a conscription bill and Davis approved it fully three months before Lincoln's first draft measure. On April 16, 1862, just after Benjamin's departure from the war office, Davis approved an act calling for the drafting of white males between eighteen and thirty-five for three years' service. At the same time, finally dispensing with the twelve months' volunteers problem, the act held into service for three years all men of that age currently in the army. Eventually the age limits were expanded to from seventeen to forty-five, with a provision for men forty-five to fifty being drafted into state militia for local defense. As in the Union, several categories of exemptions and substitutes were allowed, but still roughly 82,000 Southern men were drafted into service during the war.[20]

The reaction in the Confederacy to conscription could hardly have surprised anyone. The notion ran not only against the grain of Americans as a whole, but even more counter to the beliefs of proponents of states rights to whom a draft imposed by the central government was a direct invasion of state prerogatives. The conscription act represented to one North Carolina editor "a tendency to standing armies and military despotism." Others, while admitting the necessity of the moment, issued stern warnings. The Constitution "has, by the conscription, been set aside or over-ridden on the *plea of a war necessity*." The people might yield now, "But let them look out, henceforth, if our rulers are honest they will not abuse this usurped power." Thousands of men sought to evade the draft. They escaped into the mountains, went to the Far West, even crossed the lines into Union territory. The act created disaffection among troops already in service, too. Many regiments objected to being held in service beyond their twelve-month enlistments. The problem became acute in some commands, and out in Mississippi Breckinridge's Orphan Brigade threatened mutiny until he calmed them with a measure of rhetoric and threat. Throughout the South the enrolling officers sent to draft men became objects of scorn, vituperation, and even physical assault. Late in the war, it would take actual force to bring men in under the act. Thus the very tenets of self-determinism that lay at the heart of the Confederacy helped as well to eat away at it from within.[21]

The inheritor of this conscription problem, Benjamin's successor, was the first man appointed to the war office with some talent for the task. George Wythe Randolph brought Virginia prestige into the cabinet. Grandson of President Jefferson, born in the mansion at Monticello, six years a midshipman in the United States Navy and later prominent in Richmond militia organizations, Randolph actually had experience in arms procurement as chairman of Virginia's commission to buy weapons. Yet his appointment surprised many, and it, too, turned out not to be a happy choice, both for Randolph and Davis. A bookish man, the new secretary did not care for the war, yet served briefly in 1861, and just a month before taking the war post he received a commission as a brigadier from the President. Many believed that this new secretary, unlike his predecessors, could not be used by the President, but was distinctly his own man. Not at first. Randolph hesitated to state opinions. He forwarded his most important correspondence to Davis without comment and invariably deferred to the President in affairs relating to the armies. With the new conscription act he showed more pluck, taking on the governors squarely, and with some success. "I think we might as well drive out the common enemy before we make war on each other," he wrote to Georgia Governor Joseph E. Brown.[22]

John B. Jones, the war office clerk, lamented that Davis and his adviser Robert E. Lee made the war department into "a second class bureau, of which the President himself is the chief," and others echoed the lament. General Henry A. Wise said of Randolph that "He is not Secretary of War; he is merely a *clerk*, an underling, and cannot hold up his head in his humiliating position. He will never be able to hold up his head." Indeed, he could not. Finally in November Randolph showed independence from Davis by ordering a troop movement in the West without the President's permission. Davis required on November 14 that henceforth all correspondence regarding military strategy and officers go to his office. The next day Randolph resigned.[23]

Now, once again, Davis began the hunt for a war minister. Time was running out, however. After a year and one half of conflict, Davis still did not have a smoothly functioning war department, thanks largely to his own interference and poor judgment of men. Worse, there had been absolutely no progress in developing an efficient chain of command. Rather, the situation worsened. While Davis had Lee as his chief military adviser, the general could informally act at least in part as a general-in-chief or as much as Davis let him. But when Lee replaced Johnston at the head of the Army of Northern Virginia, no one took his place. Now the Confederate war machine stumbled along with a President functioning as chief executive, secretary of war, and general-in-chief all in one, and quite unqualified for any one of the posts, let alone all three. Congress authorized a commanding generalship on March 30, 1862, but Davis vetoed the provision "for trenching on the executive prerogative," thought Jones. It was perhaps his greatest mistake of the war, but being the man he was, Jefferson Davis could hardly do otherwise. In the months to come after that veto he would pay dearly for trying to keep the army his personal plaything. Disunity of command and a lack of continuity in war department policy thanks to no less than four secretaries before 1862 was done, left the armies in the field largely on their own. While Lincoln and Stanton spent 1862 building an army for victory, Davis built little beyond what he had at the end of 1861. And all the while that he and his succession of secretaries vied with each other, the governors, and their generals, the Confederacy was losing the Mississippi, and the war.[24]

CHAPTER 15

"I WANT TO SEE
THIS THING OVER"

Shiloh was a parting of company for many in the West. In its after-math Beauregard sickened and left the Army of Tennessee. Breck-inridge took a division and went to help defend Vicksburg, Grant lost his command to Halleck once more, and Albert S. Johnston departed this life. The Confederacy lost its hopes for Kentucky yet once again. Many things in the war changed with Shiloh, and in afteryears it would be a benchmark in the progress of the war in the West and the struggle for the Mississippi. The struggle continued.

When Halleck left Missouri to come to Grant's army, he did not like what he found. The men seemed undisciplined, the camps untidy, and the officers incapable of keeping order. That this might not be unnatural just a few days after the greatest battle yet seen in the hemisphere seems not to have occurred to "Old Brains." What did occur to him was that Grant and Buell together were now national heroes, and he wanted some of the notoriety for himself. The best way to accomplish that was to subordinate them to him in the public eye, making it appear that he had been pulling the wires all the time. It was Halleck's least admirable trait.

It did not help Halleck that as Grant drove Beauregard from the field on the second day, yet another Western hero appeared. Forty miles south of Cairo on the Mississippi the Confederates had built two fortifications that effectively controlled river traffic below that point. At New Madrid, Missouri, General Leonidas Polk erected earthworks and planted batteries on a strategic bend in the river. Nearby, on Island No. 10 in the middle of another bend, he planted another battery, with supporting earthworks on the Tennessee shore. The works on Island No. 10 and the shore redoubts were protected from attack by land by difficult swamps in the Tennessee lowlands. Obviously, the offensive down the Mississippi could not bypass these works. They had to be taken, and quickly.

The job went to yet another Kentuckian, forty-year-old Brigadier General John Pope, a career officer distinguished in the Mexican War who enjoyed excellent political friendships. They got him his stars early in the war and a command in Missouri. Haughty and tactless, he nevertheless displayed genuine talent. When Halleck ordered him to organize a small army from scattered soldiers in Missouri, Pope succeeded in doing so quickly and set off on his assignment. With Grant pressing at Henry and Donelson, Pope was to take New Madrid from the land, and then reduce Island No. 10. Against little opposition, he accomplished the former on March 13 when the Confederates evacuated New Madrid. The latter took a bit more effort. Pope's naval supports and troop transports were upriver from Island No. 10 and would have to pass it to reach New Madrid. That they could not do, yet Pope wanted to use them to cross his army south of the island and thus turn its flank and force its fall. The solution was the spade.

The river made a complete turn at Island No. 10, running north a few miles, then turning south again at New Madrid. Thus the water formed a peninsula about ten miles long. By digging a canal across the top of that peninsula, Pope crossed his naval contingent to New Madrid, entirely bypassing Island No. 10. On April 7, while Grant and Beauregard were battling the final fury of Shiloh, Pope ferried a brigade across below the island and cut off the Confederates' only line of retreat. That same day the 7,000-man garrison of the island surrendered, thus opening to Federal control another hundred miles of the mighty river, all the way to Memphis with only shore batteries at Fort Pillow in the way. Steadily the Father of Waters was becoming a Yankee highway, and a sword point driven deep into the heart of the Confederacy.

Now for a time it would be a naval war for the Mississippi, and names like Farragut and Porter supplant the Grants and the Popes, and certainly the Hallecks. There were, after all, two ends to the Mississippi, and New Orleans beckoned seductively to the Union Navy. Ever since the fall of Forts Hatteras and Clark, Gustavus Fox had envisioned an attack on the Crescent City. It was defended by two substantial masonry forts, Jackson and St. Philip, several miles below at the mouth of the Mississippi. A heavy chain stretched across the river, anchored on barges, to bar the passage of enemy ships, and three ironclads then finished or abuilding hoped to defend the city itself. Fox considerably underestimated the strength of all this, believing that a Federal fleet could easily pass the forts and take New Orleans. He made a convincing argument to Welles, who until then gave little thought to that end of the Mississippi. Then Lieutenant David Dixon Porter, with more up-to-date information available, seconded Fox's arguments. On November 14, 1861, Welles and Fox presented their plan for capture of New Orleans to Lincoln. The President approved, and so did then General-in-Chief McClellan, so long as the operation did not require more than 10,000 soldiers to garrison the city once taken. He could not spare more.[1]

This done, Welles must choose a man to lead the expedition. There were few enough at hand, for most of the competent officers not superannuated were already on post. Eventually Welles came to the name of Captain David G. Farragut, sixty years old, nearsighted, with no real experience in squadron command, and a Tennesseean as well. He hardly seemed the right man for such an undertaking, yet Farragut enjoyed good opinions among the Navy's high command. Welles needed "courage, audacity, tact, and fearless energy, with great self-reliance, decisive judgment, and ability to discriminate and act under trying and extraordinary circumstances." Fox seems to have suggested Farragut first, and Welles remembered him from the Mexican War when he heard the officer make a bold proposal to the then secretary of the navy. The urging of Porter made the selection final, for both Welles and Fox placed enormous confidence in Porter. They did not seem concerned by any conflict of interest presented in Farragut's being Porter's foster brother. As an orphaned child, Farragut was adopted and raised by the famous Commodore David Porter, in company with his own sons David and William.[2]

Welles gave Farragut the assignment, after assuring himself of the Southern-born officer's loyalty. Farragut gave a good account of himself there. "Those damned fellows will catch it yet!" he said of Southern officers who had resigned the Navy, and Welles was convinced. When presented with the plan for taking New Orleans, Farragut exclaimed that "It will succeed." His intent was to "run by the forts and capture New Orleans" with even less than the naval force being put at his disposal, such was his confidence. Farragut's flagship was to be the USS *Hartford*, the beginning of a happy association of sailor and ship that lasted the war.

Farragut rendezvoused his fleet at the Head of the Passes, the mouth of the Mississippi in the Gulf of Mexico. It was a formidable squadron. He had seventeen men of war, including the powerful *Hartford* and her sister ship *Brooklyn*. Also with him was the USS *Mississippi*, a side-wheeler that had gone to Japan with Matthew C.

Perry. There was as well a flotilla of mortar boats commanded by Porter, twenty little vessels each mounting a huge 13-inch mortar for lobbing shells in a high arch over earthworks and parapets. In all, Farragut had 181 cannon and Porter 99, including his mortars. It was a most formidable array of firepower. Yet there was a troublesome gun within, as well, for Porter began at once to politick against his brother. "Men of his age in a seafaring life are not fit for important enterprises," Porter secretly wrote to Fox; "they lack the vigor of youth." Just what Porter was about is difficult to fathom, yet that his own ambition motivated all his acts is certain. Perhaps, after all, there was some long-felt jealousy over the orphan who received more attention from his own father than Porter did.[3]

Poor New Orleans had little to resist Farragut except a general who deserved better of his superiors. Mansfield Lovell was a native of Washington, D.C., a Mexican War veteran, New York City street commissioner, and a man of greater abilities than President Davis would ever realize. To defend the most populous city in the South, Lovell had barely 500 men in his two forts. There had been more, but Secretary of War Benjamin repeatedly withdrew soldiers from New Orleans to reinforce the army in the East. Some 5,000 were taken in February 1862, leaving Lovell to face the storm of popular indignation—and Farragut. To augment his meager defenses, he constructed a series of fire rafts to send among the enemy fleet when it attacked, hoping to set afire some of the Yankee ships. A ram, the *Manassas*, was ready, expected to be terrible in battle, and two other ironclads, the *Mississippi* and *Louisiana* approached completion. Yet Lovell knew very well that against any concerted assault, he could not hold the city.

That was the sort of assault Farragut planned. The attempt to take New Orleans did not begin auspiciously, however. Back on October 11, 1861, the *Manassas* had gone downriver with six small ships to attack the USS *Richmond* and four other vessels there attempting to block the mouth of the Mississippi. In a small battle at the Head of the Passes, Commodore George N. Hollins's little Confederate flotilla routed the Federals, damaged the *Richmond* with the ram, and put the other ships to precipitate flight. The victory gave New Orleans a feeling of unwarranted security, and that same impression descended on the war department and navy department in Richmond, much to the sorrow of poor Lovell. Assuming the river to be safe from approach via the Gulf, Davis and Mallory and Benjamin assumed that any further threat to New Orleans would come only from upriver. Thus, as the months wore on, all pleas from Lovell and Hollins to strengthen the city's defenses met with little favor.

The threat became more immediate on December 3 when Federals occupied Ship Island in the Gulf of Mexico off Biloxi, Mississippi. It controlled entrance into Lake Pontchartrain, the back door to New

Orleans. At first Lovell deceived himself about the move, thinking it merely a diversion, while the main enemy attack would fall elsewhere in the gulf, perhaps at Mobile. Then too, the commander of the forces at Ship Island was Major General Benjamin F. Butler. "A Black Republican dynasty will never give an old Breckinridge Democrat like Butler command of any expedition which they had had any idea would result in such a glorious success as the capture of New Orleans," he wrote to Benjamin. It showed an insight into the political potential of victories that even Lincoln seems not to have enjoyed this early in the war. Allowing a Democrat like Butler to win a major victory could be injurious to the Republican party should Butler run for office at some later date. Since Butler himself became a leading Republican in years to come, however, the matter proved to be academic.[4]

By early March Lovell realized his danger from Butler after all, but Richmond never did. Davis was interested in armies and in the East. Benjamin knew nothing either of armies or navies. As late as April 17, Davis tried to order the *Louisiana* up the river even as Farragut knocked at the city's gates, and Mallory complied. And when Hollins proposed taking audacious steps to attack the Federal fleet with fire rafts and his rams, Richmond responded by relieving him of his command and ordering him East to supervise midshipmen in a desk job. Thus the government removed from the scene its only tried and successful river commander. Thus the Davis regime ensured the loss of New Orleans. Hollins was Lovell's last chance.

On April 18 Porter's mortar flotilla began the bombardment of Forts Jackson and St. Philip. Porter promised Welles that he would reduce the forts in two days. Six days later the forts still held, and Farragut demonstrated to Porter that most of his shells were in fact falling outside the enemy works. Farragut now directed that further time would not be wasted on the forts or the mortars. The next day, April 24, he would run his squadron past the forts, risking their fire. Porter, to excuse his own failure to silence the forts, later claimed that in fact it was he who urged this move. His duplicitous wire-pulling behind his brother's back would continue through much of the war.[5]

That night before the attack, Farragut surveyed his fleet. Suddenly he saw circling overhead a great bald eagle. "Look there, Flag-Officer," cried his clerk, "that is our national emblem. It is a sign of victory."[6]

Farragut piped all hands at 1 A.M. on April 24, and two hours later commenced the bold maneuver of running past the forts. The Confederates soon opened their guns on the passing ships, and then the fire rafts were released, as well as the *Manassas* and the other ten vessels that made up the pitiful Confederate fleet. By dawn the action was done. Farragut got all but three of his gunboats safely past the forts, and in the ensuing action with the enemy ships he destroyed eight of them and lost only one himself. It had been a daring action, at little cost, and fully justified the navy department's once-shaky confidence in Farragut. Porter's attempts to take credit for the action bore no fruit, and the Union had another hero.[7]

The loss of the forts, or rather their bypassing, made New Orleans untenable. Lovell had nothing with which to defend, even though his forces were now augmented to about 3,000 ill-equipped militiamen. He realized that any attempt to fight for the city could not succeed in the face of the combined might of Farragut's fleet and Butler's 10,000 men marching overland. It would only subject the city and its people to terrible destruction in lives and property. Instead, he returned defense of the city to the mayor and civil officials. Thus, when Farragut's fleet came in sight of the city on April 25 and he sent ashore his demand for surrender, Lovell declined to capitulate and instead evacuated his command. Unable to fight, he and the Confederacy could gain nothing by giving up what force he had. He would be censured for the rest of his career for this action though it was the only sensible course to follow. A later court of inquiry exonerated him of blame for the loss, but many in the South could not forget that he was a native of the North. Worse, the court showed the culpability of the war department and Davis in not appreciating the danger to New Orleans or listening to Lovell's pleas for help. As a result, the findings were not published for some time, and Lovell's career remained permanently marred. Only at war's end was he restored to duty, at the insistence of Johnston and Lee. Long after the war Davis would falsify his own account of the loss of New Orleans to exculpate himself from blame. The Confederate President could be a very small man at times.[8]

Farragut took the city, Butler moved in to occupy, and the Mississippi now stood closed to the Confederacy at both ends. The forts protecting the city surrendered on April 27, and the Confederate ironclads were destroyed by their own crews to prevent capture. Mary Chesnut wrote in anguish, "New Orleans is gone, and with it the Confederacy! Are we not cut in two? The Mississippi ruins us if it is lost."[9]

Much remained for Farragut. With his first prize taken, more beckoned. Welles had ordered him to go farther up the river if the combined movement under Grant and Foote had not by then cleared the upper Mississippi. Farragut should advance and attack the Confederate fortifications from the rear, supporting Foote. "If I get a successful entrance," Farragut himself told Fox, "I shall not stop until I meet Foote." But now a dilemma faced him. Which was more important, moving upriver or attacking Mobile? Both were mentioned in his orders. Finally he sent Porter to Mobile, and himself continued the conquest of the lower Mississippi.[10]

Butler brought his small army into New Orleans on May 1, 1862, and began the occupation. That freed Farragut to move ahead, and in the next week he took Baton Rouge without opposition. On May 12 a squadron of light draft gunboats went farther up the river and took Natchez, Mississippi, again without enemy resistance. Bit by bit Farragut was biting off the river. The next place for him to chew would be Vicksburg.

The captain sent Commander S. P. Lee upriver with six gunboats to exact the surrender of Vicksburg, and on May 18 Lee made his demand. "Mississippians don't know, and refuse to learn, how to surrender to an enemy," came the reply. "If Commodore Farragut or Brigadier-General Butler can teach them, let them come and try." Word that finally the enemy intended to resist his move up the river made Farragut anxious to get as much of his fleet to Vicksburg as quickly as possible. However, the river provided dangers to his larger vessels, and Confederate batteries planted high on bluffs where his naval guns could not reach offered even more impediments. On May 23, carrying 3,200 soldiers led by Brigadier General Thomas Williams, Farragut's fleet came within sight of the river bastion at Vicksburg. At once Farragut began a personal reconnaissance of the enemy's defenses, trying to discover the number and strength of the batteries on the bluffs and the type and strength of Confederate vessels that might meet him on the water. But soon his commanders determined that the city could not be taken. It was too strong, and their force and Williams's was too weak. The best they could do would be to leave a few gunboats in the vicinity to blockade the city, while Farragut and the main fleet returned to New Orleans. This made all the worse the captain's chagrin when he reached the Crescent City to find orders from the navy department directing him to exert every effort to get his fleet past Vicksburg to join with the squadron of river gunboats and ironclads under Captain Charles H. Davis, successor to the ailing Foote. Much had been happening on the river north of Vicksburg as well, and it was time for the Union to close this artery once and for all.[11]

Following Pope's victory at New Madrid and Island No. 10, the way lay clear for a naval advance toward Memphis, obstructed only by river defenses at Fort Pillow, Tennessee. Pope and Foote showed energy in pressing their advantage, and less than a week after the success at New Madrid, Foote's flotilla appeared just above Fort Pillow. But then Halleck, preparing to advance against Beauregard at Corinth, removed almost all of Pope's army, and left Foote to fend for himself. For the next several weeks Foote did little except suffer from his painfully wounded foot, and on May 9 he turned the command over to his anointed successor, Davis, fleet captain for Du Pont in the Port Royal expedition.

The very day after Davis assumed command his ability was put to a challenge greater than any faced by Foote. On that day the Confederate River Defense Fleet commanded by Captain James E. Montgomery attacked. It possessed only eight little gunboats, all converted merchant ships on the river before the war, and now indifferently armed with one gun apiece, and defended by bales of cotton, heavy timbers, and some railroad iron on the sides. It was an audacious move, and a desperate one, with no chance of success unless the Federal fleet's commander were a coward. Davis was not.

The Confederates attacked first one of Pook's city class ironclads, the *Cincinnati*. In short order Davis disabled or put out of control half of the enemy fleet, but not before they had rammed the *Cincinnati* and the *Mound City* and left the two Union gunboats sinking. Montgomery quickly saw himself outmatched and withdrew, first to Fort Pillow, and then to Memphis. Still, the bold attack completely surprised Davis, and made him wary of further advance on the Mississippi without strong reinforcement. He received it two weeks later, and in strength that the Confederates could hardly resist.[12]

Colonel Charles Ellet of Pennsylvania, bridge builder and persuasive advocate of the ram as a naval weapon, had lobbied unsuccessfully for some time for the war or navy departments to construct a fleet of light draft rams on the Mississippi to counter the vessels known to be under construction by the Confederates. Only on March 27, 1862, did Stanton finally authorize him to go to the West and start a fleet of steam rams. Ellet began at once buying suitable river steamers for conversion, and his success proved startling. In barely forty days he completed work on nine rams and two other "floating batteries," his "Ram Fleet" being ready for service by May 10. At once Stanton ordered Ellet to join Davis and cooperate in the capture of Memphis and the destruction of the River Defense Fleet.

Davis and Ellet took an immediate dislike to each other, the age-old army-navy rivalry springing up at once. Neither seemed willing to work with the other. Thus Ellet set off on his own responsibility, intent upon taking Fort Pillow and Memphis. He planned to attack on June 5 in tandem with land forces, but the Confederates occupying the fort evacuated the place and Montgomery's fleet retreated to Memphis. Halleck's occupation of Corinth had left Pillow isolated and untenable, but Memphis had to be defended if possible for its cannon foundry and other industry.

Now Davis took over. At dawn on June 6 he sent five of his ironclads and four of the Ellet rams against Montgomery's little fleet. The destruction was complete in this, the last "fleet" engagement of the Civil War. Only one Confederate vessel escaped destruction or capture. In two hours the battle was done, and the city of Memphis surrendered before noon.[13]

The Union success on the Mississippi seemed almost done, and in remarkably short time. In just four months the Federals secured the northern river from Cairo to Vicksburg and the southern part from

Head of the Passes to Vicksburg. Virtually the entire Mississippi was theirs, except for this one remaining river stronghold. With its capture Northern shipping could use the river unvexed and Confederate communications with, and supplies from, western Louisiana, Arkansas, and Texas, would be cut off. It remained only to take Vicksburg.

Two days after the Battle of Memphis, on June 8, Farragut put his squadron on the way north once more, this time to take Vicksburg for sure.

It proved a slow passage, but on June 25 the *Hartford* came within seven miles of Vicksburg to meet the *Brooklyn, Richmond,* and several gunboats and mortar boats. Later the same day General Williams and his 3,000 soldiers arrived on transports. Meanwhile Ellet and his Ram Fleet awaited just above the river city, and he and Farragut communicated with each other via couriers sent through the swamps. Farragut advised Ellet and Davis that there might be an attack soon.

On June 26 he sent Porter's mortar boats to begin a bombardment of the city that lasted for several days. Farragut planned to attack the next day. "Here we are once more in front of Vicksburg," Farragut wrote to his wife that night. "The work is rough." He feared that he could not combat the enemy guns placed on the bluffs, that the necessity for taking the city had prevented adequate preparation. "I hope for the best, and pray God to protect our poor sailors from harm."

Farragut had to postpone for another day, but early on June 28 gave the signal for his fleet to move. He intended to run past the Vicksburg batteries and link with Federal ships upriver. In darkness illuminated by the flash of hundreds of guns, the Union ships made their passage. Casualties were light, though a few ships proved unable to make the passage and returned downriver. By dawn Farragut was safely above the city and wiring to Welles for Halleck to do his part now and send from 12,000 to 15,000 men to move against the city from the land. Together the Army and Navy could seize Vicksburg.[14]

Perhaps so, but there were men on those bluffs who had other ideas. One of them was now Major General John C. Breckinridge. His performance at Shiloh, while hardly outstanding, was still as good as that of any other Confederate on the field and better than some who had been trained soldiers. As a result, he won promotion soon thereafter, and an endorsement from Braxton Bragg that the elevation was "Nobly won upon the field." Only one other politician would be raised to this rank by the West-Point-conscious Jefferson Davis. Yet there was little time for the new major general to glory in his rise. After covering the Confederate retreat to Corinth, Breckinridge acted as the army's reserve and when Halleck appeared about to advance against them, he and others advised Beauregard to withdraw. Halleck, after taking command from Grant, moved with all the speed of a terrapin in his advance on the Confederates, giving them every opportunity to escape. They did.[15]

Bragg replaced the ailing Beauregard at the army's head and knew that now Vicksburg would be threatened. He ordered Breckinridge's command there to reinforce the garrison commanded by Major General Earl Van Dorn. His soldiers arrived before him, and Breckinridge himself came into Vicksburg the very day that Farragut ran past the batteries. His command now changed from that of a corps to a division, and Van Dorn stationed him north of the city. On July 2 the Kentuckian's division moved closer to the river, and on July 4, when the combined forces of Davis and Farragut made a great bombardment of the city, Breckinridge and his Orphan Brigade nearly captured one of Porter's mortar boats that ventured too close to shore. They did not know that that same day Farragut received news that Halleck was not willing to send any troops to help in reducing the river fortress. Thus the Navy had passed the batteries to no purpose. The pitiful little force of General Williams, now on the opposite shore of the river, could do nothing. Soon he would lead his command back south to occupy Baton Rouge.

While a desultory shelling of Vicksburg continued, Breckinridge and his men settled into the oppressive heat and humidity of a Mississippi summer. Hundreds of men fell out sick, cutting the general's effectives in half. Worse, his relations with the blatantly egotistical Van Dorn deteriorated rapidly. Van Dorn, a native of Mississippi, graduated near the bottom of his class at West Point, just above James Longstreet. He had served in Texas and Virginia, then in Arkansas where he lost the Battle of Pea Ridge. A man of charm with ladies—too much for his own good, it would prove—he and his conceits managed to alienate most of his male peers. He and Breckinridge got along well at first. The two even played together, personally manning one of the city's guns during a bombardment until the enemy sent a hail of bursting shells toward them. But soon Breckinridge found Van Dorn's egotism repulsive, and their relations became stiffly formal. The Kentuckians in the Orphan Brigade felt the same. "Coxcomb, dandy, fop, ball-room beau," one of them said of Van Dorn, "and such a thing of paint, perfume, and feathers to command our Breckinridge—and us!" Most could not accept the incongruity of "having the finest-looking man in the Confederacy, and that man a Kentuckian, subordinate to one so apparently inferior in every way."[16]

But personal animosities were forgotten two weeks after Breckinridge reached Vicksburg. That day, July 15, something happened to raise the spirits of every Confederate and send Farragut into a gloom. Far up the Yazoo River, a tributary of the Mississippi, Confederate constructors had been at work for weeks on finishing a new ironclad first begun at Memphis. The vessel measured 165 feet long, 35 feet wide, and carried ten heavy guns inside a casemate protected by four and one half inches of railroad iron. She was the CSS *Arkansas*, the most formidable Southern vessel ever to ply the great river, yet her career would last barely three weeks.

Her captain, Lieutenant Isaac Brown, chose July 15 to run his vessel out of the Yazoo and straight through Farragut's fleet to the safety of Vicksburg. It was a bold stroke, took the Federals quite by surprise, and succeeded admirably. When he saw the ship coming, Breckinridge sent his Orphans toward the Yazoo to cover Brown, then climbed to the dome of Vicksburg's courthouse to watch the action. That same day he provided a squad of artillerists from his Kentucky brigade to go aboard the *Arkansas* and serve one of its guns in the firing as Farragut brought part of his fleet past the city once again. On following days Breckinridge several times detailed Kentuckians to handle the *Arkansas* guns, the Orphans reporting afterward that they performed "as Kentuckians have always and will continue to act before the enemy, whether on land or water."[17]

Farragut felt dejected by the day's events, and another repulse on July 22, when Ellet tried to ram and sink the *Arkansas* unsuccessfully, did nothing to help. The next day Welles ordered him to return to the lower Mississippi for the season, and Davis took his flotilla back to the mouth of the Yazoo. The *Arkansas* almost single-handedly had won for Vicksburg a reprieve of several months and for the Confederacy control again of nearly three hundred miles of the Mississippi. Now was the time to follow up on the success and take measures to secure that stretch of the river once more open. Yet Richmond was not prepared for this. Even though Bragg's army was close enough to cooperate, he and Davis were listening to the Kentucky muse again and planning an invasion for the fall. Secretary of War Randolph had little to do, as usual, and Van Dorn had to rely on his own resources. That meant Breckinridge.

Despite the poor condition of his division thanks to malaria and dysentery, Breckinridge took orders on July 25 to move his command south by rail to attack Williams at Baton Rouge. Success there would anchor the Confederate hold on the Mississippi below Vicksburg, protecting the mouth of Louisiana's Red River which brought invaluable supplies from the trans-Mississippi interior. The condition of his command was such that Breckinridge agreed to undertake the expedition only if the *Arkansas* could be sent downriver to cooperate with him in the attack, and Van Dorn agreed. Unwittingly Breckinridge, the untutored soldier, had conceived the Confederacy's first combined operation of land and naval forces.

Despite considerable obstacles, the Kentuckian had his pitiful little "army" in front of Baton Rouge by August 5. Already he had waited a day for the *Arkansas* to be ready. The march in the heat cost him 600 men, but still he moved the remainder through the early morning dark to the city's outskirts. An accident led to shots being fired in confusion, putting Brigadier General Ben Hardin Helm out of action and killing his aide Lieutenant Alexander Todd, brother of Mrs. Abraham Lincoln. It also alerted the Federals in Baton Rouge. Nevertheless Breckinridge attacked. Williams, himself depleted by sickness, still matched the Confederate numbers and had five gunboats tied at the city's wharves as well. Even though Breckinridge steadily pushed the Federals back to and through their own camps, he finally came to a place where he could move no farther without risking fire from the gunboats. "His presence had a magical effect upon the men," wrote an observer. Breckinridge had learned from his mistakes at Shiloh. Now, instead of leading his troops personally, he remained behind the battle line generally maintaining control of all of his units by his staff officers.

Finally ammunition ran so low that the Confederates had to use their bayonets. They closed so near the Federals that the gunboats had to stop firing for fear of hitting their own men. Yet still the *Arkansas* did not appear. Finally, with Williams killed in battle and the Federals huddling at the riverbank under the protection of the gunboats, Breckinridge could stay no more, and ordered a withdrawal until the ironclad should appear. It never did. Troubled by failing engines, the *Arkansas* barely got within four miles of Baton Rouge when she stopped. Her crew destroyed her rather than see her captured by approaching Federal gunboats.

Both sides claimed victory, yet certainly Breckinridge outfought and outgeneraled his opponent. Only the failure of the ironclad kept him from holding the city, but Breckinridge quickly perceived what Van Dorn did not realize until a few days later. Baton Rouge was not the place for their purposes anyhow. That place, in fact, was Port Hudson about ten miles up the river. Its bluffs commanded the river at a bend, unlike Baton Rouge, which would have been difficult to fortify to resist enemy fleets. On August 12 the Kentuckian began the occupation and fortification of Port Hudson, and thereby gained for the Confederacy a bastion on the river that would stand for nearly a year. The loss of the *Arkansas* opened the Mississippi to the enemy up to Vicksburg again, but the works at Port Hudson closed that door before Farragut could take advantage. Thus, though just a few weeks before the South had lost every mile of the great river except Vicksburg, now Breckinridge had reclaimed several hundred miles of water. It was to be the last significant action of the year for control of the river, and for the South by far the most important. The Congress in Richmond understood. It voted its thanks to the general from Kentucky and his little army.[18]

"It is one of the happiest moments of my life," said Farragut when he learned the fate of the *Arkansas*. Less happy was the attempt of his foster brother William D. "Dirty Bill" Porter to take credit for defeating the ironclad in battle, when in fact her own crew destroyed her. There was a wide streak of character fault in these Porters, one

39. "Little Mac," George B. McClellan, the general who claimed he could "do it all" then did almost nothing. He appears, second from right, on the Peninsula with some of his staff. (Library of Congress)

40. Part of McClellan's great Army of the Potomac, at Cumberland Landing, Virginia, in 1862. It is one of the finest armies ever fielded anywhere but without a general who can fight. (Library of Congress)

41. The Confederate Army in Virginia had several generals who could fight. One who was untried and unproven when he replaced Johnston on the Peninsula was Robert E. Lee. (National Archives)

42. One already proven is Thomas J. Jackson, the great Stonewall, who adds to his luster from Manassas by his brilliant campaign in the Shenandoah in 1862. Lee will make him his right arm, though at first he fails him on the Peninsula. (National Archives)

43. Major General Henry W. Halleck, barely competent in the field and prone to take credit for his subordinates' successes. As general-in-chief he is a little more successful. (National Archives)

44. *Armies ran on money and financing them rested in the hands of men unfamiliar with the task. Salmon P. Chase would rather have been President, but as secretary of the treasury he raised the capital to equip and run Lincoln's armies.* (Library of Congress)

45. *Poor Lucius Chittenden, whose hands almost signed away his life on a wealth of bonds never used.* (National Archives)

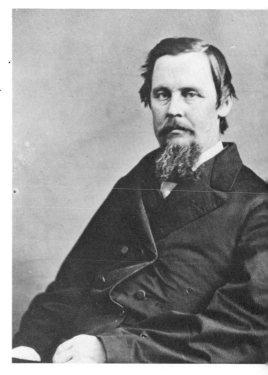

46. *The field at Cedar Mountain in August 1862, where Pope received his first hint of what Lee had in store for him at Second Manassas.* (Library of Congress)

47. *The carnage of Antietam. Dead lying in the "sunken road." It is the bloodiest single day of the Civil War, a battle without victors.* (Minnesota Historical Society)

48. *Lincoln goes to the field to try to get his general to fight. In this photograph, taken October 3 or 4, 1862, the President sits in McClellan's headquarters tent, urging him to shake the "slows." A month later "Little Mac" will leave the scene for good.* (Library of Congress)

49. *One of many slaves loyal to their masters; Silas, at right, took uniform and arms to accompany Andrew Chandler into the Mississippi Infantry.* (Courtesy of John M. Prewitt)

50. *Entering the lists for freedom. The 1st United States Colored Troops.* (U. S. Army Military History Institute)

happily not shared by their foster brother, and better, David G. Farragut. Soon after the ironclad's demise Farragut received even more cheering news when he learned of his promotion to the new rank of rear admiral. Welles ordered him back into the Gulf of Mexico to make preparations for an attack on Mobile. Farragut was more than happy to leave the river. It had been a scene of great frustration for him. In the sea he would be free of the interservice politicking, he hoped, and of the back-biting of his brothers as well.[19]

That jealousy and deviousness permeated more than the Navy on the river. As Farragut's departure turned the campaign for the Mississippi back to the Army once more, grizzled little U. S. Grant could reflect himself on the ingratitude and duplicity of his fellow officers. When Halleck superseded him in command back in April, Grant became nominally second in command. At once Halleck began taking credit for Shiloh and attempted to ease Grant out of the public eye. Meanwhile he marshaled his forces for the advance on Corinth, boasting that he would destroy the enemy in a single blow. However, Halleck took three weeks to get his campaign started and then took another month to march the twenty miles to the outskirts of Corinth. At once "Old Brains" turned timid. Having just stolen a reputation from Grant and Pope, he feared to risk it, telling his officers that "It is better to retreat than to fight," or so Grant believed. Meanwhile Grant was reduced to little better than an observer, and asked to be relieved more than once. When the move to Corinth began, Grant, often unable to see or perceive the ulterior motives in men, believed Halleck to be "one of the greatest men of the age." Less than two weeks later, however, he would complain to Halleck that "my position differs but little from that of one in arrest." On May 11 he asked to be restored to command, or else relieved entirely. He was hurt. "I have been so shockingly abused," he told Julia, "that I sometimes think it is almost time to defend myself." His spirits sinking, he told her, "I want to see this thing over." Yet he had found one friend in these trying days. Sherman. "I have never done half justice by him," Grant would write referring to Shiloh. "He was my standby during that trying day of Sunday." "In Gen. Sherman the country has an able and gallant defender and your husband a true friend."[20]

With Corinth taken, Halleck depleted his army instead of using it in a mass. He might easily have taken Vicksburg from the land, or advanced against Bragg's Army of Tennessee. Instead, he sent Buell into Tennessee to hold Nashville and spread the rest of his army through northern Mississippi and western Tennessee. Grant went to Memphis and established his headquarters, remaining to function as an army of occupation for nearly a month until Halleck was relieved of his command and brought to Washington to become general-in-chief. This left Grant the senior officer and effectively a department commander, but a resentful Halleck would not confirm the position for another four months. Meanwhile Grant found his command so widely dispersed that he had little choice but to assume a defensive posture until he could once more consolidate forces to resume the offensive. That gave the Confederates a perfect opportunity to make a move of their own, and they did.

Bragg had left 16,000 Confederates under Sterling Price at Tupelo. With Van Dorn's command that made 22,000 Rebels in Mississippi. Bragg ordered them to prevent Grant from reinforcing Buell while he made his invasion of Kentucky; yet Van Dorn, ambitious on his own hook, refused to cooperate with Price at first. But then late in September the two planned a strike against Rosecrans, now commanding a part of Grant's army, near Corinth.

Grant learned of the movement on September 7, or surmised that something of the sort was in the Confederates' minds. "I was much concerned," he said later. At once he began to concentrate all of his scattered units. When he found that Price was in Iuka, ten miles southeast of Corinth, on September 14, Grant determined to attack him before Van Dorn, coming from Vicksburg, could converge with Price. The planned attack, entrusted to Rosecrans, fizzled from bad roads, bad communications, and even a bad atmospheric condition, which kept Union supports barely three miles from the field from hearing the battle. Price held his ground, then retired. "I was disappointed," said Grant, yet he found no fault with Rosecrans at the time.[21]

For two weeks after the fight at Iuka on September 19, the Confederates combined their forces and plotted against Corinth. From their position at Ripley, fifteen miles southwest of Corinth, Van Dorn and Price moved north on September 30, and at first it looked to Grant as if they were heading for Memphis. But then he ascertained that, in fact, Van Dorn intended to attack Rosecrans at Corinth. His confidence in Rosecrans unshaken by Iuka, Grant allowed him to remain in command and take the Confederate attack. On October 3 Van Dorn struck. The Federals now occupied earthworks first built by Beauregard six months before. At first Rosecrans's center fell back, but late in the day a counterattack halted Van Dorn's advance. He renewed his attacks the following morning yet the Federals held everywhere along their line. Unable to create an advantage, Van Dorn and Price had no choice but to withdraw, defeated in their hope to take this important rail center. Grant was ready for them when they sought to retreat by way of Pocahontas, west of Corinth. Foreseeing an enemy withdrawal, Grant sent troops to block their path. Unfortunately, as he had at Iuka, Rosecrans failed to pursue vigorously. Even though Van Dorn was stopped at Pocahontas, then, Rosecrans gave him time to sidestep the place and continue south to Ripley and on to Holly Springs. Had Rosecrans acted with zeal, he and Grant would have pinched the Confederates between them and destroyed or dispersed the major enemy army in Mississippi. Vicksburg would then have been theirs for the taking. Grant's relations with Rosecrans broke down almost immediately, as the latter began politicking for a separate command. He got it late in the month, being sent to replace Buell. Grant never trusted him again. This little general had a few peculiar features and among them was a disinclination to be forgiving of those who had failed him. He would overlook failure, sometimes repeated, in his few favorite cronies. But they never sought to undermine his position behind his back. If ever he got the chance, Grant would see that men like Rosecrans were put out of action, and the war.[22]

Now it was time for more of that war. The Confederate defeat at Corinth effectively left northern Mississippi securely in Grant's hands. That, and his new appointment as commander of the Department of the Tennessee, which embraced all of that land between the Mississippi and Tennessee rivers and from Cairo as far south as he could go, changed Grant's situation. He could advance again. There was a new Confederate commander in Mississippi, Lieutenant General John C. Pemberton. There were more Southern troops coming to join him. Clearly the enemy had gone on the defensive and the way now lay open for Grant to march on Vicksburg at last. It was time to complete the conquest of the Mississippi.[23]

CHAPTER 16

"TO AID THE NATIONAL TREASURY"

One thing Grant did not have to worry about. Money. Neither he nor the other Federal commanders in the field concerned themselves with the costs of this war. That was the business of the Congress and the Treasury Department, and they were very much concerned, indeed. By the time Grant began his preparations for the move on Vicksburg late in 1862, this war was costing almost $2.5 million every day![1]

Neither North nor South began the war fiscally prepared. Furthermore, neither entirely appreciated at the outset the enormous strains that a sustained conflict would put on their treasuries. America was primarily an agricultural continent, even in the North despite its greater degree of industrialization. Agriculture did not produce national wealth. Personal income and savings were low among farmers and planters, they paid no income taxes, no excise. The Federal government raised its operating capital entirely from customs duties, sale of public lands, and other means that, by their nature, could not be expanded to meet the sudden voracious demands of major warfare.[2]

Worse, the nation's banking system, North and South, was chaotic. There had been no national bank since the days of Jackson. Indeed, he did his best to dissociate the government from banking entirely.

The Independent Treasury Act of 1846 pulled Washington out of all contact with the rest of the banking community. The treasury exclusively raised and handled its own funds, and the various state and local banks did likewise. All funds due to the government were payable only in gold, silver, or United States treasury notes, interest-bearing certificates of obligation but not actual money. To keep all Federal money in Federal hands, sub-treasuries were dotted across the country. "The less government has to do with banks and the less banks have to do with government the better for both," said one treasury official. Perhaps so, but it created a situation in which, in a time of major and immediate emergency, Washington could not tie into the nation's supply of hard money. That supply, furthermore, lay scattered among some one thousand six hundred state banks, and represented in the market by no fewer than seven thousand varieties and denominations of bank notes. Years before, when he first entered politics, Abraham Lincoln stood opposed to this disordered national fiscal policy. So did others, even in the South where Jackson's attitude catered to states' rights interests. Breckinridge, too, found the situation in dire need of reform. Yet now Lincoln was forced to begin waging a war with Jackson's banking system. It was virtually impossible.[3]

Financiers in the North looked with considerable interest on the developments leading to the outbreak of the war. The effects of such a conflict could be disastrous, or very profitable, depending upon the government's course and that of Secretary of the Treasury Salmon P. Chase. Chase had no financial experience at all, and very little understanding of the subject. He had to learn much, and quickly. He found a treasury that was almost completely depleted and heavily in debt. After Howell Cobb left the post in December 1860, John Dix, one of his successors during the remnant of Buchanan's term discovered that "the books and accounts of the Treasury Department were in such confusion that it was impossible to discover the true state of affairs without much labor." Shortly before Chase took office it was finally determined that the treasury was $8 million behind to its creditors, yet so low was the government's credit that it could only borrow the money at usurious interest. Worse, customs rates went down as imports to the troubled country declined. During the 1850s customs income made up 90 percent of the national revenue. Now they were down by half.[4]

When Chase took office, then, he saw no alternative to raising money quickly but to follow the path already marked. He would have to borrow money from the private sector of the economy, and pay interest to get it. Here, at least, he was fortunate that the North currently enjoyed a surplus of hard money on deposit; but the announcement that the treasury was going to finance the war by borrowing rather than by a special tax disturbed the financial community. It made them wonder just how solvent the government was and whether its bonds were in fact a safe investment.

Chase first estimated that $320 million would be needed for the special demands of the war in 1861, and he proposed to raise only $80 million of that from taxes and other normal sources. The remaining $240 million must come from loans; yet Chase ignored his own experience in his first months in office. In April 1861 he advertised for $8 million in bonds, and sold $7 million. The next month a similar appeal for nine brought only eight, and a call for fourteen shortly thereafter brought no response at all. Clearly the money men in the Union felt little enthusiasm for financing the war by loans. Or almost all, that is. For one financier early saw that opportunity and patriotism might both be served by an alliance with Chase and the promotion of war loans: Jay Cooke of Ohio.[5]

He was a Buckeye like Chase, though the two were not acquainted prior to the war. Just forty years old in 1861, Cooke had been in banking since the age of eighteen, showing a natural gift for finance. Chase knew others of Cooke's family well in Ohio political circles, and Jay's brother Henry supported Chase's campaigns for office in his newspapers. Chase and other Ohio politicos were not unaware of Jay Cooke's newly formed banking house of Jay Cooke and Company in Philadelphia. And Cooke knew well that there was opportunity in the coming war, particularly with a friend in the treasury. "I see Chase is in the Treasury and now what is to be done?" he wrote his brother Henry in the capital. "Can't you sell out the paper and open a banking house in Washington and be something respectable?"

At once Cooke tried to obtain business from the department, seeking a contract to handle all of the government's transfers of funds from one point to another, and making a percentage on the money in the meantime. Then he took a keen interest in the loans Chase was trying to put out. Finally, on April 19, 1861, as Baltimore rioted and Lincoln declared the blockade, Cooke wrote directly to Chase. If he could get together a syndicate to subscribe for $1 million or more of the government notes, might he keep the specie raised in his banks until the government drew it? "Our banks are full of patriotism and anxious to do all they can to aid you in carrying on the Treasury operations," he assured the secretary. He encouraged the loan program, adding that "a large debt will not hurt the cause of the Union."[6]

Thus began a relationship that was to prove important and beneficial both to Chase and Cooke, and to the Union. On July 12, having already raised considerable funds in loans for the treasury, Cooke made his bid for a major partnership between himself and Chase. He proposed opening "a first-class banking establishment" in Washington right away with a view to working very closely with the treasury. A few days later came the Union debacle at Manassas and, the day following, without request or authorization from Chase,

Cooke subscribed close to $2 million in loans from Philadelphia financiers for the government. Their friendship now cemented, Chase invited him to help raise another $50 million in loans just authorized by Congress. The relationship blossomed, and on September 4, 1861, Chase appointed Jay Cooke an official subscription agent for the so-called seven-thirty loans authorized by Congress in July. Cooke would raise millions in the days ahead, selling treasury notes that matured in three years and paid 7.30 percent interest. Cooke now showed remarkable enterprise. He avidly advertised the loans in the national press, encouraged businessmen and financiers, and took his campaign even to the lower classes. "This has been a hard day," he told Chase on September 7. "I have been at it from 8 A.M. till after 5—a continual stream, clergy, draymen, merchants, girls, boys and all kinds of men and women. Some of our citizens who came in—I mean those of mark—went out almost with tears in their eyes, so overjoyed at the patriotic scene." That scene repeated daily for months to come as Cooke sold his notes.[7]

The advent of Jay Cooke, however, hardly solved all of Chase's problems. As early as the summer of 1861 the Union war effort was costing up to $1 million every day, with costs escalating rapidly. Worse, the defeat at Manassas, and later the *Trent* crisis and the possibility of war with Great Britain, sent confidence in the government plummeting to an all-time low. Banks could not sell treasury bonds, depositors withdrew their funds, and specie, hard money, became so scarce that the government threatened to suspend payment of its debts in gold and silver. By December the Union stood at the brink of financial collapse.

It did not help that in that month Chase gave Congress a sugar-coated report that concealed the true state of the treasury. He told of the loans obtained thus far, reported the disappointing state of normal treasury income from duties and taxes, and then proposed that the Federal government take over control of the nation's monetary system. He suggested a national currency to replace the confusion of bank notes then in use, and that this new currency be backed by Federal bonds, thus in effect advancing his loan program as well. The adverse reaction among the nation's banking community was quick and vocal. The New York money market sagged immediately, as gold was withdrawn by wary investors as well as British depositors who feared war. On December 30, 1861, the New York banks finally announced the suspension of specie payments. They allowed no more gold to leave their premises. Other major banking cities followed in kind.[8]

This left Chase with no option but to suspend specie payments from the national treasury, thus bringing the finances of the North to the verge of collapse. "It is impossible," he said, "in consequence of the large expenditures entailed by the war and the suspension of the banks to procure sufficient coin for disbursements." While considering further loans and treasury note issues, Chase looked finally to strengthening the traditional sources of Federal income. Back on August 5, 1861, a direct tax was levied against each of the states, in proportion to its population. Not entirely successful, it collected just $17 million, barely enough for two weeks of war. On that same date as well, Congress authorized the first income tax, levying 3 percent on all workers with incomes of $800 or more per year. Later amendments brought about a crudely graduated tax, but still the act raised only $55 million during the war, while arousing a considerable furor. Measures like this and Chase's proposed national currency brought the nation closer to a Federal monetary system.[9]

The chief source of unborrowed revenue, however, came from the normal internal duties and taxes that dated back to the last century. Whiskey, for instance, and other forms of alcoholic beverages, all brought taxes into Washington. Then, on July 1, 1862, Congress passed the internal revenue law that revolutionized this system, and greatly expanded Chase's treasury. It taxed almost everything, and several times. A producer of raw materials paid taxes on his wares. The manufacturer who made something of them paid a tax on his finished product. And the purchaser paid a tax on the item for ownership. Silver watches, pianos, carriages, table service, everything but bare necessities paid the levy. Senator James G. Blaine complained that "Bankers, and pawn brokers, lawyers and horse-dealers, physicians and confectioners, commercial brokers and peddlers, proprietors of theaters and jugglers on the street, were indiscriminately summoned to aid the National Treasury." The law required some twenty thousand words to explain all of its provisions. It was cumbersome, and unpopular, but it worked. It could produce up to $200 million in a year.[10]

Chase needed still more. Paper money seemed the answer. With gold dwindling, some form of currency was necessary to pay the government's debts, some form that merchants and suppliers would have to regard as being "as good as gold." On December 30, 1861, the same day that the New York banks suspended their gold disbursements, Congress received a bill for the printing of treasury notes that would be treated as legal tender though not backed by hard money on Federal deposit. The cry of protest came quickly. There were sound arguments against such a move, yet its defenders replied that there was no choice. The government faced emergency, there was not enough gold abroad to provide a medium of exchange for the business of the Union to continue, and something had to be done at once. After extensive debate, the act passed on February 25, 1862, authorizing the printing and distribution of $150 million in notes. Chase did not like the measure. Years later as Chief Justice he will declare it unconstitutional. But for now he had to accept it.[11]

April came before the new notes were printed and in distribution.

That meant the North went three months and more without any currency after the suspension of gold. It proved a difficult time, yet the people and the business community survived on what they had hoarded at home and in their offices. The flood of new money eased the hardship however, and shortly the demand for the new "greenbacks" was such that in July Chase asked for another $150 million, and yet another in 1863. And for Chase himself, he finally had enough "money" to pay his department's bills.

During all this time the enterprising Jay Cooke stayed close to his new-found friend Chase. Cooke declined the offer of an appointment as assistant treasurer in Philadelphia, but did finally open a Washington office for his bank, Chase promptly becoming a depositor. The secretary again appointed Cooke a subscription agent for another $1 million in loans, and then late in 1862 he came to him for help when the Legal Tender Act almost created another crisis.[12]

From the moment the first greenbacks appeared, money men refused to take them in face value exchange for gold when it was available. Foreign debts had to be paid in gold, yet sale of foreign goods in the North by merchants brought only paper money. Gold being by far the more desirable, its price relative to the greenbacks soon began to increase, and all at once gold itself was a commodity, like wheat or cotton. Speculators began buying "gold futures," committing for gold sixty and ninety days in advance and gambling on its price at delivery. A Gold Exchange was organized, and shortly almost all foreign trade, import and export, found itself influenced and controlled by the fluctuations of the prices in effect in the "Gold Room." People could buy gold one day in the morning, hold it—more correctly the receipt for the gold "bought"—until the end of the day, and then resell to the Gold Bank if the price had gone up. They would receive in gold their profits from the sale, then pay back to the bank the greenback premium required for the transactions.

The result was considerable gold hoarding, attempts to corner the gold market, and ever rising prices as merchants raised their rates to cover potential losses. Goods ordered at one price might cost a good deal more when delivered if the gold price had increased. Meanwhile, the premium for paying gold prices with greenbacks increased. In January 1862 $100 worth of gold cost $103 in paper. By the end of the year the same gold brought $133.5 in greenbacks. Two years later the premium would double.[13]

With the leapfrogging effect of rising prices and rising gold values and rising needs, Chase had to turn to his loans once more, and now the most ambitious bond program of the war. On February 25, 1862, Congress authorized $517,780,500 in "five-twenty" bonds, notes redeemable after five years and automatically called in after twenty. They would bear 6 percent interest per annum, yet the immediate response was disheartening in the extreme. Cooke sold a few, yet Chase became so disgusted with the indifferent reception of the bond issue that he thought of asking Congress to repeal it. Then Cooke showed him a suggested means of making them more attractive, and Chase in turn made Cooke the exclusive agent for their sale. The result was much the same as in Cooke's earlier bond agency. His methods of advertising and promoting the bonds, together with the offering of them to bankers at slightly under par value encouraged a speedy sale. His virtual monopoly on the five-twenties also earned Cooke the resentment of many other Northern money men, but he and Chase bore their criticism.

At the same time, Cooke turned his advertising abilities to the support of the final leg of Chase's three-part financial program. Taxes and loans made up the first two, and the last was his December 1862 campaign for a national banking system and a national currency. Despite the rebuff his suggestion of a year before encountered, Chase now called again for Federal management of a system of national banks throughout the country, and a single national currency backed by Federal bonds. This would combat the confusion of state and local notes currently used and eliminate the widely variant exchange rates of one bank's currency for another. It took a year and one half to get his national banking act passed, but when it did the Union finally had for the first time a stable Federal monetary system. Banks, national banks, could open anywhere in the country when their owners bought at least $30,000 in United States bonds and met the required limit for capital. These bonds were then placed in the Federal treasury. Thus, besides unifying the banking of the nation, the act also forced the sale of millions in bonds, helping finance the Union war effort. Reaction was slow and suspicious, but before war's end the system was working. It contained the seeds of future monetary inequities, with most of the nation's money being concentrated in the major cities, but amid the smoke of the early 1860s it seemed suited to the nation's needs.[14]

By the end of 1862 Salmon Chase was meeting most of his debts incurred by the war and at least providing the nation with a means of exchange sufficient to keep the economy moving. He had raised in loans, bonds, demand notes, and greenbacks, over one billion dollars. That, added to the tens of millions raised in taxes, was enough to sustain the armies in the field and all of the attendant expenses they incurred, but it hardly allowed Chase to prevent an enormous increase in the national debt. Indeed, as the war progressed the deficit between government income and expenses would itself approach one billion.[15]

Perhaps the only person severely discomfited by Chase's loan policies was his registrar of the treasury, Lucius E. Chittenden. His was the unenviable task of signing every single loan bond issued. It could be done by no other, and the demand for bonds exceeded his output. Jay Cooke's brother Henry wrote in March 1863 of Chittenden, "Poor fellow! I don't see how he stands it to sign his name so many times in a day in addition to the other hundreds of signatures to checks, certificates, etc." Yet Cooke pressured Chittenden constantly for more and more bonds. Their output reached $2 and $3 million per day, and still the demand for the five-twenties could not be met. It would remain a problem throughout the career of the bonds, though Cooke obtained some relief for his customers when he struck a bargain with Chittenden that Cooke and Company bonds would be signed first, before those of the sub-treasuries.

As for Chittenden, his labors only increased, and sometime in March 1863 the cumbersome requirement for his signature nearly cost him his life. Yet his ordeal shows well the fact that no aspect of this war could be separated from the rest of it and regarded as distinct. At that time the military situation seemed stalemated. The navies were becoming increasingly interested in the activities of Confederate cruisers on the oceans. The British, still supposedly neutral, were building two mighty steam rams for the Confederate Navy. Diplomatic relations between Great Britain and the United States remained taut as a result. Everything, Army, Navy, foreign policy, involved itself in this situation, and it fell to little Lucius Chittenden and his pen to help break the situation. Nothing in this war could be far removed from finance.

Chase and Welles had learned of the construction of the two rams at the Laird Shipyard at Birkenhead. Confederate agent James D. Bulloch had contracted for them and they were to be ready for delivery in September. Now the two cabinet members, without consulting Charles Francis Adams, decided to buy the rams out from under Bulloch, thereby denying them to the Confederacy, and at the same time removing a diplomatic sore point. It was an ill-conceived measure, for Adams had been arguing against the right of Britain to manufacture ships for any country at war. If the United States bought these two, that destroyed his argument and left the British free to build for the Confederacy.

Chase and Welles decided they could pay any amount up to $10 million. Not in gold, of course, but in United States bonds. And that meant that on Friday March 13, poor Chittenden had to sign $10 million worth of bonds, even though on his best days he could barely exceed $3 million. Worse, he received little warning, and was even deceived as to the purpose for the notes. Called to the White House, he met with Lincoln, Chase, and perhaps Seward. They wanted to know how long it would take him to sign the required bonds. He replied that it could be done in four or five days if he used denominations of $1,000, the largest then issued. They gave him forty-eight hours. Chase's emissaries were to sail for England the next Monday.

Chittenden began at once. He worked for seven hours straight, but found he had signed only a bit over one fourth of the bonds necessary. His arm inflamed, sending terrible swelling and pain through his shoulder. Massage did not help. He continued for another twenty-three hours, stopping for exercise frequently to stay awake and taking medicine and stimulants. His hand went numb. Then his fingers curled in a distorted manner and he could only hold a pen between thumb and forefinger. He was only semiconscious by Sunday morning, his signature painfully slow. Yet he finished the task with time to spare and every signature legible. It cost him a nervous breakdown and, he claimed, the impairment of his health for the rest of his life. Perhaps. But without doubt it did bring great disappointment when a few weeks later most of the bonds were returned to him, the scheme to buy the rams falling through.[16]

No one in the Confederate treasury in Richmond came quite that close to bleeding for the cause, but the challenge faced by Memminger and his associates was no less acute. Indeed, their war costs were greater per capita than the North's, and their available resources less.

In fact, the Southern economy had been eroding for years before the coming of the war, the planters becoming increasingly dependent on the North and its capital. Some even found good cause to support secession in order to escape their debts to Yankees. By 1861 the South owed the North some $400 million. Worse, Northern banks held the financing and future of the annual cotton crops. By leaving the Union and repudiating its debts, the South would be free to attempt financing its crops on its own through the high British demand for cotton.

However, that brought with it a concomitant problem. By leaving the Union, the Confederacy abandoned what financial system and structure it had, cutting itself off from its only major source of funds. The South had to raise large sums of money quickly, and did not even enjoy the meager tax and duty system of the North. Memminger faced an enormous challenge.[17]

Many then and later argued that he was not the man for the job, yet his ties to important financial interests at home and abroad made him probably the best choice available to Davis. Since the South did not have a significant financial community, it had few experienced men of finance to take the treasury portfolio. Memminger would have to do.

Just staffing his department offered the new secretary a substantial challenge. He had to organize completely the offices of the treasurer and registrar, first and second auditors, comptroller, and assistant secretary of the treasury. To Memminger himself fell responsibility for collecting all forms of public revenue, managing public credit, sale of public property, and oversight of payment of just debts of the Confederacy. In later days, adjusting to the needs of the conflict, Memminger would stretch his organization to include a war tax office, a special office for produce loans, and another to manage treasury notes.

Mints, customs houses, and national depositories also became his province, all requiring an organization hitherto unknown in the South.[18]

The immediate demands on Memminger in his first months in office taxed him greatly. He had to have money. Unlike Chase, Memminger correctly looked first to taxes. He expected import and export duties to provide a substantial revenue, since the Confederacy had retained all of the United States tariff laws. However, Memminger saw beyond these measures, expected to bring in $25 million in 1861, to other forms of income, perhaps because, despite his optimistic prediction, he realized that a Federal blockade would cripple duty income. In fact, 1861 produced only $1,270,875 in import duties and a mere $1,300 from exports.[19]

Memminger wanted a national tax to finance the war and get the Confederacy on a stable economic base. It was hardly a popular notion to a Congress bent on sustaining the idea of states' rights. One of those rights was taxation, and the central government's attempt to usurp that right boded ill. As a result, though Memminger repeatedly urged taxes for the first two years of the war, he achieved only mixed results. "When war is waged upon a country and its citizens are called to the defense of their homes," he told Congress, "it is every man's duty to contribute of his substance to that defense. . . . Taxes afford the only certain reliance under all circumstances." Loans only brought contribution from certain parts of the economy. Duties also brought money only from a few. "But direct taxes pervade the whole body politic, and bring forth the contributions of the willing and of the unwilling."[20]

Unfortunately, the most "unwilling" were Congressmen themselves. On May 10, 1861, Memminger asked for a direct tax to raise $15 million in hard money by October 1, using the existing system within each state for tax collection. Quotas should be established for each state. Instead Congress only authorized him to collect information for a possible tax assessment. He did so with dispatch, however, and late in July once more asked for a tax, this time a specific levy on the value of slaves, land, stock, and investments, all to be taxed at 54 cents for every $100 value. On August 19 the Congress obliged him, by now realizing that this war would be too long to finance on customs duties alone. Delays set in however, and not a cent was collected before April 1862. But in the five months following Memminger realized over $10 million in taxes, and another $6 million by the end of the year. It was not an effective tax even then, for Congress left it up to the states to collect the money, and in the event they could not collect it, then the states themselves were to pay up to their assigned quota. In fact, only South Carolina, Mississippi, and Texas, actually collected the money from their citizens. The other states obtained loans and secured them with state treasury notes, thus competing with Richmond in the limited loan market.[21]

Memminger never stopped his push for an equitable and effective tax, and part of the reason was loans. In order to give the impression of solvency needed to convince investors to loan money to the Confederacy, he had first to have a working treasury and a government with working capital paying its debts. Shortsighted at first in thinking that the war would be brief and cost little, Congress preferred that it be financed in the main by loans and interest-bearing treasury notes. Memminger feared both, knowing that a sustained program of printing paper money must lead inevitably to runaway inflation and a lack of confidence in the government. The Congress would have otherwise, and he had no choice but to obey.

The loan precedent, of course, came in February 1861 when Alabama loaned the new nation $500,000. At first Memminger accepted the idea of loans, knowing it would take time to build the machinery for taxation, and that money was needed right away. As a result, he approved of the February 28 measure to raise $15 million in loans from citizens by offering "five-ten" bonds that would pay 8 percent. With high expectations he announced the availability of the bonds to the public in March, and even hoped to sell $1 million of them in New York! By October the entire $15 million in bonds had been purchased, thanks chiefly to hearty support from the South's banking institutions.

Memminger did not wait upon success, but immediately proceeded to ask Congress for another loan, this time for amounts up to $50 million in twenty-year bonds at 8 percent. At the same time Congress authorized the first issue of paper money, $20 million in treasury notes. This whole package was known generally as the Produce Loan, thanks to Memminger's desire that the bonds be given in return for cotton. The government could then sell the produce to raise money as needed, a novel idea that worked well. Some planters offered their entire crop and so pleased was Congress that in August it doubled the authorized limit to $100 million. By the end of the year, in cotton alone the Confederate treasury could boast 417,000 bales, along with substantial quantities of such other produce as rice and molasses. Though problems arose, largely due to the blockade, and subscriptions slackened by the end of 1861, Congress felt sufficient confidence in this measure to extend its limit yet again. In April 1862 they raised it to $250 million. Storage became a major problem as the cotton accumulated, and Memminger found some difficulty with a few unscrupulous planters who promised the cotton for the bonds but then later sold it instead.[22]

As for the treasury notes, Memminger did not favor them. A fiscal policy based on loans secured with notes that were themselves secured by other loans, was dangerously unstable. Yet the Confederacy desperately needed a medium of exchange, and one hopefully uniform throughout the country. Like the North, it had at the outset only the confusing myriad of state and local bank notes in varying denominations and soundness. Unfortunately, the lure of making more money by printing it eventually seduced the Congress into producing extravagant sums with so little backing in hard money that the "shinplasters" became next to worthless by war's end. They started small, with a $2 million issue in March 1861, but that did not last long. On August 19, even as Congress gave Memminger his tax on property, it also authorized the printing and distribution of $292 million in treasury notes. The following April they called for another $128 million and $140 million more in October. Never did the Congress make these notes legal tender, however. They were always obligations of the government, redeemable from two to five years after "the ratification of a treaty of peace between the United States and the Confederate States of America." In other words, holders of the notes only got hard money if the South won the war. As a result, not being required to accept the notes as legal tender, many bankers and merchants required bank notes instead, or even barter. The resulting chaos to the South's economy proved catastrophic. And the value of the treasury notes themselves steadily declined. By April 1862 a dollar in gold cost $1.40 in treasury notes and $3 by the end of the year. Before war's end that would increase twentyfold.[23]

Memminger had his detractors, like every member of the Davis court. He "should never have been appointed," said John B. Jones in January 1863. "He is headstrong, haughty, and tyrannical when he imagines he is dealing with inferiors, and he deems himself superior to the rest of mankind." President Davis, however, felt absolute faith in his secretary. "He bore an unimpeachable character for integrity and close attention to duties," said Davis, "and proved himself entirely worthy of the trust." Yet some, Jones among them, began by 1863 to suspect that Memminger was using his position to profit personally.[24]

Certainly he showed foresight. He, too, proposed a national Confederate Bank as Chase did in the North, yet Memminger appreciated its need much sooner. In April 1861 he suggested establishing a national institution along the lines of the Bank of England, a single authority that would set standards nationwide. If each state contributed $1 million and an additional $1 million were raised by private subscription, the bank would start with capital assets of $14 million, more than enough to back from $25 to $40 million in treasury notes. During 1862 the suggestion was repeated again, and expanded to include a form of stability in currency and uniformity in banking practice that even the North did not have. Memminger would not succeed in launching his Bank of the Confederate States. The old Jacksonian notions against a central bank were too strong, Congress's vision of the economic needs of the country too short. Happily, at least, Memminger received admirable cooperation from the many existing state banks in securing loans. Some even loaned him their bank note paper for the printing of the Confederate treasury notes.[25]

Memminger did establish something of a Confederate bank abroad, however. The blockade made shipment of specie to England uncertain at best, and yet the Confederacy had to be able to pay promptly for its foreign purchases. The solution seemed to be to deposit Confederate funds abroad, and in January 1862 Memminger offered to the John Fraser and Company firm of Charleston the opportunity to have its affiliate Fraser, Trenholm and Company of Liverpool, England, become a foreign depository. The appointment was accepted in March, and for the rest of the war Fraser, Trenholm remained the South's bankers abroad. Later Memminger created depositories in Bermuda, Nassau, and Havana, and in January 1863 began operations in France with the Erlanger Loan. Memminger commissioned the Paris firm of Erlanger and Company, to sell Confederate bonds in Europe to the sum of $15 million, backed by cotton. Successful at first, the full $15 million was never raised, but still it greatly enhanced Confederate capital abroad.[26]

As 1863 dawned, Memminger and the Confederate treasury were doing far better than anyone might have expected in 1861, but not nearly so well as the infant nation needed. On the face of it, the numbers looked good. In two years of war the treasury's receipts ran slightly greater than its total expenditures, which is more than Salmon Chase could say. But too much of its receipts were in paper, not gold, and even more of the expenditures were paid in worthless scrip. On top of that, exclusive of the cost of war on land and sea, the new national government was costing in the neighborhood of $300 million a year, all of that an expense that Southerners had never borne under the old Union. Only a remarkable willingness of the Southern people to support this war with their money, and the speculative interest of foreign investors, kept the treasury going. That and the imperious Mr. Memminger. Like Chase, he would never be popular, but he kept the cause from dying of an acute case of empty pocket.

CHAPTER 17

"I HAVE COME TO YOU FROM THE WEST"

As costly as the war became, Lincoln would pay the price in money, and even in men, without flinching. What galled him was the cost in time. Time, that element of which, to listen to him, his general McClellan seemed never to have a surfeit. Indeed, McClellan began to make and take his own time. After his nearly disastrous defeat on the Peninsula, he stayed put at Harrison's Landing on the James for two months without making a move. Lincoln, finally assured that Little Mac was going to do nothing, ordered the army withdrawn from the Peninsula late in July. With characteristic sloth, McClellan took a month to follow his orders. His soldiers ravaged the Peninsula, looting among others the home of Edmund Ruffin. "This house belonged to a Ruffinly son of a bitch," one scrawled on a wall. Even more than before Little Mac resented the interference of the government with his army, regarding it and himself as above the petty politicians. Because of him, this same attitude permeated many of his own officers, planting the seeds of a possible mutiny. "Would that this army was in Washington to rid us of incumbents ruining our country," wrote his corps commander Major General Fitz John Porter. Such words bordered dangerously on treason.[1]

While McClellan dawdled on the Peninsula, things happened in northern Virginia. Lincoln learned a valuable lesson from the Union defeats in the Shenandoah that past spring. Divided command promoted nothing but discord and confusion. As a result, just the day after the Seven Days battles began, on June 26, he consolidated the armies of Frémont, Banks, and McDowell, along with several other smaller commands, into the new Army of Virginia. It faced a twofold mission: to protect Washington, and to be ready to move to McClellan's support as he faced Richmond. Little Mac's prompt defeat effectively removed the latter responsibility, but still Lincoln wanted this new army between the capital and the enemy, and should McClellan ever be persuaded to move, the two armies might yet combine to deliver a heady blow to Lee. Of course, this new army required a commander.

Certainly the President could not, would not, turn to either Frémont or Banks. Both failed him in the Shenandoah Valley, and both were in fact political generals. However much he would yield to the pressure to give high appointments to influential politicos, Lincoln could not offer a major army command to one of them. The position was simply too important. No, he needed a proven professional, a man with victories. Grant would have been the obvious choice, but Halleck was politicking against him, and Old Brains himself, of course, was coming to Washington as general-in-chief shortly. That left another man of the Western army to consider, the hero of Island No. 10, John Pope.

One thing could be said for Pope from the first. He understood how to maneuver for promotion and high command. It helped that the forty-year-old general knew Lincoln before the war. Indeed, then a captain, he accompanied the President-elect on part of his journey to Washington in February 1861. During the next two months he campaigned shamelessly for promotion, obtaining the influence of several prominent Illinois men close to Lincoln. It won him a brigadier's commission in May, but not the congratulations of all of his brother officers. Old Samuel Heintzelman thought the promotion an "outrage."

Still Pope performed well in his first year as a general. He commanded a portion of Missouri under Frémont and Halleck for a time, then took over the so-called Army of the Mississippi and with it reduced New Madrid and Island No. 10, in the process winning another star. The resultant public outcry of approval for those victories was in part orchestrated by Pope himself. He exaggerated the numbers of his enemy, and engaged newspaper reporters at his headquarters to write stirring accounts of his accomplishments. A crafty general in these early days of the war could use the press to his advantage, and Pope did it perhaps better than any. He was a West Point man, handsome, conceited, yet one with a proven tendency to fight. Right now, with time slipping away and working on the side of the Confederacy, Lincoln needed most of all a man who would fight.[2]

Pope's assumption of command of his army of 47,000 scattered men did not produce immediate acclaim among the military establishment in the East. To some it came as an affront. He had been Frémont's junior in Missouri. Now Frémont was to serve under him instead. The Pathfinder would not stand for it. He despised Pope, and asked to be relieved of command. The relief was mostly Lincoln's for it allowed him to remove Frémont from active disservice for the rest of the war. Unfortunately, it brought another even more incompetent commander to the fore in Frémont's place, yet another alumnus of Missouri defeats, Franz Sigel. For all the misery Sigel will cause the Union war effort, still he demands a measure of grudging admiration. Clumsy, inept, often unintelligible in his poor English, still he showed a staying power that kept him in active and important commands, defeat after miserable defeat, long after most of the rest of the fraternity of politically appointed incompetents had been relieved. Sigel took command of Pope's I Corps, and another of the political inepts that he would outlast, Nathaniel Banks, led the II Corps, while McDowell, the only real soldier of the lot, headed the oversized III Corps.

These Western men like Pope knew how to fight, that was sure, but they knew brag as well, and of a manner that invariably offended the more refined sensibilities of the Eastern officers. Pope did not take long to alienate many in his new command. On July 14 he issued an address to "the Officers and Soldiers of the Army of Virginia." Intended to infuse them with martial ardor, it succeeded only in outraging many, and offending most. "I have come to you from the West," he said, "where we have always seen the backs of our enemies—from an army whose business it has been to seek the adversary, and to beat him when found, whose policy has been attack and not defense." The inference was obvious that soldiers in the East did not fight as well, nor were they led as well, as those in the West. Until now. "I presume that I have been called here to pursue the same system, and to lead you against the enemy." He found too much talk in the army of holding positions, of supply bases and lines of retreat. "Let us discard such ideas." The best position for a soldier was in the face of the enemy. "Let us look before us and not behind. Success and glory are in the advance. Disaster and shame lurk in the rear."[3]

In fact, it was an excellent address, concise, even stirring to those few not offended by its implications. He simply made it at the wrong time and to the wrong people. It obviously criticized McClellan and his officers, yet Pope's army was led largely by men Little Mac had nurtured. Fitz John Porter was incensed by the address. "Gen Pope," he said, "has now written himself down what the military world has long known, an ass. His address to his troops will make him ridiculous in the eyes of military men." "Humbug" and "bag of wind," others called him. He had two very marked failings said another observer: "First, he talked too much of himself, of what he could do and of what ought to be done; and, secondly, he indulged, contrary to good discipline and all propriety, in very free comments upon his superiors and fellow-commanders." Montgomery Blair, another Western man, said he was simply "a braggart and a liar." One of his fellow generals spoke for many, alas, when he said that he did not care for John Pope "one pinch of owl dung."[4]

Yet owl dung or no, Pope had the new command now, and Lincoln wanted him to act. "I think the best way to defend Washington is to attack Richmond," Pope told the Committee on the Conduct of the War in Congress. Lincoln did not quite let him undertake that ambitious a task, but instead gave him three charges. Defend the capital. Protect the Shenandoah. Draw away from Richmond part of Lee's army then facing McClellan. That, it was hoped, would allow Little Mac to attack once more or else himself withdraw to join with Pope. In that event, Pope would hold himself subordinate to McClellan. Pope, however, intimated in every possible way that McClellan was a weak sister who could not be counted upon. He expected to win any forthcoming victories on his own.[5]

Early in July, even before issuing his bombastic address, Pope began concentrating his scattered units in the region of Warrenton, east of the Blue Ridge and about thirty miles southwest of Washington. He wanted to repair and advance along the line of the Orange and Alexandria Railroad, using it as his supply line. The move would take him as far south as Gordonsville, where the Virginia Central linked with the Orange and Alexandria. Then he could threaten Charlottesville as well, thereby controlling Richmond's principal rail routes to the Shenandoah and the West. Certainly such a move would force Lee to weaken his army in Richmond to combat Pope's threat, and that in turn would allow McClellan to move from Harrison's Landing and attack with some assurance of success. Pope only agreed to undertake the maneuver, however, if he had Lincoln's assurance that McClellan would be positively ordered to attack at the right time. Yet Lincoln, finally disgusted at Little Mac's sloth, ordered him to leave the Peninsula after Pope began his campaign, thus negating a major part of the plan. Instead, McClellan was now to bring his army to Aquia Creek, a tributary of the Potomac just above Fredericksburg. This would put him within cooperating distance of Pope but also left Lee free to bring his entire army out of Richmond without threat to the capital. With an abler general in command on the Peninsula, the original pincers plan was far better.

Pope went forth with unbounded confidence, but his subordinates began to let him down immediately. He sent a cavalry command to take Gordonsville and destroy the rail junction there, but the officer in charge took five days to accomplish a two-day task, and even then only got within ten miles of Gordonsville. By having taken so long, the move allowed Lee to send Jackson and 12,000 men to Gordonsville, securing the vital junction and immediately thwarting Pope's plans. "It has been a great mistake," complained Pope, "and may possibly lead to serious consequences." Meanwhile he moaned to one of his generals that "I have heard so much talk of retreating since I took command of this army that I hardly know what to believe."

Worse, Pope encountered a situation with his command in northern Virginia that he had not faced in Missouri and Tennessee. So much of the citizenry behind his lines were in sympathy with the army ranged against him that "I find it impossible to make any movement, however insignificant the force, without having it immediately communicated to the enemy." He found a constant intercourse, verbal and by letter, between Virginians and Marylanders in his rear and those in Richmond. "A thousand open enemies cannot inflict the injury upon our arms which can be done by one concealed enemy in our midst." As a result, he asked Lincoln for permission to issue an order calling for the arrest of every male living within and behind his lines! Those willing to take an oath of allegiance to the Union would be unmolested. Those who would not were to be sent beyond Federal lines to the Confederates. Should they return, or should they take the oath and then violate it, they would be treated as spies and shot. On July 23 Lincoln allowed him to promulgate the order.

The furor in Virginia was instantaneous, and Pope became in one motion the most hated Federal commander of the season. Men captured in future operations from his army would often be ill treated, spat upon, even starved, solely because they were "Pope's men." His order also called for seizure of the property of disloyal citizens, which his soldiers had already been doing in fact for several days. On July 13 a party of Federals, after burning a railroad bridge near Culpeper, stopped at the home of Colonel Alexander Taliaferro of the 21st Virginia Infantry and forced his wife to provide them breakfast. Afterward they searched the house, took the silver service and table utensils, broke the china, and pulled from her finger a diamond ring. When a few days later Pope issued another order directing that soldiers no longer be detailed to guard Rebel homes from depredations, his vilification became complete. There were threats, and promises, across the lines that should he be captured, Pope could expect little mercy from the outraged husbands and brothers of the helpless who suffered under his declarations. In fact, Pope was merely recognizing earlier than most in this war that it was a conflict, not just of armies, but of peoples, that the Confederate citizenry as well as its soldiers had to be defeated.[6]

But Pope's chances of defeating even just the soldiery of the South were dwindling now, without his really knowing it. Robert E. Lee, victor on the Peninsula, showed a confidence now that he might have lacked before; and with a Jackson at his side who was rested at last from his valley rigors and up to his old speed and daring, Robert E. Lee was not going to wait for Pope to come to him. He saw a chance to regain part of Virginia, and an opportunity to test his newly reorganized Army of Northern Virginia.

In the wake of the Seven Days, Lee evaluated the flawed performances and the stellar ones among his commanders, as well as the cumbersome command structure throughout the army. It was time for a streamlining and reorganization. There were too many division commanders for Lee himself to cope with personally. Yet Confederate law did not allow for formal army corps, only divisions. Further, a major general commanded a division and a full general, Lee, commanded an army. There was no established intermediate rank for the leader of something bigger than a division and smaller than a corps. Congress would in time correct the situation, but for now Lee himself informally amended the law. He divided his army into two wings, not actually called corps. One he gave to Jackson, and in it the divisions now commanded by Ewell, A. P. Hill, and Jackson's old division led by Charles Winder. The other wing Lee gave to Longstreet despite his poor performance during much of the Seven Days. Lee sensed a stability in Longstreet that he needed in his high command. Longstreet's divisions were those of David R. Jones, Lafayette McLaws, and Daniel H. Hill and Richard H. Anderson. Longstreet's old division also became a part of his wing. J. E. B. Stuart, now a major general, would command all of the army's cavalry, two divisions, one led by Lee's nephew Fitzhugh Lee, and the other by a fiery South Carolinian recovered from his Manassas wound, Wade Hampton.[7]

Lee's move gave a simplified and more direct system of command to the army. He would deal directly only with Jackson, Longstreet, Stuart, and one or two minor commands not a part of the wing structure. They in turn dealt with all of the divisional leaders. Lee had in short taken a great step toward executive management. And now to manage.

Pope's apparent movement in northern Virginia afforded Lee an opportunity and a quandary. First, with McClellan in his front and indisposed to action, Lee entertained thoughts of moving north to defeat Pope and then renewing the attack on Little Mac. It was with this in mind that Lee sent Jackson to Gordonsville to secure his rail communications. As July marched on and Lee became even more convinced that the Army of the Potomac would not advance, he reinforced Jackson with A. P. Hill's division, giving Stonewall about 24,000 men. While Lee demonstrated at Richmond in hopes of preventing McClellan from leaving, he now hoped that Jackson might be able to repeat his series of victories in the valley by attacking and defeating each of Pope's corps in turn before they all united. On August 7, 1862, Jackson moved north from Gordonsville.

His intelligence informed him that only Banks was currently at Culpeper, some thirty miles north of Gordonsville, and that Pope was slowly concentrating the remainder of his army toward the same place. He must strike quickly. He did not. Hot weather slowed the march and, worse, Jackson's own orders, confused and not fully communicated to all his subordinates, made further delays. It revealed a peculiarity of Stonewall's already evident to those with him in the Shenandoah. He kept his own counsel and showed an absolute reluctance to advise with others or take them into his confidence. Only with Lee did he speak freely.[8]

As a result Jackson was a day late in reaching a place called Cedar Mountain just south of Culpeper, and once there he found more than he expected. John Pope had finally taken the field personally. Lincoln held him in Washington as a general adviser until Halleck arrived to take over as general-in-chief. Thus it was July 29 when Pope finally left to join his army. Four days later, having watched carefully the movement of Jackson to Gordonsville, he advised Halleck that he expected to take that place and Charlottesville within the next ten days. Jackson did not scare him. Particularly if he could get his three corps combined. It took some doing, and McDowell required frequent urging to get his command moving toward Culpeper. Pope had reports that Jackson numbered 50,000 at Gordonsville. He did not credit the information—McClellan would have accepted and perhaps doubled it —but still gave increasing urgency to his communications to his commanders. He wanted to move against the enemy on August 6.[9]

Banks and his II Corps was then just northwest of Culpeper near Sperryville, and the bulk of McDowell's III Corps rested near Warrenton. Pope wanted Banks to move south toward Cedar Mountain while McDowell came along the Orange and Alexandria directly to Culpeper. Sigel would move behind Banks. Pope had been hearing rumors that Richmond was to be evacuated. That, and his easy victories out on the Mississippi, gave him a species of overconfidence enjoyed by no other Federal commander in the field. He knew that he would defeat Lee. It could not be otherwise. Even though McClellan's ordered departure from the Peninsula would free Lee to bring his entire army to face him, Pope possessed absolute confidence.[10]

Pope intended, from his position near Cedar Mountain, to send cavalry raids around Jackson and thus force him out of Gordonsville without actually giving battle. "I can easily make the position at Gordonsville untenable," he wrote to Halleck. However, he reckoned without the audacity of Jackson.[11]

Even before receiving word from Lee to do so, Stonewall determined to attack the departed Federal corps individually if possible. By August 8, only Banks's corps and another division were at Cedar Mountain, with Sigel expected late the next day, and McDowell still on the way. Anticipating this, Jackson marched north out of Gordonsville on August 7. But of course his slow march meant that the attack planned for August 8 could not take place until the next day. Meanwhile, his movement did not especially alarm Pope. Admitting the possibility that Jackson intended a major attack, he was far more certain that the enemy merely proposed a reconnaissance in force. Still he tried to hurry his absent forces to Cedar Mountain just in case. Leave their baggage behind, he told his commanders. "Celerity of movement and the preservation of your men for effective service are of all things desirable." They could live off the land and enough provisions to carry or drive on the hoof, rather than burden themselves with a commissary train of wagons.[12]

By 8 A.M. August 9, Pope realized that Jackson was going to attack and probably on his right flank. The Confederates were still a few miles off, so that morning he sent Banks and his corps forward to delay the enemy while the remainder of the army continued its march to consolidate. Banks moved to place his left on Cedar Mountain and his center and right on the open ground northwest of it. Jackson drove in the Federal cavalry sent in advance and moved immediately to meet Banks's main line. Banks attacked first, on orders from Pope. He caught two of Jackson's brigades unready and drove them back steadily during the afternoon until A. P. Hill arrived and stabilized a line that was close to disintegration. Jackson, whose orders had been garbled and incomplete all day, finally managed to launch a counterattack. He enjoyed a considerable advantage of numbers over Banks now, and drove him back with heavy loss from Cedar Mountain. Then Banks, too, obtained relief when a fresh division joined him and stopped the enemy advance. There the battle stopped at stalemate.

Late that night, however, Jackson received intelligence that another enemy corps was arriving to support Banks. That meant that the rest of Pope's army could be close as well. All at once his advantage disappeared, and now Jackson found himself heavily outnumbered. His chance to defeat each enemy corps in succession had disappeared. He stayed in Banks's front on August 10, caring for the wounded and burying the dead and then withdrew the next day.[13]

As happened frequently in these earlier days of the war, both sides claimed the victory, and neither won it. Jackson wired to the capital just before he withdrew that "God blessed our arms with victory." Lee responded in kind, telling Stonewall that "the country owes you and your brave officers and soldiers a deep debt of gratitude." In fact, Jackson fought arguably his worst battle of the war. With nearly 20,000 men to Banks's 8,000, Jackson should have overwhelmed the Federals. Instead, after muddling his own march to Cedar Mountain and costing himself an extra day on the road, Stonewall conducted a confused and uncoordinated offense which only Hill's arrival prevented from becoming a defeat.

As for Pope, he performed little better, having taken too long in the first place to consolidate his army, thus leaving Banks isolated and ripe for attack. Worse, during the fight he did not reinforce Banks sufficiently with troops close at hand, and himself did not go to the battleground. Nevertheless, he too claimed the victory. The day after the fight, while Jackson still remained in his front, he promised Halleck that he would do the best he could, admitting that he might be "forced to retire." Suddenly even Pope had to speak of lines of retreat, even he, the hero from the West. But his confidence was not all gone. "I hope, however, for better things," he advised. When Jackson withdrew back to Gordonsville, Pope's confidence increased, and on August 16 he published for his army a congratulatory address including a word of thanks from Halleck. "Cedar Mountain will be known in history as one of the great battle-fields of the war," said the general-in-chief, and to that Pope added the grandiose prediction that "Cedar Mountain is only the first of a series of victories which shall make the Army of Virginia famous in the land." Both North and South regarded Pope's address as pure bombast.[14]

Both North and South learned something from Cedar Mountain, too. Lee recognized that Jackson could no longer hope to stop Pope entirely on his own. Should the Army of Virginia advance farther, Jackson would have to be heavily reinforced to meet the threat. However, McClellan's continuing lack of movement urged Lee to take the risk of sending Longstreet to join Jackson, leaving little more than two brigades and some local defense militia to hold the capital. Should McClellan finally decide to attack, Richmond was his. Here Washington had helped by ordering Little Mac to leave the Peninsula some time before, yet it was only on August 14 that troops began to embark for Aquia Creek. Thus McClellan's sloth might actually have worked to Union advantage, if only he had taken another few days to obey the orders he had already ignored for almost a month. On August 13 Lee ordered Longstreet north. Two days later Richmond would have been helpless. Of course, McClellan still believed that Lee had 200,000 or more in the capital, so it is entirely probable that had he stayed on the Peninsula he still would have been too fearful to attack. The story becomes redundant after a time. For a full year every Federal operation in Virginia is affected adversely by this one general's timidity. He complains to his wife that he is called "Quaker" and "procrastinator." He is.[15]

Pope, with less good sense than McClellan, and far more daring, also faced some new realities in the wake of Cedar Mountain. He finally had his army together and believed himself in a strong position along the Rapidan River. However, the news that McClellan was finally leaving the Peninsula, and that Lee was concentrating in his front changed the picture materially. Now he was outnumbered, or nearly so, and soon discovered Lee's intention to attack him on the

Rapidan when a copy of the Confederates' battle plan fell into his hands. Pope had already consulted with Halleck about the enemy buildup and now realized that he could no longer remain on the Rapidan, a position in which Lee could easily turn his flank and cut him off from Washington. Consequently, on August 18 he began pulling his army back along the line of the Orange and Alexandria to the Rappahannock River, a far more defensible position. Lee followed and only the rising waters of the river prevented each from getting at the other for a few days.[16]

Now it was Lee's turn to capture information. Stuart, in a brief raid, took Pope's headquarters baggage, and gathered with it correspondence showing that McClellan was expected to come and reinforce Pope. That meant that Lee's time to effect anything before the enemy greatly outnumbered him was very limited. Portions of the Army of the Potomac were already at Fredericksburg, and Aquia, just twenty-five miles away, with more disembarking at Alexandria. If McClellan should move with dispatch, Lee would be in a bad way.

But one thing Lee could always do was count on Little Mac not to do anything with speed. It was that belief which largely led the Confederate general to conceive a plan so bold as to verge on foolhardiness. Indeed, with variations, it was to be his only battle plan of the war for offensive operations. He would divide his army in the face of the enemy and reunite it with Pope in between. Lee ordered Jackson to move up the Rappahannock as far as Salem, about twenty-five miles. There he was to cross and move directly for the Orange and Alexandria at Bristoe Station, far in Pope's rear. Meanwhile Lee would divert Pope along the river to keep him in place and then follow with Longstreet's command. With his rail communications cut, Pope would have no choice but to retreat, and in doing so he would be withdrawing right into the waiting arms of the Confederates who would stand squarely between him and Washington. The boldness of the plan rivaled Jackson's in the Shenandoah Valley. The one potential spoiler would be McClellan. Should he reinforce Pope, or should he divine the intent of the move and reach Bristoe first, Lee ran the risk of putting himself between two Federal armies. But McClellan would be predictable. He was the best general the Confederates had.

On August 25 Jackson started his march, and now he entirely redeemed himself for his lackluster performance during the Cedar Mountain operations. He covered the distance to Salem in a single day, at the expense of scores of men who dropped exhausted from heat stroke and thirst. Yet the men cheered him as they passed. "Old Jack" brought legend in train. The men knew it. And he knew their stuff and fiber. "Who could not conquer with such troops as these?" he asked. The next morning, even though he had outmarched his wagons and many of the men did not eat, he led them forth again, east through Thoroughfare Gap in the Blue Ridge. "Close up, men, close up! Push on, push on!" came the relentless exhortations from Stonewall. They reached Gainesville, then passed beyond and took Bristoe, having marched over fifty miles in two days. Upon capturing the railroad town, the Confederates immediately began derailing incoming Federal trains loaded with supplies for Pope's army. Pope, meanwhile, knew that something was happening. Shortly after noon on the day Jackson left, Pope got word that his lookouts had spotted about 20,000, "a considerable column of infantry and cavalry and artillery," leaving Culpeper and moving toward the west. At first he believed that Jackson was returning to the Shenandoah. Later in the day he changed his opinion and suspected that, in fact, Jackson was only acting to screen the movement of the rest of Lee's army due west into the valley. The next day, as Jackson was marching toward Bristoe, Pope's intelligence system broke down, providing him little good information until well into the evening, when Jackson's advance captured Bristoe and began derailing trains.

This left Pope with an enormous problem. Not only did he find himself suddenly cut off from Washington. He still did not know what Longstreet's wing was doing and continued to fear a movement into the valley. Worse, he had lost confidence in his own high command, excepting only McDowell. Banks's corps was broken down, and Sigel, he told Halleck, "is perfectly unreliable." He wanted another commander for that corps, and Halleck promised it would be done when the crisis passed. Early on August 27 Pope informed the general-in-chief that he would withdraw his army to the vicinity of Gainesville. "Whether the enemy means to attack us or not I consider doubtful," he said. Still Pope did not see that he and not the valley was the object of Lee's maneuver. Halleck did and immediately advised the general to hold his grip on the Orange and Alexandria. Then came confirmation that Jackson had moved on to Manassas and that his entire command was with him. Pope and McDowell saw beyond the threat to the opportunity thus afforded. Jackson was separated from Lee, and therefore vulnerable. At once Pope ordered his army back from the Rappahannock and began sending them to positions that would put them between Jackson and Longstreet's column still back near Salem. His orders were almost impeccable, his dispositions excellent. "If you are prompt and expeditious," he told one of his generals, "we shall bag the whole crowd."[17]

Yet Pope made a few mistakes, and his worst was the failure to send a force to Thoroughfare Gap sufficient to deny access to Longstreet. Had he done so, Jackson would have been truly alone. As it was, he regained Bristoe easily, driving Jackson in on Manassas Junction. Sigel and McDowell gathered at Gainesville and Banks at Warrenton. Heintzelman's corps from the Peninsula finally arrived now and took post between the two, and Fitz John Porter's V Corps also

arrived to join Banks. They effectively placed a wall of Federals
fifteen miles long separating Jackson and Longstreet.

Jackson knew he had a problem, yet acted coolly. He spent the better part of August 27 replenishing his rations and ammunition from
the abundant Federal supplies at Manassas and valiantly trying to
keep his soldiers from disorganized looting. That done, he destroyed
the remainder of the supplies, leaving Manassas a shambles. Now he
faced his real challenge. The opposing armies formed something of a
gigantic T, Pope providing the vertical, and a twenty-five-mile line
from Jackson, through Sigel and McDowell at Gainesville, to Longstreet, making the horizontal. Stonewall had to find ground where he
could withstand what Pope might throw at him until Lee and Longstreet arrived. His obvious choice was to move northwest. That would
mean meeting only Sigel and McDowell at first, since Heintzelman
and Banks and Porter would have much farther to march to reach
him. It would also, though indirectly, bring him closer to Longstreet,
shortening the distance to be covered before they came together. Indeed, should Pope face him in battle, it would give Longstreet an opportunity to come directly into the Federal rear. The ideal ground for
his stand Jackson already knew well. It was Stony Ridge, seven miles
to the northwest, an excellent place for defense. Barely two miles
from it sat Henry Hill. The old Bull Run battleground. Jackson had
come back to the scene of his first glory.

On August 28 Pope concentrated his army on Manassas, hoping to
bag Jackson there, only to find him gone and the junction a mess.
Then came intelligence that A. P. Hill had been seen at Centreville,
and now Pope ordered his corps to march there, assuming that Jackson's entire command was there esconced. Indeed, poor Pope almost
wandered with his corps over the countryside, looking to find where
Jackson really was, the situation made worse by the fact that he failed
to use his cavalry well in reconnaissance. It was nearly 6 P.M. that
evening when one of McDowell's divisions was marching from
Gainesville toward Henry Hill on its way to Centreville, that Jackson was finally found. They did not expect him.

Stonewall had the bulk of his command behind the crest of Stony
Ridge. As a result, when the division of Rufus King marched along
the Warrenton Turnpike below the ridge, the Federals did not suspect
that 20,000 Confederates watched them. Indeed, all they saw was a
lone Confederate, leisurely walking his horse back and forth along
their line of march, well within rifle range. "Sometimes he would halt,
then trot on briskly, halt again, wheel his horse and pass again along
the front of the marching column, or rather along its flank." The
horseman was Jackson himself. With uncommon boldness he reconnoitered the enemy in their full view, they thinking little of the soli-
tary horseman. Then he turned and rode back to the crest of the ridge

to his staff. "Bring up your men, gentlemen," he said in his queer squeaky voice. They would attack.[18]

The Confederates swooped over the ridge and down onto the unsuspecting Yankees but found that they made an admirable resistance. For four hours the fighting went on, King valiantly holding his ground until nightfall when he withdrew in the direction of Gainesville. Now, at last, Pope knew where Jackson was, and he intended to attack him at dawn. Heintzelman would move from Centreville to join in an assault to be initiated by Sigel. Porter would come north in addition, and the recently arrived IX Corps of Major General Jesse Reno would come along behind Heintzelman. Thus Pope would have Jackson's command assaulted from three sides and, as he told Halleck, "I do not see how it is to escape without heavy loss." The problem was that Pope had spent two days marching his army about, almost aimlessly, and they were tired. Worse, he did not even know where whole divisions were at the moment, thinking McDowell's corps intact when in fact the divisions of King and James B. Ricketts—who commanded a battery on this field a year before—were entirely out of place for McDowell to follow his orders. Further, Pope still ignored Longstreet. He believed that the Confederate had been driven back through Thoroughfare Gap by Ricketts, whom McDowell thoughtfully sent to stop his passage. He was right, but Longstreet merely outflanked the gap and was even then marching toward Gainesville. Only ten miles separated him from Jackson.[19]

The next day commenced the Second Battle of Bull Run, or Manassas. All told Pope had nearly 70,000 soldiers under his command, while Jackson and Longstreet—should they succeed in combining—would number only about 50,000. Yet Pope had nearly lost the battle before he started. Despite his absolute lack of confidence in Sigel, he ordered the German to open his attack on Jackson. Sigel struck twice, managing both assaults ineptly, and Jackson drove him back easily. Worse, still deceiving himself about Longstreet, Pope now realized that he was coming, but put his earliest arrival at dusk of the next day. In fact Longstreet was extending Jackson's right flank by noon, completely unknown to the Federals. Reno and then Heintzelman joined Sigel in attacking Jackson's Stony Ridge line, and some attempt was made to turn Stonewall's vulnerable left flank, but Pope failed to coordinate his assaults and the Confederates repelled every one. When the fighting ended at sunset Pope, without his knowledge, lay in a most unenviable position, in large part due to his own mismanagement. The corps of Heintzelman, Reno, Sigel, and McDowell were all aligned facing Jackson. Porter was more than a mile to the south, held there by conflicting orders. Thus there was a wide gap in the Federal line precisely where Longstreet sat poised. Lee tried three times that day to get Longstreet to attack, to wheel on his left and take Pope in his unsuspecting flank. Three times Longstreet persuaded Lee that the time was not right.

The next morning Pope believed that Jackson was withdrawing and ordered another general attack. It took Lee by surprise, but the Confederates held their ground. Porter was called in from the far left to make the assault on Jackson's right, and he succeeded for a time in driving Stonewall back, but then Longstreet's artillery, still unknown to the Federals, opened and disrupted him completely. Now was the time for Lee and Longstreet. There was no disagreement. Five divisions, 25,000 men, fresh and rested, began their advance straight into the unprotected flanks of Sigel and Porter. The effect was electric. Pope's left caved in, then Jackson began his own attack, pushing the Federals back. By nightfall Pope's army had been forced in upon itself and was desperately holding onto Henry Hill, where Jackson had held so well thirteen months before. But here Pope stayed and Lee could not move him further. That night the Federals began their retreat to Centreville, leaving the field to Lee. There was no rout this time, no panic and disorder. Pope was beaten, but he retired as an army. That morning he had sent Halleck a boastful message relating a great victory. Now he had to send more sober tidings. Halleck sought to comfort the beaten general, but there was little consolation. His casualties in the three days' fighting, and including a rearguard action at Chantilly, came to 16,000. Lee's losses just exceeded 9,000. And once more a beaten Federal army was retreating to Washington.[20]

Hovering over the whole campaign, like a dark specter, was a man not present on the battlefield. McClellan. As all through this troubled year 1862 in the East, he is the decisive factor. After taking his time in getting his army off the Peninsula and to Aquia and Alexandria, McClellan did little to aid Pope as he faced the advancing columns of Jackson and Longstreet. Even when Halleck, exasperated at dealing with Little Mac and a bit afraid of him, gave him absolute discretionary power to move his troops, McClellan held two full corps at Alexandria that might well have given Pope the battle. Indeed, they finally arrived, but only after the fight was done. The first day of the battle, August 29, Lincoln asked McClellan what ought to be done. Little Mac's sage reply was "to leave Pope to get out of his scrape," or else concentrate both armies. Of course, by then it was too late. Lincoln was incensed by McClellan's conduct all during Pope's campaign. It appeared that he deliberately dragged his feet and resisted cooperation, almost in the hope of Pope's defeat. Little Mac even confided to his wife his belief that if Pope were defeated then he would regain his overall command in Virginia. Certainly Lincoln believed that there had been some deliberate attempt against Pope. Stories came from independent sources of McClellan's officers, particularly Porter, refusing to cooperate with Pope and obey his orders. Pope, anxious for excuses, greatly, and unjustly, elaborated the theme to the point of the eventual cashiering of Porter from the army. Pope could not save himself, however, and Lincoln had to replace him, though he cast no censure on the Kentuckian's conduct of the campaign. An unsuccessful general simply had to be replaced. And the greatly disorganized Army of Virginia and the portions of the Army of the Potomac with it had to be rebuilt. There was, alas, only one man for that job.[21]

"He has acted badly in this matter," Lincoln said of Little Mac, "but we must use what tools we have. There is no man in the Army who can . . . lick these troops of ours into shape half as well as he." The President was not blind to what he felt McClellan had done. "I must have McClellan to reorganize the army and bring it out of chaos," he told Welles, "but there has been a design, a purpose in breaking down Pope, without regard of consequences to the country. It is shocking to see and know this; but there is no remedy at present. McClellan has the army with him." On September 2 Little Mac resumed command in Virginia. Three days later Lincoln relieved Pope of further duty and steeled his resolve to attempt again to work with McClellan. He intended, however, that the appointment only be temporary. He would use the little Napoleon to get his army back in fighting shape. Then he would find a man who did not fear to use it. Lincoln had to have a victory and soon. He had a great purpose in mind.[22]

CHAPTER 18

"THE DEATH KNELL
OF SLAVERY"

"War is a terrible necessity at best," wrote Colonel Owen Lovejoy of Princeton, Illinois. Yet he, like many of his stripe, regarded this war as not only necessary, but beneficial. The preservation of the Union was a laudable goal, to be sure. But Lovejoy saw higher aims, a greater purpose, an almost holy mission. Abolition.[1]

He was born in 1811 in Maine, into a family of stern moral values and upright example. From youth he idolized his older brother Elijah. They worked and swam and read the Bible together. Both boys studied the ministry, as had their father. Elijah, nine years Owen's senior, went west to Missouri in 1827, and Owen longed for the day when he might join him. All of the Lovejoy men fell easy prey to the persuasions of the influential itinerant abolitionists of the day, particularly Theodore Weld and William Lloyd Garrison. Elijah took it most to heart.

Soon after his move to St. Louis, Elijah Lovejoy began writing antislavery editorials for a local religious newspaper. Missouri was not the place for that, and angry opponents destroyed his press as they did those of other abolition editors all across the country in the decades before the war. And like the other outraged editors, fired by their abolition zeal and their constitutional rights, Lovejoy determined to continue his work. He moved to Alton, Illinois. Claiming that, in fact, he supported voluntary emancipation rather than enforced abolition, Lovejoy was rapidly impelled to the more radical position by the outrages he saw committed by slaveholders against Negroes, free and slave.

His arrival in Alton did little to soften his stand, for as soon as the remnant of his press and type from St. Louis arrived, a new mob destroyed them and threw them into the Mississippi. Alton was only a few miles from St. Louis, and the mob from Missouri could easily follow him. Undaunted, Lovejoy started again, brought his brothers, including Owen, to work with him and told the people of the city boldly that he was "the uncompromising enemy of Slavery, and so expected to live, and so to die." By mid-1836 he was in operation again, edging ever closer to a true abolition position as he saw less and less chance—and merit—in gradual emancipation or African colonization of manumitted blacks. By the following spring he announced his commitment to abolition of slavery by Congressional action. It cost him his life.

By the summer Lovejoy and his family were not only vilified by slavery men throughout the West but also subjected to physical assault. He kept a rifle by his bed. Owen and John Lovejoy, in the next room, maintained three loaded pistols. The people of Alton from time to time attempted to guarantee their safety, but when Lovejoy organized a meeting in Alton to be attended by the leading antislavery lights of the country, the proslavery forces felt the gauntlet thrown in their faces. The convention met in October 1837. Already another press had been destroyed sometime before, and the incessant peril of their lives affected Lovejoy's wife. He was tempted to give it up, but Owen persuaded him to continue. A mob in September destroyed yet another press. The town fathers asked the Lovejoys to leave, fearful for their safety. Elijah refused and ordered another press. "The contest has commenced here; and here it must be finished. Before God and you all, I here pledge myself to continue it, if need be, till death. If I fall, my grave shall be made in Alton."

Late on November 6, 1837, the next press arrived. Lovejoy, Owen, and several supporters guarded it in a warehouse, expecting another mob. They came the next evening, armed. Persuasion failed as the drunken mob started to batter its way into the building. The defenders opened fire, killing one of the rioters. Then there came a lull, and Elijah Lovejoy stepped outside to see if the mob had left. It had not. From hiding came shots and the editor reeled back inside the warehouse, mortally wounded. Two days later he was buried, as he had promised, in Alton. Alone in a room with the casket before the funeral, Owen Lovejoy, who had seen his brother's murder, sank to his knees and swore to himself. "I shall never forsake the cause that has been sprinkled with my brother's blood."[2]

Nor would a host of others. Lovejoy's death made him a great martyr to the antislavery cause. Indeed, like so many martyrs, he did more for the movement by dying than he ever would have in life. Men like Wendell Phillips and John Brown were so moved that they resolved to dedicate their lives to the ending of slavery. Therein lies the heart of the vigor, the resilience, the unshakable resolve of the abolitionists in the days to come. Theirs was not merely a political or ideological issue. It was emotional and spiritual. There can hardly be a better analogy than that of the early Christians. Oppression drove them closer together. The murder of Lovejoy and others, rather than discouraging their followers, gave them instead greater determination. In their martyrs' blood they swore, as did Owen Lovejoy, renewed allegiance. Most of the early abolitionists also suffered personal injuries, humiliations, loss of property, impoverishment, and every manner of harm short of death. Thus for the leaders of the movement this was no mere abstract cause. They had suffered for it, bled for it personally. Slavery had done them a personal wrong. Just as the disciples spread in their gospels the stories of Christ's humiliations and death, so did the abolitionists ably publicize their wrongs endured, winning converts while reassuring the faithful. It helped that there was good ground for their message. Even though proponents of Congressional abolition were few, the number of those opposed to the institution of slavery, North and South, was legion. Most favored emancipation, the voluntary freeing of slaves by their masters. Others preferred the purchase of slaves by organizations such as the American Colonization Society, which then shipped the blacks to a new home of their own in Africa. Yet others, though few, suggested government purchase of slaves to be then manumitted. Thus the slaveholders would not suffer an enormous loss of capital assets with no recompense.

From all this raw material, the abolitionists could hope to draw converts, just as Elijah Lovejoy had been converted himself to abolitionism. And to this his adherents added something unknown even among the early Christians. They attempted to meet in secret, to work gently and gradually toward their goal. The abolitionists, however, brought an urgency and militance to their cause. They pushed and fought in the open. They wanted action at once and delighted in provoking their enemies. What is more, with the open support of most of the American churches, their movement possessed not only social and political and economic potential, but also religious overtones as well. Like Elijah and his namesake of old, then, these men came to regard themselves as prophets, the keepers not just of an idea, but of an eternal truth created by God. So unshakably convinced were they of their rightness, that they would die for it before they would yield. Most slave proponents, and even those in the middle, failed to appreciate the power of these seeming fringe fanatics. A few, Breckinridge among them, however, recognized that the force of reason and argument might not be sufficient to combat a moral idea. He stood closer to the mark, for the abolitionists, few as they were, few as they would ever be, were unconquerable. They could not be defeated politically for their realm was not exclusively politics. They could not be silenced in the press. They could not be muzzled in the pulpit. And they could not be silenced in death. Unsuspected even by themselves, the abolitionists, these dedicated men like Lovejoy, zealous, emotional, and not infrequently a bit imbalanced, heralded the most potent social movement in the Western world since the time of Luther.

By the opening of the Civil War, the disciples of Lovejoy had come far toward their goal, yet with far to go. Just as James continued to spread the good news in the wake of his brother Jesus' death, so did Owen Lovejoy take on his brother's mantle. He spoke from the pulpit as a Congregational minister at Princeton, Illinois, organized public meetings to further the movement, and at some personal risk used his own home as a station on the much publicized "underground railroad," spiriting fugitive slaves from the South away from the slave catchers who tried to enforce the despicable Fugitive Slave Law of 1850. Yet he, unlike his brother, came to realize in the 1850s that the movement needed a political base, and the repeal of the Missouri Compromise provided one, for it united in opposition a host of outraged men, not necessarily abolitionists, but almost all antislavery sentiments. The Republican party.

Lovejoy became at once one of the chief organizers of the new party in Illinois, and it was largely through his influence and persuasion that the far less committed Abraham Lincoln was brought into its embrace. The Rail Splitter did not stand second to anyone in his personal opposition to slavery, yet he was fearful of aligning himself with a party so committed to the radical step of abolition. Ever the politician, Lincoln feared the consequences it might have on his hopes for the Senate seat he would contest with Douglas in 1858. Finally, however, Lovejoy prevailed. Lincoln became a Republican, but emphasized continually that "I now do no more than oppose the *extension* of slavery." For the next six years, as the war came, the abolitionists like Lovejoy would work on Lincoln to change that. And when finally he was elected, they and the wing of the Republican party that they composed, called Radicals, believed that the hour of deliverance was at hand. Only days after the opening guns at Fort Sumter, Charles Sumner, himself a powerful martyr for the cause, went to the Executive Mansion and told the new President that "under the war power the right had come to him to emancipate the slaves."[3]

And when war came, many like Lovejoy awaited it anxiously. He and Sumner and others regarded this as the final opportunity to erase America's shame by swift, bold movement. A stroke of the pen is all that was needed, as Sumner told the President. Abolition could be accomplished. Indeed, it would help subdue the Confederacy. Frederick

Douglass, the most prominent freedman in the nation and an ardent proponent of emancipation, declared that "The simple way, then, to put an end to the savage and desolating war now waged by the slaveholders is to strike down slavery itself, the primal cause of the war." Shortly thereafter Douglass suggested war policy, making abolition a weapon of reprisal against the South. "Sound policy, not less than humanity, demands the instant liberation of every slave in the rebel States." Therein lay the hint of a change that took place in the abolition movement, and in the Republican party. With the advent of war came an opportunity for something more than an end of slavery. Men of ambition, as well as conviction, saw in the abolition movement an avenue to power. The Republicans, still a minority party in 1860, could use abolition as an issue to achieve not only their moral goals, but permanent political ascendancy as well. For both ends, many of them welcomed the war as a genuine godsend.[4]

They were the Radicals. Their origins went back to the formation of the party itself. Though never formally distinguished by a hard line from the rest of the party, still their attitudes made them generally discernible as, indeed, after awhile they came proudly to identify themselves as Radicals. The early and most powerful national lights in the party were the rallying point for these men. Sumner, Seward, and Chase, all represented Radicalism in the popular imagination long before the new party even organized. Seward, in fact, was far more conservative in character than the others, but in the popular mind he stood firmly with them. Sumner was the real leader, the true devoted zealot, abolitionist first, Republican second. As for Chase, while few ever questioned his genuine commitment to the cause, there was no denying that he, more than the others, saw it as a vehicle to power. Thus in its own hierarchy, the Radical wing of the party represented factions even within itself. Other lesser luminaries also enjoyed prominence in Radical ranks, among them Benjamin Wade, John Hale of New Hampshire, Zachariah Chandler of Michigan, and Henry Wilson from Massachusetts. As Lincoln took office all of them but Seward and Chase sat in the Senate, forming a powerful block of influence in the upper house. Meanwhile, equally influential Radicals formed a vocal minority in the House of Representatives. Joshua Giddings, George W. Julian of Indiana, the indomitable Thaddeus Stevens of Pennsylvania. And Owen Lovejoy of Illinois.[5]

Following his part in forming the Republican party in his state, Lovejoy won election to Congress in 1856 and reelection two years later. Like his brother before him, he spoke out powerfully, and at once, quickly identifying himself as among the most forceful of the orators espousing abolition. "What Achilles' wrath was to Greece, slavery is to our country," he said in the House; "the prolific spring of woes unnumbered. Not the discussion, not the agitation of the subject of slavery, but the existence of slavery itself." Thereafter his voice was seldom still when the subject of slavery came up. The Kansas troubles, Lecompton, Harpers Ferry, every topic touching on the peculiar institution usually heard his words of counsel, of admonition, of demand. In 1858 he took a small part in the Lincoln-Douglas debates, to the extent that some accused Lincoln of being Lovejoy's tool. Not so, yet the Rail Splitter's oratory did reflect a gradual shift in his position toward going beyond the mere prevention of slavery's expansion. Undoubtedly Lovejoy and fellow Republicans like him were slowly influencing the President-to-be.

"No one can intimidate me," declared the abolitionist during his second term, and as he won increasingly the attention of the party at large, the Radical faction began thinking of him for a place in 1860. Some believed that he should have the vice-presidential nomination, and a few impractically looked even higher. But Lovejoy himself had no such plans. Indeed, as 1860 approached, he was disillusioned if anything by the loss of his younger brother Joseph from abolitionist ranks. Once in sympathy with Owen and Elijah, Joseph Lovejoy by 1859 stood almost directly opposed to their principles. "Slaveholders have a complete vindication of their present position," he wrote, "they are entitled to be looked upon as benefactors to the country and to the human race." American slavery is "a redemption," he said, "a deliverance from African heathenism."

The tension in Congress on the eve of Lincoln's election reached such a stage that many gentlemen took their seats rather uncomfortably due to the pistols in their pockets. One representative from Georgia actually had his hand on his pistol, the hammer cocked during one heated day in the House, his intended object Lovejoy. Yet he spoke fearlessly on, friends telling him that the Southerners in his hearing "acted like a turkey on a hot grate." When Lincoln came to office, then, he found in Lovejoy a potent ally yet, like the rest of the Radicals, a troublesome one. He wanted to reunite the Union. That was all. They wanted an end to slavery. If it could be accomplished by the restoration of the Union, fine. If not, many were inclined to "let the erring sisters go," taking the stink of slavery with them. Yet Lincoln and the Radicals would have to work together for either to accomplish their individual aims. It would not always be a smooth partnership.[6]

For the abolitionists and the Radicals, the war opened great vistas. Sumner was not jesting when he made his suggestion to Lincoln. The outpouring of Northern support for the war said to him that his great object could be accomplished. "This generous & mighty uprising of the North seems to menace defeat to the rebels & the extinction of Slavery in blood." Joshua Giddings felt the same. "The first gun fired at Fort Sumpter [sic] rang out the death knell of slavery." And a onetime Democrat, Carl Schurz, soon to become a political general, told the President's private secretary that "What we could not have done in many lifetimes the madness and folly of the South has accomplished for us. Slavery offers itself more vulnerable to our attack than at any point in any century." As a result, once the war began, most of the Radicals at once became its most ardent supporters. More, they opposed compromise by which the South would be brought back into the Union on the basis of the prewar status quo. Lovejoy now declared for "a vigorous prosecution of the war." That determination became even more pronounced after he, along with some other Congressmen, rode out to Bull Run to watch the expected defeat of the Rebels. Seeing the humiliating defeat of the national forces, Lovejoy commandeered an ambulance and personally drove two wounded soldiers to a hospital. Shocked, he readily accepted the offer of a colonelcy on the staff of Frémont in Missouri.[7]

He reached St. Louis while the furor still raged over Frémont's premature emancipation of the state's slaves. Lovejoy certainly sympathized with Frémont's action, and when Lincoln repudiated the order and later removed the general from command in Missouri, it was a measure of the distance between Lincoln and the abolitionists. Any attempt at accomplishing their aims at this stage of the war threatened the loyalty of Missouri, Kentucky, and Maryland, as well as the western portion of Virginia and east Tennessee. To win his war, Lincoln had to keep that territory, even if it meant delaying emancipation attempts until the border was securely in Federal hands. Slaves had worn their chains in American for two and a half centuries. Better let them wear them a year or two more until the North was certain of victory, rather than attempt emancipation too soon, lose the border, the war, and thereby any chance of ending slavery as well. The Radicals did not see this. Lincoln failed to recognize the true character of the war, they charged. Worse, some even attacked the President's character. Lincoln's attitude toward slavery, charged Ben Wade, "could only come of one, born of 'poor white trash' and educated in a slave State." Lovejoy, however, saw the greater end. Deploring Lincoln's act, still he remained quiet, recognizing that President and Radicals must stay on good terms for their mutual benefit.[8]

Following the debacle at Manassas, many of the Radicals tacitly admitted Lincoln's position that the war must be won first before slavery could be abolished. As a result, they pressed him constantly for advance, attack, victory. When McClellan came to the East, most took heart, expecting that this brilliant young general would be their deliverance and that of millions of blacks. Thus no one except Lincoln was more disillusioned when Little Mac showed his true nature and delayed doing anything. By late October they were visiting the President demanding action or the general's removal. Lincoln, cannily using their demands to his own ends, conveyed their sense of urgency to McClellan, and thereby tried to persuade him to move against the enemy. He did not, and thus began a year-long feud between Little

Mac and the abolition wing of the Republican party, with Lincoln in the middle, and often pulling the strings.[9]

Meanwhile the abolitionists in Congress did not abandon their pressure to attack slavery as well as the Confederacy. The Massachusetts Democrat turned general, Benjamin F. Butler, gave them their first opportunity. Commanding at Fort Monroe in May 1861, he refused to return three runaway slaves to their Confederate master, calling them "contrabands of war" to which the Virginia officer lost all claim when he and his state rebelled. The term contraband stuck to escaped slaves for the rest of the war. More profound, his policy encouraged thousands of slaves to flee to Federal lines, creating a considerable problem for Union commanders hard pressed to care even for their own men but an opportunity for Owen Lovejoy.

On July 8, 1861, in Lincoln's special session of Congress, he introduced a resolution proposing that Butler's policy be made regulation throughout the army. No fugitive slaves would be returned; the existing Fugitive Slave Law should be repealed. His measure failed of passage, excepting the part approving Butler's course, but he and other Radicals were much disappointed when Congress insisted on refusing to encourage slaves to escape to Union lines. They were further incensed when Lincoln ordered Halleck to replace the abolitionist Hunter as Frémont's replacement. The whole Missouri experience represented a setback to their war aims. Lovejoy, however, restrained himself from outwardly attacking the President as did many of his colleagues. He too, like so many of these Western men now faced with war, gravitated away from the extreme fringe. An extremist he was on abolition to be sure, but one who recognized that strength lay in the middle. He had to remain a good bedfellow with the center in order to bring it to his great purpose. He, like Lincoln, could wait a little longer.[10]

Still, Lovejoy would not go too far toward the center. When, after the Manassas defeat, the House passed a resolution by John J. Crittenden declaring that the purpose of the war was solely to preserve the Union, and not to abolish or interfere with slavery in the South, Lovejoy like a few other Radicals abstained. And as the special session ended, he unequivocally declared that his desire was to confiscate all Rebel property as a blow against the rebellion. That meant slaves as well as land and cotton. On the final day of the session such an act, the first Confiscation Act, did pass, making prizes of war of any property used in rebellion against the United States, including slaves who worked on fortifications or in military support services. It was a start.[11]

When Lovejoy returned to Washington for the first regular session of the Thirty-Seventh Congress, he brought with him a renewed determination to make this war one against slavery as well as disunion, to persuade Lincoln that destroying the former meant necessarily the

end of the latter. Indeed, he wanted to enlist black troops in the army
that they might fight for their own freedom. "If we can subjugate the
rebels without Negroes, we can do it quicker with them," he argued.
"I do not expect to get rid of a system like that without trouble: but
inasmuch as the cancer must be cut out, inasmuch as we are on the
table and the knife is ready, and our life depends upon our submit-
ting to the operation, I say carry the knife to the bone even though it
creates a soreness which it will take a generation to recover from."
The people were gradually coming to be ready for such a move, he
believed. "President Lincoln is advancing step by step just as the cautious swimmer wades into the stream before making a dive." The
Chief Executive, said Lovejoy, "will make a dive before long."[12]

Lovejoy experienced bitter disappointment, then, when Lincoln
repudiated Secretary of War Cameron's suggestion to arm black soldiers in December 1861. Together with other members of the House,
he struck back by passing an endorsement of Frémont's premature
emancipation of the previous August, and approving of Cameron's
plea for Negro troops. Further, they passed a resolution asking that
slaves of Rebels be emancipated wherever the Union had military jurisdiction. This was to be only the beginning. The abolitionists in the
Republican party had given Lincoln nine months. Now they had no
movement toward emancipation, and certainly no move by McClellan
that looked toward an early end of the war. In the session to come
they would depart far more from the administration policy, despite
Lincoln's urgings that they keep "the integrity of the Union prominent
as the primary object of the contest on our part."[13]

In the first several weeks of the session a host of bills aimed at slavery appeared in Congress. A bill was introduced to abolish slavery in
the District of Columbia. Lovejoy proposed a law to prohibit Union
commanders from returning fugitive slaves. More confiscation bills
came in, and on December 20 he almost succeeded in getting passed
a resolution liberating all Rebels' slaves as well as confiscating all
forms of property. The Radicals were on the offensive.

Soon they attacked Halleck, suspected of proslavery leanings.
Then, in the wake of the embarrassing disaster at Ball's Bluff, Virginia, the previous October, Lovejoy supported a move to create a
Committee on the Conduct of the War, eventually to become the
most powerful, and dread, body in Congress, a sort of star chamber
that could, and did, investigate any and every general and military
operation. It would ruin many careers, but Lovejoy saw in it a means
to use the threat of the committee to encourage the generals to fight,
and to fight against slavery. Wade, Chandler, Julian, and other Radicals dominated the committee. While Lincoln approved of its aims, he
would in time come to deplore its harsh methods.[14]

The committee would be especially suspicious of McClellan, and
only in part because of his military sloth. He was a Democrat, a po-

tential demagogue, a man popularly spoken of among the opposition for the 1864 nomination, and therefore as great a threat to the Radicals and abolition as the rebellion itself. Many believed, erroneously, that McClellan as President would pursue a peace policy that would allow the Confederacy to remain outside the Union. That did not do justice to Little Mac's genuine devotion to the Union and belief in winning the war. However, whether he won the war or lost it, McClellan in the White House could be relied upon not to strike a blow at slavery. Indeed, in the aftermath of his failure on the Peninsula, and well aware that he was now at war with the Radicals as well as the Confederates, Little Mac actually made so bold as to suggest war policy to Lincoln, making his position on slavery clear. When the President visited his general at Harrison's Landing in July, McClellan handed him a letter.

"While general-in-chief, and directing the operations of all our armies in the field," McClellan would recall, "I had become deeply impressed with the importance of adopting and carrying out certain views regarding the conduct of the war." He put these views in his letter. The Constitution, he said, must never be abandoned. The Union must be preserved "whatever may be the cost in time, treasure, and blood." Once successful in the South, secession would spread like a plague. "Let neither military disaster, political faction, nor foreign war shake your settled purpose to enforce the equal operation of the laws of the United States upon the people of every State."

Now Lincoln must make war policy, he said. "This rebellion has assumed the character of war; as such it should be regarded, and it should be conducted upon the highest principles known to Christian civilization." They must not war upon the people of the South, only against their armies and their government. "Neither confiscation of property, political executions of persons, territorial organization of States, or forcible abolition of slavery should be contemplated for a moment." Private property must be protected. "Pillage and waste should be treated as high crimes." "Military power should not be allowed to interfere with the relations of servitude, either by supporting or impairing the authority of the master." Of course, contraband slaves recognized by Congressional act must be received. Further, should slaves be appropriated for government work, their owners ought to be paid for them. He even recognized that this means, and military necessity, could and perhaps should work emancipation in the border states.

Having settled on this policy, Lincoln should then publish it to the world, thus garnering the support of the loyal in America, North and South, and the respect of foreign nations. It would also help in recruiting and, with Little Mac's highly developed notion that there could never be enough men in arms to meet a foe who was always more numerous, recruiting assumed almost paramount importance. "A

declaration of radical views, especially upon slavery, will rapidly disintegrate our present armies." Only in closing did McClellan actually
address military subjects, soundly suggesting the need for a general-
in-chief—Halleck had not yet been appointed—and hinting, though
not suggesting, that he would gladly assume the post.[15]

It was an altogether remarkable letter, and meant more than met
Lincoln's eyes as he read it. He then put it in his pocket without comment. The Radicals had been on the offensive against McClellan for
over six months, because he was slow, because he was a Democrat,
and because he was soft on slavery. In January Wade and Chandler
all but accused him of cowardice to his face. Then the general's onetime friend Stanton, now very cozy with the Radicals, showed the
lesser side of his nature by turning against him when he became secretary of war. In the wake of Ball's Bluff the Committee on the Conduct of the War crucified General Charles P. Stone, never informed
him of the charges against him, and kept him imprisoned for half a
year. Finally, at the Radicals' insistence, Lincoln diffused somewhat
McClellan's hold on his army by enforcing a reorganization into
corps, with mostly Republican generals at their head. All this and
more gave Little Mac ample cause to despise the Radicals, and when
he brought about his own defeat on the Peninsula, it was easy for him
to look to them as the cause. "I have lost this battle because my force
was too small," he wrote on June 28. He could not be held responsible
for his heavy casualties. "I have seen too many dead and wounded
comrades to feel otherwise than that this Government has not sustained this army. If you do not do so now the game is lost. If I save
this army now, I tell you plainly that I owe no thanks to you or any
other person in Washington. You have done your best to sacrifice this
army."[16]

The Harrison's Landing letter was McClellan's counterattack on the
Radicals and their policy. He, like they, took the battle directly to the
President, and he challenged every aspect of their program. Confiscation, arbitrary arrest, vindictive war against the entire South and not
just its armies, abolition, and even the punitive policy of encouraging
portions of Southern states that were largely loyal to splinter and join
the Union. Western Virginia was even then being maneuvered toward
separate statehood, and east Tennessee might be next. In short,
McClellan presented in brief compass a brilliant statement of the war
aims of the large mass of conservatives in the North, and upon no
subject more so than slavery. But his timing was terrible. He could
only suggest such a policy, and launch such an attack on the Radicals,
from a position of strength, from a major victory. Failing that,
McClellan had no base of power. Instead, Lincoln gave Pope, well
liked by the Radicals, the command in Virginia and called Little Mac
away from the Peninsula. Clearly the abolitionists in Congress had
come of age. They had the power to meet and best the Union's most

popular general. Now perhaps they had the power for a great change, for emancipation.

Lovejoy acted as a leader in the House in the push for emancipation. Knowing that Lincoln still favored African colonization as a remedy, or a gradual compensated emancipation, Lovejoy felt willing to compromise by accepting the latter as a start. In March he voted to support a compensation measure proposed by the President, offering Federal money to any state that might itself adopt a policy of gradual abolition. It was a cautious measure, indicative of Lincoln's approach to the problem. By not being Federally enforced, the measure did not violate the rights of any state. Still, Kentucky objected even to this while, on the other hand, the most hardcore abolitionists objected to compensation. There must be emancipation plain and simple. Yet Lovejoy saw the better road. The extremes, withdrawn to themselves, got nowhere. By compromise, by finding the middle ground, there lay the road to progress. Admittedly the advance was slower than he wished, but any start was better than none, and he, unlike so many others, understood the extreme difficulty that faced Lincoln on any emancipation move. "Let no one belittle this great act of the President," he said of this tentative step. "It is great in underlying principle." Thereafter, said Lovejoy, "Mr. Lincoln is a historical personage."[17]

Their partnership traveled a rocky path, however. When Major General David Hunter started arbitrarily freeing slaves under his military jurisdiction at Hilton Head and Port Royal, South Carolina, in April and May, Lincoln repudiated the action, saying it was a species of activity that only the President might exercise. In the face of great indignation from the Radicals, still Lovejoy stood with Lincoln. He saw this not as a defeat, but as a means of clearing the way for greater things. Indeed, to suit his purpose in introducing and passing a bill abolishing slavery in all Federal territories, Lovejoy proposed a resolution thanking McClellan for the taking of Yorktown. Little Mac himself was grateful. "Even the Abolitionists seem to be coming round," he told his wife, "judging, at least, from the very handsome resolutions offered by Mr. Lovejoy in the House." In fact, Lovejoy made the resolution merely to better his image with conservatives in hopes of winning their support for his territorial bill. Eventually it passed, and Lincoln signed it into law on June 19.[18]

Now Lovejoy and the abolitionists believed that they had Lincoln well on the way to achieving their aim. He had gone this far. It was time to press the issue. The public sentiment in the North seemed generally favorable to the territorial and District of Columbia abolitions. The next step was the nation.

As for Lincoln, he still favored some less extreme step than emancipation by Federal decree, but his options were dwindling. The border state politicians continued to reject even gradual emancipation.

McClellan's defeat on the Peninsula seemed to argue for some bold strike against a symbol of rebellion other than its armies. That could only mean slavery. Northern politicians wanted to enlist Negro soldiers as a further blow at slavery. Lincoln could not continue to resist. Indeed, he did not wish to. Years before he had proclaimed himself as opposed to slavery as any abolitionist. His reluctance until now to move on a general emancipation was based chiefly on political considerations, fears that it would actually harm the war effort. By the summer of 1862, however, he was almost ready.

On June 18 Lincoln spoke privately with his Vice-President, Hannibal Hamlin of Maine. He was certain that now the time was near when he could issue a proclamation emancipating all slaves in the states in rebellion. Hamlin, delighted, was sworn to secrecy, and Lincoln told no one else for some time, even though the attacks on him continued from Radical abolitionists. Yet many saw that soon the President would have no choice. Jay Cooke, even then avidly selling bonds for Chase, told the treasury secretary that Lincoln would have to emancipate either in the manner of Hunter or else with a Congressional bill. Another, more virulent, confiscation act was then in Congress. Yet another attempt on July 12 to get some compromise from the border state men failed. Lincoln had already now discussed his proposed emancipation measure with most of his cabinet, and on July 13 for the first time he intimated to Lovejoy that the time might be near. By this time he was determined. "I was in my best judgment, driven to the alternative of either surrendering the Union or issuing the emancipation proclamation."[19]

Now it was a matter of when. On July 22 the full cabinet discussed the measure. There was not complete unanimity, Blair predictably objecting and warning that it would cost Lincoln heavily in the fall elections. But the rest agreed with the President's policy. Seward suggested that it would be politic to withhold the announcement until the Union had a significant victory on the battlefield. Issue the proclamation in strength, not weakness, he said. Lincoln agreed. He would wait, and continue to suffer the criticism of the Radicals who did not know what he was sitting on. They had come a long way together. Their aims, Lincoln's, and those of millions of blacks, were finally about to meld in a single great purpose. Lovejoy would stay with the President during the trying weeks ahead as the Rail Splitter anxiously awaited that necessary victory. Pope did not give it to him in August in Virginia. And that meant that the hopes of all, as September dawned, rested upon the one man seemingly least qualified to bring them victory, a man who, had he known what rested on his success or failure, might have been even less anxious than usual to come to combat.

George Brinton McClellan.

CHAPTER 19

"HE HAS GOT THE 'SLOWS,' MR. BLAIR"

Robert E. Lee rather considerably discomfited Lincoln's plans for Little Mac. The President only wanted McClellan temporarily in command in Virginia again in order to rebuild the army. Then he would find another man who could lead it back into Rebeldom to meet the enemy on their own ground. Instead, Lee brought the war to McClellan. Invasion of the North.

Lee's victory over Pope at Second Manassas invigorated the Confederacy. Coming as it did on the heels of the Peninsula success, it made up considerably for the dismal news from the West. More importantly, it demanded that Lee follow on his advantage, largely to make up for those failures in Tennessee and Mississippi. "Our victorious troops in Virginia," said a Charleston editorial, "must be led promptly into Maryland." Lee must strike McClellan before he reorganized his army, and drive the Union government into Pennsylvania. "When the public buildings in Washington shall have been razed to the ground, so as to forbid the hope of their ever again becomming the nest of Yankee despotism, then, at last, may we expect to see the hope of success vanish from the Northern mind, and reap the fruit of our bloody and long continued trials."[1]

Confederate pressure for an invasion of the North dated back to the euphoria over Jackson's success in the Shenandoah, that valley which itself offered such a promising avenue for invasion into western Maryland. Further, Lee faced the necessity of making some sort of move after Pope's retreat. He could not stay where he was. To go east would bring him too close to the strongly fortified Washington. Going south left too much of Virginia open again for invasion. A move west to the Shenandoah looked better, but a reverse there could cut Lee off from Richmond. Thus, strictly military persuasions dictated that, if he were to capitalize at all on his victory, he must carry the war into the enemy's country and move north. Further, Lee hoped that he might be able to remain in western Maryland for some time, posing a continual threat to Washington, and thereby keeping Richmond secure. Then too, he and Davis believed that a considerable Confederate sentiment existed in Maryland. The presence of his army would rally thousands to its banners. On September 3, just two days after the last action with Pope at Chantilly, and one day after McClellan's restoration to command, Lee decided to invade. The next day he secured President Davis's approval of the bold plan, even as his army was on its way to the Potomac.[2]

Lee faced many decisions as he rode toward Leesburg where he staged his army. There were several Potomac crossings available. Which to use? Moving west of the Blue Ridge, by way of Harpers Ferry, he might be as far north as Hagerstown, Maryland, before McClellan could mount any real resistance. On the other hand, if he crossed east of the Blue Ridge, it would pose a greater threat to Washington, and then he would still be in a position to move west to Hagerstown unimpeded. At the same time, such a move would protect his line of communications via the Shenandoah. Moving with swiftness, Lee poised the Army of Northern Virginia on the banks of the Potomac by September 5. As they crossed they cheered, and the army's bands broke into "Maryland, My Maryland."

Lee was making far more of a gamble than he knew and an unwise one at that. The victory over Pope had been costly. His army had no time to reorganize itself after the heavy fighting at Cedar Mountain and Manassas. Ewell, one of Jackson's finest division commanders, was out of the war for a while with a leg that would be amputated. Another of Jackson's commanders, General Charles S. Winder, lay killed at Cedar Mountain. The men wore rags. Many had no shoes, rations were short, animals were exhausted and broken down. The army was reduced to no more than 50,000, and it still did not have a truly efficient organization. Of course Lee felt it necessary to strike north while the Federals were disorganized, but they were hardly more disorganized than he. Furthermore, the knowledge that McClellan was back in command alone should have told Lee that he had a little time on his hands. However long he took to reorganize, Little Mac would take longer. However slowly he moved into the North, McClellan would react more slowly. The Confederacy undoubtedly needed a grand bold gesture to show the world its strength and ability to defend itself. Such an invasion fit the need, but only if it proved successful. A defeat in the North would be worse than no invasion at all. And the will of the Federal soldier to defend his own homeland was a quantity as yet untested, unknown. Taken all together, the risks were too great, the necessity not sufficiently compelling at this moment, for Lee's move to be prudent.

It took until September 7 to complete the crossing of his army. That done, Lee moved straight for Frederick, Maryland. From this point he entertained ideas of a move farther north to Harrisburg, Pennsylvania, an important railroad hub, then east to threaten Philadelphia, Baltimore, and even Washington. His plans were not set, too hastily formed. He was making his strategy even as he rode Maryland's dusty summer roads, but wisely he used his cavalry under Stuart to buy him time for planning. Stuart took his horsemen east and made demonstrations very close to Washington itself to mask Lee's movement, then crossed the Potomac and set up a screen nearly twenty miles long behind which McClellan's cavalry could not penetrate.

Predictably, Washington and McClellan were mightily disturbed. Reports came first of Stuart's ride toward the capital, and then on September 5 and 6 came scattered and largely inaccurate accounts of crossings of large numbers of the enemy on the upper Potomac. McClellan's cavalry commander, Brigadier General Alfred Pleasonton, reported late on September 5 that a Confederate deserter claimed that Lee and his entire army were moving into Maryland. Enemy numbers were reported at 30,000 to 40,000, and during the next day more reports came in confirming the deserter's tale.

Halleck faced a problem at once. He had a garrison of 12,000 at Harpers Ferry, commanded by Colonel Dixon S. Miles. If Lee really had crossed north of Leesburg, then Miles was entirely cut off from Washington. Miles himself confirmed this and was pulling in his outposts, while Halleck said late on September 5 that "I find it impossible to get this army into the field again in large force for a day or two." Harpers Ferry, he admitted, might well be attacked and overwhelmed before then. As for McClellan's army, several of its corps and division commanders were even then being relieved of command to face charges preferred by Pope. Thus almost the first task facing Little Mac was to get his high command in shape. McDowell was to be relieved of the I Corps by Major General Joseph Hooker, a dashing division commander in whom McClellan had much confidence. Little Mac begged that Porter and Major General William B. Franklin be retained in their commands at least for the present emergency, postponing their relief "until I can see my way out of this difficulty." Halleck agreed.[3]

At once McClellan began ordering his corps across the river from Virginia, unaware that he narrowly missed being replaced as army commander. The President frankly did not want him, nor did he believe that the general was capable of meeting the threat. Once before, just prior to ordering the Army of the Potomac to leave the Peninsula, Lincoln had spoken to Major General Ambrose E. Burnside, offering him McClellan's command. The Rhode Islander felt intense loyalty to McClellan, and declined. The same happened again now, Burnside urging the President that Little Mac could meet and defeat Lee. Several discussions with Halleck followed, and finally the President admitted that he had no other alternative in the emergency but to give McClellan command of the army even then going into the field. Lincoln personally told Little Mac that he would leave Washington to lead the campaign, though with typical bravado McClellan later claimed that no one gave him orders to assume command. He just took it, believing that if he failed he would be put to death![4]

On September 6 McClellan began slowly moving northwest from Washington, feeling his way toward Lee. An immediate problem was Miles and his garrison at Harpers Ferry. Dangerously exposed there, Miles could do good service if somehow he might be joined with the Army of the Potomac. By September 11 McClellan felt that he had to have Miles with him, for he was at his old game again. Writing to Halleck that day, Little Mac said with confidence that "All the evidence that has been accumulated from various sources . . . goes to prove most conclusively that almost the entire rebel army in Virginia, amounting to not less than 120,000 men, is in the vicinity of Frederick." Obviously, he said, Lee was risking everything on a great battle in the North. "They intend to hazard all upon the issue of the coming battle." He believed Lee knew the Confederates to be superior to the Federals by fully one fourth. Worse, in the aftermath of Lee's victories, the Rebels would undoubtedly fight well. McClellan spoke of the possibility of defeat, even of the loss of Washington. He was covering all of the potential disasters that he foresaw, then begging for more soldiers. Halleck sent what he could. In fact, McClellan was lying. He had only one report that put the enemy as high as 120,000, and that came secondhand, from a Pennsylvania clergyman who passed through Frederick. Hardly a trained observer. A telegraph operator in Maryland estimated Lee at 100,000, but in fact the only estimates that came from a reliable source, Major General John E. Wool, placed the Confederates at between 30,000 and 75,000. Little Mac should have known better than to accept figures from any but trained military observers, but such was his nature that he seized at the highest figure anyone could offer, even from an itinerant preacher.[5]

Lee certainly had no objection to McClellan's ravings. Indeed, he counted on it. "He is an able general," said the Virginian as he rode through Maryland, "but a very cautious one. His enemies among his own people think him too much so. His army is in a very demoralized and chaotic condition and will not be prepared for offensive operations—or he will not think it so—for three or four weeks. Before that time I hope to be on the Susquehanna." Until then, Lee had much to do.[6]

On September 7, as the Virginian occupied Frederick, Davis sent him instructions to announce in a proclamation to the people of Maryland just why the Confederate Army was there. It was a diplomatic move in part, designed to prove that Confederate aims were not for conquest, nor to overthrow Federal authority in what remained of the old Union. "The Confederate Government is waging this war solely for self-defense," said Davis. "It has no design of conquest." Rather, "we are driven to protect our own country by transferring the seat of war to that of an enemy." The next day Lee would go further when he suggested to the President that "The present position of affairs, in my opinion, places it in the power of the Government of the Confederate States to propose with propriety to that of the United States the recognition of our independence." Both Davis and Lee were making politics here in Maryland. Lee issued the proclamation, but nothing came of his suggested peace movement. Indeed, though he could report to Richmond from day to day that "nothing of interest" was happening, he did find that the expected outpouring of sympathy for the South did not materialize. Rather, the merchants of Frederick closed their stores to the Rebels, and Lee had to quarantine the city except by special pass.[7]

Soon Lee prepared to leave Frederick and continue his campaign. Now he split his army, sending Jackson to capture Miles at Harpers Ferry and Longstreet on to Hagerstown. That left only Stuart's cavalry and a division led by D. H. Hill to cover the twenty miles between those two points. Lee outlined his intentions in Special Orders No. 191 on September 9, including detailing Hill to act as rear guard, and several other small detachments ordered to cooperate with Jackson. The army was then to converge on Hagerstown once Harpers Ferry and the line of the Baltimore and Ohio had been taken. Through a clerical oversight, involved with the still imperfect organization of the army, two copies of the order were sent to D. H. Hill instead of one. The first he read and kept. The second someone in his headquarters wrapped around three cigars and put into a pocket or saddlebag. Sometime during the next three days that little package fell unnoticed to the ground, and on September 13, when McClellan moved into Frederick in the wake of Lee's departure, a Federal soldier found it. Little Mac was overjoyed.[8]

"Here is a paper with which if I cannot whip 'Bobbie Lee,' I will be willing to go home," McClellan boasted to General John Gibbon. The lost order showed that Lee had divided his army and that only Hill and Stuart stood between the Federals and the isolated halves of the

Confederates. The general wired to Halleck of his find but instead of proposing the opportunity thus afforded, he used the discovery instead to reinforce his complaints that Lee had his entire army with him and must certainly number "120,000 men or more." Little Mac must have more men.[9]

A quick march now could have put McClellan squarely between Jackson and Longstreet. He might not have bagged Stonewall, who could withdraw into the Shenandoah, but certainly by taking Harpers Ferry and thus denying Jackson access to Longstreet, McClellan might then have turned to the wing marching to Hagerstown and overwhelmed it. Little Mac had over 80,000 men in his army, yet he delayed more than half a day before he pushed two corps, Burnside and Franklin, forward toward Turner's and Crampton's gaps along the South Mountain range. It was dawn on September 14 when the Federals moved, and by that time warning was already on its way to Lee that McClellan was coming. He may even have been told of the finding of the lost order, for McClellan was careless in letting people around Frederick know what he had found. As a result, Lee saw at once his danger. He ordered Hill to move at once to Turner's Gap, and turned Longstreet around and started him toward Hill's support. Farther south the division of Lafayette McLaws would have to cover Crampton's Gap.[10]

While all this took place, Jackson moved on Harpers Ferry. The command marched more slowly than expected, for Lee wanted Stonewall to be at Harpers Ferry on September 12 and have it surrounded. Instead it was not until September 15 that Stonewall got the divisions of A. P. Hill, A. R. Lawton, Richard H. Anderson, John G. Walker, and John R. Jones, in place and ready. He opened a bombardment of the little river town the day before to keep Miles in place. It did not require much. Miles, remembered chiefly for his drunkenness at First Manassas, made almost no attempt to defend his position. Harpers Ferry was dominated by Maryland Heights to the north, Loudoun Heights on the east, and Bolivar Heights on the west. Instead of establishing himself on those high places, he kept all of his garrison drawn into the town where enemy artillery could easily pound him into submission. By late September 14, Miles was surrounded, and only 1,200 cavalrymen managed to boldly find their way out. Franklin was supposed to come to Miles's aid after passing Crampton's Gap, but Miles did not know it, for McClellan did not tell him. Thus, with little hope in holding out, the Federals in Harpers Ferry capitulated the next morning after a token resistance in which Miles took a mortal wound.[11]

"Through God's blessing," Jackson reported to Lee, "Harpers Ferry and its garrison are to be surrendered." He took 11,000 prisoners, and a great quantity of small arms and supplies. It came as welcome news to Lee, and he could use some, for the day before, September 14, had not been a good one. D. H. Hill was a bit tardy getting his division fully up to Turner's Gap in time to meet the threat from Burnside's advancing corps. Noon arrived before Hill was prepared to meet the Federals, and just barely did he beat them to the gap. Arraying his brigades along the forward crests of the two slopes leading down to the gap, he awaited Burnside's attack. McClellan himself commanded personally in the assault against Hill. As a result it was tentative at best, though some spirited fighting took place, and Hill managed to hold out long enough for Longstreet to arrive with the bulk of his command. Still heavily outnumbered, the Confederates managed to stay in place well after dark until Little Mac sent Federals around both of their flanks and Longstreet had no option but to withdraw. That same evening McClellan was able to do something he had never done before. He sent Washington a message announcing a victory. "It has been a glorious victory," he said. "The troops behaved magnificently." Indeed, he so exaggerated his small success that he wrote his wife that "God has seldom given an army a greater victory than this." Every moment added to the importance of the battle at South Mountain, said he. "How glad I am for my country that it is delivered from immediate peril!" Lincoln thanked Little Mac for his victory, such as it was, and advised him to pursue the enemy, but McClellan would take his time, sending out more announcements of his triumph and, in an undeniable display of childish bravado, even wrote to old General Scott boasting of his battle just to aggravate that old wound.[12]

McClellan would never learn that winning a campaign took more than posturing and boast. And he did not show such anxiety about informing Washington of how McLaws's division had completely baffled Franklin at Crampton's Gap, though losing the position in the end. Yet still he now undeniably held the advantage if only he could move swiftly enough to take it. Jackson and Longstreet were separated, and Jackson behind his schedule in capturing Harpers Ferry. Had Little Mac pushed forward immediately on September 15, he might have hit Longstreet alone. But Burnside was slow to advance, and McClellan ordered Franklin to stay in place instead of pursuing Lee to Sharpsburg. Only well into the afternoon did the commanding general order Franklin forward, having wasted half a day's time. When Franklin did move, he found that Lee had withdrawn to a strong position on a high ridge beyond a small stream, Antietam Creek. Lee had had time to choose his own ground, and now McClellan would have to drive him from it.[13]

Lee entered Sharpsburg on September 15, and there received the news of Jackson's capture of Miles's garrison. At once he ordered Longstreet and Jackson both to concentrate at this place, a little town of little consequence. It faced on the west the bending course of the Potomac, running roughly north to south. Parallel to the river and three miles east of it flowed the Antietam. The position looked good to Lee because the creek was crossable only at a few spots, and high ground on his side would give him excellent coverage of Federal assaults. It also afforded easy access to Jackson, who could march up the Virginia side of the Potomac and cross at a ford immediately behind the right of Lee's line. This same ford, however, would be Lee's sole avenue of retreat should he meet a reverse. In the event of a lost battle, he could hardly expect to get his entire army safely across one ford with any sort of enemy pursuit. The ground was a high risk, just like the entire campaign. That campaign now lay in shambles even with the victory at Harpers Ferry. Lee's only hope was to get his army together again and win a great and smashing victory. Anything less, even a drawn battle, was for him a loss, for it would leave him no choice but to retire to Virginia once more.

By late on September 15 Lee could see the first advance of the Army of the Potomac appearing across the Antietam. Franklin and his corps approached from the southeast, facing the right of his line. Burnside and Edwin V. Sumner's corps moved in from the east, facing his center and left. Soon Lee discovered a dreadful flaw in his choice of position, for there were high places on McClellan's side of the Antietam that would allow his artillery to range with its fire over most of the Confederate line. Yet even now Lee believed that he would not be attacked, at least not until September 17. That would give ample time for Jackson to come.[14]

He was right, as usual when Lee gauged McClellan. Though much of his army was on the Antietam by the afternoon of September 15, McClellan decided that it was too late to attack, even though Lee had barely 19,000 Confederates which the Federals outnumbered by between two and three to one. McClellan knew where Jackson was, too, and that delay would give Stonewall time to join his commander. But he still deluded himself that Lee had 120,000, or so he claimed. More probable is that McClellan, for all his abilities, lacked genuine moral courage.

September 16 dawned with dense fog over the impending battlefield. Little Mac welcomed it, for he as yet had no plan of attack. Indeed, this would be his first real attempt to plan and conduct a set piece battle, for all his actions on the Peninsula had been defensive, all the planning done by Johnston and Lee. The general rode all over the field, sometimes personally selecting positions for the units that came up, looking at the ground and peering across the Antietam at Lee, who was altogether delighted to wait another day to fight. By mid-afternoon Little Mac had an idea of what he wanted to do, but barely more than that. He intended first to attack Lee's left. Once Hooker's corps had crossed the creek and driven the Confederate flank back toward the center, Burnside was then to attack Lee's right by crossing a stone bridge. If both attacks were fruitful, then he

would send an assault against Lee's center. It was a terrible plan.
From local people McClellan could learn that Lee's only escape was
by way of that one ford behind his right, and there is where the Federals should have attacked first. Driving Lee's right away from that
ford, McClellan would have him trapped. Better, it would also cut off
the only avenue by which Jackson could reinforce the main army.
Worst of all, McClellan's whole approach was almost fatally tentative.
As he actually described his plan, he would attack on Lee's left "at
least to create a diversion, in favor of the main attack, with the hope
of something more, by assailing the enemy's right—and, as soon as
one or both of the flank movements were fully successful, to attack
their center with any reserve I might then have in hand." There was
not a syllable of certainty or confidence in the whole outline, and he
admitted that he had no sure plan to have a reserve "in hand" when
its time might come.

By the late evening of September 16 Hooker got his corps across
the Antietam and in position for its attack on the morrow. There was
some skirmishing in the process, but nothing developed. Then some of
the troops with which Hooker tangled were withdrawn to the center
of the field as others took their place. Jackson. Pushing hard from
Harpers Ferry, he had brought two divisions across the Potomac ford
to Lee that morning, with the divisions of McLaws and Anderson still
on the way. With certainty they would reach the field early on the
next day and be in time for the battle. All day Lee anxiously turned
his glance toward the road leading to Harpers Ferry. There lay his
salvation, and Jackson did not disappoint him.

Hooker attacked with the first dawn on September 17, the Battle of
Antietam was fairly begun. Though none yet knew it, this would be
the bloodiest single day of the entire Civil War. Heavily outnumbered, Jackson's line fell slowly back until the gamecock John B.
Hood delivered a fierce counterattack. McClellan sent Major General
Joseph K. F. Mansfield forward to Hooker's support with his XII
Corps, but Mansfield fell killed in the movement and Hooker took a
painful wound soon thereafter. All at once Little Mac had a serious
command vacuum on his right just as the first fighting of the day gave
him an initial advantage. Hooker had three divisions, two of them
commanded by old familiar names in this war. The first belonged to
now General Abner Doubleday, still gleefully returning those first
shots from Charleston a year and one half before. Another division
followed General Ricketts, with his own grudge to settle. The other
looked for leadership to General George Gordon Meade and, as senior
officer, Meade took over after Hooker's wound. The Confederate
counterattack considerably disorganized the I Corps, and Meade
withdrew it from the action to recompose. Meanwhile, Mansfield's division commanders continued the attack on Jackson, and slowly drove
him back past a Dunkard church. Despite the loss of two of his gen-

erals, and McClellan's failure to do anything to fill the command void thus created, this first part of his battle plan was going well. Already Lee was in trouble.

Now was the time for Edwin V. Sumner's II Corps to enter the contest just to the left of Mansfield's battling divisions. Fresh and anxious for the fight, Sumner chafed at being held in reserve by McClellan as the early guns of the battle went off. Finally McClellan let him go, and with an impetuous charge Sumner drove his corps straight into a place called the West Woods, just above the church. His leading division, Major General John Sedgwick's, met a fire from three sides after Mansfield's divisions backed out of the line to regroup, and almost at once Sedgwick was in deep trouble. Sedgwick faced no alternative but to withdraw, and in so doing forced the division on his left to follow suit. Jackson pressed his advantage and recovered some of the lost ground, and already McClellan's ineptitude in battle tactics revealed itself. Not only did he fail to coordinate the assaults by his corps and division commanders but, worse, he did not press Burnside's anticipated attack on Lee's other flank. That left half of the Army of the Potomac inactive, and allowed Lee, behind the Antietam, to skillfully shift troops away from his unthreatened right to the endangered left.

Sumner's other division belonged to Brigadier General William H. French, and in the rush to attack, it became sidetracked and did not follow Sedgwick into the fray. Rather French struck off to Sedgwick's left, near the center of Lee's line, and here encountered D. H. Hill. Their fighting grew rapidly in intensity, augmented when Israel B. Richardson brought another Federal division to French's assistance. Other Confederate troops reinforced Hill, but gradually the Southerners fell back until they reached a sunken road which gave them excellent cover. There some of the most ferocious fighting of the war would take place in the next hour. Hundreds would bleed and die in the fight for this one country path, soon to be called Bloody Lane. It is the bloodiest single spot on that bloodiest day.

Hill held against ever mounting Federal assaults. General Richardson fell with a mortal wound, yet his men finally managed to outflank the enemy in the road, and Hill was forced to pull back. But still he bought time, and his valiant resistance against very heavy odds only served to increase the caution of McClellan, who spent most of the day thus far well behind the lines giving little real direction to the battle.

Lee now faced a desperate situation. His entire left had been brutally assailed and, despite the check given to Hooker and Mansfield, the fall of Bloody Lane left him no alternative but to pull back that half of his army, ever contracting his lines. Worse, the Federal artillery, the best managed arm of McClellan's army this day, dealt terrible blows to the Confederate guns, at one time putting all but a dozen out of action, many of them permanently. Lee had no reserves left, every unit being sent into the defense or else facing Burnside along the Antietam to repel his attack. Only the division of A. P. Hill, left at Harpers Ferry to parole prisoners and secure the captured booty there, offered the promise of fresh troops. Yet Hill had miles to march to the sound of the guns, and a successful assault by Burnside might well cut him off by taking Boteler's Ford, the only route across the Potomac. The survival of the Army of Northern Virginia depended now upon McClellan.

Little Mac did not fail Lee. While the fight on his right developed largely without his direction, he held units out of it for a reserve, then piece by piece allowed them to go into the battle. And Burnside, originally supposed to create a diversion for the main attack, was kept idle for the first three hours of the day even though a "diversion" in military parlance was supposed to precede the main attack. Only around 10 A.M. did Little Mac finally order Burnside to move, and by then the bulk of the fight against Jackson had died down, allowing Lee to move units to his right to face the new threat.

On top of that, Burnside did not manage his part of the battle at all well. Even as McClellan withheld Franklin from following up on the success at Bloody Lane, which would have crippled Lee, Burnside fumbled his assignment. Without bothering to conduct a sound reconnaissance of the Antietam, he began sending his divisions in senseless attacks across that exposed stone bridge, each one easily repulsed by Jones's division and what remaining artillery Lee could mass. A Confederate brigade commander serving with distinction in the defense was Robert Toombs. It was well after noon when finally the Federals took the bridge and began crossing over, at the same time finally discovering that they could have walked across the shallow stream at many places close by. Burnside did not, then, get in formation to continue his advance until about 3 P.M. When he did send his IX Corps forward at last, Lee could not resist, and was driven back into Sharpsburg.

Now, yet again, McClellan had the opportunity to inflict a crushing defeat. His cavalry chief, Pleasonton, reconnoitered across the Antietam and discovered that Lee had weakened his center in order to protect his flanks. Pleasonton, seconded by Brigadier General George Sykes, begged McClellan to attack. Porter's fresh V Corps lay immediately opposite Lee's center. In a single swift move across the creek, with an excellent crossing in Union hands already, Porter could drive straight into Sharpsburg, split Lee in two, and virtually surround Jackson with his back to an uncrossable Potomac. There was a chance that part of Longstreet's wing might be able to escape across Boteler's Ford, but not if Burnside pressed his advantage. Little Mac had a chance virtually to destroy the Army of Northern Virginia, and with it the eastern Confederacy, for barely a division would then stand between him and Richmond. Yet situated as he was in a command post fully two miles from the battlefield, McClellan chose to do nothing. He barely had any conception of what was happening except the reports that came back to him, and they were, of necessity, half an hour old by the time they reached him. Thus he prejudiced his chances of capitalizing on any such advantage as Pleasonton discovered even before the battle began. He left it almost entirely to his corps commanders, and the reasons are not hard to divine. Years later in writing his memoirs, the usually boastful McClellan, delighting in placing himself at the center of activity in his narration, wrote his description of Antietam almost as if he had not been there. The only personal reference to himself is a ride he took to the right of his line well into the afternoon, and after that had ceased to be the main scene of activity. He gave few orders, and studiously avoided being at the scene of principal activity. Unconsciously, McClellan was preparing his own personal lines of retreat. If he failed of victory or, worse, suffered a defeat, he would be able to cast the blame on the commanders actually on the field. If he did not give them guidance, then he could not give them directions that would prove to be in error. Like Joseph E. Johnston, McClellan felt a mortal fear of taking "a shot." After the battle was done, however, and in the years to come, he would fire many a round at the generals who he left to fend for themselves in the fight.[15]

Then came something with which Little Mac felt more comfortable. A Confederate success. A. P. Hill could not have arrived at a better time. Even with the lack of leadership from his commanding general, and despite his own sloth, Burnside was slowly pressing Lee more and more. But in so doing he exposed his own left, near Boteler's Ford. And there came Hill, unexpected, to hurl himself against the enemy. Completely surprised, Burnside could not stand where he was, and drew back to Antietam Creek. By 5 P.M. the battle was done.

Lee knew the measure of McClellan better, perhaps, than he would any other Federal general. Indeed, after the war he reputedly admitted to a daughter that "McClellan was the only Genl. Father dreaded," and as well, when asked who he thought the ablest soldier was that he faced during the war, Lee said "McClellan by all odds!" Not very likely, but if Lee did utter such nonsense, it was hardly a compliment. Lee was human, like any general, with a measure of pride, a pride wounded by defeat. Yet McClellan never defeated him, nor even gave him a serious challenge. Indeed, on September 18 Lee stayed on the field at Sharpsburg, surprising all his generals except Jackson by expressing a willingness to continue the battle rather than withdraw. He was willing because he knew McClellan, and knew he could beat him. Therein lies the hidden motivation in any highly suspect remark about Little Mac being the best Union general. Lee always defeated McClellan, therefore he had beaten the best. Despite later defeats at the hands of other Northern commanders, Lee could remain in his mind unconquered since he was never beaten by McClellan.[16]

Certainly McClellan did not defeat Lee at Antietam. Of course the battle effectively ended the invasion of the North, and on September 19 Lee began a leisurely withdrawal toward Virginia with barely a hint of a Federal pursuit. In fact the invasion was doomed from the start, ill advised and poorly planned. Setting that aside, however, this vicious and bloody fight along the Antietam can only be regarded as an enormous tactical and moral victory for Lee. Having got himself into a position in which the virtual existence of his army faced the greatest peril of the war, and with it the Confederate cause in Virginia, he managed to hold his position against considerable odds and withdraw his army badly battered but intact. The casualties were terrible. More than one fourth of his army felt the sting of Federal lead, and for McClellan losses surpassed 12,000 in killed, wounded, and missing.

But of course the campaign was a defeat for Lee, and no one crowed more in victory than Little Mac. "The spectacle yesterday was the grandest I could conceive of," he wrote his wife on September 18. "Those in whose judgment I rely tell me that I fought the battle splendidly and that it was a masterpiece of art." Warming to his theme, he would go on in the days ahead to say that "I feel some little pride in having, with a beaten and demoralized army, defeated Lee so utterly and saved the North so completely. Well, one of these days history will, I trust, do me justice." "I feel that I have done all that can be asked in twice saving the country."[17]

McClellan remained north of the Potomac for the rest of the month, reorganizing and attempting against some odds to reequip and clothe the men. Meanwhile he feuded incessantly with Halleck, resentful that the general-in-chief had not sent effusive congratulations for the victory at Antietam. Little Mac resolved not to visit Washington if he could avoid the den of vipers he perceived there. As a result what little communication there was between Lincoln, Halleck, and the Army of the Potomac broke down. Twice during October Washington ordered McClellan to cross the Potomac and go after Lee, who was then refitting and substantially rebuilding his army in the Shenandoah. Twice McClellan procrastinated. Lincoln himself went to visit the army and to urge the general to action, without any success. Gazing out across the Army of the Potomac, now reinforced to 120,000 or more, the President sarcastically referred to it as "only McClellan's bodyguard."[18]

Finally in the last week of November, the army crossed the Potomac and marched into Virginia once more, concentrating around Warrenton. McClellan made the movement sufficiently slow that Lee was able to send Longstreet from the Shenandoah to get between the

Federals and Richmond. Then, on November 7, a courier arrived from Washington. He went first to Burnside, and after some persuasion got him to accompany him to Little Mac's headquarters. He handed McClellan an order relieving him of command and directing that the reluctant Burnside take his place. McClellan was stoical, calm, hardly surprised, though to the end of his days he would never be able to face the reasons for his dismissal. Always in his mind it was a conspiracy of Halleck and the Radicals, with the President's acquiescence. Never could he admit to himself that it came, instead, from his own doing. Lincoln meant his reappointment to be temporary, but the qualified success at Antietam had bought McClellan another opportunity. "I said I would remove him if he let Lee's army get away from him," Lincoln told Francis P. Blair, "and I must do so. He has got the 'slows,' Mr. Blair."[19]

However much he disappointed the men in Washington, the general enjoyed almost unqualified support in the army, and now the Union faced its final danger from McClellan. Incensed, many of the army's officers drank to quench their anger, and then talked of leading their soldiers on the capital to depose Lincoln and install McClellan as dictator. Little Mac himself became aware of this widespread sentiment. "Many were in favor of my refusing to obey the order, and of marching upon Washington to take possession of the government." To his everlasting credit, McClellan manfully resisted what must certainly have been a strong temptation, one that appealed not only to his well-developed megalomania, but also to his bitterly hurt feelings. His patriotism did not waver, and he discouraged all such talk, remaining with the army for several days after his relief in order to calm his officers. Then he left for his home in Trenton, New Jersey, never to take the field again. Like many unsuccessful generals, he would spend the war "awaiting orders."[20]

CHAPTER 20

"RIDE ON MASSA JESUS"

The comings and goings of one Yankee general meant little to the three and one half million Negroes living as slaves in the Confederacy. Life for them had changed little since their ancestors' arrival on the slave ships of generations and centuries before. It was a life of toil, not always unremitting, of meager education, of little challenge, of almost no goals. Americans were indeed a distinct people in the world by the middle of this century, but the slave was not a part of that new person. Denied the ethic and opportunity of individual achievement—or failure—that whites had, denied the mobility, the property, the learning, and the freedom, to be a part of the American mainstream, the slaves were doubly chatteled. Intentionally prevented from acquiring the attributes necessary to make their way on their own, they depended as much on their masters as their owners did upon them. One fourth of the entire Southern population had barely the education to sign a name or skills requisite for more than common labor. Should they be suddenly loosed upon society, many feared not only from the slaves, but for them as well. What would they, could they, do?

It was a question that faced Lincoln and his generals in the field almost from the first days of the war. When Benjamin F. Butler occupied Hampton Roads in May 1861 and garrisoned Fort Monroe, when the Federals took Port Royal and New Orleans and Corinth, and a hundred cities more, the neighborhood slaves came in pairs and in twenties. They came for succor, for food, for freedom. No one was ready for them. The blacks expected emancipation; the generals often could give them nothing but a meal and directions to go back the way they came. Yet wherever Lincoln's armies went to stay, there slavery disintegrated spontaneously. To tens of thousands of blacks, the coming of the Yankee soldiers brought the day of "Jubilo." It would not be that easy for white or black.

It may have been inevitable that this war would bring emancipation in train with Union victory, but certainly Lincoln did not begin it with a conscious plan for forced abolition nor any idea of how to deal with the slaves that would flock to his forces. Indeed, the phenomenon seems to have taken most Federals by surprise. It happened first to Butler at Fort Monroe, and to him fell the honor of designating the slaves who sought his sanctuary as contrabands. The day after his arrival, Butler found three black men who came into his lines, runaways, asking for shelter.[1]

Butler was not an abolitionist. Indeed, in Maryland the previous month he loudly proclaimed his intention to honor the rights of slaveholders, a stand that brought criticism from the antislavery faction in his own state. Now in Virginia he saw the blacks who began coming into his lines solely in military terms, hence the sobriquet of contraband. He learned that Confederates used the slaves to work on fortifications. That made them as much a part of Rebel war efforts as a gun or a wagon, and therefore just as confiscatable. Butler's intent, never emancipation, was to accept runaway slaves and thereby deny the enemy of its labor force. For the next year and one half, this would be the chief rationale for accepting the trickle of blacks that soon became a flood.

When the Federal minions came near, many farmers and slaveholders selected their better blacks and sent them deeper into the interior where they would be safe. This "refugeeing" became a common sight in the South in 1861, and at times as many as two thousand slaves were on the road at a single time with their masters "running the negroes." When the dread sound of "Yankees coming" met the ears of the plantation lords, they removed what they could, and no property was more mobile than that which walked on its own legs. Further, in time the Confederate authorities would themselves insist on removing Negroes to keep them out of enemy hands where they might be used for military purposes. Many slaves, with deliverance so near, did not wait to be moved, but removed themselves instead toward Federal lines. Others, considered too old or feeble to be worth taking, were left for the Yankees if they wanted them. General David Hunter called them "fugitive masters," those who abandoned their blacks and fled, and some anonymous slave gave song to the owner's departure.

> *Say darkeys hab you seen de massa,*
> *Wid de muffstash on he face,*
> *Go 'long de road sometime dis mornin'*
> *Like he gwine leabe de place.*
> *He see de smoke way up de river*
> *Whar de Lincum gun-boats lay;*
> *He took he hat, an' leff berry sudden,*
> *And I spose he's runned away.*
> *De massa run, ha, ha!*
> *De darkey stay, ho, ho!*
> *It mus' be now de kingdum comin',*
> *An' de yar ob jubilo.*

That many slaves, in fact, did not covet their freedom is certain. Some, told fearful stories by their masters, expected Yankees to breathe fire and devour poor darkeys alive. "They got long horns on their heads and tuskes in their mouths and eyes sticking out like a cow. They're mean old things," said one Tennessee slave. Yet the overwhelming majority of the slaves looked with anticipation to the coming of Mr. Lincoln's soldiers. Freedom might be an unknown, but slavery was not, and there must be something better.

Many of the slaves, particularly those in the less populated mountainous regions, barely knew that there was a war, much less that their freedom might be in the offing. One old Virginia man, whose only recollection of war came from that in 1812, heard Union guns and exclaimed, "Well, I 'clare 'fo' Gawd, dere's dem damn Britishers again." But most knew what was happening, and had a notion of why it was happening. Indeed, thanks to their informal grapevine, many slaves knew the latest war news before their masters. And almost all understood instinctively that the sound of the Yankee guns in the distance could mean freedom. As the cannon raged at Manassas in July 1861, one old slave woman worked in her kitchen making dinner. When now and again she heard the boom of a fieldpiece the old woman said lowly to herself, "Ride on Massa Jesus."[2]

However they came into the Federal lines, and for whatever reasons, the escaped slaves offered an enormous problem to their new benefactors. Butler's contraband statement was hardly a proclamation of emancipation, but it moved in that direction by denying the Fugitive Slave Law. Butler put them to work on his own fortifications, caring not only for the men, but also their wives and children who invariably came with them. Thus he made tacit admission that the slave was more than contraband, else why give sanctuary to a child or woman who could hardly serve a military purpose for the enemy.

Soon came the first confiscation acts, and contrabands became Federal policy. Their management required its own bureaucracy both within the army and in the war department, and in time the government required that the slaves be paid. Miserable wages to be sure, but still the first time that most of them ever received anything for their toil. By the end of 1862 over 15,000 slaves came under the aegis of Fort Monroe alone. And when the second confiscation measure passed that summer, they were all automatically declared free.[3]

The care of these newly freed men, soon to be called freedmen, attracted the notice of more than the war department. A variety of humanitarian and religious organizations in the North almost immediately organized to uplift the black spiritually and intellectually even as the military made use of his muscle. Groups like the American Missionary Association, the Friends Association of Philadelphia, and the United States Christian Commission, sent their messengers of enlightenment in the path of the conquering armies to commence at once the work of remolding the slave into the white man's idea of a useful member of society. Often they came with little more than good intentions and Bibles. They did much good, and some harm, but how else were they to commence the work of undoing over two centuries of slavery except by trial and error?

To Port Royal went the Gideonites. When Du Pont's fleet captured the South Carolina town and its vicinity, including Beaufort and Hilton Head, he found some ten thousand slaves left behind by their masters. At once Butler's problem at Fort Monroe was amplified tenfold, and a simple contraband policy was not going to be enough for the management and care of this virtual city of blacks. Were they to be free, or remain slaves, work for wages, or work at all? What about all of the plantation land abandoned by their owners, and the crops that needed tending? Could these blacks be made soldiers? Might they be educated, given land, made independent? A hundred questions that Americans never squarely faced before appeared as Du Pont steamed victoriously into the harbor. Port Royal would be their answering ground.[4]

At first the Federals had to contend with the variety of impulses motivating the Negroes at Port Royal. Most wanted freedom. Many wanted revenge, and looted and destroyed aimlessly after their masters left. First the Yankees had to bring order, and particularly keep them from destroying the cotton crops and fields. That produce would be needed to help keep King Cotton from forcing England to recognize the Confederacy, and these Negroes here could work for their own freedom by tending the cotton that would be sent abroad to appease hungry textile mills. It was one of the largest crops within living memory.

First Chase's treasury department sent agents to Port Royal, their chief interest being the cotton. They made employment for some of the slaves in ginning, baling, and hauling the crop for shipment, but most of the blacks remained indolent, and many badly clothed and ill fed. Clearly more had to be done for them. Chase met the challenge by sending a special agent to see to the slaves' employment and set them to work planting a crop for the coming year. He sent north for people to come and educate the slaves, and at once a host of well-intentioned relief societies such as the Port Royal Relief Committee were formed. They sent money and clothing and food, and books and teachers. Here at Port Royal the Union government would erect its first major laboratory for the education and patriation of the Negro slave.

The goal was to make the slaves—and legally they were still slaves —self-supporting. The same organization used in the fields before the war continued, except that the Yankee reformers had to cast themselves in the somewhat ironic roles of overseers. There was not enough money to pay the field hands at first, but they did receive food and clothing, and the beginnings of an education. Scores of women brought their brand of New England civilization, including schoolroom and church, to the freedmen, mixing with the rudiments of reading and writing a good deal of utterly useless information quite lost on the slave and his situation. Yet it was a gesture in good faith, done in all charity. They taught the blacks how to support themselves, though hardly lavishly. They learned self-rule, something of the laws that governed free men, and in the apportioned leavings of their former masters they owned land for the first time. The Port Royal experiment brought them to the threshold of citizenship.[5]

Yet there were those, particularly General David Hunter, who wanted to append a responsibility to that new status. Military service. Simon Cameron's report to Congress in December 1861 had advised the employment of Negro soldiers in the war, and met with sound condemnation from all but the more outspoken abolitionists like Sumner and Lovejoy. Yet the idea took hold almost from the first shot, for what retribution could be more just than to use as a weapon against the slaveholders' conspiracy the very people that it sought to keep enslaved? Besides the poetic justice of the subject, it could also encourage the three millions and more of slaves in the South to run away or rebel, themselves becoming an army within the Confederacy, a threat from inside as potent as that from without.

Hunter started the move with vigor in his May 9, 1862, order emancipating the slaves within his military jurisdiction in Florida, Georgia, and South Carolina, and authorizing their arming as soldiers. Indeed, he ordered a conscription of all black males between the ages of eighteen and forty-five. Over 500 men were drafted at once and the beginnings of a Negro regiment started. The slaves were largely reluctant to come, fearing that they might just be exchanging one master for another, bond slavery for military servitude. The abolitionists in the North hailed Hunter's action, but of course Lincoln had to repudiate it or risk disaster in the border slave states. Yet the idea of black soldiers would not go away. It cropped up again in August, when Lincoln declined the offer of two Negro regiments from the West, and then on August 22, 1862, General Butler, who so often seemed to be at the center of the freedmen's issue, began raising a Negro regiment in New Orleans. Lincoln did not try to stop him. Indeed, three days later the war department quietly authorized the commander in South Carolina to raise up to 5,000 black soldiers, though only for guard duty. By November, however, the 1st South Carolina Volunteers was nearing completion. Indeed, Hunter's successor, General Rufus Saxton, began using the men of the still incomplete regiment in coastal raiding operations and reported them to be good soldiers. That same month they took their first wounds in their own battle for freedom. "How can I expect to get my freedom," said one escaped slave, "if I'm not willing to fight for it?" In time tens of thousands would be willing.[6]

This put all the more pressure on Lincoln to effect some general emancipation of the slaves. They were working, and fighting, and bleeding for the Union. Were they not entitled to enjoy the blessings of freedom? The enlistment of black soldiers only increased the pressure on Lincoln from the Radicals, and that pressure, the unwillingness of the border states to accept the President's suggestion of gradual voluntary state emancipation, the raising of black troops, and McClellan's questionable success at Antietam, all came together to make September 1862 the right time. And it was not too soon for, strange to contemplate, there were those in the Confederacy who thought to preempt the Rail Splitter with an emancipation of their own.

For the slave in the Confederacy, the war brought little change except that, in many cases, the "massa" went off to the war and his "missus" now ran the farm or plantation. Labor remained their life. Only those close to the war areas really felt the influence of the conflict. But as the war went on, eventually the hunger and deprivation that reached every aspect of Southern society finally made the slave a part of the war, too. If it did not, then the necessities of the military did. Thousands of slaves were impressed, or rented, from nearby plantations to erect fortifications and act as teamsters and in other noncombatant roles. Indeed, often when white soldiers were required to dig and carry, they protested vigorously at being forced to do Negroes' work.

From the first the Confederacy's leaders made emphatic their position that slavery was the best and natural status for the Negro. "Our new government is founded," said Alexander H. Stephens in March 1861, "upon the great truth, that the negro is not equal to the white man; that slavery—subordination to the superior race—is his natural and normal condition." Editorials elaborated, saying that "The idea of the equality of race is a figment." "Why is it that the negro thrives in servitude, multiplies in numbers, and improves from generation to generation?" The answers were simple. "Left to himself, the negro would perish if placed in conflict with the white man. . . . When emancipated and removed from the crushing competition of a superior race he demonstrates his utter incapacity for self-restraint, grows idle and thriftless, indulges his passions without the slightest check, descends step by step down to the original depths of his ignorant and savage instincts, and at length is debased to nearly the state in which he is found in the wilds and jungles of Africa."[7]

Yet however much the Confederacy sought to justify slavery, and thereby itself, the institution presented some difficult problems for Davis and his government. From the first diplomatic envoys sent word that across the Atlantic "the public mind here is entirely opposed to the Government of the Confederate States of America on the question of slavery." The Southern emissaries tried to avoid the subject entirely when possible. "You often hear expressed the regret that slavery exists amongst us," wrote Slidell from Paris, "and the suggestion of a hope that some steps may be taken for its ultimate but gradual extinction." Indeed, just a few days after Antietam, Slidell talked with the Earl of Shaftesbury who suggested that President Davis "in some way present the prospect of gradual emancipation." Coming unsolicited from Richmond, said the earl, such a policy would lead immediately to recognition and "to more decided measures to put an end to the war." Slavery, it seemed, was the only obstacle to foreign intervention or so thought many.[8]

Indeed, there was a rising sentiment within the Confederacy against slavery. For the most part it was merely the continuation of a minority opinion long felt, and little affected by the war. "I hate slavery," wrote Mary Chesnut the month after first Manassas. "I say we are no better than our judges in the North, and no worse. We are human beings of the nineteenth century and slavery has to go, of course. All that has been gained by it goes to the North and to Negroes. The slave owners, when they are good men and women, are the martyrs. I hate slavery."[9]

Even as the war progressed, there existed a substantial movement to improve the condition of the slaves, and right some of the injustices done them during past decades. Indeed, it was a major step simply to admit that there had been abuses. Spurred chiefly by religious groups, measures came from state legislatures repealing the old statutes prohibiting slave literacy. They gave legal recognition to slave marriages. In time the separation of mothers from their children by sale was prohibited. Law forbade the exclusion of Negro testimony in some cases, and the strictures against slaves assembling together fell away. In time many in the religious community began to regard Confederate reverses on the battlefield as punishment from God for slavery, and for the old prohibitions against teaching blacks to read the Bible. "I am not sure but this very law is one of the many reasons why God is withholding, in a degree, his smiles from the righteous struggles we are waging with our cruel foes," speculated one editor.[10]

Strangely, many of the recipients of these abuses expressed a willingness to take arms to keep themselves and their brothers in bonds. Among many free Negroes and slaves, allegiance to master and to the South actually outweighed the desire for personal freedom. Early in the war, even before the first guns, many plantation owners suggested putting their chattels under arms to help defend the South. In April 1861 a regiment of 1,400 free Negroes organized itself in New Orleans and drilled with white troops. Another company presented itself in Richmond that same month, as did yet another black organization in Mobile. Some of the states authorized the raising of black soldiers, Tennessee in the summer of 1861 even calling for a draft if necessary. Some slaveholders suggested raising a virtual army of 100,000 or more.

All companies formally tendered to the war department were turned away, avoiding the unanswerable inconsistency of a nation fighting to uphold the idea of racial inequality yet allowing its inferiors to fight for it. Still many blacks did travel with the armies, usually as body servants and cooks, and frequently they grasped fallen weapons and fired them at the Federals, the enemies of masters and a system so thoroughly ingrained in them that they would fight not to be free. As for the free Negroes who offered themselves in regiments, for many there was little to distinguish them from whites except their color. Some prospered in trade, and many even owned slaves themselves. Thus the age-old impetus of self-interest took hold. How rapidly the freed Negro in the South became American.[11]

The pressure, and expedience, of some formal Confederate move toward emancipation gradually mounted. As with every other aspect of the war, North and South, no issue stood alone. Intertwined in emancipation were diplomacy, economics, labor, the military, the church, and the very nature of the South and the Confederacy. Yet none was ready for the step that Abraham Lincoln would take on September 22, 1862.

Prepared since the summer, and already read to the cabinet a few days before, Lincoln's Preliminary Emancipation Proclamation needed only a victory. Antietam, however dubious, served the purpose, and the President waited less than a week before he made his announcement. He declared all of the Confederate states except Tennessee, some Federally occupied portions of Virginia and Louisiana, and the forty-eight counties designated as "West Virginia," to be in rebellion. Having said that, he went on to "declare that all persons held as slaves within said designated States and parts of States are, and henceforward shall be, free." Further, he asked that they not revolt against their masters, except in self-defense, yet promised that they would find sanctuary within Federal lines, and all who wished should be received in the armed forces.

The document said far less than it implied. Lincoln did not by words seek to change the character of the war from one to sustain the Union to a holy endeavor for freedom. In fact he made it plain that he was still waging the conflict solely to reunite the sections. Further, in his proclamation he still made a bid for compensated emancipation. It was not to take effect until January 1, 1863, and of course it technically only freed slaves in those places under Confederate control, in other words in places where Lincoln's proclamation could not be enforced. Slaves held in the border states and in occupied areas remained slaves.

There was immediate dissatisfaction with the measure from many quarters. The abolitionists found it far too little. Seward complained that "We show our sympathy with slavery by emancipating slaves where we cannot reach them and holding them in bondage where we can set them free." Abroad the reaction was much the same. "There seems to be no declaration of a principle adverse to slavery in this proclamation," complained Lord Russell, and the London *Spectator* acidly commented that "The principle is not that a human being cannot justly own another, but that he cannot own him unless he is loyal to the United States." Many denounced the proclamation as purely an attempt to win military support by enlisting Negroes.[12]

In fact, most of the measure's critics misunderstood the document and Lincoln's motivation, particularly with reference to just which slaves were freed. They did not see that as a military measure, a punitive measure against the Confederacy, the proclamation should naturally affect only those in rebellion. Why penalize loyal men in Kentucky and Maryland? Further, to emancipate in the border states only endangered their still shaky stability in the Union, particularly at this moment with Bragg's Confederate Army invading Kentucky and driving toward the Ohio. Lincoln justified the document solely on military necessity, an exercise of his war powers. Indeed, he would confess that he felt in normal times such a proclamation would be unconstitutional.[13]

Certainly the people of the Confederacy thought it a violation of the Constitution. Jefferson Davis would in later years cite the proclamation as "the fullest vindication of their own sagacity in foreseeing the uses to which the dominant party in the United States intended from the beginning to apply their power." Like most of his fulminations, this conclusion was fallacious. Lincoln clearly issued the proclamation in reluctance and, once determined to issue it, tempered its provisions considerably. The border states were still offered the opportunity of gradual emancipation, and had the seceded states put down their arms and returned to the Union, there is no reason to suppose that emancipation would have been made a precondition to their acceptance. Indeed, prior to issuing this preliminary proclamation, Lincoln published to the world his policy on this war. "My paramount object *is* to save the Union, and is *not* either to save or to destroy slavery," he wrote. "What I do about slavery, and the colored race, I do because I believe it helps to save the Union." He made it clear that this was his official concept of his duty. Personally, he had not changed his oft-expressed "wish that all men every where could be free." But so far as this war was concerned, "If I could save the Union without freeing *any* slave I would do it; and if I could save it by freeing *all* the slaves I would do it; and if I could save it by freeing some and leaving others alone I would also do that." Clearly, Lincoln's was a conservative, reluctant policy of emancipation, which even he questioned in its legality. Yet he conceived a very broad mantle of war powers for the presidency, and would exercise as much or as little as would suit his great end.[14]

Some in the South, like old Edmund Ruffin, greeted the proclamation with delight. "I am glad that this proclamation has been issued," he wrote on September 28. He believed that it would "cause the loss of favor . . . in the states of Mo, Ten, Ky, & Md., I think this proclamation will serve to do our cause good. It will convert thousands of Unionists to Secessionists." Like many in the South, Ruffin believed that the document sought to foment servile insurrection, even though Lincoln explicitly counseled the slaves to patience and nonviolence.[15]

The Rail Splitter was keeping faith with his announced policy of March 1861. There had been no war then, and he promised to do nothing to interfere with slavery where it already existed. It still existed in Kentucky, Maryland, Missouri, Delaware, and in the occupied portions of the Confederacy, and he did not now tamper with it there. Only in that territory still actively in rebellion did he strike at Southern labor and economy. In a war, all aspects of society that contribute to war's effort are fair targets for attack, and next to armies themselves, labor and economy stand paramount along with industry. The rebellious states might avoid that threat if they would cease their revolt before January 1, 1863.

In its way, the proclamation struck at the Confederacy in yet one way more. Diplomacy. As the summer of 1862 wore on, the sentiment in Great Britain and France for trying to end the war in America steadily increased, not out of sympathy with either side, but because of their own self-interest. Both nations were being hurt in their carrying trade, and France for one wanted to enlarge her foothold in North America. Yet this did not necessarily mean that the two powers sought some solution that was against the interests of the Union. Indeed, Lincoln's earlier moves toward emancipation brought some approval across the Atlantic, among the peoples and their governments, particularly in France. But things were brewing in Britain that to some augured ominous things for Lincoln and his Union.[16]

By the summer of 1862 cotton had become scarcer than any Englishman could remember, barely 10 percent of the previous summer's supply sat ready for the looms. Lord Russell at one point asked, in effect, that Lincoln lift the blockade to allow cotton to reach Europe safely. Failing that, the threats of intervention grew increasingly, aggravated by McClellan's defeats on the Peninsula and Pope's failure at Manassas. The South appeared to be maintaining itself militarily. Many in London, among them the chancellor of the exchequer, William Gladstone, believed that now the Confederacy had earned its independence.

Russell kept his views more quiet but steadily explored the feeling in France and his own country. He did not look to armed intervention, but only an offer of mediation at first, an attempt to negotiate a peace settlement between the combatants. He hoped to have all his information marshaled for a cabinet meeting to decide the issue in October. Palmerston, commenting on the disaster at Manassas, speculated that Washington and Baltimore might fall to Lee next. "If this should happen would it not be time for us to consider whether in such a state of things England and France might not address the contending parties and recommend an arrangement upon the basis of separation?" Russell went further, asserting that no such capture of a major Northern city was necessary. "The time is come for offering mediation to the United States Government with a view to the recognition of the independence of the Confederates." Should mediation fail, he said, then Britain ought to recognize the Confederacy on its own. First France must be won to the idea, and then Russia and the other European powers. Britain would not act alone.

Palmerston constantly kept options open. On October 2 he suggested mid-October as the best time to make the offer of mediation, knowing that Lee was then invading the North. Should Lee achieve a success in his campaign, the Federals might be the more ready to negotiate. Should McClellan prevail, then they could withhold the offer and await further events. The whole plan was conditioned, not on what was best for the Confederacy, but what served England's interests. They did not dare try to intervene on behalf of a failing cause. Indeed Palmerston, in informing Gladstone of the contemplated offer, declared that even if the North rejected and the South accepted a proposal for an armistice, Great Britain should only "acknowledge the Independence of the South, but we ought, Russell and I imagine, to declare the maintainance of our Neutrality." Nothing said about entering the war on the side of the Confederacy. Indeed, some like Gladstone actually feared that the South might be too successful, thereby making the Confederates unreasonable at the peace table.

Then came word of Antietam. Not an overwhelming victory for the North, yet it clearly was a defeat for the South, and at once Palmerston abandoned any immediate plans for mediation or recognition. Certainly, had there been any willingness to go to war with the Union, that too he put aside, for only with the Lincoln government on its knees would he risk war. The wrong move could cost Britain enormous losses in trade and perhaps Canada as well.[17]

Observers then and later believed that Antietam was a turning point, that the victory saved the Union by preventing British recognition of the Confederacy and, therefore, armed intervention. Nothing is further from the fact. Paramount is Britain's concept of her own interests. She did not want an overwhelmingly victorious Confederacy, for the carrying trade and grain exports of the North were just as vital as the cotton from the South. Canadian interests were considerably intertwined with Yankee banking and investment. An utter Union defeat would injure Britain economically whereas Confederate defeat, in fact, would not. England and France's best opportunity lay simply in ending the blockade. That way Southern cotton would be free to come abroad once more, Southern indebtedness to foreign banks would still be binding, and Northern produce and merchant trade would remain uninterrupted. Despite widespread sympathy with the Confederate cause, there was even more prevalent antipathy toward slavery, yet to the rulers in London and Paris, ideology was not the prime issue. Mediation and peace served their purposes. War with the North did not.

Thus, Antietam aside, the issue to come before Palmerston's cabinet that October would have been only the offer of mediation. That alone was a process that would have taken weeks to bring about, and if Seward found it to his purpose, he could well have delayed it longer. The offer being rejected by the North, then formal recognition of the Confederacy was the next step. This, to be sure, would have ended diplomatic relations between the Union and Britain and France, for Seward so instructed Adams. Yet even that did not mean war nor any form of foreign aid for the Confederacy not already being provided. Further, Palmerston always insisted that Britain, France, and Russia act in unison, yet the czar's government was decidedly biased toward the Union, which could only serve to slow any move toward armed action.

Given the condition of trans-Atlantic communications, all of this could not have been accomplished in less than three months, even admitting the almost impossible event in which Palmerston would actually go to war. Of three major campaigns that would take place in that period, the Union would undisputedly triumph in two. Thus, even if Palmerston's cabinet had gone ahead and discussed mediation in

October, or even offered it, Northern successes by the end of the year would have effectively removed the conditions which Palmerston himself set for recognition.

In sum, there was never really a chance of European recognition and armed intervention in behalf of the Confederacy, with or without Antietam. Indeed, Palmerston's own position on recognition was that, once granted, Britain and the other powers should remain neutral. Further, the cabinet was divided on the subject, at least one member being opposed to any interference at all in America. And then came Lincoln's Preliminary Emancipation Proclamation. However much Russell and other upper class Britons may have derided the measure, it met with wide acclaim among the working class people in the nation. The same thing happened on the Continent. British immigrants in the North sent glowing reports home of their life in the Union, their feelings toward slavery and the proclamation. And in an attempt to relieve some of the hardship caused by the cotton shortage, and the resultant unemployment, the Northern public were sending assistance in money and even ships loaded with foodstuffs. Public opinion decidedly favored the Union, and Palmerston and his government could hardly ignore that potent factor.[18]

Thus the long-held contention that Antietam provided a watershed in the Civil War, that the Confederacy's hopes for success came their closest to realization but for that battle, simply does not stand. As implied by Palmerston on more than one occasion, Britain's interests would not allow armed intervention until Confederate successes were so overwhelming that, in fact, foreign aid would not be needed. There is even the possibility that, the extremity being reached, England's benefit would best be served by intervening on behalf of the Union. Certain it is that Antietam was no turning point militarily or diplomatically, for how can there be a turning point in a cause that was lost from its inception?

Yet this is hindsight. For the men of 1862, the cause did not seem lost, the Union saved. The armies marched on and so did their generals. Now Joe Johnston, too, went to the West, his faith in the cause unshaken. Breckinridge was already there, his faith never certain. So was Grant, his determination on Vicksburg fixed. In the East McClellan at last was on the shelf, and there at least a turning point for Union fortunes. He passed from the field without a revolt. However insufficient as a general and a man, he proved a true patriot, and still to be heard from before the war was done. The idealists like Lovejoy and the Radicals they nurtured felt their muscles flexing, their power growing, their once spiritual cause being transformed by fortune and opportunity into a political party with a driving will to attain and maintain ascendancy. In policy they stood beyond their President, and always he must seek to moderate their desires. Their counterparts to the South, the old nationalists so long determined to have their own

Southern nation, had it now, embattled, increasingly impoverished and, most disillusioning of all, ever more tending toward centralized power in Richmond. Their ideals of extreme personal, local, and state autonomy were being dashed as Davis and his ministers frantically gathered authority in the capital in the struggle for survival.

One man, of course, lay beyond all these cares. The Reverend Williamson Jahnsenykes, the prophet of 1808, rested peacefully in his Massachusetts grave, unaware of the terrible struggle he foretold, of the rise of an "Illinois Republican" who made of Antietam his own turning point, for his own purposes. Hesitatingly, unwillingly, uncertainly, that Illinois Republican took a halting step toward transforming political rebellion into social revolution. Like so many others in this war, North and South, he moved falteringly toward the center, the surest abode of compromise, settlement, and peace. It was to be a long journey.

And he still had far, far to go.

DOCUMENTATION BY CHAPTER

INTRODUCTION

1. Williamson Jahnsenykes [William Jenks], *Memoir of the Northern Kingdom, Written, A.D. 1872 . . . in Six Letters to His Son* (Boston, 1808), p. v.
2. Ibid., pp. 2, 14, 23, 24, 26–28, 29, 31–33.
3. Ibid., pp. 38–39, 40, 41, 42, 43, 45–47.
4. Ibid., pp. v–vi.
5. *The Monthly Anthology, and Boston Review*, V (December 1808), pp. 683–84.

CHAPTER ONE

1. Alexander Brown, *The Genesis of the United States* (Boston, 1890), I, pp. 339–40.
2. Warren M. Billings, ed., *The Old Dominion in the Seventeenth Century* (Chapel Hill, N.C., 1975), pp. 22–23.
3. Francis Jennings, *The Invasion of America: Indians, Colonialism, and the Cant of Conquest* (Chapel Hill, N.C., 1975), pp. 15ff.
4. Richard Slotkin, *Regeneration Through Violence: The Mythology of the American Frontier, 1600–1860* (Middletown, Conn., 1973), pp. 217, 370–71.
5. Willie Lee Rose, *A Documentary History of Slavery in North America* (New York, 1976), pp. 15–16, 17; Winthrop D. Jordan, *White Over Black, American Attitudes Toward the Negro, 1550–1812* (Chapel Hill, N.C., 1968), pp. 72–73.

6. Rose, *Slavery*, pp. 19–20; Jordan, *White Over Black*, pp. 73–80.

7. Jordan, *White Over Black*, pp. 315–21.

8. Henry Wilson, *History of the Rise and Fall of the Slave Power in America* (Boston, 1872), I, pp. 3–5; Jordan, *White Over Black*, pp. 321–27.

9. Wilson Carey McWilliams, *The Idea of Fraternity in America* (Berkeley, Cal., 1973), pp. 259–66; David M. Potter, *The South and the Sectional Conflict* (Baton Rouge, La., 1968), pp. 65–67.

CHAPTER TWO

1. William C. Davis, *Breckinridge, Statesman, Soldier, Symbol* (Baton Rouge, La., 1974), pp. 46–47.

2. Mobile, Alabama, *Daily Register,* May 30, 1875.

3. Manuscript speech of Edward Marshall, 1877, in John C. Breckinridge Papers in possession of Dorothy T. Breckinridge; John W. Forney to Breckinridge, September 20, 1853, Breckinridge Family Papers, Library of Congress; *United States Review,* IV (September 1856), p. 150.

4. Lexington, *Kentucky Statesman,* January 20, 1854; Davis, *Breckinridge,* pp. 102–19; Breckinridge to Robert J. Breckinridge, March 6, 1854, Breckinridge Family Papers.

5. Alexander H. Stephens, *A Constitutional View of the Late War Between the States* (Philadelphia, 1868–70), I, p. 274.

6. H. W. Beers to Breckinridge, August 18, 1855, Breckinridge Family Papers; Davis, *Breckinridge,* pp. 140–46, 170–71.

7. Samuel S. Cox, *Union—Disunion—Reunion: Three Decades of Federal Legislation, 1855 to 1885* (Providence, 1885), pp. 410–11; Breckinridge to William A. Duer, January 5, 1857, John C. Breckinridge Papers, New-York Historical Society, New York.

8. United States Congress, *Congressional Globe* (Washington, 1857), 35th Congress, 1st Session, part 3, p. 3041; Robert M. Myers, ed., *The Children of Pride* (New Haven, 1972), p. 325.

9. Breckinridge to William Bigler, May 7, 1859, William Bigler Papers, Historical Society of Pennsylvania, Philadelphia.

10. Breckinridge to Robert J. Breckinridge, January 30, 1860, Breckinridge Family Papers; Breckinridge to Theodore O'Hara, January 19, 1860, Frederick M. Dearborn Collection, Houghton Library, Harvard University, Cambridge, Mass.

11. J. D. Hoover to Franklin Pierce, December 25, 1859, Franklin Pierce Papers, Library of Congress; Lexington, *Kentucky Statesman,* February 28, 1860.

12. Breckinridge to James B. Clay, May 9, 31, 1860, Thomas J. Clay Papers, Library of Congress.

13. Benjamin F. Butler, *Butler's Book* (Boston, 1892), pp. 144–46,

148; William K. Scarborough, ed., *The Diary of Edmund Ruffin,* I (Baton Rouge, La., 1972), pp. 435, 438.

14. Louisville, Kentucky, *Courier-Journal,* May 18, 19, 1875, November 17, 1887; Jefferson Davis, *Rise and Fall of the Confederate Government* (New York, 1881), I, p. 52.

15. Breckinridge to G. Nelson Smith, June 28, 1860, Breckinridge Papers, Dorothy T. Breckinridge; Breckinridge to S.L.M. Barlow, June 30, 1860, S.L.M. Barlow Papers, Huntington Library, San Marino, Cal.; J. Henly Smith to Alexander H. Stephens, August 18, 1860, Alexander H. Stephens Papers, Library of Congress; Varina H. Davis, *Jefferson Davis, Ex-President of the Confederate States of America: A Memoir by His Wife* (New York, 1890), I, p. 685.

16. New York *Times,* July 11, 1860; Scarborough, *Diary of Edmund Ruffin,* I, pp. 458, 481.

17. Stephens to Smith, October 13, 1860, in U. B. Phillips, ed., *Correspondence of Robert Toombs, Alexander H. Stephens and Howell Cobb* (Washington, 1913), p. 501.

CHAPTER THREE

1. Charleston, South Carolina, *Mercury,* July 20, 1860.

2. Scarborough, *Diary of Edmund Ruffin,* I, pp. xv–xl *passim.*

3. Frank Moore, comp., *The Rebellion Record* (New York, 1861), I, Documents, p. 2; Scarborough, *Diary of Edmund Ruffin,* I, p. 512.

4. Robert E. Rodes to Francis H. Smith, January 13, 1861, Rodes Alumni File, Virginia Military Institute, Lexington; *Rebellion Record,* I, Documents, pp. 7–8.

5. *Rebellion Record,* I, Documents, pp. 9–10.

6. U. S. War Department, *War of the Rebellion. Official Records of the Union and Confederate Armies* (Washington, 1880–1901), series I, volume 1, p. 103 (hereinafter referred to as *O.R.*).

7. John Thompson to his father, February 1861, John Thompson Letters, Public Record Office, Belfast, Northern Ireland; Samuel W. Crawford, *The Genesis of the Civil War* (New York, 1887), p. 104; Abner Doubleday, *Reminiscences of Forts Sumter and Moultrie in 1860–'61* (New York, 1875), p. 62.

8. *O.R.,* I, 1, p. 2.

9. Crawford, *Genesis,* pp. 109–11.

10. *O.R.,* I, 1, pp. 3, 252; Crawford, *Genesis,* pp. 148–49; William H. Trescott, "Narrative," *American Historical Review,* XIII (April 1908), p. 546.

11. *O.R.,* I, 1, p. 133.

12. *O.R.,* I, 1, pp. 132–37; Crawford, *Genesis,* pp. 185–86.

13. Allan Nevins, ed., *The Diary of George Templeton Strong* (New York, 1953), III, p. 89.

14. Mobile, Alabama, *Daily Advertiser,* January 12, 1861; *O.R.,* I, 1, pp. 134–44.

15. Doubleday, *Reminiscences,* p. 114.

16. Thompson to his father, February, 1861, Thompson Letters.

17. Crawford, *Genesis,* p. 295; Philip Auchampaugh, *James Buchanan and His Cabinet on the Eve of Secession* (Lancaster, Pa., 1926), p. 156.

18. John G. Nicolay and John Hay, *Abraham Lincoln: A History* (New York, 1890), III, p. 398.

19. Ibid., p. 377; *O.R.,* I, 1, pp. 190–91.

20. Robert M. Thompson and Richard Wainwright, eds., *Confidential Correspondence of Gustavus Vasa Fox* (New York, 1920), I, pp. 3–31 *passim;* William H. Ellison, "Memoirs of Hon. William Gwin," *California Historical Quarterly,* XIX (December 1940), pp. 362–66.

21. *O.R.,* I, 1, pp. 59, 285, 291, 297, 301; Crawford, *Genesis,* pp. 494–96; C. C. Buel and Rossiter Johnson, eds., *Battles and Leaders of the Civil War* (New York, 1884–87), I, p. 76.

22. Scarborough, *Diary of Edmund Ruffin,* I, pp. 563, 584, 588; *Battles and Leaders,* I, p. 76.

23. Doubleday, *Reminiscences,* pp. 145–46.

24. *Rebellion Record,* I, Documents, pp. 53–54.

25. W. A. Swanberg, *First Blood: The Story of Fort Sumter* (New York, 1957), p. 324.

CHAPTER FOUR

1. Charles Francis Adams, *An Autobiography* (Boston, 1916), p. 75.

2. Burton J. Hendrick, *Lincoln's War Cabinet* (Boston, 1946), pp. 65–66.

3. *Rebellion Record,* I, Documents, p. 63.

4. Ibid., pp. 65–70.

5. Ibid., p. 71; Charleston, South Carolina, *Mercury,* April 19, 1861.

6. *Rebellion Record,* I, Documents, pp. 78–79.

7. E. B. Long, *The Civil War Day by Day* (Garden City, N.Y., 1971), p. 65.

8. Kenneth M. Stampp, *And the War Came* (Baton Rouge, La., 1950), pp. 156–57, 205, 223, 245–46.

9. James G. Randall and David Donald, *The Civil War and Reconstruction* (Boston, 1969), pp. 173–75.

CHAPTER FIVE

1. Robert E. Lee to John MacKay, October 2, 1847, R. E. and G. W. C. Lee Papers, U. S. Army Military History Institute, Carlisle Barracks, Pa.

2. James I. Robertson, Jr., *The Stonewall Brigade* (Baton Rouge, La., 1963), pp. 7–8, 11; *O.R.*, I, 2, p. 862; Mary Anne Jackson, *Memoirs of Stonewall Jackson* (Louisville, Ky., 1895), p. 168.

3. John Coxe, "Wade Hampton," *Confederate Veteran*, XXX (December 1922), p. 460; John Coxe, "The Battle of First Manassas," *Confederate Veteran*, XXIII (January 1915), p. 24.

4. Douglas S. Freeman, *Lee's Lieutenants* (New York, 1943–44), I, p. 712n.

5. *O.R.*, I, 2, pp. 718–21; Fairfax, Virginia, *Herald*, June 3, 1904.

6. Mary Boykin Chesnut, *A Diary from Dixie* (Boston, 1949), p. 175.

7. Joseph E. Johnston, *Narrative of Military Operations* (New York, 1874), pp. 30–31.

8. U. S. Committee on the Conduct of the War, *Report of the Joint Committee on the Conduct of the War* (Washington, 1863), part II, p. 38 (hereinafter cited as *C.C.W.*); Donald Mitchell, *Daniel Tyler: A Memorial Volume* (New Haven, 1883), p. 49.

9. Milledge L. Bonham to P. G. T. Beauregard, August 27, 1877, Milledge L. Bonham Papers, South Carolinian Library, University of South Carolina, Columbia.

10. Gilbert E. Govan and James W. Livingood, *A Different Valor: The Story of General Joseph E. Johnston* (Indianapolis, 1956), pp. 46–47; *O.R.*, I, 2, p. 478.

11. Jackson, *Jackson*, p. 175; John N. Opie, *A Rebel Cavalryman with Lee, Stuart and Jackson* (Chicago, 1899), p. 25; D. B. Conrad, "History of the First Battle of Manassas and the Organization of the Stonewall Brigade," *Southern Historical Society Papers*, XIX (1891), p. 87.

12. Johnston, *Narrative*, pp. 37–38; Alexander R. Chisolm, Notes on Blackburn's Ford, Alexander R. Chisolm Papers, New-York Historical Society, New York.

13. Thomas Goldsby, "Fourth Alabama Regiment—Official Report," July 29, 1861, clipping in M. J. Solomons Scrapbook, William Perkins Library, Duke University, Durham, N.C.; Bradley T. Johnson, "Memoir of the First Maryland Regiment," *Southern Historical Society Papers*, IX (1881), p. 482; James McHenry Howard, *Recollections of a Maryland Confederate Soldier* (Baltimore, 1914), pp. 34–35.

14. Johnston, *Narrative*, p. 41.

15. *C.C.W.*, II, p. 39; Samuel P. Heintzelman Diary, July 20, September 1, 1861, Samuel P. Heintzelman Papers, Library of Congress; M. A. De Wolfe Howe, *Home Letters of General Sherman* (New York, 1909), p. 202; Oliver O. Howard, *Autobiography* (New York, 1909), I, p. 152; Mitchell, *Tyler*, pp. 56–57.

16. Howe, *Home Letters*, p. 202; Oliver O. Howard to his wife, July 20, 1861, Oliver O. Howard Papers, Bowdoin College Library, Bruns-

wick, Maine; Howard, *Autobiography,* I, p. 152; New York *Times,* July 24, 1861.

17. G. Moxley Sorrell, *Recollections of a Confederate Staff Officer* (New York, 1905), p. 93; Thomas Pelot to Lalla Pelot, September 15, 1861, Lalla Pelot Papers, Duke University.

18. Thomas Jordan to Jubal Early, July 8, 1861, P. G. T. Beauregard Papers, Duke University; A. C. Myers to William Porcher Miles, June 17, 1861, William Porcher Miles Papers, Southern Historical Collection, University of North Carolina, Chapel Hill; E. Porter Alexander, *Military Memoirs of a Confederate* (New York, 1907), pp. 32–34.

19. *O.R.,* I, 51, part 2, p. 689.

20. *C.C.W.,* II, p. 201.

21. Charleston, South Carolina, *Mercury,* July 25, 1861; Samuel W. John, "The Importance of Accuracy," *Confederate Veteran,* XXII (August 1914), p. 343; Goldsby, "Report," Solomons Scrapbook; Chesnut, *Diary from Dixie,* p. 88.

22. J. W. Pelot to Lalla Pelot, September 15, 1861, Pelot Papers.

23. Joseph E. Johnston to Jefferson Davis, August 3, 1861, Joseph E. Johnston Papers, Duke University; John B. Jones, *A Rebel War Clerk's Diary* (New York, 1961), p. 37.

CHAPTER SIX

1. Davis, *Rise and Fall,* I, pp. 640–48.

2. Alexander H. Stephens to Linton Stephens, February 23, 1861, Alexander H. Stephens Papers, Southern Historical Collection.

3. Davis, *Rise and Fall,* I, pp. 230–31.

4. Long, *Civil War Day by Day,* p. 38; Davis, *Rise and Fall,* I, pp. 232–36.

5. Davis, *Rise and Fall,* I, pp. 669–70.

6. William Y. Thompson, *Robert Toombs of Georgia* (Baton Rouge, La., 1966), pp. 164–65.

7. Davis, *Rise and Fall,* I, pp. 242–43; Edward A. Pollard, *Life of Jefferson Davis* (Philadelphia, 1869), p. 181.

8. Chesnut, *Diary from Dixie,* pp. 10–11; Joseph T. Durkin, *Stephen R. Mallory, Confederate Navy Chief* (Chapel Hill, N.C., 1954), pp. 108–30 *passim.*

9. William C. Harris, *Leroy Pope Walker, Confederate Secretary of War* (Tuscaloosa, Ala., 1962), pp. 20–22.

10. John H. Reagan, *Memoirs, with Special Reference to Secession and the Civil War* (New York, 1906), pp. 109–10.

11. Robert D. Meade, *Judah P. Benjamin, Confederate Statesman* (New York, 1943), pp. 161–62.

12. Thomas C. DeLeon, *Four Years in Rebel Capitals* (Mobile, Ala., 1892), p. 37.

13. Reagan, *Memoirs*, pp. 124–27; Report of the Postmaster General to the President, April 29, 1861, Theron Wierenga, comp., *Official Documents of the Post Office Department of the Confederate States of America* (Holland, Mich., 1979), I, pp. 1–13.

14. Meade, *Benjamin*, pp. 167–69; William H. Russell, *My Diary North and South* (New York, 1954), pp. 95–96.

15. Thomas C. DeLeon, *Belles, Beaux and Brains of the '60's* (New York, 1909), pp. 83–84; Russell, *Diary*, pp. 101–2.

16. Henry C. Capers, "The First Official Order," *Southern Bivouac*, I (May–June 1883), p. 394; Richard C. Todd, *Confederate Finance* (Athens, Ga., 1954), pp. 25–27.

17. United States Navy Department, *Official Records of the Union and Confederate Navies in the War of the Rebellion* (Washington, 1896), series II, volume 2, p. 69 (hereinafter referred to as *O.R.N.*).

18. Frank E. Vandiver, *Rebel Brass* (Baton Rouge, La., 1956), pp. 43–45.

19. Wilfred Buck Yearns, *The Confederate Congress* (Athens, Ga., 1960), pp. 12–15, 32–33.

20. John Echols to Francis H. Smith, February 28, 1861, John Echols File, Alumni File Room, Virginia Military Institute, Lexington.

21. Rudolph Von Abele, *Alexander H. Stephens* (New York, 1946), pp. 198–200.

CHAPTER SEVEN

1. John Y. Simon, ed., *The Papers of Ulysses S. Grant* (Carbondale, Ill., 1969), I, pp. 359–60.

2. Horace Porter, *Campaigning with Grant* (New York, 1897), p. 342; *Papers of . . . Grant*, II, pp. 3–4.

3. *Papers of . . . Grant*, I, pp. 359–60, II, pp. 27–28; U. S. Grant, *Personal Memoirs* (New York, 1885), I, pp. 235–36.

4. Hans Christian Adamson, *Rebellion in Missouri* (Philadelphia, 1961), pp. 126–27; William E. Parrish, *A History of Missouri, Volume III, 1860 to 1875* (Columbia, Mo., 1973), pp. 24–25; *Rebellion Record*, I, Documents, pp. 408–10, 412.

5. *Papers of . . . Grant*, II, p. 69; Grant, *Memoirs*, I, pp. 249–51.

6. Albert Castel, *General Sterling Price and the Civil War in the West* (Baton Rouge, La., 1968), pp. 6, 28, 32, 35, 44–45, 64–65; Adamson, *Rebellion*, p. 257; *Rebellion Record*, II, Documents, p. 496.

7. *Papers of . . . Grant*, II, pp. 80–82, 105, 142.

8. Castel, *Price*, pp. 48–56; *Rebellion Record*, II, Documents, pp. 497–98.

9. *Papers of . . . Grant*, II, p. 311.

10. William C. Davis, *The Orphan Brigade* (Garden City, N.Y., 1980), p. 3.

11. "For His Own Side," *Southern Bivouac*, II (February 1884), p. 277.

12. *Papers of . . . Grant*, II, pp. 186, 190, 191, 196–97.

13. Grant, *Memoirs*, I, pp. 269–71.

14. Ibid., pp. 273–81; *Papers of . . . Grant*, III, p. 136.

15. Grant, *Memoirs*, I, p. 284.

CHAPTER EIGHT

1. Davis, *Breckinridge*, pp. 261–63, 278–79, 283–85; undated clipping in John S. Jackman Diary, Library of Congress; Louisville, Kentucky, *Journal*, October 14, 1861.

2. Thomas L. Connelly, *Army of the Heartland* (Baton Rouge, La., 1967), pp. 62–64.

3. United States Congress, *Congressional Record* (Washington, 1921), LXI, Part 7, 67th Congress, 1st Session, pp. 7, 393.

4. Chapter VIII, Volume 60, Clothing Account Book, Co. C., 4th Kentucky Volunteers, 1862–1864, p. 222, Record Group 109, National Archives, Washington, D.C.

5. *Papers of . . . Grant*, IV, pp. 112–19.

6. Grant, *Memoirs*, I, pp. 285–86.

7. Ibid., pp. 287–88; *Papers of . . . Grant*, IV, pp. 96, 99, 103–4.

8. *Papers of . . . Grant*, IV, pp. 124, 129, 149, 153.

9. Ibid., p. 157; Grant, *Memoirs*, I, pp. 294–98.

10. *Papers of . . . Grant*, IV, pp. 203, 207, 211–12; Grant, *Memoirs*, I, pp. 303–7.

11. Grant, *Memoirs*, I, p. 310; *Papers of . . . Grant*, IV, p. 218; Bruce Catton, *Grant Moves South* (Boston, 1960), pp. 177–78.

12. Davis, *Orphan Brigade*, pp. 63, 69.

13. *Papers of . . . Grant*, IV, pp. 229, 271.

14. Grant, *Memoirs*, I, pp. 326–28; *Papers of . . . Grant*, IV, pp. 320–21.

15. Grant, *Memoirs*, I, pp. 317, 328–29; *Papers of . . . Grant*, IV, p. 349.

16. Grant, *Memoirs*, I, p. 333; *Papers of . . . Grant*, IV, p. 443, V, pp. 13–14.

17. Davis, *Breckinridge*, p. 303.

18. Jackman Diary, April 6–7, 1862; *Papers of . . . Grant*, V, p. 17; Connelly, *Army of the Heartland*, p. 157.

19. Davis, *Breckinridge*, p. 305.

20. Ibid., pp. 305–8, 310.

21. Ibid., p. 311.

22. Grant, *Memoirs*, I, p. 342.

23. *Papers of . . . Grant*, V, p. 47.

CHAPTER NINE

1. John Niven, *Gideon Welles, Lincoln's Secretary of the Navy* (New York, 1973), p. 322.
2. Ibid., p. 359.
3. Ibid., p. 359.
4. Robert E. Johnson, *Rear Admiral John Rodgers, 1812–1882* (Annapolis, Md., 1967), pp. 155–56.
5. Ibid., p. 158.
6. Robert McBride, *Civil War Ironclads* (Philadelphia, 1962), pp. 49–50.
7. John D. Milligan, *Gunboats Down the Mississippi* (Annapolis, Md., 1965), pp. 18–24; Johnson, *Rodgers*, p. 166; McBride, *Ironclads*, pp. 52–53.
8. Gideon Welles, "The First Iron-Clad Monitor," *Annals of the War* (Philadelphia, 1879), p. 20.
9. H. Ashton Ramsay, "Most Famous of Sea Duels: The *Merrimac* and *Monitor*," *Harper's Weekly*, February 10, 1912, p. 10.
10. William C. Davis, *Duel Between the First Ironclads* (Garden City, N.Y., 1975), p. 5.
11. Niven, *Welles*, pp. 364–65; United States Congress, *Congressional Globe* (Washington, 1861), 37th Congress, 1st Session, p. 347.
12. William N. Still, *Iron Afloat* (Nashville, Tenn., 1971), pp. 18–19; John S. Wise, *The End of an Era* (Boston, 1902), pp. 191–93; *O.R.N.*, II, 1, p. 757; 2, p. 152; Jones, *War Clerk's Diary*, p. 52.
13. Davis, *Duel*, pp. 16–17; James F. Baxter, *The Introduction of the Ironclad Warship* (Cambridge, Mass., 1933), pp. 269–70.
14. Allen Gosnell, *Guns on the Western Waters* (Baton Rouge, La., 1949), p. 11; Charles G. Summersell, *The Cruise of the CSS* Sumter (Tuscaloosa, Ala., 1965), pp. 14–17.
15. Summersell, *Sumter*, p. 177.

CHAPTER TEN

1. Norman B. Ferris, *Desperate Diplomacy, William H. Seward's Foreign Policy, 1861* (Knoxville, Tenn., 1976), pp. 3–4.
2. Roy P. Basler, ed., *The Collected Works of Abraham Lincoln* (New Brunswick, N.J., 1953), IV, pp. 317–18.
3. Ferris, *Desperate Diplomacy*, pp. 21–22.
4. Ibid., pp. 3–31.
5. Charles F. Adams to William H. Seward, May 17, 1861, National Archives.
6. Ferris, *Desperate Diplomacy*, p. 51.
7. Ibid., pp. 110, 138, 143.
8. Paul Pecquet du Bellet, *The Diplomacy of the Confederate Cabi-*

net of Richmond and Its Agents Abroad (Tuscaloosa, Ala., 1963), pp. 30–32.

9. *O.R.N.*, II, 3, pp. 214–16, 219–21.

10. Ibid., p. 221.

11. Ibid., pp. 278–80.

12. John W. DuBose, *The Life and Times of William Lowndes Yancey* (Birmingham, Ala., 1892), II, pp. 621–22; *O.R.N.*, II, 3, pp. 273–74.

13. Lynn M. Case and Warren E. Spencer, *The United States and France: Civil War Diplomacy* (Philadelphia, 1970), pp. 190–91; Norman B. Ferris, *The* Trent *Affair: A Diplomatic Crisis* (Knoxville, 1977), pp. 18–19.

14. Ferris, Trent *Affair*, pp. 21–26; Case and Spencer, *United States and France*, pp. 192–94.

15. Ferris, Trent *Affair*, p. 47.

16. Niven, *Welles*, pp. 444–45; Ferris, Trent *Affair*, pp. 70–71.

17. Ferris, Trent *Affair*, pp. 132–33, 184–85.

18. New York *Times*, December 29, 1861; Ferris, Trent *Affair*, p. 191; *O.R.N.*, II, 3, p. 484.

CHAPTER ELEVEN

1. Phillips, *Correspondence*, p. 586.

2. Govan and Livingood, *A Different Valor*, pp. 68–71.

3. T. Harry Williams, *Lincoln and His Generals* (New York, 1952), p. 26; George B. McClellan, *McClellan's Own Story* (New York, 1887), pp. 66–67.

4. Williams, *Lincoln and His Generals*, pp. 44–45.

5. McClellan, *McClellan's Own Story*, pp. 176–77.

6. Rowena Reed, *Combined Operations in the Civil War* (Annapolis, Md., 1978), pp. 36–39.

7. Michael C. C. Adams, *Our Masters the Rebels* (Cambridge, Mass., 1978), pp. 111, 113.

8. Williams, *Lincoln and His Generals*, pp. 55–56, 65.

9. Govan and Livingood, *A Different Valor*, p. 96.

10. *O.R.N.*, I, 6, pp. 776–77.

11. Ibid., pp. 780–81; *O.R.*, I, 5, part 2, p. 391.

12. Dinwiddie B. Phillips, "The Career of the Iron-Clad Virginia," *Collections of the Virginia Historical Society*, New Series, VI (1887), p. 201.

13. Ibid.

14. Catesby ap R. Jones, "Services of the 'Virginia' (Merrimac)," *Southern Historical Society Papers*, II (February–March 1883), p. 68.

15. Samuel Dana Greene, "I Fired the First Gun and Thus Com-

menced the Great Battle," *American Heritage*, VIII (June 1957), pp. 13, 102.

16. John Taylor Wood, "The First Fight of Iron-Clads," *Battles and Leaders*, I, p. 701; Davis, *Duel*, p. 118.

17. Govan and Livingood, *A Different Valor*, pp. 114–18.

CHAPTER TWELVE

1. *O.R.*, I, 5, pp. 965–66.
2. Henry Kyd Douglas, *I Rode with Stonewall* (Chapel Hill, N.C., 1940), p. 20.
3. Ibid., p. 65.
4. Govan and Livingood, *A Different Valor*, p. 126.
5. Ibid., p. 156; George W. Tainter to Herman P. Harrington, April 16, 1929, in possession of Elliot A. Billings, Falmouth, Mass.
6. Gustavus W. Smith, *The Battle of Seven Pines* (New York, 1891), p. 104.
7. *O.R.*, I, 11, part 3, pp. 685–86.
8. Dabney H. Maury, *Recollections of a Virginian* (New York, 1894), p. 161; R. M. Hughes, *General Johnston* (New York, 1897), pp. 154–55.
9. Francis W. Pickens to Bonham, July 7, 1861, Bonham Papers.
10. McClellan, *McClellan's Own Story*, p. 452.
11. John N. Ware, "Enroughty, Darby, and General McClellan," *American Heritage*, VII (February 1956), p. 120.

CHAPTER THIRTEEN

1. Virginia Clay-Clopton, *A Belle of the Fifties* (New York, 1905), p. 168.
2. William J. Kimball, *Starve or Fall, Richmond and Its People* (Ann Arbor, Mich., 1976), p. 36; Louis Manarin, ed., *Richmond at War* (Chapel Hill, N.C., 1966), p. 77.
3. Jones, *War Clerk's Diary*, pp. 22–23.
4. Chesnut, *Diary from Dixie*, pp. 68–69, 82, 83.
5. Mrs. Eugene McLean, "A Northern Woman in the Confederacy," *Harper's New Monthly Magazine*, CXXVIII (February 1914), pp. 443–44; Chesnut, *Diary from Dixie*, pp. 81, 83, 85, 86; Jones, *War Clerk's Diary*, p. 34.
6. McLean, "A Northern Woman," p. 444.
7. Jones, *War Clerk's Diary*, pp. 75–76.
8. Ibid., p. 77.
9. Ibid., pp. 77–78.
10. Ibid., pp. 79–80, 83, 84, 86.

11. Kimball, *Starve or Fall*, pp. 122–23.

12. Samuel J. T. Moore, *Moore's Complete Civil War Guide to Richmond* (Richmond, Va., 1978), p. 50; Chesnut, *Diary from Dixie*, pp. 115–16.

13. Kimball, *Starve or Fall*, p. 127.

14. Moore, *Guide*, pp. 64–68.

15. Ibid., pp. 72–74; Chesnut, *Diary from Dixie*, p. 100.

16. Moore, *Guide*, p. 73; Clay-Clopton, *Belle*, p. 175.

17. Chesnut, *Diary from Dixie*, pp. 365, 368–70; Clay-Clopton, *Belle*, pp. 174–77. This play took place February 5, 1864.

18. Clay-Clopton, *Belle*, p. 178.

19. Jones, *War Clerk's Diary*, pp. 79, 102, 105, 108; Clay-Clopton, *Belle*, p. 179.

20. Chesnut, *Diary from Dixie*, pp. 121, 126–28, 280; Kimball, *Starve or Fall*, pp. 129–30.

21. Jones, *War Clerk's Diary*, pp. 180, 182; Douglas O. Tice, "Bread or Blood," *Civil War Times Illustrated*, XII (February 1974), pp. 12–19.

22. Clay-Clopton, *Belle*, p. 173.

CHAPTER FOURTEEN

1. Jones, *War Clerk's Diary*, p. 34.

2. Williams, *Lincoln and His Generals*, p. 7.

3. J. W. Schuckers, *The Life and Public Services of Salmon Portland Chase* (New York, 1874), p. 374.

4. David Donald, ed., *Inside Lincoln's Cabinet: The Civil War Diaries of Salmon P. Chase* (New York, 1954), p. 12; Randall and Donald, *Civil War and Reconstruction*, pp. 322–24.

5. Harold Hyman and Benjamin P. Thomas, *Stanton: The Life and Times of Lincoln's Secretary of War* (New York, 1962), pp. 125, 134–37.

6. Henry P. Beers, *Guide to Federal Archives Relating to the Civil War* (Washington, 1962), pp. 242–43.

7. Hyman and Thomas, *Stanton*, pp. 152–53; Randall and Donald, *Civil War and Reconstruction*, pp. 331–33.

8. Hyman and Thomas, *Stanton*, pp. 161, 387.

9. Fred A. Shannon, *The Organization and Administration of the Union Army 1861–1865* (Cleveland, Ohio, 1928), I, pp. 259–61; Long, *Civil War Day by Day*, p. 325.

10. Shannon, *Organization*, I, p. 64; *Harper's Weekly Illustrated Newspaper*, August 10, 1861.

11. Shannon, *Organization*, I, p. 69; *O.R.*, III, 1, p. 681.

12. Hyman and Thomas, *Stanton*, p. 151.

13. Grady McWhiney, *Southerners and Other Americans* (New York, 1973), p. 84.

14. Harris, *Walker*, pp. 20–23.

15. Ibid., pp. 26, 56–58, 61, 74, 80–81; McWhiney, *Southerners*, p. 87.

16. Jones, *War Clerk's Diary*, pp. 42–46.

17. Ibid., p. 46.

18. Rembert Patrick, *Jefferson Davis and His Cabinet* (Baton Rouge, La., 1944), pp. 172–73, 177–79.

19. Henry P. Beers, *Guide to the Archives of the Confederate States of America* (Washington, 1968), p. 134.

20. Ibid., 237; *O.R.*, IV, 3, p. 1101.

21. Memory F. Mitchell, *Legal Aspects of Conscription and Exemption in North Carolina, 1861–1865* (Chapel Hill, N.C., 1965), pp. 10, 13–14.

22. Patrick, *Davis and His Cabinet*, pp. 123–25.

23. Ibid., pp. 126–28.

24. Jones, *War Clerk's Diary*, pp. 71–72.

CHAPTER FIFTEEN

1. Niven, *Welles*, pp. 379–81.

2. Charles L. Lewis, *David Glasgow Farragut* (Annapolis, Md., 1943), II, p. 8.

3. David D. Porter to Gustavus V. Fox, March 28, April 8, 1862, Gustavus V. Fox Papers, New-York Historical Society, New York.

4. Lewis, *Farragut*, II, p. 41; *O.R.*, I, 6, p. 832.

5. Lewis, *Farragut*, II, pp. 51–52.

6. Ibid., p. 53.

7. Ibid., pp. 55–63.

8. Charles I. Dufour, *The Night the War Was Lost* (Garden City, N.Y., 1960), pp. 344–52.

9. Chesnut, *Diary from Dixie*, p. 215.

10. *Correspondence of . . . Fox*, I, p. 303; *O.R.N.*, I, 18, p. 8.

11. *O.R.N.*, I, 18, pp. 491–92.

12. Milligan, *Gunboats Down the Mississippi*, pp. 66–68.

13. Ibid., pp. 72–76.

14. Lewis, *Farragut*, II, pp. 97–100.

15. "Confederate Rag-Bag," *Historical Magazine*, 3rd Series, II (August 1873), p. 92.

16. E. Porter Thompson, *History of the Orphan Brigade* (Louisville, Ky., 1898), pp. 117–21; Robert G. Hartje, *Van Dorn: The Life and Times of a Confederate General* (Nashville, Tenn., 1967), pp. 200–1.

17. Davis, *Breckinridge*, p. 318; Davis, *Orphan Brigade*, p. 113.

18. Davis, *Breckinridge,* pp. 318–23; Breckinridge to Earl Van Dorn, August 7, 1862, Breckinridge Papers in possession of John M. Prewitt.

19. Lewis, *Farragut,* II, p. 126.

20. Grant, *Memoirs,* I, pp. 372, 377; *Papers of . . . Grant,* V, pp. 102, 111, 114, 116, 124, 140.

21. Grant, *Memoirs,* I, p. 405.

22. Ibid., p. 415.

23. *Papers of . . . Grant,* VI, p. 186.

CHAPTER SIXTEEN

1. United States Congress, *Congressional Globe* (Washington, 1862), 37th Congress, 3rd Session, part 1, p. 286.

2. Randall and Donald, *Civil War,* p. 340.

3. Bray Hammond, *Sovereignty and an Empty Purse, Banks and Politics in the Civil War* (Princeton, N.J., 1970), pp. 19–20.

4. New York *Herald,* February 14, 1861; Hammond, *Banks and Politics,* pp. 30–31.

5. Hammond, *Banks and Politics,* pp. 42–43.

6. Ellis P. Oberholtzer, *Jay Cooke, Financier of the Civil War* (Philadelphia, 1907), I, pp. 131–36.

7. Ibid., pp. 143–44, 147–49, 158–59.

8. Hammond, *Banks and Politics,* pp. 141–42.

9. Oberholtzer, *Cooke,* I, p. 172.

10. James G. Blaine, *Twenty Years in Congress* (Norwich, Conn., 1886), I, p. 433.

11. Hammond, *Banks and Politics,* pp. 184–86.

12. Oberholtzer, *Cooke,* I, p. 191.

13. Ibid., pp. 213–14.

14. Robert P. Sharkey, *Money, Class, and Party* (Baltimore, 1959), pp. 226–31; Hammond, *Banks and Politics,* pp. 289–90, 293–94.

15. Long, *Civil War Day by Day,* p. 727.

16. Oberholtzer, *Cooke,* I, p. 231; Otto Eisenschiml, "Did an Anonymous Englishman Save the Union?," *Civil War Times Illustrated,* V (August 1966), pp. 13–17; Frank Merli, *Great Britain and the Confederate Navy* (Bloomington, Ind., 1970), p. 184.

17. Richard L. Lester, *Confederate Finance and Purchasing in Great Britain* (Charlottesville, Va., 1975), pp. 3–7.

18. Todd, *Confederate Finance,* pp. 3–5.

19. Ibid., pp. 121–23, 125.

20. Ibid., p. 130.

21. Ibid., p. 133.

22. Ibid., pp. 26–27, 34–35.

23. Ibid., pp. 116–19, 198.

24. Jones, *War Clerk's Diary*, pp. 153–54; Davis, *Rise and Fall*, I, p. 242.

25. Todd, *Confederate Finance*, pp. 19–21.

26. Ibid., pp. 50–51.

CHAPTER SEVENTEEN

1. Williams, *Lincoln and His Generals*, p. 148; William K. Scarborough, ed., *The Diary of Edmund Ruffin*, II (Baton Rouge, La., 1976), pp. 419–20.

2. Warren G. Hassler, *Commanders of the Army of the Potomac* (Baton Rouge, La., 1962), p. 56.

3. *Rebellion Record*, V, p. 552.

4. Hassler, *Commanders*, p. 62.

5. *C.C.W.*, I, p. 282.

6. *O.R.*, I, 12, part 3, pp. 484, 485, 500–1, part 2, p. 52; *Rebellion Record*, V, Documents, pp. 45–46.

7. Freeman, *Lee's Lieutenants*, I, pp. 671–74.

8. Ibid., II, pp. 13–15.

9. *O.R.*, I, 12, part 3, pp. 527, 530–31, 535.

10. Ibid., pp. 535–36, 537.

11. Ibid., p. 536.

12. Ibid., pp. 548, 551.

13. Ibid., p. 553; Freeman, *Lee's Lieutenants*, II, pp. 42–45.

14. *O.R.*, I, 12, part 2, pp. 132–35, 185.

15. McClellan, *McClellan's Own Story*, p. 470.

16. *O.R.*, I, 12, part 3, pp. 590–91.

17. Freeman, *Lee's Lieutenants*, II, pp. 87–91; *O.R.*, I, 12, part 3, pp. 652–53, 668, 684, 685, 704.

18. Freeman, *Lee's Lieutenants*, II, pp. 107–8.

19. *O.R.*, I, 12, part 3, pp. 720–21.

20. Ibid., pp. 741, 749.

21. McClellan, *McClellan's Own Story*, p. 515.

22. Williams, *Lincoln and His Generals*, p. 162; Gideon Welles, *Diary of Gideon Welles* (Boston, 1909–11), I, p. 113.

CHAPTER EIGHTEEN

1. Edward Magdol, *Owen Lovejoy, Abolitionist in Congress* (New Brunswick, N.J., 1967), p. 292.

2. Ibid., pp. 4–5, 11, 15, 22–24, 26.

3. *Collected Works of . . . Lincoln*, II, pp. 322–23; David Donald, *Charles Sumner and the Coming of the Civil War* (New York, 1960), p. 388.

4. Philip S. Foner, *The Life and Writings of Frederick Douglass* (New York, 1950–55), III, pp. 94, 125.

5. Hans L. Trefousse, *The Radical Republicans* (New York, 1968), p. 507.

6. Magdol, *Lovejoy*, pp. 177, 218, 220, 225, 226, 235, 237, 242.

7. Trefousse, *Radical Republicans*, pp. 168–69; Magdol, *Lovejoy*, pp. 280, 290.

8. Trefousse, *Radical Republicans*, pp. 176–77.

9. Ibid., p. 180.

10. Magdol, *Lovejoy*, pp. 282–83.

11. Ibid., pp. 284–85.

12. Ibid., pp. 300–2.

13. *Collected Works of . . . Lincoln*, V, pp. 35–53.

14. Magdol, *Lovejoy*, pp. 309–12.

15. McClellan, *McClellan's Own Story*, pp. 487–89.

16. Trefousse, *Radical Republicans*, pp. 186–91; *O.R.*, I, 11, part 1, p. 61.

17. Magdol, *Lovejoy*, p. 324.

18. Ibid., pp. 330–34; McClellan, *McClellan's Own Story*, p. 355.

19. Trefousse, *Radical Republicans*, p. 223; Oberholtzer, *Cooke*, I, p. 197; *Collected Works of . . . Lincoln*, VII, pp. 281–82.

CHAPTER NINETEEN

1. Charleston, South Carolina, *Mercury*, September 6, 1862.

2. Douglas S. Freeman, *R. E. Lee* (New York, 1934–35), II, pp. 350–53.

3. *O.R.*, I, 19, part 2, pp. 184–85, 186, 187, 188–90.

4. Williams, *Lincoln and His Generals*, pp. 163–65; McClellan, *McClellan's Own Story*, pp. 549, 551.

5. *O.R.*, I, 19, part 2, pp. 214–15, 230, 233, 248, 254–55.

6. *Battles and Leaders*, II, pp. 605–6.

7. *O.R.*, I, 19, part 2, pp. 598–99, 601–2, 603.

8. Ibid., pp. 603–4.

9. John Gibbon, *Personal Recollections of the Civil War* (New York, 1928), p. 73; *O.R.*, I, 19, part 2, pp. 281–82.

10. Freeman, *Lee*, II, pp. 369–70.

11. Freeman, *Lee's Lieutenants*, II, pp. 194–99.

12. *O.R.*, I, 19, part 1, p. 951, part 2, pp. 294–95; McClellan, *McClellan's Own Story*, p. 612.

13. *O.R.*, I, 19, part 2, pp. 296, 297.

14. Freeman, *Lee*, II, p. 380.

15. McClellan, *McClellan's Own Story*, p. 601.

16. R. E. Lee, Jr., *Recollections and Letters of General Robert E. Lee* (New York, 1905), pp. 415–16.

17. McClellan, *McClellan's Own Story,* pp. 612–13.

18. John G. Nicolay and John Hay, *Abraham Lincoln: A History* (New York, 1914), VI, p. 175.

19. Warren G. Hassler, *General George B. McClellan, Shield of the Union* (Baton Rouge, La., 1957), pp. 316–18; Williams, *Lincoln and His Generals,* p. 177.

20. Frederic E. Ray, *Alfred R. Waud, Civil War Artist* (New York, 1974), pp. 39–41; McClellan, *McClellan's Own Story,* p. 652; Hassler, *McClellan,* pp. 327–29.

CHAPTER TWENTY

1. Louis S. Gerteis, *From Contraband to Freedman* (Westport, Conn., 1973), pp. 12–14.

2. Bell I. Wiley, *Southern Negroes* (New Haven, 1938), pp. 4–19 *passim.*

3. Gerteis, *Contraband,* pp. 18–19, 22.

4. Willie Lee Rose, *Rehearsal for Reconstruction* (New York, 1976), pp. xii–xiv.

5. Ibid., pp. 16–17, 407–8; Gerteis, *Contraband,* pp. 50–52; Wiley, *Southern Negroes,* pp. 177–79.

6. Rose, *Rehearsal,* pp. 146–51, 190–94.

7. Robert F. Durden, *The Gray and the Black: The Confederate Debate on Emancipation* (Baton Rouge, La., 1972), pp. 7–8, 10, 11.

8. Ibid., pp. 15, 16, 17.

9. Chesnut, *Diary from Dixie,* pp. 122–23, 164.

10. Wiley, *Southern Negroes,* pp. 166–69.

11. Ibid., pp. 147–50.

12. Randall and Donald, *Civil War,* p. 381.

13. Ibid., pp. 382–83.

14. Davis, *Rise and Fall,* II, p. 190; *Collected Works of . . . Lincoln,* V, pp. 388–89.

15. Scarborough, *Diary of Edmund Ruffin,* II, pp. 453, 455–56.

16. Case and Spencer, *United States and France,* pp. 320–22.

17. Frank L. Owsley, *King Cotton Diplomacy* (Chicago, 1959), pp. 337–38; John Prest, *Lord John Russell* (Columbia, S.C., 1972), p. 395.

18. Philip Van Doren Stern, *When the Guns Roared* (Garden City, N.Y., 1965), pp. 157–58.

INDEX

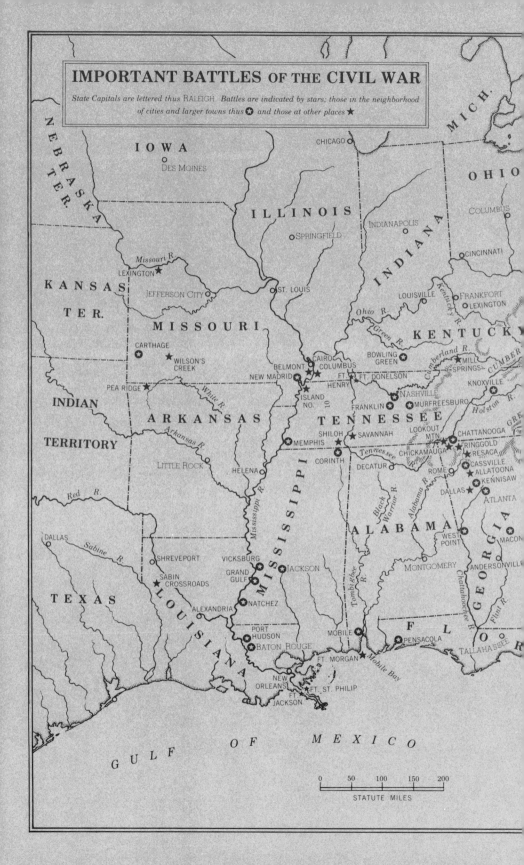

IMPORTANT BATTLES OF THE CIVIL WAR

State Capitals are lettered thus RALEIGH *Battles are indicated by stars; those in the neighborhood of cities and larger towns thus* ⊛ *and those at other places* ★